DESTINATION RECOMMENDATION SYSTEMS

Behavioural Foundations and Applications

DESTINATION RECOMMENDATION SYSTEMS
Behavioural Foundations and Applications

Edited by

Daniel R. Fesenmaier

Professor and Director
National Laboratory for Tourism and eCommerce
School of Tourism and Hospitality Management
Temple University
Philadelphia, Pennsylvania, USA

Karl W. Wöber

Associate Professor
Institute for Tourism and Leisure Studies
Vienna University of Economics and Business Administration
Vienna, Austria

Hannes Werthner

Professor and Head
Department for Information Systems
University of Innsbruck
Innsbruck, Austria

www.cabi.org

CABI is a trading name of CAB International

CABI Head Office
Nosworthy Way
Wallingford
Oxfordshire OX10 8DE
UK

CABI North American Office
875 Massachusetts Avenue
7th Floor
Cambridge, MA 02139
USA

Tel: +44 (0)1491 832111
Fax: +44 (0)1491 833508
E-mail: cabi@cabi.org
Website: www.cabi.org

Tel: +1 617 395 4056
Fax: +1 617 354 6875
E-mail: cabi-nao@cabi.org

A catalogue record for this book is available from the British Library, London, UK.

Library of Congress Cataloging-in-Publication Data
Fesenmaier, Daniel R.
Destination recommendation systems: behavioural foundations and applications/Daniel R.
Fesenmaier, Karl W. Wöber, Hannes Werthner.
      p. cm.
Includes bibliographical references and index.
ISBN-13: 978-0-85199-023-1 (alk. Paper)
ISBN-10: 0-85199-023-1 (alk. Paper)
1. Travel--Computer network resources. 2. Tourism--Computer network
     resources. 3. Internet. 4. World Wide Web. I. Wöber, Karl W.
     II. Werthner, H., 1954– III. Title.
G149.7.F47 2006
910.285'4678–dc22

2005032292

ISBN-10: 0-85199-023-1
ISBN-13: 978-0-85199-023-1

Typeset by SPi, Pondicherry, India.
Printed and bound in the UK by Biddles Ltd, King's Lynn.

Contents

Contributors

Ulrike Bauernfeind is a PhD candidate and a research and teaching assistant at the Institute for Tourism and Leisure Studies, Vienna University of Economics and Business Administration. Her research interests include website evaluations, usability, decision-support systems and recommender systems.

Dario Cavada is an IT Consultant with many years of experience in the Hospitality Industry. He has been working in the eCommerce and Tourism Research Laboratory group as an IT expert. His research interests include recommender methodology and tourist support during all the phases of travel using web technologies and mobile devices.

Benedict G.C. Dellaert is Meteor Research Chair and Professor at the Department of Marketing, Maastricht University, the Netherlands. Previously he was at Tilburg University, the Netherlands, and the University of Sydney, Australia. He holds a Master's degree in Technology Management and a PhD in Technical Sciences (Urban Planning) from Eindhoven University of Technology, the Netherlands. His research interests are in consumer decision-making, customization and personalization, tourism and retailing. His work has appeared in journals such as *Annals of Tourism Research, Journal of Marketing Research, Journal of the Academy of Marketing Science* and *Leisure Sciences*.

Dr Daniel R. Fesenmaier is a Professor at the School of Tourism and Hospitality Management, Temple University, and Director of the National Laboratory for Tourism and eCommerce. His research interests include travel decision-making, travellers' spatial behaviour, influence of technology on travel behaviour and the development of tourism marketing information systems.

Dr Thomas Franke completed his doctoral thesis at the Bavarian Research Network for Information Systems (FORWIN) in Nuremberg. His main research topics are advising systems using recommendation engines, soft computing methods like genetic algorithms or expert system approaches applied to the field of travel decision-making and leisure planning. At the moment, Dr Franke is working as Executive Assistant to the Board of Management at Norisbank in Nuremberg.

Klaus Grabler is a managing partner of Manova, an Austrian company specializing in solving analytically sophisticated market research problems, and in developing decision-support systems for managers. Between 1992 and 2002 Grabler was an Assistant Professor at the Institute for Tourism and Leisure Studies, Vienna University of Economics and Business Administration, and a member of the DieToRecs (EU 5th framework project # IST-2000-29474) project team.

Dr Ulrike Gretzel is an Assistant Professor at the Department of Recreation, Park and Tourism Sciences at Texas A&M University and Director of the Laboratory for Intelligent Systems in Tourism. Her research focuses on persuasion in human–technology interaction, the representation of sensory and emotional aspects of tourism experiences and issues related to the development and use of intelligent systems in tourism.

Dr Gerald Häubl is the Canada Research Chair in Behavioural Science, the R.K. Banister Professor of Electronic Commerce and an Associate Professor of Marketing at the University of Alberta School of Business. He is a faculty affiliate of the Sloan Center for Internet Retailing at Vanderbilt University and a research fellow of Pennsylvania State University's eBusiness Research Center. Professor Häubl is the founder and current director of the Institute for Online Consumer Studies. His primary areas of research interest are consumer decision-making, the psychology of preferences, consumer search for products and information and interactive decision aids for consumers.

Dr Yeong-Hyeon Hwang is an Assistant Professor at the Division of International Tourism, Dong-A University, Korea. His research interests include use of en route travel information and travellers' behavioural changes induced by new information technologies. He is involved in several research projects related to the development of ubiquitous tourism systems.

Dae-Young Kim is a PhD candidate, lecturer and research assistant in the Department of Hospitality and Tourism Management, Purdue University, West Lafayette, Indiana. His research interests include hospitality and tourism marketing, convention management, advertising channel effectiveness, online emotional engagement and information technology in tourism system.

Josef A. Mazanec is a Full Professor of Business Administration and Director of the Institute for Tourism and Leisure Studies of the Vienna University of Economics and Business Administration, WU Wien. He was a visiting scholar at the Alfred P. Sloan School of Management, MIT (1992), Vice-Rector for Research of the WU Wien (1997–2002) and Speaker of the Joint Research Program on Adaptive Information Systems and Modelling in Economics and Management Science (1997–2001). His research interests are in consumer behaviour, strategic marketing, decision-support systems and management science applications in hospitality, leisure and tourism.

Nader Mirzadeh is a technical leader at the Computer Architecture and Parallel Systems Group at the University of Amsterdam, the Netherlands. His research interests include databases, query processing and flexible query management.

Nicole Mitsche is a lecturer in Tourism at the School of Arts, Design, Media and Culture at the University of Sunderland in the UK. Her research interests include intelligent travel or destination recommendation systems (decision-support systems), website evaluation, user search behaviour and popular festivals.

Cristian Morosan is the Program Director for Information Technology and Tourism with the National Laboratory for Tourism and eCommerce at Temple University. His research interests include travellers' information search, technology adoption behaviour, tourism website effectiveness and persuasive technologies in tourism.

Quang Nhat Nguyen is a PhD candidate at the International Graduate School in Information and Communication Technology, University of Trento. His research interests include machine learning, decision-making support, personalization and recommender systems and development of adaptive mobile systems.

Dr Joseph T. O'Leary is Professor and Head of the Department of Recreation, Park and Tourism Sciences at Texas A&M University. His research interests involve knowledge management and analysis of large national and international studies of travel and recreation behaviour.

Dr Bing Pan is a Visiting Assistant Professor at the Department of Hospitality and Tourism Management in the School of Business and Economics, College of Charleston and the Head of Research in the Office of Tourism Analysis. Dr Pan is responsible for conducting travel and tourism research projects supporting state, region and local tourism agencies. His research and teaching interests include the uses of information technologies in the tourism industry, information systems, online behaviour and consumer behaviour in tourism.

Dr Francesco Ricci is a senior researcher and the technical director of the eCommerce and Tourism Research Lab at ITC-irst. He recently coordinated the DieToRecs (Intelligent Recommendation for Tourist Destination Decision-making) IST project and he is the main designer of the Trip@dvice technology. His current research interests include recommender systems, constraint satisfaction problems, machine learning, case-based reasoning and software architectures.

Hildegard Rumetshofer is Area Manager for Innovation and Research Cooperation at the Institute for Applied Knowledege Processing at the University of Linz. She has worked for several European companies as a research assistant and project manager. Her current research work is related to decision-making and reasoning, especially in the context of user-centred, intelligent e-learning systems.

Dr Erwin Schaumlechner is a Project Manager and Software Development Manager for Tiscover AG, a leading destination management system (DMS) provider, operating one of the world's largest families of destination portals. Dr Schaumlechner is responsible for the execution of research projects in consideration of the integration of the research results into the company's array of products. His research interests include the development of destination management systems, tourism portals and content management systems as well as the manifold possibilities of touristic information exchange between providers.

Dr Olivierio Stock has been at ITC-irst since 1988 and has been its Director from 1997 to 2002. His activity is mainly in artificial intelligence, natural language processing, intelligent interfaces and cognitive technologies. He is the author of about 160 published papers and author or editor of 10 volumes, and member of the editorial board of a dozen scientific journals. He has been Chairman of the European Coordinating Committee for Artificial Intelligence, President of the Association for Computational Linguistics and of the Italian AI Association and is an ECCAI Fellow.

Dr Adriano Venturini is manager and co-founder of eCTRL Solutions, a company specialized in providing and developing recommendation technologies for the eTourism sector. eCTRL Solutions has acquired the rights to commercially exploit Trip@dvice, the recommendation technology for web portals developed in ITC-irst to support the tourist decisional process with personalized recommendations. Dr Venturini is responsible for extending Trip@dvice and integrating it in next-generation tourism portals. His current research interests are in tourism recommender systems (particularly in case-based reasoning methodologies and in intelligent query management), in software architectures (component-based development, web and distributed architectures) and in the data integration area (mediator architectures, XML).

Dr Hannes Werthner is a Professor at the University of Innsbruck, Department for Information Systems, founder and president of the eCommerce Competence Center (EC3) in Vienna, and the scientific coordinator of the Austrian Network for e-tourism (ANET). His research activities cover decision-support systems, simulation, artificial intelligence, e-commerce and Internet-based information systems, especially in the field of tourism.

Dr Karl W. Wöber is an Associate Professor at the Institute for Tourism and Leisure Studies, Vienna University of Economics and Business Administration. His main research interests include information technology for tourism and hospitality marketing, tourism statistics, benchmarking methodologies, decision support and expert systems and strategic planning.

Zheng Xiang is a PhD/BA student at the Fox School of Business and School of Tourism and Hospitality Management at Temple University. He is also working as a research assistant at the National Laboratory for Tourism and eCommerce. His research interests include information systems for destination marketing organizations, strategic planning and travellers' information search behaviour.

Massimo Zancanaro has been working as a researcher in the Cognitive and Communication Technologies Division at ITC-irst since 1993. His primary interest is in the field of intelligent interfaces and in particular language-based interfaces. During the past few years, he has specialized in the application of IT to the domain of cultural heritage with a particular focus on the design issues related to mobile audio-based hypermedia. He has been a member of several programme and organization committees of conferences and workshops in the field. Since 2001, he has lectured in electronic commerce at the University of Trento and, in 2004, Computer–Human Interaction at the International PhD School in the same university.

Dr Andreas H. Zins is an Associate Professor at the Institute for Tourism and Leisure Studies, Vienna University of Economics and Business Administration. Dr Zins is active in research in the fields of consumer behaviour, marketing research, marketing management, information behaviour, travel expenditures, social impacts and leisure attractions.

Foreword

There have been a number of issues in the study of travel and tourism that have elicited research interest, but there are few that are more significant than the study of how travel decisions are made. Since there are so many stages or pieces to the travel system, the challenge includes the destination focus as well as all the other products contained. Understanding these decisions captures the attention of both the researcher and the practitioner. On the one hand, the issue is interesting to understand from a theoretical point of view. On the other hand, it has enormous implications for the largest economic activity in the world. The growth of information technology and computer applications as they relate to travel decisions has increased the need for improved understanding and new attention to this area since few of the previous travel decision models reflect this in their model structure.

This is not a simple undertaking for at least three reasons. In a recent bestseller written by Thomas Friedman, *The World is Flat*, one of the most dramatic changes he discusses is the flattening of the information access hierarchy from a vertical to a horizontal structure. Virtually anyone with a computer and access to the World Wide Web has the ability to search, access and sort through enormous amounts of information from around the world. This ability to access information has already begun to show up as a change phenomenon in the travel arena in terms of how people gather information about where to go and what to do (e.g. more options and choices to consider), but also as the way in which people have traditionally used information sources, shifting people more to consider web-based sources as their first place to search, supplanting word of mouth as the first place to gather suggestions on possible destinations and products. Similarly, online purchasing of travel continues to rapidly increase. At this point, there is no evidence this will slow.

Behaviour has already changed and will continue to be altered. Patterns that were identified in past research will probably become less stable and no longer be appropriate for planning, management, marketing and policy. As the new behaviours develop – making choices, purchasing, etc. – the manner in which they are examined in the travel decision model framework must be reconsidered under the research microscope. Will travellers consider all information available (a possibility that is virtually impossible already) or will they establish rules and guidelines for themselves to make evaluation more easy? Will providers assist in that winnowing process? What will be included and excluded? How important is understanding the information presented going to be in making a choice? Will sociodemographic characteristics make a difference in how this process is dealt with? As experience-based systems develop that include new sensory and personality-based ingredients, what will be the impact on behaviour? Will the proliferation of new equipments like integrated hand-held devices and broadening wireless access affect search and decision behaviour? The list of new questions goes on and on.

We are at a seminal point in thinking about new ways to examine Destination Recommendation Systems both in terms of theoretical and practical needs and implications. The material in this publication takes us in an exciting direction, which forces a re-examination of assumptions and the planning of a new knowledge trajectory that will probably reshape the future of world travel.

Joseph T. O'Leary

Introduction: Recommendation Systems in Tourism

Recommendation systems have become an essential tool in online marketing. Today, recommendation systems are deployed on hundreds of different e-commerce sites and support millions of consumers in their search for products. Recommendation systems are seen as one of the fastest growing domains of Internet applications and are expected to become increasingly sophisticated and effective. Tourism is no exception to this trend; indeed, tourism is especially affected by the explosion in availability of information on the Web as it has become one of the most important e-commerce categories. Also, the tourism industry is very fragmented and even very small providers of tourism products such as bed-and-breakfast establishments have started to make information available online. Hwang *et al.* (2003) reported that over 70 million travel-related web pages were retrieved as a result of a simple search on Google.com. However, these sites typically provide lists of information and have been relatively poor in aiding users during the planning of where, when and how to go on vacation and what to do at a certain destination (Delgado and Davidson, 2002). Thus, there seems to be a particularly great need for decision support in the form of recommendations on tourism websites.

Designing recommendation systems for the tourism industry is extremely challenging. Tourism experiences are complex composites of tourism products and services, which suggests that there are many opportunities for bundling various elements of the value chain (i.e. destinations, accommodations, attractions, etc.) with the help of recommendation systems. Therefore, travel-related recommendations must refer to a variety of products (locations, attractions, activities, etc.) in order to provide a meaningful picture of the proposed trip. In addition, variety seeking is especially pronounced in tourism; that is, tourists do not necessarily want to go to a place where everybody else goes because of a fear of crowds and the resulting inconveniences. Therefore, the most 'popular' items might not be considered attractive in the context of tourism. Finally, consumption in tourism occurs in three stages – prior, during and after the trip – and, therefore, travel recommendation systems should incorporate a series of mechanisms necessary to support all stages of the travel consumption process.

There are a variety of existing travel-related recommendation systems where, perhaps, the most widely known include Expedia.com, Orbitz.com, Travelocity.com and TisCover.com. Each of these systems employs a variety of approaches to structuring or organizing one's search for travel products. Interestingly, these systems largely serve travellers *after* they have already decided many aspects of the trip including destination, travel group and data by facilitating the booking process. From commercial, technical and theoretical perspectives this focus on the functional aspects of travel are understandable; today's systems are excellent at facilitating transactions but extremely poor at supporting the search for experience goods. Imagine, for example, trying to find an exotic destination in Expedia.com or any other destination recommendation system that is 'just right' without having extensive knowledge of the destination. However, it is expected that these and emerging edu-entertainment systems will become more 'inspirational', enabling prospective travellers to better 'imagine', even pre-sample, several components of a trip.

Defining Recommendation Systems

It is often necessary to make choices without sufficient information or knowledge of the alternatives. In such instances, consumers often rely on recommendations from family, friends or experts (e.g. sales assistant) to make a decision. Recommendation systems guide behaviour by suggesting products or information relevant to consumers, thus mimicking and at the same time enhancing this social process of giving and receiving from others. Consequently, the value of recommendation systems lies in their ability to provide consumers with relevant options without the requirement that users specify exactly what they want. Häubl and Trifts (2000) define recommendation systems as software tools that make recommendations based on learned information about the user's preference function. Recommendation systems vary in sophistication, ranging from simple retrieval or filtering applications to comprehensive recommendation systems (Spiekermann and Paraschiv, 2002) and are often classified into content-based vs collaborative filtering systems (Balabanovic and Shoham, 1997). Collaborative filtering systems infer a user's preferences from other, similar people's preferences (Ansari *et al.*, 2000), and mimic social processes such as word of mouth, assuming that the evaluation or opinions of others are an important information source consumers use in their decision-making process (Kim and Kim, 2001). In contrast, content-based filtering assumes that characteristics of an item determine the user's liking of the item. Thus, content-based recommender systems provide suggestions based on an analysis of the content of the items a user has searched for or purchased in the past (Kim and Kim, 2001). Recommendation systems can also be distinguished depending on whether they are memory-based, i.e. they compare users against each other directly using correlation or other measures, or model-based, which means they derive a model based on historical data (Breese *et al.*, 1998; Pennock *et al.*, 2000; Burke, 2002). Schafer *et al.* (2001) provide a more comprehensive classification of recommendation systems based on: (i) the type of user input; (ii) the recommendation method; (iii) the existence and type of community input; (iv) the presentation of the recommendation; and (v) the degree of personalization (see Fig. I.1). However, hybrid systems that incorporate a variety of approaches are becoming increasingly popular (and blur the distinction between systems) as they promise to reap the benefits of the different methods while overcoming their inherent drawbacks (Pennock *et al.*, 2000; Burke, 2002).

Designing Destination Recommendation Systems: An Overview

This book discusses a number of topics that are especially relevant for understanding how to design effective destination recommendation systems. For example, Hwang, Gretzel, Dellaert, Häubl, Pan and Fesenmaier (in Chapters 1–5, this volume) argue that a thorough understanding of consumer behaviour, especially information search and decision-making-related behaviour, is fundamental to the design of effective travel recommendation systems. In

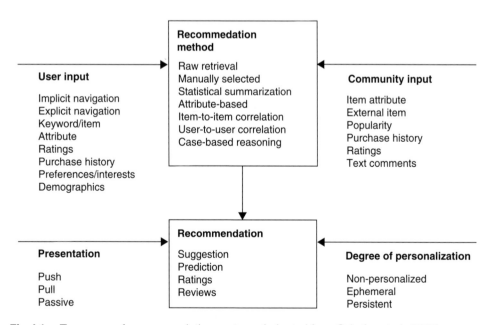

Fig. I.1.   Taxonomy of recommendation systems (adapted from Schafer *et al.*, 2001).

order to be able to truly support consumer decision-making, recommendation systems have to acknowledge that decision-making processes vary across:

- decision problems (simple vs complex, well-defined vs ill-defined, etc.);
- contexts (time, location, etc.);
- social situations (group vs individual, degree of accountability, etc.); and
- individuals (prior knowledge, cognitive capacity, degree of motivation, etc.).

Furthermore, as suggested by Dellaert and Häubl (in Chapter 4, this volume) improvement in recommendation system design can only be achieved if these systems explicitly incorporate a number of perceptual factors influencing consumer choice. Therefore, effective profiles should not only contain basic demographics and information about what the user is looking for but also information about the personality, values, attitudes and involvement of the user, as well as the knowledge the user brings to bear. In addition to personal characteristics of the user, the specific characteristics of the decision to be made have to be accounted for. Existing consumer behaviour literature suggests that taking the context in which the recommendation takes place into account can greatly enhance the perceived quality and increase the likelihood of acceptance for recommended alternatives. However, it is clear that studies are needed to examine the nature and extent to which recommendation systems actually influence traveller choices.

The chapters included in Part II (Chapters 6–12, this volume) elaborate on the framework proposed in Chapter 5, providing discussion of critical methodologies and considerations for destination recommendation design. In Chapter 6, Ricci *et al.* describe the development of Trip@dvice, a case-based reasoning approach to destination recommendation. The methodology, it is argued, provides an excellent foundation for supporting the decision-making and information search processes underlying travel. The authors use Trip@dvice as the engine for destination recommendation prototype systems called NutKing and DieToRecs, which introduce the notions of 'seeking inspiration' where it is assumed that users require visual cues describing the destination rather than more typical text-based descriptions.

Building on the innovations proposed in Chapter 6, Zins and Grabler argue that most recommendation systems are much too complicated and that alternative approaches to guide traveller decision-making are needed. They propose an interesting and novel solution by developing a typology of six decision styles – (i) highly predefined travellers; (ii) accommodation-oriented travellers; (iii) recommendation-oriented travellers; (iv) geography-oriented travellers; (v) price-oriented travellers; and (vi) activity-oriented travellers – which can be combined with other user information to provide highly personalized recommendations. Gretzel *et al.* propose an alternative typology based upon travel personalities and demonstrate that they can be used quite effectively in easing the information burden while providing useful destination recommendations. Josef Mazanec builds upon the findings described in the previous three chapters to propose a complementary approach to case-based reasoning as discussed in Chapter 6. Specifically, neural network techniques are used to build an adaptive system capable of 'learning' user preferences.

Chapters 7–9 focus on three critical issues in the design of destination recommendation system interfaces. Gretzel, in Chapter 10, suggests that the highly structured queries typical of recommender systems are not effective in eliciting user preferences. Indeed, she argues that because of the experiential nature of tourism people most often think of travel within the context of stories. Therefore, integrating narrative design into destination recommendation systems may enhance the quality of the recommendations while improving the persuasiveness of the overall website. Design issues are further explored in Chapter 11, where Xiang and Fesenmaier consider the role of metaphors in enhancing navigation and the interactivity between recommendation systems and the traveller. Furthermore, they argue successfully that because of the experiential nature of travel, metaphors can be used very effectively to communicate a range of hedonic attributes or benefits of a destination. Chapter 12 posits that destination recommendation systems design should be based upon the notions underlying online games, i.e. the central element of design is play. This chapter gives a basic overview of the play and playfulness literature, and provides a number of interesting examples where play is used as an organizing principle. It argues that these components must be extended to destination recommendation systems in order to substantively improve user experience.

Part III introduces four distinctly different systems that have been developed based upon the notions outlined in the previous chapters. Wöber, in Chapter 13, discusses the development of a search engine for European destinations. Ricci *et al.* (Chapter 14) and Zins and Bauernfeind (Chapter 15) further elaborate the components of DieToRecs, while Franke (Chapter 16) describes the various design challenges underlying the development of TourBO. Finally, Ricci and Nguyen (Chapter 17) describe MobyRek, a system that is tailored for on-the-move travellers. It is hoped that detailed discussion of these destination recommendation systems will encourage further innovation in such optimization strategies as well as the design of user interfaces.

Part IV focuses on the future of recommendation systems for travellers. The authors discuss the expected evolution of these systems and argue that they will become normal everyday tools, much like other systems (i.e. stoplights, warning lights, etc.) that enable us to interpret and navigate our environment. A very interesting example of such a system is provided with the goal of pointing the direction for future development.

Final Thoughts

A number of excellent books have been written such as Donald Norman's *The Design of Everyday Things* and Michael Dertouzos' *The Unfinished Revolution* that enable us to appreciate the role of recommendation systems in our lives.

Indeed, 'simple systems' such as an oil gauge, a stop light on a busy street, or the whistle of a teapot are important but transparent recommendation systems guiding our lives. As communication systems evolve and new systems used to access the Internet merge and emerge, it is clear that recommendation systems are becoming even more essential to providing and/or creating an environment that enables us to easily and successfully manage the potential opportunities and threats it contains. The travel industry, an important part of the world economy and our lives, has been a leader in the growth of the Internet but has not kept pace as partners in the changing Internet environment. However, it is clear that the development of Internet technologies can easily be adapted for use by tourism-related organizations. This book represents such an effort whereby scholars from a number of disciplines combine their talents to collaborate on the development of new technologies that will guide further development of the Internet for the travel industry.

It is important to recognize the impact that the Internet has had on the travel industry. Beginning only slightly more than a decade ago, the Internet has become the primary source for travel information worldwide, enabling access to well over a billion web pages describing hundreds of thousands of destinations. Most of these websites have enabled potential travellers to learn about destinations and book travel and accommodations while offering very little customer support, let alone enabling travellers to actually understand the destination. Travel recommendation systems such as those discussed in this book represent an important development and growth in travel-oriented systems in that they are customer-focused and, therefore, offer increased access to the traveller. The tremendous growth of high-speed and wireless access will create further means to support the tourist. However, virtual communities, blogs and a variety of other informal self-organizing systems are now emerging that have the potential to substantially disrupt the direct relationship between customer and destination, thereby creating new challenges for Internet marketing. It is certainly exciting to be part of this evolving system. We sincerely hope that you enjoy reading this book as much as we have enjoyed putting it together.

I Behavioural Foundations for Destination Recommendation Systems

1 Information Search for Travel Decisions

YEONG-HYEON HWANG, ULRIKE GRETZEL, ZHENG XIANG AND DANIEL R. FESENMAIER

1. Introduction

One of the most important behavioural processes underlying travel decision-making can be generally described as the information search and processing. Travel decisions require a large amount of internal as well as external information and potentially encompass a number of information search, evaluation and integration tasks and activities. Travellers often actively seek information as part of their travel-planning effort, considering it an important component of the travel experience. Travel information available to individuals has a substantial influence on different aspects of travellers' decision-making, particularly on destination choice (Crompton, 1979; Snepenger et al., 1990; Mansfeld, 1992; Um and Crompton, 1992; Gursoy and Chen, 2000; Jeng and Fesenmaier, 2002). Many studies have indicated that the main function of information search is to support decision-making and product choice by reducing risk and uncertainty (Bettman, 1979; Vogt et al., 1993; Gitelson and Kerstetter, 1994). Research on travellers' information search and processing behaviour has a long history and has made substantial contributions to tourism marketing (Fodness and Murray, 1998; Vogt and Fesenmaier, 1998; Bieger and Laesser, 2004; Gursoy and McCleary, 2004).

With the exponential growth of the amount of information available to consumers on the Internet, issues related to consumer information search and processing behaviour need to be re-examined and reinterpreted within this context (Hoffman and Novak, 1996; Dholakia and Bagozzi, 2001; Ratchford et al., 2003). It has been commonly accepted that the manner in which consumers search for, process and use information is a complex phenomenon that is not completely understood, which implies that the assumption that the Internet will lead to better consumer decision-making may not be completely warranted (Peterson and Merino, 2003). In tourism, there is an increasing interest in studying travellers' information search behaviour in the digital environment. For instance, it has been realized that although the enormous amount of information available on the Internet at one's fingertips can greatly help travellers in planning trips and/or formulating expectations about tourism experiences, it can also lead to information overload, making it difficult and sometimes frustrating for travellers to find relevant information (Good *et al.*, 1999; Pan and Fesenmaier, 2005). It has also been recognized that the potential capacity of the Internet, which can be used to create more interactive and vivid search experiences, has not been fully exploited by tourism marketing websites. To a certain degree this can be attributed to a mismatch between the inherently experiential nature of travel and tourism products and the way in which tourism websites are promoting their products (Cho *et al.*, 2002; Gretzel and Fesenmaier, 2002b). Obviously, it can be expected that a better understanding of travellers' online information search and processing behaviour will potentially lead to a better design of online marketing information systems and, consequently, to an enhanced marketing performance.

Understanding how travellers acquire and process information is important for marketing travel and tourism products because it is during the information search process that marketeers can influence travellers' decision-making (Schmidt and Spreng, 1996). Since the top goal of a destination recommendation system is to provide travel information users with guidance about what destination and other trip-related products, understanding travellers' information search behaviour in the online environment is essential to the design of the system. The goal of this chapter is threefold: (i) to provide an overview of foundational research on travellers' information search and processing, focusing on travellers' search and processing strategies and factors influencing the behaviour; (ii) to provide an illustration of the digital information environment, specifically the Internet, and its implications for travel information search behaviour; and (iii) to discuss the implications regarding how to integrate travellers' behavioural factors into the design of human-centric destination recommendation systems, especially the potential approaches a destination recommendation system can take to accommodate the various information-processing strategies of prospective travellers.

2. Travel Information Search and Processing

There have been three major theoretical streams in consumer information search literature (Srinivasan, 1990; Schmidt and Spreng, 1996; Gursoy and McCleary, 2004): (i) the psychological/motivational approach; (ii) the economics (functional) approach; and (iii) the consumer information-processing approach (see Bieger and Laesser, 2004 for a comprehensive review). These approaches offer a diversity of perspectives with which to describe consumer information search behaviour. Travel information search and processing traditionally had been assumed to be a problem-solving task with the goal of reducing the level of uncertainty and enhancing the quality of a trip (Fodness and Murray, 1997; Vogt and Fesenmaier, 1998; Bieger and Laesser, 2004). It has also been explained by travel motivation theory in the proposition of people being 'pushed' by their own internal forces (motivation) and 'pulled' by the external forces (stimuli) of the destination attributes (Leiper, 1990; Cha *et al.*, 1995). Researchers in tourism have proposed a number of frameworks and perspectives to study travel information search and processing behaviour. The following provides an overview of the most significant approaches to information search within the context of travel planning.

2.1 Travel information search and processing models

With its roots in consumer information processing theory (Bettman, 1979; Assael, 1984), the process-based perspective of travel information search and processing has a long history and a prominent presence in tourism research (Woodside and Lysonski, 1989; Leiper, 1990; Um and Crompton, 1992; Vogt and Fesenmaier, 1998; Crotts, 1999; Correia, 2002). Based on this view, travel decision-making consists of several stages of information search and processing (see Fig. 1.1). Travellers begin the information search process by utilizing internal memory sources to list product alternatives after recognizing a purchase need. If this initial list of alternatives is satisfactory, the evaluation phase can begin. If, on the other hand, the list derived from internal memory is not satisfactory, individuals start searching for information using

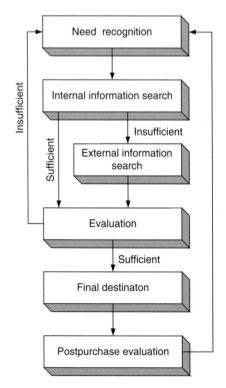

Fig. 1.1. A general framework of travel information search and processing (adapted from Crotts, 1999).

external sources such as personal sources (e.g. friends and relatives), commercial sources (e.g. brochures and advertisements), non-commercial sources (e.g. virtual travel communities) and experiential sources (e.g. inspections and pre-purchase visits). Once a satisfactory amount of information is accumulated, the various alternatives are evaluated and subsequently selected or eliminated. The destination choice set model can be seen as a special consideration of this model within the context of destination choice (Crompton, 1992).

As depicted in the process-based model, it is generally understood that travellers use two different information sources to acquire knowledge for decision-making: internal and external. By definition, internal information search involves memory and occurs prior to external search. External information search refers to everything but memory when searching for information (Peterson and Merino, 2003). Internal information includes an individual's personal experiences and past information search results. External information is almost always actively acquired through personal sources, marketeer sources, neutral sources and experiential sources (Crotts, 1999). Research has also been conducted in order to understand the level of importance of various information sources within the decision-making process (Leiper, 1990; Correia, 2002; Bieger and Laesser, 2004). As illustrated in Fig. 1.2, the travel decision-making process is classified into three stages: the pre-decision stage, the decision stage and the post-decision stage. Within this framework, the pre-decision and post-decision stages can be differentiated in terms of the level of importance of various information sources, suggesting that the process-based view and the source-based view can be combined (Bieger and Laesser, 2004). For example, information from marketeer or professional sources such as tour operators or travel agencies only plays a significant role before a definite trip decision, mainly for non-standardized tours. Travellers also actively acquire information from direct sources such as destinations,

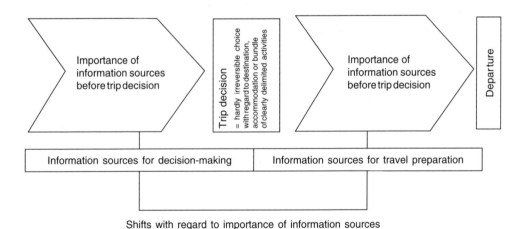

Shifts with regard to importance of information sources

Fig. 1.2. Process framework of information sources (adapted from Bieger and Laesser, 2004).

hotels and so forth, but these sources may not be considered neutral. Therefore, trust in, and neutrality towards, these information sources need to be established. After a trip decision has been made, information from sources such as relatives or friends becomes more important and often discriminates actual travel behaviour. In general, source credibility can be considered the strongest predictor of type of information sources used (Kerstetter and Cho, 2004).

Understanding the uniqueness of travel and tourism products has always been of primary interest to tourism researchers, because these products mostly are intangible personal service products, which can induce functional, financial, physical, psychological and social risks (Teare, 1992; Lovelock and Wright, 1999). Traditional perspectives of travel information search focus on functional needs, which are defined as motivational efforts directed at, or contributing to, a specific purpose. According to this perspective, the search for information enables travellers to reduce their uncertainty and to enhance the quality of a trip (Teare, 1992; Fodness and Murray, 1997; Bieger and Laesser, 2004). Vogt and Fesenmaier (1998) expanded the conventional functional information search perspective by identifying four additional needs: hedonic, innovation, aesthetic and sign (see Fig. 1.3). This model posits that information needs other than functional needs capture psychological, sociological, aesthetical and symbolic experiences of information searching. Based on this model, it is understood that not everyone who collects information actually intends to travel, and many of the travel information search motivations can

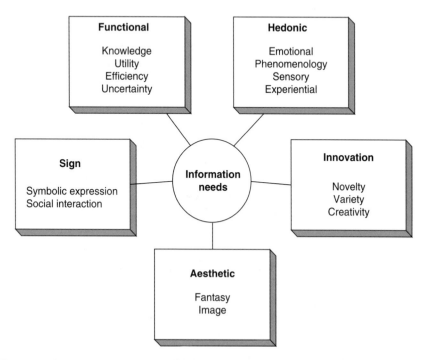

Fig. 1.3. An information needs model (adapted from Vogt and Fesenmaier, 1998).

be considered as leisure and recreation-based. Therefore, this model expands the view of travel information search process from a strict marketing context into a broader one of communication.

Perhaps one of the most important issues relating to traveller information search is the distinction between ongoing vs pre-purchase information search (Bloch *et al.*, 1986). Pre-purchase information search efforts are those that aim at increasing product-related knowledge to inform a specific purchase decision. Ongoing search, on the other hand, provides additional benefits by focusing on the future use of the obtained information as well as satisfaction with the search activity itself. The focus of information environments, therefore, needs to be different for customers who are in a pre-purchase information search situation as opposed to those who are in an ongoing information search mode because of the differences in products and search attributes stressed by the two search strategies. Most research on travel information search and processing considers pre-purchase information search as the key component in decision-making (Vogt and Fesenmaier, 1998; Bieger and Laesser, 2004).

Research focusing on strategies of information acquisition also suggests that there are two basic strategies of information search: holistic (i.e. alternative-based) and analytical (i.e. attribute-based). This distinction indicates whether an individual prefers interdimensional or intradimensional material such as books and ads (Tversky, 1969; Payne, 1976; Bockenholt and Hynan, 1994). An interdimensional process or an alternative-based search is identified as transitions between two different attributes for the same alternative, whereas an intradimensional process or attribute-based searching behaviour is distinguished as transitions between two alternatives for the same attribute. Information-processing strategies, compared with information search, focus on the actual use of the information obtained during the search process. That is, once information about alternatives is collected either by internal or external search, or by a combination of both, individuals evaluate the various alternatives by categorizing, evaluating, organizing and retaining or ignoring the information (Assael, 1984). Individuals are known to selectively pay attention to information, using different strategies such as interdimensional and intradimensional processing, to deal with the information obtained (Tversky, 1969; Payne, 1976; Bockenholt and Hynan, 1994; Bettman *et al.*, 1998). For example, a prospective traveller might use interdimensional processing and look at multiple attributes of a single destination before considering another destination, or use intradimensional processing, which involves evaluating a single attribute (e.g. price) across available alternative destinations before taking into account another attribute. This information processing continues until a consumer reaches a certain threshold of confidence about the decision. Whenever information deficiency is felt, the individual will search for more information and integrate this new information into that retained from previous searches.

2.2 Factors influencing travel information search and processing

Research has identified a series of factors influencing travellers' information search and processing patterns, encompassing several aspects of the information environment (e.g. the level of difficulty of the choice task, number of alternatives, complexity of the alternatives), traveller characteristics (e.g. education, prior product knowledge, involvement, family life cycle, socio-economic status) and situational variables (e.g. previous satisfaction, time constraints, perceived risk, composition of travelling party) (Fodness and Murray, 1998; Vogt and Fesenmaier, 1998; Gursoy and McCleary, 2004). While it is not the intention of this chapter to elaborate on each of these, the following provides a brief overview of these factors and their effects on information search and processing behaviour.

Travellers' characteristics, in particular sociodemographic variables, have been widely used to explain information search behaviour (Gitelson and Crompton, 1983; Etzel and Wahlers, 1985; Capella and Greco, 1987; Vogt and Fesenmaier, 1998). In terms of age, existing research indicates that older travellers tend to rely more on family and past experience as information sources (Capella and Greco, 1987), and are more interested in satisfying hedonic, aesthetic and sign needs in the information search process (Vogt and Fesenmaier, 1998). Also, more educated travellers with higher levels of income tend to search for more information (Gitelson and Crompton, 1983; Etzel and Wahlers, 1985), and women are more likely to consider functional aspects in their information search than men (Vogt and Fesenmaier, 1998).

Travellers' knowledge is an important construct that influences information search and processing behaviour (Park and Lessig, 1981; Brucks, 1985; Park *et al.*, 1988). Interestingly, a number of different perspectives have been suggested regarding the relationship between knowledge and information search behaviour. A negative relationship would imply that the more knowledge a traveller can draw on, the less information seeking will occur. In contrast, a positive relationship suggests that as people acquire more knowledge they will be more actively involved in the information search process because they can better or more easily interpret information and, thus, derive more benefits from information than people with limited knowledge. Studies also suggest an inverted U-shaped function where a positive relationship exists up to moderate levels of knowledge, and a negative relationship at moderate to high levels of experience or knowledge (Punj and Staelin, 1983; Alba and Hutchinson, 1987; Moorthy *et al.*, 1997). Knowledge and previous experience have been included in several studies within the context of travel information search (Manfredo, 1989; Snepenger *et al.*, 1990; Perdue, 1993). A study conducted by Kerstetter and Cho (2004) demonstrated that prior knowledge may be a multidimensional construct, and that when addressed independently, it does influence individuals' search for vacation information.

Travel information search and processing also depend on individuals' level of involvement (Finn, 1983; Celsi and Olsen, 1988; Jamrozy *et al.*, 1996). For example, as the perceived risk involved in the decision task increases, situational involvement rises accordingly, and individuals tend to invest more resources in external information search (Murray, 1991). That is, highly involved travellers are likely to use more criteria, search for more information, use more information sources, process relevant information in detail, make more inferences and will form attitudes that are less likely to change (Celsi and Olsen, 1988; Fesenmaier and Johnson, 1989; Manfredo, 1989; Perdue, 1993).

Personality has also been identified as a factor with considerable influence on information search and processing strategies. For example, individuals' differences in the complexity of the causal explanations they reach to make sense of their environments suggest that personality influences the extent and nature of information search and integration patterns. Also, individuals with a tendency to postpone decisions when faced with difficult choices or conflicts have been found to engage in search patterns that are different from those used by individuals who are not indecisive (Ferrari and Dovidio, 2001).

Trip characteristics such as travel group composition are important explanatory variables of travel information search behaviour. Travel group composition, for instance, has been found to influence the information search strategy selected (Fodness and Murray, 1997). Family groups tend to use media as information sources more than other types of travel parties, and are more likely to be involved in extensive search processes in order to assure satisfaction of all the members (Gitelson and Crompton, 1983). Travel purpose also influences information search strategies. Fodness and Murray (1998) found that those travelling for vacation purposes were the most likely to rely on their personal experience to plan their trips. In addition, they were able to find evidence for a relationship between mode of transportation and types of travel information sources used. Further, length of travel has been identified as a factor that influences the use of travel agents as an information source (Snepenger *et al.*, 1990). Finally, empirical evidence suggests that there is a relationship between travel distance and information search strategies. For example, Pennington-Gray and Vogt (2003), among others, have found that out-of-state visitors are more likely to obtain travel information at welcome centres than in-state residents.

3. The Digital Information Environment and Information Search

Although systematic study of the Internet as an information source has been limited (Ratchford *et al.*, 2003), many articles have described the various aspects and attributes of the Internet in terms of its capacity to store, transfer and communicate information (Ainscough and Luckett, 1996; Hoffman and Novak, 1996; Good *et al.*, 1999; Dholakia and Bagozzi, 2001). On the technical side, the basic relationships underlying information technology advancement have been described as following several 'laws' such as Moore's Law, Metcalf's Law and Gilder's Law (Ruefli *et al.*, 2001). From the communication and marketing perspective, the Internet provides certain capabilities such as inexpensively storing vast amounts of information in different virtual locations available on a 24 × 7 basis to consumers and supporting and facilitating several forms of interaction (Peterson and Merino, 2003). This digital information environment has significant impact on consumer information search behaviour and it is evident that consumers will increasingly rely on the Internet when searching for product information (Ratchford *et al.*, 1996; Peterson and Merino, 2003). Thus, it entails special consideration in the context of consumer decision-making, especially in relation to the strategies employed in information search and processing. More specifically, the impact of these emerging Internet-based information environments on consumer behaviour can be summarized as follows:

- *Ubiquitous information access and computing.* Given access to the Internet, information is available to consumers from anywhere at any time. Thus, Internet-based information search environments literally eliminate any temporal and spatial limits of consumer information search activities.
- *Reduction of information cost.* In digital environments, consumers can search for and acquire information at a very low cost (Bakos, 1997). Economists have speculated that this characteristic will result in a market where retailer location is not material and consumers are fully informed about prices and all available alternatives, minimizing retailer profits (Bakos, 1997; E. Brynjolfsson and M.D. Smith, 1999, unpublished data).
- *Interactive communication.* Being an interactive media, the Internet also supports and facilitates one-to-one, one-to-many, many-to-one and many-to-many interactions, with different levels of interactivity (Hoffman and Novak, 1996). These interactions can be characterized according to their origination and interface, depending on whether they involve human-to-human, human-to-machine, machine-to-human or machine-to-machine origins and interfaces (Peterson and Merino, 2003).
- *Volitional control.* Compared with traditional media such as print materials and television, consumers have greater control over all aspects of the information acquisition process in the digital information environment (Dholakia and Bagozzi, 2001). For example, consumers can decide which website to visit, which places within the website to enter, how long to stay online and at a specific website.
- *Information overload.* Owing to the Internet, people have access to more information than ever before. However, too much information from too many sources may lead to information overload due to the cognitive costs associated with information processing (Bettman *et al.*, 1991; Hibbard, 1997; Good *et al.*, 1999). Literally, no surfing in the chaotic information space is possible without some guidance technology such as information retrieval (IR) or information filtering (IF) mechanisms that reduce the whole information space to a manageable amount of information.

It is argued that the characteristics of digital information environments necessitate the development of information search models, which take the specifics of the technology, the characteristics of the user and the particularities of the user's interaction with the information system into account. During the last decade, consumer researchers have been studying these issues from different perspectives. For example, from a communication point of view, the Internet can be seen as a distributed, interactive and networked multimedia, which can increase the likelihood for consumers to experience an optimal state called 'flow' (Hoffman and Novak, 1996). Dholakia and Bagozzi (2001) exemplify another stream of research by looking at consumer information search on the Internet as a goal-setting and goal-striving process.

The concept of 'flow' stems from motivational psychology and has been used to denote 'the episodes when life is heightened, when one is deeply involved and mental energy is highly focused on the activity or experience' (Csikszentmihalyi, 1990; Kubey and Csikszentmihalyi, 1990). In an online environment, flow is 'the state occurring during network navigation which is: (i) characterized by a seamless sequence of responses facilitated by machine interactivity; (ii) intrinsically enjoyable; (iii) accompanied by a loss of self-consciousness; and (iv) self-reinforcing' (Hoffman and Novak, 1996, p. 57). Digital environments can increase the likelihood of experiencing flow largely due to the novelty and challenges to consumers, the interactivity of the environment as well as the volitional control consumers have been endowed with (Hoffman and Novak, 1996; Novak *et al.*, 2000). As a result of flow, consumers may gain a high level of learning, a greater behavioural control and self-efficacy and an overall positive subjective experience.

The Mind-Set Formation and Influence (MSFI) model proposed by Dholakia and Bagozzi (2001) succeeds in integrating at least some of the most relevant factors of consumer search behaviours on the Internet (see Fig. 1.4). According to this model, website selection, length of website visit and information obtained depend on one's mindset (i.e. one's specific cognitive orientation). Four different mindsets of the information seeker have been identified: deliberative, implemental, exploratory and hedonic. A deliberative mindset represents a cognitive orientation with a focus on collecting and processing information, while an implemental mindset is defined as the state in which a consumer's focus is oriented towards the smooth action execution for goal achievement. An exploratory mindset refers to the state of mind in which a consumer focuses on new experiences, and a hedonic mindset represents a state where the individual pays attention to the sensory elements of the experience. Both deliberative and implemental mindsets are more goal-oriented, whereas exploratory and

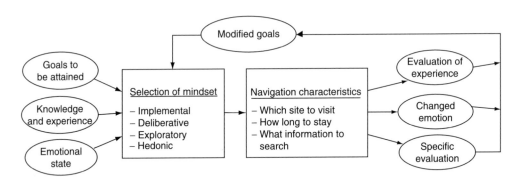

Fig. 1.4. Mind-Set Formation and Influence (MSFI) model (adapted from Dholakia and Bagozzi, 2001).

hedonic mindsets focus more on the search experience itself (Dholakia and Bagozzi, 2001).

Three antecedent factors combine to determine the consumers' mindset when they start using the Internet. For example, consumers wanting to perform their banking activities online may fall into an implemental, action-focused mindset, whereas those wanting to plan for a vacation a few months later may start from an exploratory mindset, browsing through a number of websites in order to accumulate information for future decision-making. Thus, an individual's mindset can vary from time to time depending on goals to be attained, relevant knowledge or experience and the emotional state at the time the search process occurs. Also, mindsets can change during the actual search process as the result of the interaction with the information source and/or the information found. This model of consumer mindset formation and influence is parsimonious and has the potential to explain a variety of consumer behaviours in digital environments.

The above discussion places a strong emphasis on providing optimal information search experience for consumers. Experiences stem from the interaction between an individual and an object or environment and integrate both psychological and emotional conditions that go beyond the passive reception of external stimuli and the subsequent interpretation of the sensation (Li *et al.*, 2001; Cho *et al.*, 2002). For example, shopping in the real world (with searching for information as one of its core components) itself is often a complex, rich and hedonic experience. Further, successful or memorable experiences enable one to experience intense emotions; thus, transforming the product into something greater than the sum of product attributes, because emotions play a crucial role in attention, planning, reasoning, learning, memory and decision-making (Picard, 1998). In addition, users respond to experiences in different ways and the information gained through this interaction can be used to customize each online search experience so that it becomes appropriate for the individual user (Shedroff, 2001).

The importance of integrating the experiential aspects of information search processes into the digital information environments becomes especially apparent when looking at the specific characteristics of travel. Travel is inherently experiential. For example, decisions regarding destination choice often contain emotional and affective content (Mansfeld, 1992), and travellers have heterogeneous information needs (Vogt and Fesenmaier, 1998). In contrast to consumer goods, which typically comprise a usually well-defined range of tangible or searchable attributes and, to a lesser extent, intangible or experiential aspects, travel and tourism products such as vacations and destinations are complex bundles of experiences with only a small set of tangible components. Further, consumers usually learn about products prior to the actual purchase mainly through an assessment of what consumption experience the product can offer and how well it can meet expectations with respect to the experience desired by the consumer (Hoch and Deighton, 1989). Due to the complex experiential nature of the tourism product and substantial geographical distances, inspection or trial prior to the purchase decision is almost impossible, thus affecting the consumers' ability to learn and create correct expectations about the actual consumption experience. Thus, travel and tourism products can be seen as 'experience goods' on the Internet because: (i) full information on 'dominant' attributes of these products cannot be known without direct experience; and (ii) information search for 'dominant' attributes is more costly and difficult than direct product experience (Klein, 1998).

4. Implications for Travel Recommendation Systems

Understanding travel information search and processing has numerous managerial implications for modelling travellers' search behaviour and, ultimately, developing technologies to create optimal search experiences. Generally, it is understood that many people are highly involved in information search for travel planning for a variety of reasons ranging from functional (e.g. detailed price information) to hedonic (e.g. destination images). The nature and type of information sought depend to a large degree upon the individual's personal characteristics and the stage within the travel-planning process. For example, some findings regarding the influence of travel and destination knowledge and/or experience on information source use are especially interesting and relevant for the context of designing destination recommendation systems. First, inexperienced travellers to a destination are likely to search for more information than repeat visitors to minimize the risk involved in visiting an unknown destination (van Raaij, 1986). Second, experienced travellers are known to use different information sources from those used by naive travellers. Inexperienced tourists appear to rely more on professional sources than experienced tourists (Woodside and Ronkainen, 1980; Snepenger *et al.*, 1990). This can be interpreted as resulting from a greater tendency of experienced travellers to seek variety and, thus, more novel information. This is also in concordance with Vogt and Fesenmaier's finding (1998) that experienced tourists tend to have higher innovation needs than inexperienced tourists.

Understanding travellers' individual characteristics such as personality and mindset has some significant implications as well. Especially the MSFI model (Dholakia and Bagozzi, 2001) suggests that consumers' navigation behaviour and its direct consequences can be understood, and potentially modelled, based on a number of psychological and cognitive characteristics, which largely determine the nature of their Web search experience. For example, there is a substantial variation in the way people process information, where some potential travellers evaluate destination on a holistic basis, while others use attribute-based processes, which will lead to a variety of 'mindsets' that can impact their online search behaviour such as navigation strategies. Thus, it will be highly desirable for an information system to learn beforehand about what 'mindset' a prospective traveller possesses when coming to visit, such that it can provide relevant content and functionality accordingly and, consequently, create a pleasant and enjoyable experience.

The recognition of travel and tourism products as 'experience goods' has important implications for accommodating travellers' information search on the Internet. Most of the current travel websites are designed based on the assumption that the individuals actively compare product attributes when purchasing the product and, thus, fail to provide content and functionality that can address the experiential aspects of the products. This will result in unsatisfactory search experiences for travellers. However, in order to make travel products searchable using current technologies, experiential aspects have to be translated into tangible attributes (Klein, 1998). Traditionally, marketeers have been trying to bridge this information gap and the resulting uncertainty with the provision of extensive verbal descriptions of mostly tangible factors, such as amenities afforded by a hotel room, supported with photographs as visual cues, or by establishing destination and company brands. However, this approach is very limited in terms of actually representing tourism experiences (Gretzel and Fesenmaier, 2002a,b). Thus, it is crucial for the success of an online information system to provide innovative ways in which tourism experiences can be conveyed and communicated. For example, making the search process itself an experience requires two different steps: (i) designing experience into the search process; and (ii) the experiential representation of search results. According to Klein (1998, p. 196), this could be achieved by creating online 'virtual experiences'.

Linking together research related to travel information search and processing strategies and the context of destination choice and theories on consumer behaviour in the digital environments will reveal important implications for accommodating travel information search in the digital environment. In addition, to provide attribute-based travel information, an intelligent travel recommendation system can be used by a destination marketing organization to: (i) enable potential visitors to 'experience' the destination; (ii) simplify the decision-making process by identifying destinations that meet specific needs and desires; (iii) facilitate the purchase of products and services at any time and any place; and (iv) encourage potential visitors to revisit a destination again and again through customer relationship management techniques. Thus, it is critical that experiential aspects of the travel experience be fully integrated into any destination recommendation system. Various strategies may be implemented that enable potential users to effectively and efficiently obtain 'important' non-verbal (i.e. non-text) cues regarding the attractiveness of potential destinations.

Chapter Summary

Travel decisions can be described as evolving and dynamic information processing, requiring a large amount of information. With the enormous amount of information available on the Internet, travellers are able to obtain detailed information about almost any destination worldwide. However, this does not guarantee that travel information search is a satisfactory experience. Thus, understanding and integrating behavioural models of travel information search into system design will enhance the likelihood of the success of travel recommendation systems. This chapter has provided an overview of the relevant literature on travel information search and processing within the context of digital information environments.

2 Travel Destination Choice Models

YEONG-HYEON HWANG, ULRIKE GRETZEL, ZHENG XIANG AND DANIEL R. FESENMAIER

1. Introduction

Travel decision-making involves a complex and multifaceted decision process (Park and Lutz, 1982; Moutinho, 1987; Woodside and MacDonald, 1994; Tay *et al.*, 1996; Dellaert *et al.*, 1998a; Fesenmaier and Jeng, 2000; Jeng and Fesenmaier, 2002). Among the many aspects of a trip that require the consideration, evaluation and elimination of alternatives, choosing a destination represents one of the core decisions to be made. Travel, by definition, represents a spatial movement from an original location to one or more destinations, and tourism products and services (attractions, accommodations, activities) are closely tied to these destinations. Also, this central role of destination choice implies that the selection of a travel destination is one of the first decisions made in the trip-planning process and influences all subsequent decisions (Jeng and Fesenmaier, 2002). Thus, travellers' destination choice forms an essential part of their entire trip-planning process and has long been recognized as an important topic by researchers in tourism.

In its simplest form, destination choice can be defined as a process of choosing one destination among a number of alternatives for the purpose of fulfilling the travel-related needs at hand. Following from research in consumer behaviour, travellers are understood to follow a funnel-like procedure of narrowing down choices that involves a series of well-defined stages: (i) recognition that there is a choice to be made; (ii) formulation of goals and objectives; (iii) generation of alternative set of destinations; (iv) search for information about the properties of the alternatives under consideration; (v) judgement or choice among these alternatives; (vi) action taking; and (vii) providing feedback for future decision-making. The most basic model of destination choice can be easily translated into content and functions for destination recommendation systems.

©CAB International 2006. *Destination Recommendation Systems: Behavioural Foundations and Applications* (eds D.R. Fesenmaier, K.W. Wöber and H. Werthner)

However, modelling travellers' destination choice and ultimately making real-time suggestions based on behavioural 'predictions' for individual travellers still present challenges for developing destination recommendation systems. There seems to be several factors that could make this type of prediction difficult. First, destination choice involves high-risk, ill-defined choice situations where outcomes have unknown probabilities due to the intangible and experiential nature of tourism, and the ultimate choice of a final destination depends more or less on the quality and quantity of information available to, and used by, a traveller (Wahab *et al.*, 1976; Snepenger *et al.*, 1990; Fodness and Murray, 1997). For example, the term 'destination' itself lacks a commonly agreed definition because: (i) the spatial extension of a destination is known to be a function of the traveller's distance from the destination; and (ii) a destination is not only a geographical entity but can also be a collection of activities or experiences (Ricci and Werthner, 2002). Second, several issues related to the decision-making process may contribute to the complexity of modelling destination choice as well. For example, it is understood that, in addition to functional or utilitarian elements, destination choices often contain emotional and affective content (Mansfeld, 1992). For instance, the exact cost of a tour package might be considered a functional element, whereas promotional messages, and family and friend influences, act as emotional elements in the choice process. Destinations may also have attributes that are inherently fixed to the brand that so far cannot be readily varied to model destination choice behaviour (Crouch and Louviere, 2001). Third, a modelling approach requires not only the application of general goal-achievement rules such as utility maximization but also the integration of situational and environmental factors such as trip characteristics (Hwang and Fesenmaier, 2001; Jeng and Fesenmaier, 2002).

The primary goal of a destination recommendation system is to guide travellers in terms of the destination and other trip-related products. Thus, an in-depth understanding of how travellers make choices in regard to the destinations they are planning to visit is of great importance to designing a successful recommendation system, because human-centric computing involves designing, developing and implementing information technology that reflects the needs and lifestyles of its human users (Silverman *et al.*, 2001). This chapter provides an overview of the destination choice models that have been developed to describe the process and strategies travellers use in trip planning. In addition, it discusses travellers' individual sociodemographic and psychological factors that will influence the travellers' trip-planning process as well as the effect of the decision frames in which travellers are making these decisions.

2. Destination Choice Models

The recognition that destination choice is the central aspect of trip planning has led to an impressive amount of research, and many conceptual approaches to understanding travel destination choice have been proposed. In general, these approaches can be conceptualized into four different frameworks: (i) choice set models, which focus attention on the process through which individuals reduce a large set of potential destinations to a single one (Um and Crompton, 1991; Crompton, 1992; Crompton and Ankomah, 1993; Ankomah *et al.*, 1996); (ii) general travel models, which are based upon consumer theory and focus on the processes individuals follow when they try to identify and select a travel destination (Moutinho, 1987; Woodside and MacDonald, 1994); (iii) decision net models, which examine the travel decision at an aggregate level and focus attention on the relationships between the various 'facets' of travel planning (Dellaert *et al.*, 1998b; Fesenmaier and Jeng, 2000; Jeng and Fesenmaier, 2002); and (iv) multidestination travel models, which reflect the variety of approaches used to explain travel patterns involved in trips with more than one destination as well as the strategies employed by individuals when 'bundling' together destinations (Lue *et al.*, 1993; Stewart and Vogt, 1997; Tideswell and Faulkner, 1999).

The choice set model approach (see Fig. 2.1) defines destination choice as a 'sorting out' process (Um and Crompton, 1990, 1991; Crompton, 1992; Crompton and Ankomah, 1993; Ankomah *et al.*, 1996), whereby the 'early consideration set' is created when a prospective traveller eliminates from consideration those destinations that are 'not available' based upon practical constraints such as knowledge, time and budget. The second stage in the decision process occurs when the prospective traveller further reduces the choice set by excluding: (i) 'inept' alternatives, those destinations that the prospective traveller is aware of but rates poorly; and (ii) 'inert' alternatives, those destinations of which the traveller is aware but has no interest in

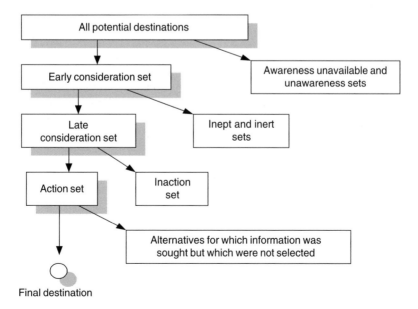

Fig. 2.1. Structure of choice set model (adapted from Crompton and Ankomah, 1993).

(Um and Crompton, 1990; Crompton, 1992; Crompton and Ankomah, 1993). According to this framework, the evaluation criteria used to narrow down the various sets of alternatives include demographic and psychological characteristics of the decision-maker, situational constraints and destination stimuli (Ankomah *et al.*, 1996). Also, Um and Crompton (1990) argue that a prospective traveller relies more on passively obtained information in the early stages and searches for information more actively in the later stages. In other words, the prospective traveller actively seeks information only for those alternatives included in the 'action' set, i.e. those destinations considered as being attractive and within current constraints. It is this action set that is then used as the basis for selecting the final destination. The choice set model approach also anticipates that travellers are more likely to take into account the positive aspects of alternative destinations (described as 'facilitators') in early stages of the destination choice process, whereas negative aspects (described as 'inhibitors') are more prominent in later stages (Um and Crompton, 1992).

A number of general travel models developed based upon consumer behaviour theory have been proposed (see Moutinho, 1987 for an excellent review). This approach takes a comprehensive perspective in that its scope is not limited to the destination per se but rather incorporates many aspects of pre- and postpurchase decision-making processes including preference structure formation, information search and postpurchase evaluation. Woodside and his colleagues (Woodside and Lysonski, 1989; Woodside and MacDonald, 1994), for example, proposed a general model of travellers' choice whereby situational factors (i.e. personal characteristics and social structure) and marketing factors (i.e. product design, price and advertisement) establish the decision context (see Fig. 2.2).

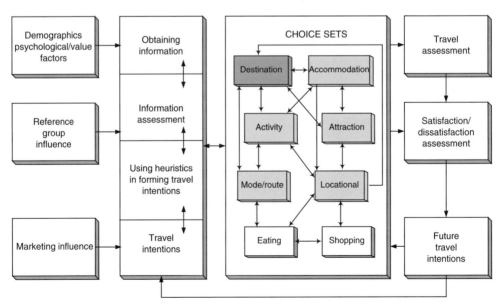

Fig. 2.2. Tourism service decision process (adapted from Woodside and MacDonald, 1994).

The decision to travel is a complex process, which requires the solution of a number of 'sub-decisions' or 'facets' including destination, travel party, attractions to visit, timing and route (Moutinho, 1987; Jeng and Fesenmaier, 2002). This research suggests that the overall structure of these sub-decisions is hierarchical in that the decisions made later in the process are contingent upon those made earlier. In addition, travel decision-making is assumed to have a net structure, implying that one sub-decision relates directly or indirectly to all other sub-decisions (Moutinho, 1987; Fesenmaier and Jeng, 2000; Jeng and Fesenmaier, 2002). Based on this conceptualization of travel decision-making, Fesenmaier and Jeng (2000) and Jeng and Fesenmaier (2002) proposed a multistage hierarchical trip decision net model (see Fig. 2.3). According to this model, the overall travel decision consists of core, secondary and en route decisions. Core decisions are usually planned ahead of time, in detail, and include making choices with respect to the primary destination, date and length of the trip, nature of the travel party, type of accommodation, route and budget. Secondary decisions are tentative in that they are considered before the trip but remain largely flexible to accommodate the possibility of change. Secondary decisions include the selection of secondary destination(s), activities and attractions to visit. En route decisions are those considered during the trip, such as the selection of restaurants and stores. The decision net model implies that prospective travellers in different decision stages confront different choice tasks and, thus, require different types of information. However, the hierarchical dependency between

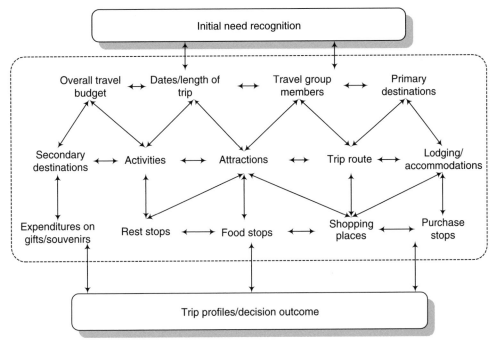

Fig. 2.3. A decision net of tourism travel (adapted from Fesenmaier and Jeng, 2000).

sub-decisions posited by the decision net model allows one to narrow down the range of subsequent choices and the respective information needs based on the outcome of previous stages in the decision-making process.

Most of the research on travel destination choice focuses on the selection of a single destination. A number of scholars have argued, however, that the assumption of a single destination trip is often fallacious and oversimplistic (Fesenmaier and Lieber, 1988; Lue et al., 1993, 1996; Oppermann, 1995; Stewart and Vogt, 1997; Tideswell and Faulkner, 1999). This line of research indicates that people tend to visit more than one destination for several reasons and, at the same time, they also take into consideration the constraints and opportunities associated with visiting these multiple destinations. First, tourists visit several destinations in order to satisfy diverse needs and reduce risk and uncertainty. From an economic rationalistic point of view, travellers may combine visits to several destinations in the course of a single trip to reduce the overall cost of travel and to maximize the use of time, money and other resources associated with the travel (Kim and Fesenmaier, 1990; Tideswell and Faulkner, 1999). Travellers' propensity to visit multiple destinations on a single trip is also compounded with the inclusion of visits to friends and relatives in travel itineraries. This variety-seeking and multiple benefit-seeking behaviour exists not only in relation to destination choice but also within the context of selecting activities (Fesenmaier and Lieber, 1988; Bristow et al., 1995; Dellaert et al., 1997, 1998a). Variety seeking, and thus multidestination travel, tends to increase with the size of the travel group as each individual is likely to have different expectations regarding the trip. Thus, a large travel group may tend to visit more destinations than a small travel group in order to satisfy the members' diverse needs (Fesenmaier and Lieber, 1985; Lue et al., 1993). Second, the probability of taking a multidestination trip also depends on a series of constraints or opportunities such as travel mobility, time constraints, destination familiarity, types of travel arrangement and spatial configurability of multiple destinations. In general, for example, the higher the travel mobility (e.g. when a personal car is available as opposed to just air transportation), the higher the tendency towards multidestination trip behaviour (Cooper, 1981; Debbage, 1991; Tideswell and Faulkner, 1999). Also, the spatial and opportunity-related configuration of destinations as well as the origin of the traveller can have an effect on the likelihood of selecting multiple destinations (Fotheringham, 1985; Kim and Fesenmaier, 1990; Gunn, 1994; Jeng and Fesenmaier, 1998).

3. Factors Influencing Destination Choice

The destination choice models described above provide insights into the specific nature of travel-planning behaviour. These models have been used to explain and predict destination choice under certain circumstances based on different assumptions and/or premises. For example, many of the studies related to choice modelling in tourism assume that travellers are rational decision-makers who try to maximize the utility and, thus, assess costs and benefits of their actions before committing themselves to choosing a specific destination (Wahab *et al.*, 1976; Schmoll, 1977), while some acknowledge the role of constraints on destination choice (Woodside and Lysonski, 1989; Um and Crompton, 1992), or even consider destination choice a compulsory sub-decison among other travel-related decisions (Moutinho, 1987). Despite the diversity of the approaches, these models have one thing in common: travellers' destination choice process has been approached as a functional or utilitarian decision-making activity that is influenced by a number of psychological and non-psychological variables. An analysis of the literature discussing the general forms of travel destination choice models indicates that the variables used to explain and predict one's destination choice can be classified into two broad categories: (i) decision-maker's personal characteristics; and (ii) travel characteristics (Fig. 2.4). Personal characteristics encompass socio-economic characteristics as well as one's psychological and cognitive traits. Travel characteristics include situational factors that make the travel distinguishable from other travels. As depicted in Fig. 2.4, individual characteristics influence destination choice in both direct and indirect ways, while the effect of travel characteristics on the travel destination choice is rather direct.

3.1 Decision-maker's characteristics

In order to understand travellers' destination choice, sociodemographic and psychological characteristics have been widely used as explanatory variables for evoked set formation, categorization of alternative destinations and antecedents of information processing (e.g. Mayo and Jarvis, 1981; Woodside and Lysonski, 1989; Um and Crompton, 1991; Woodside and MacDonald, 1994). Sociodemographic characteristics such as age, education, income and marital status are often employed as surrogates for determining the travel decision-maker's resources and constraints. However, the explanatory power of sociodemographic variables with respect to variations in destination choice seems to be rather limited (Fesenmaier and Lieber, 1985).

Psychological and cognitive variables with potential impacts on the destination choice process include personal values, knowledge and experience

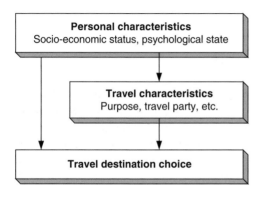

Fig. 2.4. Factors influencing destination choice.

related to a destination or travel in general, personality (i.e. locus of control, risk avoidance, etc.) and attitude towards certain destinations, as well as involvement in the trip-planning process. The structure of an individual's value system provides the basis for deriving intentions and directing human behaviour. Woodside and Lysonski (1989) argue that personal value systems influence travellers' destination awareness. In contrast, Um and Crompton (1991) describe personal values as an internal input that initiates the formation of an evoked set from an awareness set. In empirical studies, Madrigal (1995) has shown that personal values are a better predictor of choice between group tours and individual tours than personality, and Zins (1998) has utilized personal values as an antecedent variable for hotel choice.

Knowledge is an important cognitive domain that influences destination choice (Snepenger *et al.*, 1990). Knowledge, often obtained through direct experience, can be represented either as travel knowledge in general or as knowledge of alternative destination(s), or both. In each case, knowledge influences the range of alternatives considered. Further, previous experience with a destination plays an important role in terms of how a destination is categorized during decision-making processes with respect to how well it could perform when selected as a travel destination (Woodside and Lysonski, 1989). Also, differences in the choice of destinations and attractions between first-time visitors and repeat visitors are prevalent. First-time visitors tend to choose destinations that are easily accessible, while experienced visitors are more likely to consider destinations with low accessibility (McKercher, 1998). In addition, repeat or more experienced visitors may want to visit novel destinations since they have already visited well-known destinations within a region or attractions within a specific destination. In this sense, repeat visitors are more selective and less prone to visit multiple destinations (Oppermann, 1992; Decrop, 1999; Hwang *et al.*, 2002). This discrepancy can be explained by looking at the difference in perceived risk of the two groups of travellers. Repeat visitors with better knowledge about what to expect from or at the destination perceive less risk than first-time visitors and, thus, encounter less uncertainty in their destination choice process. Destination familiarity can, of course, not only be acquired through previous experience but is also dependent on the amount and type of information obtained about the destination (Tideswell and Faulkner, 1999).

Personality, which can be defined as 'the reflection of a person's enduring and unique characteristics that urge one to respond in persistent ways to recurring environmental stimuli' (Decrop, 1999, p. 106), is a 'complex outcome of a person's learning, perceptions, motivations, emotions, and roles' (Mayo and Jarvis, 1981, p. 109). Plog (1994) suggested two fundamental personality dimensions that are of importance within the context of tourism: allocentricism and psychocentricism. Allocentric travellers, who exhibit a self-assured and venturesome personality, are more likely to choose exotic destinations, while psychocentric travellers, whose centre of attention is focused on self-doubts and anxieties, are thought to prefer familiar destinations (Plog, 1994; Ross, 1994). Griffith and Albanese (1996) have shown that Plog's model can be used to characterize travellers in terms of their psychographics and suggested practical use of these traits to make destination recommendations. Further, personality traits related to locus of control and sensation seeking or risk avoidance, which influence an individual's decision-making style, play of course an important role in any decision-making process but are of particular importance for destination choice processes because of the high levels of uncertainty involved (Roehl and Fesenmaier, 1992).

Knowledge and/or perceptions of the characteristics of various destinations, the destination images created through exposure to advertising and marketing efforts and the fit between conceptions of the destinations with personal values and beliefs result in particular attitudes towards these places. These attitudes towards certain destinations are significant determinants of whether or not a destination is considered an alternative and how it is evaluated in later stages of the destination choice process. Research by Fishbein and Ajzen (1975), among others, relates personal attitudes to subsequent behaviour, arguing that they play an important role in understanding destination choice. The attitude–behaviour model provides explanations for human behaviour based on individual attitudes and the behavioural intentions that can be derived from them (Ajzen and Fishbein, 1980; Ajzen, 1991). Within the context of destination choice, Um and Crompton (1990) have operationalized attitude towards alternative destinations as the difference between the magnitude of the perceived facilitators and the magnitude of the perceived inhibitors, and have argued that destinations with higher attitude scores are more likely to be included in the evoked set and, ultimately, to be selected as the final destination. However, a study by Ajzen and Driver (1991) indicates that leisure travel as a form of planned behaviour involves not only behavioural control in accordance with personal attitudes but also interactions between social groups. Therefore, destination-related decisions involve not only the allocation and negotiation of different personal aspects (personal preference and utility) but also a consideration of many different social resources (social group, companionship).

Consumer involvement can be interpreted as the perception of personal importance in relation to an object. In a complex decision and choice situation there is a greater need to develop commitment and stronger attitude in order to accomplish the task. On the other hand, simple and routine decisions require relatively low consumer involvement (Reid and Crompton, 1993). Fesenmaier and Johnson (1989) used the individual's trip-planning involvement as the basis for segmenting the Texas travel market. They found that low-involvement travellers tend to have a shorter planning horizon, while the medium–high involvement travel group showed a longer trip-planning horizon. It is important to note that the longer the planning horizon, the more destination alternatives can be considered and the more extensive can their evaluation be. In addition, the results of their study indicated that low-involvement tourists take shorter, getaway types of trips that involve less resource constraints and less risk factors, whereas highly involved tourists tend to take longer vacations, which require extensive cognitive efforts, advance planning and entail more resource constraints and risk factors.

Many researchers argue that travel decision-makers' individual characteristics do not operate in a vacuum. To a certain degree, travel decision-
makers' characteristics are also affected by forces outside the individual
travellers. As suggested by Ajzen (1991), an individual's subject norm can
be influenced by his or her perceived behavioural expectations of some important referent individuals or groups such as spouse, family and friends.
For example, Mayo and Jarvis (1981) classified these external forces into four
major groups: role and family influences, reference groups, social classes,
and culture and subcultures. Other researchers such as Woodside and Lysonski (1989) and Schmoll (1977) considered market stimuli and travel stimuli
as important external factors that can potentially influence travel decision-
makers' cognitive and psychological characteristics.

3.2 Trip characteristics

The complexity of the destination-related decision-making process stems
from the fact that it depends on the specifics of the situation in which it occurs. Trip characteristics appear to be the most important determinants of
the context in which destination decisions (or sub-decisions) are taken. These
trip characteristics include travel purpose, length of travel, distance between
origin and destination, and travel group composition, as well as related factors such as travel mobility. Thus, one's evaluation criteria for alternative
destinations vary from one task to another as the context of the trip changes.
Travel purpose can be generally defined as one's stated needs or motives
for travel and can be used to classify trips into two broad categories: business and leisure. Leisure travel, which is often referred to as vacation travel
or pleasure travel, can be further divided into subcategories based on the
specific purpose and/or length of travel, for instance as getaway trip, family
vacation, etc. Travel purpose is, oftentimes, closely connected to activities
and settings (e.g. visits to cultural heritage sites) and, therefore, significantly
constrains or defines the range of alternative destinations considered.

The nature of the travel group is also an important influence factor. Alternative destinations considered by a person who plans to go on a family vacation, for example, are probably different from those considered for a trip with
friends. The characteristics of the travel party also impact the geographical
range of alternative destinations taken into account in that they influence the
mobility of the travel group. A family with children tends to take short vacations at easily accessible destinations. In contrast, couples without children
are more likely to choose destinations with modest accessibility (McKercher,
1998). It has also been shown that the nature of the travel party defines the
degree of heterogeneity in the group with respect to interests. That is, as
the travel party size increases, the number of needs to gratify is likely to
increase accordingly and, thus, multidestination travel is more likely to occur
(Fesenmaier and Lieber, 1985, 1988; Lue *et al.*, 1993).

The time available for a trip constrains the geographical range of the
trip. Thus, travellers with limited amounts of time available tend to prefer

nearby destinations. In contrast, travellers with more time tend to prefer more distant destinations (McKercher, 1998). In this sense, the length of trip constrains the range of alternatives that will be considered. Consequently, whether a destination will be considered an alternative is a function of the length of the trip and also the distance from home to a destination, a factor that has been included as a key variable in aggregated destination choice models (Kim and Fesenmaier, 1990; Lo, 1992). In general, the number of trips generated from a region increases to a certain threshold distance and starts to decrease after that point (McKercher, 1998). Variations in the threshold distance appear to be attributable to trip characteristics as well as personal characteristics. In disaggregated models, cognitive distance instead of physical distance has been emphasized to account for circumstances in which individuals use mentally measured proximity or distance to evaluate alternatives.

Travel mobility is not only a function of the nature of the travel group but also depends on the transportation mode a traveller uses during a trip (Tideswell and Faulkner, 1999). Alternative destinations, which a traveller with a rental car or personal car can think of, might be unavailable to travellers who use, for instance, only public transportation. Travel mobility has an impact on the flexibility of the travel itinerary and is positively related to not only the number of destinations but also the number of attractions and activities that can be integrated into the trip. Thus, the transportation mode used can also explain certain tendencies towards multidestination travel as travellers with greater mobility are better equipped for visits to more than one destination (Cooper, 1981).

4. Decision Frames

Decisions can be framed in various ways depending on personal preferences for certain decision-making strategies and the needs or constraints derived from the specific trip-planning situation. Specifically, the number and type of decision criteria taken into account will vary based on the nature of the trip to be planned. Trips defined around a specific activity, such as golfing, for instance, will strongly influence the frame in which the decision has to be made. For such a trip, beach access at the destination might be desired but might not be perceived as being as important as in the case of a typical summer, sun and beach vacation. Also, it can be assumed that personal characteristics influence one's need, ability and/or willingness to take certain criteria into consideration. A low annual household income, for instance, will probably encourage the adoption of a decision frame that incorporates price as a main criterion. Further, personal cognitive styles can greatly influence the amount of information included in the decision-making process and especially the number of alternatives considered by the individual decision-maker (Hunt *et al.*, 1989; Driver *et al.*, 1990).

Further, destination decisions can be taken at different levels in the travel-planning hierarchy, i.e. one can select a main destination, a secondary

destination or places within a destination such as attractions and restaurants. Given the impact of choosing a main destination on decisions with
respect to lower-level facets of a trip, being in the process of selecting the
main destination of a trip implies that many characteristics of this trip are
still undetermined. In contrast, if the main destination has been chosen and
the decision-making process refers to finding one or more secondary destinations, one can assume that many important characteristics of the trip have
already been outlined and that the range of destination alternatives in the
consideration set will be rather limited. At the most specific level, destination
decisions involve choosing places to visit at a destination. This latter form of
destination decision can be characterized by a high level of constraints and,
consequently, a relatively small number of alternatives to be considered.

Depending on the specificity of the destination decision, the amount
and type of information taken into account in the decision-making process
will vary. It can be assumed that more specific destination decisions require
more specific information. If no destination decision has been made, the information sought will be in the general form of destination alternatives and
will often be more image-based than factual. If a main destination has been
selected, the destination decision will focus on secondary destinations in
proximity to the main destination. Such a decision requires image-related
information as well as more specific details about distances and activity and
attraction portfolios to evaluate destination complementarities. Finally, those
decisions that involve selecting places or attractions at a specific destination
will to a large extent include detailed and more functional information in the
form of opening hours, prices, admission restrictions, etc.

5. Implications for Travel Recommendation Systems

The literature on travel destination choice models establishes a substantial
theoretical foundation for designing destination recommendation systems
by providing an in-depth understanding of travellers' decision-making behaviour. Despite the complexity of decision-making involved in destination
choice, there is some degree of regularity and predictability in the travel-
planning process that computer-based systems can utilize to reflect the personal and individual differences in how travel decisions are made. A variety
of techniques or procedures can be used to achieve predicting destination
choice by using independent variables including individual characteristics
such as demographics, price and cultural background, and trip-related characteristics such as destination attractiveness and travel cost (Louviere and
Hensher, 1983; Ben-Akiva and Lerman, 1985; Fesenmaier, 1990; Jeng and
Fesenmaier, 1996).

This literature suggests that: (i) a destination is the primary anchor for
travel planning; (ii) factors effecting destination choice are consistent but
the nature and extent of impact vary substantially, depending upon traveller characteristics and the nature of the trip; and (iii) the extent to which
places or destinations may be bundled depend on the length of the trip and

the spatial organization of potential destinations. From a marketing point of view, this leaves the issue wide open with respect to how a destination recommendation system makes 'suggestions' for travellers; i.e. a recommendation system can tap into different aspects and/or stages of the process of destination choice when a traveller is searching information on the Internet (which will be extensively discussed in Chapter 3, this volume). For example, based on the destination choice set model and research in consumer behaviour, it is understood that although travellers' consideration sets are primarily memory-based and memory-driven, they can be altered with external information. Thus, a common practice used by destination recommendation systems is to provide relevant alternatives that could potentially fit into the travellers' consideration set by using certain preference elicitation techniques. Also, a recommendation system should aid the traveller in narrowing down the choice alternatives and eventually identify the destination he or she wants to visit.

Chapter Summary

Travel decision-making has been seen as a complex and multifaceted decision process and is critical for understanding travellers' trip-planning activities. It includes decisions regarding destination, attractions, timing, transportation and activities. Among the many sub-decisions that comprise a trip decision, destination choice has been considered the core component. Based on this recognition, a substantial amount of research has been devoted to study travel destination choice. A modelling approach that aims to explain and predict choice outcome is fairly complicated and challenging. It requires not only the application of general goal-achievement rules such as utility maximization but also the integration of situational and environmental factors. This chapter has provided an overview of the models that have been developed to describe the process and strategies travellers use in trip planning.

3 Information Search and Navigation on the Internet

BING PAN AND DANIEL R. FESENMAIER

1. Introduction

Travellers have adopted the Internet as one of their primary sources for travel information (Weber and Roehl, 1999; Lake, 2001; TIA, 2002). However, travellers are often overwhelmed by the huge amount of information online and not able to locate the information they intend to find (Pan and Fesenmaier, 2000). Thus, trip planning on the Web can be a frustrating experience (Radosevich, 1997; Stoltz, 1999). Using artificial intelligence and expert system techniques, travel recommendation systems have been promoted as a proactive way to facilitate travel information search and trip planning (Hwang and Fesenmaier, 2001; Klicek, 2001; Ricci and Werthner, 2001). However, the usefulness of these systems is still unclear.

In Chapters 1 and 2 relevant behavioural research in consumer studies and tourism research were considered as they inform the designing of travel recommendation systems. This chapter focuses on understanding trip planners' information processing in computer-mediated environments (CME). Different from information processing on printed media or television, when planning a trip online, a traveller needs to interact with a computer through a web browser. The interaction between a travel information searcher and the Internet can be viewed at different levels: (i) the interaction between a user and a computer; (ii) the interaction between an information searcher and an information system; and (iii) the interaction between a navigator and a hypertext system. There are many research pieces in these areas that may deepen our understanding of trip planning online. This chapter starts with a review of the literature in these areas; different views on usability issues are then discussed followed by the results and the implications from an online trip-planning study.

2. Human–Computer Interaction Models

Travellers search information on the Internet through the use of a computer. Thus, behavioural models in human–computer interaction (HCI) can deepen our understanding of this process. Traditional HCI literature is based on information-processing theory, which views human beings as information processors (Card *et al.*, 1983; Preece *et al.*, 1994). The human information processor is composed of the perceptual system, the motor system and the cognitive system, along with their own memories and processors. The perceptual system includes every sense of the human being and their relevant buffer memories. The cognitive system consists of a mechanism that receives information from perceptual system and memory to generate appropriate responses, whereas the motor system is responsible for carrying out actions according to responses from the cognitive system. Card *et al.*, (1983) proposed the goals, operators, methods and selection rules (GOMS) model, which describes the process of interaction between a user and a computer. The user sets up goals to determine what he or she wants to achieve. The operators are the elementary efforts needed to achieve the goal, such as keystrokes. The user determines the procedures for achieving the goal, which consists of operators and other relevant goals. The user then follows selection rules to determine which method to apply if several methods exist.

Norman's execution–evaluation cycle (1990) is another influential model which guides the design of information systems. According to this model, the stages of interaction include establishing the goal, forming the intention, specifying the action sequence, executing the action, perceiving the system state, interpreting and evaluating it, respecting the goals and intentions. Norman argued that problems always arise when there is an evaluation gulf whenever the physical representation of the system cannot match the expectation of the users. Furthermore, the user and the system each describes the task in different languages: a user uses 'task language' while a system uses 'core language', which is the computerized representation of the task (Dix *et al.*, 1998, p. 105). The two languages are not identical and the discrepancies often cause communication problems between the user and the system.

3. Cognitive Information Retrieval Models

Travel information search on the Internet can be viewed as an information retrieval process. According to Jacob and Shaw (1998) there are two paradigms dominating most information retrieval research. The physical paradigm is based on an analogy to mechanical systems that does not take users' cognitive mode into account. On the other hand, the cognitive perspective of information retrieval argues that 'any processing of information, whether perceptual or symbolic, is mediated by a system of categories or concepts which, for the information-processing device, is a model of his world' (De Mey, 1977, pp. xvi–xvii). Cognitive information retrieval views information as subjective instead of objective in that information only makes sense when

it is assimilated into the mental model and knowledge structure of the information receiver. Accordingly, effective information retrieval depends on the
congruence between the cognitive structure of an individual user and the
knowledge representation of the information system (Shera, 1965). Since
each individual's idiosyncratic mental model is influenced by many sociocognitive variables and is hard to capture and analyse, it is easier to explore
the shared mental model and knowledge representation of a user group or
knowledge domain (Allen, 1996).

Similarly, Ingwersen (1992) argued that in the information retrieval process, data in the information system has been transformed into information
in relation to the mental model of the user and, subsequently, the knowledge
state of the user is changed. The concept of 'polyrepresentation' of information can be applied to both the user's mental model and the system's information space. The linkage between different representations of knowledge
states of the users and the systems can reduce the uncertainty by eliminating
lexical ambiguity and providing contextual information. Furthermore, the
interaction between a user and an information system is mediated by the
user interface. Users always need to generate queries to match the system's
language (Beaulieu, 2000), which represents compromises between their
information needs and the need to adapt to the information system itself.
Mental models can be represented either as the different metaphors or
affordance of a computer system (Norman, 1988) or as the interrelationship
between different concepts in the information user's mind and information
space (Carley and Palmquist, 1992).

4. Research on Navigation on the Internet

Travellers search a variety of websites on the Internet for a trip-planning task
(Pan, 2003). The Internet is an interactive hypertext system where information nodes are 'hyperlinked' according to their semantic relevance (Boechler,
2001). Different from traditional information retrieval, travel information
search process is a navigation process in the hypertext space, both among
different websites and inside a specific one. For information searchers,
traversing through the web space involves information processing and learning, and judgements of semantic relevance according to information searchers' knowledge states and search goals. Accordingly, the success of finding
travel related information on the Internet is determined by the ease of navigation and understanding of information content on web pages.

Research on hypertext systems showed that there are three ways to
carry out information search tasks in a hypertext system: (i) the user can
traverse through a set of links to reach relevant nodes; (ii) the user can navigate through the documents using a representation interface (such as using
a graphic bookshelf to represent the organization of online books); and (iii)
the user can query all documents through keyword search to locate relevant
documents (Conklin, 1987). The main advantage of hypertext is that a large
amount of information can be accessed rather quickly and the organization

of the information is relatively flexible. However, hypertext does not have a conventional structure that leads the user through documents and the user is completely unrestricted in terms of where to go and which hyperlink to click; thus, hypertext-based systems require more cognitive effort.

Two different theories have emerged that provide explanations for hypertext navigation: (i) information-foraging theory (Pirolli and Card, 1999); and (ii) a cognitive model of web design and navigation (Bollen, 2001). In an analogy to food-foraging behaviour of living organisms, information-foraging theory is a general model describing how people use different strategies and technologies to search for information in response to the changing information environment. Information searchers organize information in clusters in order to minimize information search cost and use filtering methods to single out documents that are more relevant (Fig. 3.1). Furthermore, they use proximal cues to identify important information for further exploration or consumption. The concept of information scent is a construct that describes how information searchers identify valuable information from 'snippets' of proximal cues (represented by link anchors on the Web). In an empirical study, the value of information scent was measured by vectors of words in the documents in relation to the information searchers' intention. The decision of which link to click on a web page depends on the value of information scent of each link (Chi *et al.*, 2001). In contrast, Bollen (2001) proposed a cognitive model of web design and navigation whereby he argued that shared knowledge is necessary for hypertext navigation (Fig. 3.2). In addition, he argued that a user's expertise, navigation strategies, domain knowledge and mental models, along with hypertext network structure, all contribute to hypertext navigation. The mental models of the users are represented in their navigational path and the model of the system is represented by the hyperlink structure of the websites. In explaining the navigation process, Kim and Hirtle (1995) argued that the users of a hypertext system need to perform several tasks at the same time: informational tasks, which is reading and understanding the contents presented in the linked nodes; navigational tasks, which is planning and searching through links; and also management and negotiation of the previous two tasks. Failing the second task may lead to disorientation in a hypertext system.

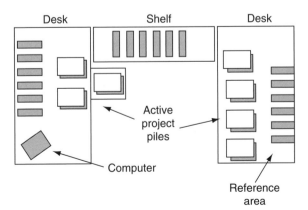

Fig. 3.1. Information in clusters: the physical layout of a business office (from Pirolli and Card, 1999).

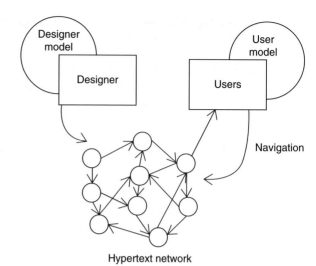

Fig. 3.2. Hypertext design and use is shaped by users' and designers' mental models (from Bollen, 2001).

5. Usability Issues in Searching Information on the Internet

Various models in HCI literature view different mental models, or languages, and understanding of tasks between a user and a computer system contribute to usability problems in the interaction process (Dix *et al.*, 1998). For example, Abowd and Beale (1991) proposed an interaction model that comprises four major parts (the user, the system, the input and the output) (Fig. 3.3). When a user's mental model is congruent with the conceptual model of the designer that is embodied in a computer, the interaction between a user and a computer will be smooth and successful (Norman, 1990). Similarly, the cognitive information retrieval literature, similar to the constructivist view of learning, views the degree of congruence between the mental model of information users and the semantic model of the information systems as determining the usefulness and efficiency of the system (Beaulieu, 2000).

Hypertext is a special type of information retrieval system. The complexity of hypertext navigation may induce additional usability problems.

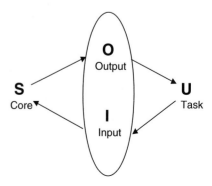

Fig. 3.3. A human–computer interaction model (from Abowd and Beale, 1991).

According to Nielsen (1995), hypertext usability includes five aspects: easy to learn, efficient to use, easy to remember, few errors and pleasant to use. However, Smith (1996) argued that since hypertext is designed to encourage exploration and browsing, traditional measures of computer system usability, such as the time it takes to complete a task and the number of mistakes made in the process, are not appropriate. Instead, he proposed a measurement of 'lostness' as the number of information items inspected compared with the number of items nominally needed to make a decision. To explore the nature of usability problems, Wang and Pouchard (1997) showed that users had problems understanding the syntax and semantics of search engines. More than 30% of the subjects did not click any links returned from the search engine on a university home page. They suggested that providing context-sensitive help and automation of query terms would reduce this type of errors. Another study conducted by Bilal (2000) with middle school students showed that the students always used natural language to perform information search that is not supported by the search engine. Many times they were searching information on the concepts that were either too broad or too narrow. These results suggest that the semantic meanings of concepts are a major factor contributing to usability problems when users are searching information on the Internet.

Mental models are a central concept in explaining the difficulties and usability problems during the interaction process. However, different researchers define mental models through different perspectives. According to Norman, a mental model is 'the model people have of themselves, others, the environment, and the things with which they interact. People form mental models through experience, training and instruction' (Norman, 1988, p. 17). Furthermore, Johnson-Laird (1983) suggested that mental models are the basic structure of cognition: 'mental models play a central and unifying role in representing objects, states of affairs, sequences of events, the way the world is, and the social and psychological actions of daily life' (p. 397). However, mental models are incomplete and constantly evolving and are usually not accurate representations of a phenomenon (Kearsley, 2001). They are parsimonious, typically contain errors and contradictions and provide simplified explanations of complex phenomena. Jacob and Shaw (1998), on the other hand, define a mental model as an 'internal cognitive structure that the individual constructs, explicitly or implicitly, to represent a particular target domain, be it an event, an activity, an object, or a subject area' (p. 158). They argued that the concept of mental models subsumes several related constructs such as scripts (Schank and Abelson, 1977), schemata (Rumelhart, 1980) and frames (Minsky, 1986).

According to Anderson (2000) knowledge can be divided into declarative knowledge and procedural knowledge. Declarative knowledge represents our understanding of concepts and ideas and the relationships between them; procedural knowledge stands for the knowledge of accomplishing a task. In other words, declarative knowledge is about 'what' and procedural knowledge is about 'how'. The concept of mental models in the HCI literature (Norman, 1988) mostly refers to procedural knowledge, while mental models in communication research typically refer to declarative knowledge (Carley and Palmquist, 1992). According to Sasse (1997), most empirical research on mental models in the procedural knowledge sense is separated from theoretical frameworks. Most of these studies tried to direct users through metaphors and analogies in the instructions before the experiments, which are actually secondary mental models based on the researchers' understanding of the system (Borgman, 1986; Frese *et al.*, 1988). On the other hand, semantic mental models in communication literature are closely related to human memory. According to Collins and Quillian (1972), human beings have a networked semantic memory in which networked nodes and links among these nodes represent concepts and their relations. Since the Web is mainly text-based, and Internet browsers have relatively fewer functions (bookmarks, printing, history list and Back and Forward buttons), which are easier to learn compared with frequent use of Internet browsers, mental models based upon declarative knowledge are much more important in information search on the Internet. Semantics deal with different concepts or different keywords regarding one concept. Therefore, the concept of a semantic mental model can be used to differentiate the concept of mental models in the declarative knowledge sense (following Carley and Palmquist, 1992) from more traditional perspectives of mental models in HCI (Norman, 1990). According to Carley and Palmquist (1992), there are three major ways to elicit mental models: content analysis, procedural mapping and task analysis. The second and third are used to elicit users' mental models in the procedural knowledge sense. Content analysis is used to extract mental models in the declarative knowledge sense and has a long history in communication research, and more recently has been used in research on the Internet (Bauer and Scharl, 2000; Haas and Grams, 2000).

Additionally, satisfaction is another major indicator of success of information technology and information systems and is determined by many elements (Mahmood *et al.*, 2000). The background knowledge and experience of the user with computers, the Internet and other information retrieval systems can influence their web search behaviour (Hsieh-Yee, 2001). Since a mental model is an important construct in explaining information searchers' navigation behaviour, it is argued that the congruence between the mental models of information searchers and the semantic model of information space contributes to the overall effectiveness of travel information search on the Internet. In addition, research showed that product knowledge and information search experience could influence their information search efficiency (Hsieh-Yee, 2001).

6. Travel Information Search on the Internet

Following the HCI and cognitive information retrieval literature, travel information search on the Internet is the interaction between information searchers and the information space (the part of the Internet related to tourism and travel destinations) in the context of trip planning. This section describes a conceptual model for travel information search and trip planning on the Internet and further details the results of a trip-planning study and its design implications.

Travel information space contains different types of information provided by various parties in the tourism industry who are marketing their tourism products and who communicate with travellers. Three components define this interaction: a travel information searcher, the interface and the travel information space (Fig. 3.4). Travellers' situational factors, knowledge and skills regarding travelling and the travel information space contribute to effective travel information search. Travel information space refers to all the travel-related web pages on the Internet that potential travellers can access. The interface consists of search engines, the information structure of websites and various metatags and link structures, which are used to facilitate the information search.

Jeng (1999) argued that the goal of travel planning could be seen as a hierarchical structure of sub-goals. Following the concept of semantic mental models, the goals can be represented as a network of sub-problems, which need to be solved (Network A in Fig. 3.5). In Network A different nodes represent different sub-goals in which different darkness of the nodes represents different rigidity and centrality levels (the darker nodes represent more central and rigid sub-decisions). For example, 'Travel Partners' is generally rigid

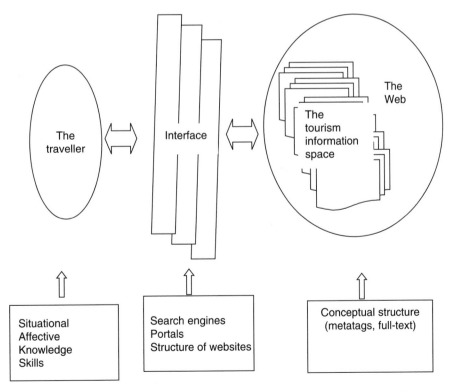

Fig. 3.4. Travellers interacting with the Internet when searching for information.

and central to the overall travel plan, and is difficult to change. On the other hand, one's choice of 'Rest Stops' usually changes according to other aspects of the trip. These sub-goals are interrelated and are constraints to each other. This is the most general level of a travel information searcher's semantic mental model prior to their information search and consists of various sub-goals in different domains. However, this level of semantic mental model is too general and not sufficient for exploring one's semantic structure, which

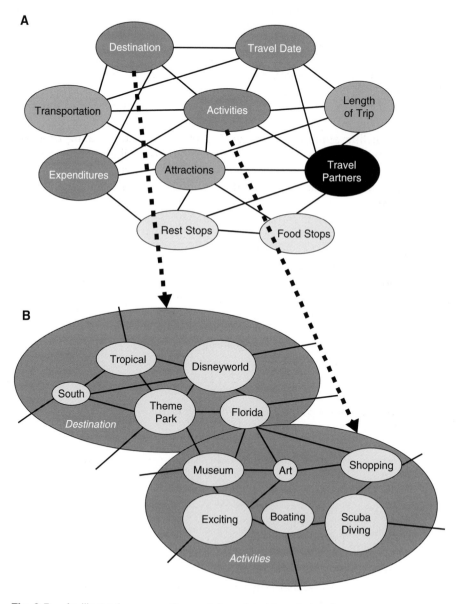

Fig. 3.5. An illustrative semantic mental model of travel planning.

can be compared with the language and vocabularies in the travel information space. Therefore, if we 'zoom in' to see the details of each node, one can see that each sub-goal has a cluster of related concepts and ideas and may include nouns, adjectives, and verbs. Network B of Fig. 3.5 is an illustration of two clusters, destinations and activities. When searching for travel information on the Internet, one's choices of links are determined by the value of relevance of the link anchors; in other words, the value of information scent, which is perceived cost and value of information source from proximal cues (Card *et al.*, 2001). For example, 'Theme Parks' is the most significant concept in this semantic network. If 'Theme Parks', 'Tropical', 'South', and 'Florida' appear on the same page and they are equally visually prominent, most likely the information searcher will click on the link of 'Theme Parks'. However, not every click is equally important. Some clicks are intended to reach certain destination web pages on which the travel information searcher stays for a longer period of time. According to Kim and Hirtle (1995), information seeking on the Web involves reading/understanding and navigating, and the two processes happen simultaneously. Since attribute information regarding alternatives are needed in the decision-making process, the destination page is usually a content page describing attributes of different alternatives (Nakayama *et al.*, 2000), whereas click-through web pages are index pages and the content is limited. For example, a travel information searcher with a mental model as in Fig. 3.5, will likely click through 'South', 'Florida', 'Theme Parks' rather quickly in order to reach the 'Disneyworld' page and then spend a much longer time reading its content. In this example, the former pages constitute navigational pages and the latter are reading pages. Accordingly, the travel information search can be represented as 'episodes' whereby each episode contains one destination or content page. The rest of pages in the 'episode' are index pages in which the travel information searcher clicks through quickly in order to reach the destination or content page.

Importantly, during the navigation process, the mental model of the travel information searcher and the representative semantic network continues to change. For example, after the destination choice has been made (e.g. the travel information searcher decides to go to Disneyworld in Florida), the searcher's semantic network will change accordingly. Some destination concepts and ideas (Disneyworld and Theme Parks) will disappear and some related concepts emerge and become more central (e.g. Hotels and Motels). Travellers' mental models are dynamic and contingent upon their decision-making process. After a certain period of searching and travel planning on the Internet, the information searcher will stop when all the goals are satisfied or the travel information searcher encounters obstacles (fatigue, no relevant information or time constraint). The result of the planning effort is a 'sub-space' of the overall travel information space, which represents the results of the interaction between the mental model of the travel information searcher and the travel information space. Clearly, the semantic model of the travel information searcher plays an essential role in this process. If the traveller's mental model and the concepts and keywords in the travel information space do not match, the information searchers will not find the information they are looking for. It is clear, then, that the travel information searchers' mental models represent their background knowledge, information search tasks and their understanding of the Internet as a travel information source. Furthermore, travel information is obtained by searching travel information space based upon one's idiosyncratic mental models. Finally, these mental models continue changing during travel information search on the Internet based on the information they encounter and sub-decisions they make.

A recent study by Pan (2003) shows that the travel information search follows a hierarchical structure, in which the process can be divided into different 'chapters' (Fig. 3.6 denotes a semantic graph of a trip-planning process and Fig. 3.7 is a translated hierarchical map). One chapter denotes one aspect of travel planning, e.g. selecting a hotel, an attraction or a transportation method. Furthermore, one chapter can be divided into different 'episodes'. For example, to make an accommodation choice, the planner may consider several alternatives by visiting different hotel websites. Each alternative considered is one episode of the accommodation chapter. Their mental foci at each chapter and episode are different. However, there are commonalities in the chapter level since results show that more than half of the subjects make their accommodation choice first.

In Pan's study (2003), the travel information searchers were generally satisfied with their online trip-planning process. The information searchers were also highly adaptive; when they encountered navigation problems (e.g. broken links), they simply ignored them and took them for granted. However, the mismatch of semantic mental models was evident. The travellers used more subjective and experiential keywords to describe their background knowledge and their informational needs; alternatively, online travel information is dominated by a marketing and promotion language, which focuses on profitable attractions and price information. The points of interests shown on websites are also different from travellers' interests. In general, there are still great discrepancies between these two types of mental models.

Surprisingly, research results show that greater mismatches of mental models actually lead to more satisfactory information search process. Findings also demonstrated that different from other types of information search, travel information search is not totally functional; encountering novel and exciting information can boost planners' current emotional states. A more congruent match of semantic model actually means the users are more likely to encounter routine information and confirm their expectations and thus make the trip-planning process less fun. Mandler (1975) indicated that novel and incongruent information leads to arousal. When the arousal happens in a positive and pleasant context, positive feeling will occur. Travel planning happens in a positive context since travelling is a leisure activity. When novel and incongruent information is encountered, the subjects will achieve a more positive feeling.

The research results of the study by Pan and others (Zhang and Von Dran, 2000) indicate that the satisfaction of travel information search may be determined by two factors: hygiene and motivator. Satisfying the functional

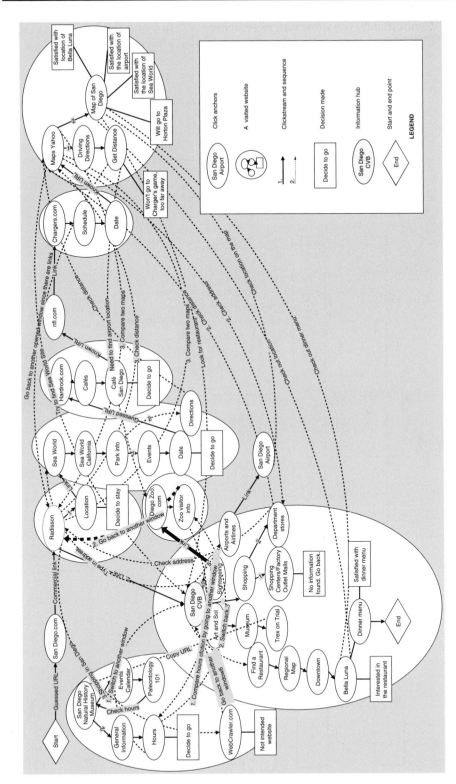

Fig. 3.6. Clickstream semantic map of subject #13.

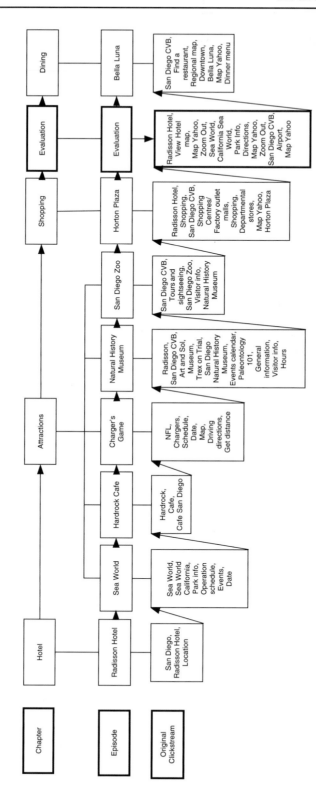

Fig. 3.7. A hierarchy of travel information search for subject #13.

needs of travellers is the hygiene factor, without which information searchers will feel frustrated and unsatisfied; on the other hand, novel and exciting
information they encountered beyond the travel information searchers'
semantic models is the motivator, which satisfies the information searchers' hedonic needs. Only when both the functional and hedonic information
needs are satisfied can the travel information searcher achieve a higher level
of satisfaction.

In general, travel information search and travel planning are more experiential and hedonic. Travel planning on the Internet is an integral part of
the travelling experience. The previous discussions indicate that the users'
satisfaction with information systems surpass the traditional view of functional needs in terms of finding relevant information but is moving towards
fulfilment of hedonic needs. These findings indicated that navigation is not
usually a major usability problem that may lead to unsatisfactory information search. The actual alternative evaluation on a certain web page influences
their satisfaction to a greater degree. In other words, the content of the websites is more important than their structure. This finding poses important
implications for the research and design of information technology since the
focus should be switched more on providing exciting and novel content as
well as fitting the users' mental models to satisfy their functional needs.

7. Implications for Designing Travel Recommendation Systems

The research literature clearly indicates that in order to design better travel
information recommendation systems, we need to understand how the
users' mental models change with time and their influence on users' satisfactory information search, both in terms of semantic mental models and
procedural mental models. More specifically, we need to understand what
types of information they are looking for and how they understand the
travel information search system. Various methods could be used to assess
different mental models. Interviews, verbal protocol and semantic network
analysis on the transcriptions of interviews can be used to abstract the users'
semantic mental models. In terms of procedural mental models, we need to
make certain that the users understand the functions of different parts of the
recommendation system, and the way to achieve different functions. Stages
of information seeking need to be taken into consideration when designing a
recommendation system, and different stages of information seeking require
different mental models. Therefore, it is essential to identify the stage in the
information search process in order to design a dynamic and useful system.

The importance of both hedonic and experiential aspects of travel planning indicates that recommendation systems not only provide relevant
functional results but also exciting and novel choices that are beyond traveller expectations. Customization and personalization is widely recognized
as a way to design better interface of information systems. The underlying
assumption is that once we acquire a better knowledge of the individual
characteristics of each user, we can customize the interface according to their

preference and mental models. However, this research showed that the total match of two models does not necessarily lead to a higher level of satisfaction. Pleasant surprise, which is beyond the user's mental model, is necessary. Hence, it is important to provide enjoyable 'surprises' that the travel information searchers do not anticipate. Beyond finding the perfect mental model of information users, more focus can be put on producing novel and exciting information that represents the characteristics of the destination.

The keywords in the travel information searchers' semantic mental model represent their connections with the designated destination. They are also the concepts and keywords associated with the destination as a brand. Thus, narrative design appears to be an important aspect of website design (Nielsen, 1999). By using a storytelling style, travel information providers can incorporate travellers' language and concepts to provide a more powerful persuasive marketing language.

Chapter Summary

Travellers plan a trip using a variety of information sources including the Internet. Since travel recommendation systems are a part of the information environment a trip planner will encounter online, the understanding of trip-planning behaviour on the Internet is essential to provide guidance to the design of useful systems. When travellers plan trips on the Internet, their interaction with the Internet can be viewed at different levels: between a user and a computer, a user and an information retrieval system, and a navigator and a hypertext system. This chapter has reviewed relevant research in human–computer interaction (HCI), cognitive information retrieval, hypertext navigation and trip planning on the Internet. This chapter argues that in order to design better travel information recommendation systems we need to understand how the users' mental models change with time and their influence on users' satisfactory information search, both in terms of semantic mental models and procedural mental models. The hedonic and experiential aspects of travel planning on the Internet indicate that travel recommendation systems should not only provide relevant results but also exciting and novel choices that are beyond the traveller's expectations.

4 Tourist Decision-making and Travel Destination Recommendation Systems

BENEDICT G.C. DELLAERT AND GERALD HÄUBL

1. Introduction

The Internet has dramatically increased the amount of travel destination information that is easily available to tourists. It would be a daunting task if tourists aimed to access, order and understand all this information when searching for suitable travel alternatives. Fortunately, travel destination recommendation systems (TDRSs) offer a promising way to assist tourists in dealing with the Internet's information overload. Such systems have the potential to assist tourists in their decision-making not only by reducing their search efforts but also by improving the quality of their decisions (e.g. Häubl and Trifts, 2000; Häubl and Dellaert, 2004; Häubl et al., 2004). It is not surprising, therefore, that TDRSs have become an integral part of many Internet travel services (e.g. Fesenmaier et al. in the introduction to this book).

Despite extensive research on tourist decision-making (e.g. Woodside and Lysonski, 1989; Crompton, 1992; Mansfeld, 1992; Dellaert et al., 1998a; Fesenmaier and Jeng, 2000), little is known about the specific case of tourists' decisions when faced with the opportunity to use a TDRS. First, because it is not known on what grounds tourists decide whether or not to use a TDRS and, second, the process by which tourists select a destination may be quite different when using a TDRS. This chapter aims to begin to conceptualize these two important tourist decision processes in the context of TDRSs.

2. Tourists' Decisions to Use a TDRS

In our analysis, we highlight the role of TDRSs as a technology that tourists can choose to use when making their travel destination decisions. When they are offered access to this technology, tourists first need to decide whether or not they wish to make use of it. In this section we develop a conceptual model of this initial decision. To do so, we draw on previous research that has investigated drivers of individuals' intentions to use information technology in a professional work environment (e.g. Davis *et al.*, 1989; Venkatesh *et al.*, 2003), and of consumers' intentions to use new technology-based self-services (e.g. Dabholkar, 1996). We then integrate these findings into a tourist decision-making framework by drawing on the extended choice model framework proposed by McFadden (1986).

There are several important findings that emerge from this literature. One main finding is that when evaluating a technology, individuals consider both the *outcome* of the technology and the *process* by which the technology operates (e.g. Davis *et al.*, 1989). The outcome aspect typically is captured in a dimension such as 'usefulness' or 'performance' in models of individuals' intentions to use a certain information technology. We suggest that, in the context of a TDRS, this dimension can best be captured by a construct that represents the tourist's evaluation of the destination that is recommended by the system. The process by which the technology operates tends to be evaluated on two additional dimensions: ease of use (or lack of effort) and enjoyment (or fun to use) involved in working with the technology (e.g. Dabholkar 1996). In the domain of tourism, Dellaert and Wendel (2004) found a similar split in tourists' evaluations of the use of the Internet as a travel information channel, and it would appear likely that tourists tend to evaluate the process by which a TDRS provides its recommendations on these two dimensions as well. Over time, individuals are expected to form relatively stable beliefs about how a technology performs on each of these three criteria (i.e. usefulness, ease of use and enjoyment). Individuals' beliefs about the criteria are then expected to influence their attitude towards the technology (Dabholkar, 1996). Figure 4.1 summarizes the main structure of this model.

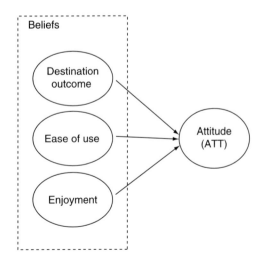

Fig. 4.1.   Tourist attitude towards using a TDRS.

The relative role of individuals' beliefs, attitude and behavioural intention in their decisions to use a technology may vary, for example, depending on situational differences or an individual's experience with the decision process (Dabholkar, 1994). However, two relatively robust findings are that beliefs about the technology's usefulness may have a direct effect not only on an individual's attitude towards the technology but also on the individual's intention to use it, and that the ease of using a technology may affect the evaluation of the technology's usefulness (e.g. Davis *et al.*, 1989).

Research on individuals' use of information technology and self-service technology has largely limited itself to modelling individuals' attitudes towards, and their stated intentions to use, a certain technology rather than their actual choices of whether or not to use the technology. Therefore, to capture the element of choice, we develop an explicit model of individuals' choice behaviour with respect to using a TDRS. In line with McFadden (1986), we suggest that tourists' choices to use a TDRS are based on the utility they attach to using a certain TDRS, and that this utility in turn is based not only on tourists' attitude towards, and beliefs about, TDRSs in general but also on a weighted evaluation of: (i) directly observable characteristics of the TDRS; and (ii) the characteristics of other available destination choice channels (e.g. travel agents or travel brochures). Figure 4.2 summarizes these three choice components in a graphical model.

More formally, we expect that a tourist i's decision to use a certain $TDRS_j$ is based on the utility V_{ij} he or she attaches to using this TDRS. This utility is then influenced by: (i) the observable characteristics of the TDRS such as access speed, design and regional focus, X_{TDRS}, and (ii) the tourist's attitude towards using a TDRS, ATT_i, which in turn is affected by his or her relatively stable beliefs with respect to a TDRS's usefulness, ease of use and the enjoyment involved in using a TDRS. This can be expressed as

$$V_{ij} = \beta_{TDRS}X_{TDRS} + \gamma ATT_i \qquad (4.1)$$

The probability that a tourist will choose to use a certain TDRS can then be expressed as the probability that V_{ij} will exceed the utility V_{other} of the best alternative way of making a travel destination choice that is available. If we

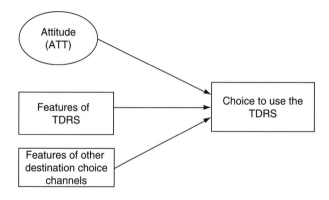

Fig. 4.2. Tourist choice to use a TDRS.

allow for some error in the modelling of these utilities (ε_{ij} and ε_{other}), the probability of choosing to use a certain TDRS is expressed as

$$P(\text{TDRS}_j) = P(V_{ij} + \varepsilon_{ij} > V_{other} + \varepsilon_{other}) \qquad (4.2)$$

3. Tourists' Destination Choices in the Context of a TDRS

We now focus on tourists' destination choices, once they have selected a TDRS as their decision channel. TDRSs typically present tourists with a ranked list of recommended destinations based on some type of preference input, e.g. from experts or from the tourist himself or herself. Thus, when choosing a destination in the context of a TDRS, a tourist is faced with the problem of selecting the most attractive destination from a list of destinations that are ranked in order of (expected) attractiveness. This decision problem can also be thought of as a search process in which the tourists' goal is to find the most attractive destination from the total list of possible destinations. Tourists go through this list in a sequential fashion (i.e. one alternative at a time), but always have the option of going back and choosing any alternative from the list.

More formally, we conceptualize this destination choice process as an iterative process with two sequential steps that are repeated until a destination is selected (cf. Dellaert and Häubl, 2004). In each iteration of the process, tourists first decide whether or not they wish to continue with the search process for the most attractive destination. This decision represents the first step in each iteration, and we label it the *search continuation choice*. If tourists decide to continue their search, they look at the next alternative in the list and compare it to the most attractive destination they had already found in the list. This comparison represents the second step of the process, and is labelled *destination choice*. If tourists decide not to continue their search, they select the most attractive destination that they have seen so far. Figure 4.3 graphically represents the proposed two steps in the process. We now discuss each step in greater detail.

3.1 Search continuation choice

At each decision stage t, the consumer calculates the expected utility of the most attractive uninspected alternative in the recommendation list (e.g. Weitzman, 1979). Typically, when recommendations are provided to the tourist, this alternative will be the next in line in the ordered list of suggested destinations. The expected utility of this alternative is then used, along with its expected distribution, as input in calculating the expected benefit of looking at this next alternative. This benefit (ΔU_t) is the expected difference between the most attractive alternative that was already observed in the list and the expected utility of the next alternative. The cost of further search (c) is then compared

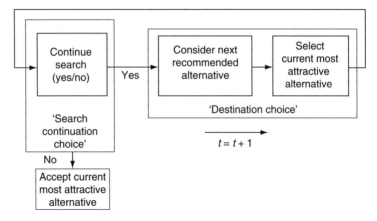

Fig. 4.3. Tourist destination choice process when using a TDRS.

with this expected difference (e.g. Weitzman, 1979; Hauser and Wernerfelt, 1990) and the search is continued if c is lower than ΔU_t.[1] This search process continues until the cost of search outweighs the expected benefits of looking at the next alternative.

3.2 Destination choice

Traditionally, tourists' preferences for a destination are modelled using a random utility model (e.g. Ben-Akiva and Lerman, 1985; Louviere, 1988; Haider and Ewing, 1990). This type of model assumes that tourist choices can be represented as a process in which tourists evaluate the attributes of the alternatives in terms of the utility that these attributes can provide. The (part-worth) utilities associated with each of the attributes are then assumed to be integrated cognitively into one overall utility for every destination alternative. The utility function describing this evaluation consists of two main parts: (i) a deterministic component representing the systematic utility that the tourist derives from the alternative's attributes; and (ii) a random error component capturing the errors in modelling this systematic utility. Such random errors can be due to various sources, such as measurement errors, omitted explanatory variables and unobserved variations in taste.

Then, by applying the simple choice rule that the alternative with the highest utility is selected, the approach allows one to express the choice probability of each available alternative. This probability is modelled as a function of the attributes of the alternative and the attributes of the other alternatives in the comparison set. For example, the well-known logit model

---

[1] This strategy is optimal if one can assume that the value of learning about other alternatives (further down the list) does not outweigh the benefits of searching the next most attractive alternative.

arises if one is willing to assume that the random error components in the utilities of the alternatives follow independently and identically distributed Gumbel distributions (e.g. Ben-Akiva and Lerman, 1985). In the case of the destination choices, tourists choose in every iteration of going through a list of recommended destinations whether or not to select a certain new alternative over the previously most attractive destination. In this way, tourists sequentially choose the destination that they find most attractive from among those that they have already examined.

4. The Impact of TDRSs on Tourist Choices

The conceptual models proposed in this chapter constitute a possible framework for further theoretical and empirical research on the effect of TDRSs on tourist decision-making. Although there is considerable evidence in the literature to support the proposed decision components and their sequence, this previous research was conducted largely outside the domain of tourist destination decision-making. An important next step, therefore, would be to investigate the empirical validity of the proposed structure and the relative importance of the various components in a tourism context. Some indicative conclusions, however, can already be drawn from the emerging body of work investigating the impact of recommendation agents on individuals' product choices. We briefly review a number of key results from this research, and discuss their implications in terms of our proposed model structure.

Häubl and Trifts (2000) examined the benefits to consumers of receiving personalized product recommendations. They compared consumers' product choices from sets of 54 products when consumers did and did not receive such recommendations based on their stated preferences. This research found significant reductions (of approximately 50%) in the number of products that consumers looked at when they were offered an ordered list of recommendations. At the same time, Häubl and Trifts also found that personalized recommendations allowed consumers to make significantly better purchase decisions. For example, consumers who received recommendations were significantly less likely to choose a product that was objectively dominated by another available product.

In a later study, Häubl and Dellaert (2004) report similar findings in the context of an experiment involving tourists' hypothetical choices of holiday homes from lists of 500 possible homes. Their results indicate that use of an electronic recommendation system allowed tourists to search less, but at the same time improve the quality of their decisions. Tourists who used a recommendation system were significantly more likely to choose a holiday home option that was close to their stated preference. With regard to effort, Häubl and Dellaert observed that tourists who had access to a recommendation system spent significantly less time searching and looked at fewer holiday home options than did those who were not provided with such a tool.

If we relate these findings to our proposed conceptual model, they are especially relevant for tourists' decision whether or not to use a TDRS. It is likely that, over time, tourists will come to realize that a TDRS can be quite useful when making destination choices and, therefore, that their attitude towards TDRSs and their intention to use such systems will increase. At a decision-process level, their destination choices and search continuation choices are also affected. It appears reasonable to expect that tourists using a TDRS will consider fewer destinations and will be more likely to choose only pareto-optimal destinations (i.e. destinations that are not dominated by any other destinations). This mechanism would intensify competition between destinations. As a consequence, especially those destinations that have no (or only a few) unique characteristics could be forced to compete strongly on price in order to be considered by tourists using a TDRS. Also, a stronger split between popular and less popular destinations could occur in the market if tourists only consider 'top' destinations that are high on their recommended list.

At the level of the online travel service provider, there are likely to be important competitive effects of offering TDRS access. One potential key benefit to travel service providers is that offering buyers a TDRS may increase customer loyalty. This effect is quite relevant considering that in the online world the competition is 'only a click away'.

Over time, online consumers can grow to be very loyal shoppers (Brynjolfsson and Smith, 2000; Johnson *et al.*, 2003). This shift occurs because, even when it is easy to navigate from one Internet vendor to the next, individuals prefer to shop using interfaces that they know. In particular, once somebody has learned to use one electronic interface, the time and effort required to use that interface is greatly reduced. As a result, customers are hesitant to switch to another interface where they would have to learn new skills and invest more time and effort to complete the same task. This type of loyalty is often referred to as 'cognitive lock-in'.

Given the emphasis that online buyers place on the ability of electronic interfaces to save them time and simplify their lives (Bellman *et al.*, 1999), it should not be surprising that providing (personalized) recommendations has the potential to further enhance customer loyalty. One of the key strengths of a TDRS is its ability to reduce the time and effort required for a tourist to make a decision (cf. Häubl and Trifts, 2000; Häubl and Dellaert, 2004). This suggests that a travel service provider should be able to increase the switching cost for the customer by offering access to a TDRS because, once a tourist is familiar with the TDRS, this will result in an even greater reduction in time and effort than experience with a website alone could provide (Murray and Häubl, 2003).

5. Conclusion

In this chapter we have proposed conceptual models to describe two important components of tourist decision-making when TDRSs are present: (i) tourists' choices to use a TDRS; and (ii) tourists' destination choices when using a TDRS. The proposed models are strongly rooted in previous research on individuals' use of information technology (e.g. Davis *et al.*, 1989), consumer choice theory (McFadden, 1986) and individuals' search and choice behaviour (e.g. Hauser and Wernerfelt, 1990).

An important next step would be to examine the performance of the proposed models in the empirical context of tourist destination choices. For example, it would be interesting to investigate the degree to which normative models of tourist destination choice in ordered lists of recommendations align with actual tourist decision processes in connection with a TDRS. Another interesting question would be whether tourists using a TDRS recognize the improvements in decision quality and the reductions in decision effort that this technology offers them, or whether their perceptions of the impact of a TDRS on their decisions are biased in some way. For example, it may be difficult for tourists to compare decision effort and outcomes across different types of destination choice support options.

Finally, it could also be interesting to investigate if tourists' preferences may be influenced by the use of a TDRS. In our analysis so far, we have assumed that tourist preferences are stable and do not change as a result of the particular decision support process that is used. There are some indications, however, that the technology used to generate the recommendations given in a TDRS may affect tourists' preferences for different alternatives. For example, Häubl and Murray (2003) found that in the context of consumers' product choices, the selective inclusion of attributes in a recommendation system has a systematic and persistent effect on consumers' preferences for different product attributes. We hope that our conceptual analysis and discussion in this chapter will offer a useful starting point for such future analyses.

Chapter Summary

This chapter argues that, in the context of tourists' use of information technology, it is more important to understand tourists' actual choices of whether or not to use the technology than their attitudes towards, and their stated intentions to use, a certain technology. Following from this understanding, three conceptual models are proposed to examine tourists' choice of TDRSs: (i) tourists' attitude towards using a TDRS is conceptualized as a function of the destination recommended, the perceived usefulness and the level of enjoyment of the system; (ii) tourists' choice to use a TDRS is determined by their attitudes towards the system, the features of the system and the features of other destination choice channels; and (iii) the destination choice process when using a TDRS is described as an iterative process involving two sequential steps that are repeated until a destination is selected. Empirical evidence indicates that recommendation systems can have a significant impact on tourist choices. It is thus concluded that future research should focus on empirically testing the proposed models and investigating how tourists' preferences will be influenced by the use of a TDRS.

5 A Behavioural Framework for Destination Recommendation Systems Design

Ulrike Gretzel, Yeong-Hyeon Hwang and Daniel R. Fesenmaier

1. Introduction

The emergence of information technology and its relatively fast and wide adoption within the tourism industry has led to an explosion in the availability of destination-related information. The Internet now provides access to over 161 million travel-related web pages (Google, 2004), enabling potential travellers to obtain detailed information about almost any destination worldwide. This enormous amount of information available at one's fingertips can greatly help travellers in planning trips and/or formulating expectations about tourism experiences. At the same time, it can lead to information overload, making it difficult for information seekers to find relevant information (Pan and Fesenmaier, 2002). Fortunately, information technology also provides the means for building systems that can simplify the decision-making process by identifying destinations that meet specific needs or desires and by enabling potential visitors to 'experience' the destination prior to a purchase. These systems vary in sophistication, ranging from simple retrieval or filtering applications to comprehensive recommendation systems (Spiekermann and Paraschiv, 2002). Whereas the more basic forms of such decision aids have been widely adopted and integrated into search engines and database query systems, the latter have only been implemented to a certain extent and are still lacking vital elements before they can match or even exceed the quality of human recommendations (Häubl and Trifts, 2000). It is argued here that in order to develop into more helpful and successful decision-making support tools these systems have to become truly human-centric in their design and functionality.

Human-centric computing involves designing, developing and implementing information technology that reflects the needs and lifestyles of its human users (Silverman et al., 2001). A number of systems have emerged over the last 10 years that offer the promise of such human-centric computing. For example, an interactive system developed for museum use, AlFresco (Stock, 2000), offers the opportunity for a visitor to experience a 'unique' visit to a museum based upon personal interests, questions and movement through the museum. Others, including Hruschka and Mazanec (1990) as well as Vanhof and Molderez (1994), have outlined possible strategies for developing travel counselling and recommendation systems, which enable potential travellers to 'easily' identify destinations of interest. The focus of more recent research has been on adaptive systems, which learn and adapt to the specific needs of the user (Loban, 1997; Mitsche, 2001; Ricci and Werthner, 2001). Human-centric computing requires, of course, a profound understanding of the human behaviours it tries to mimic and/or enhance (Silverman *et al.*, 2001). A rich literature has emerged in the fields of consumer behaviour, information search and processing, and human–computer interaction that provides behavioural foundations for the development of human-centric systems. Systems related to travel and tourism, however, face an additional challenge in that they have to take the peculiarities of travel behaviour into account in addition to gaining insights from general theoretical frameworks and, thus, should thoroughly engage with existing research in tourism. Studies indicate, for example, that travellers often actively seek information as part of their travel-planning effort and consider it an important component of the travel experience. These studies also suggest that the information search process involves different hierarchical steps depending upon a number of personal and situational factors (Jeng and Fesenmaier, 2002). However, so far, the various relevant findings of the travel and tourism literature have never been integrated and conceptualized in a way that can be translated into guidelines for recommendation system design. This chapter proposes a behavioural framework of travellers' interactions with destination recommendation systems that takes the specific characteristics of travel information search and decision-making into account. In addition, it outlines several design guidelines for destination recommendation systems that follow from the discussion of the various behavioural components.

2. A Behavioural Framework for Destination Recommendation Systems

Based on the review of the travel destination choice and information search and processing literatures presented in the previous chapters, a behavioural framework can be conceptualized which integrates the factors that shape an individual's interaction with a destination recommendation system (DRS) (Fig. 5.1). The model assumes that individuals access a DRS to learn about alternative destinations. The nature of the information searched for will depend on two main factors: (i) the structure of the decision task to be accomplished; and (ii) the context in which this trip decision will be taken. The structure of the decision task and the information needs derived from

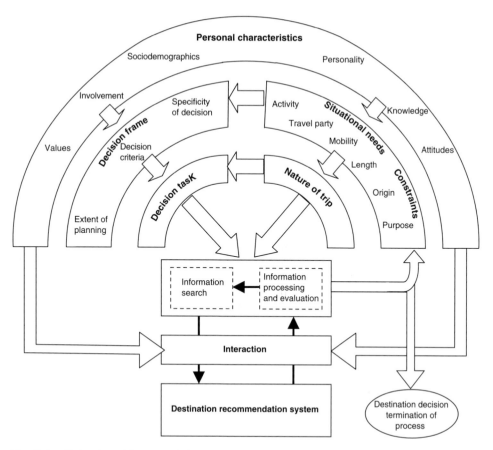

Fig. 5.1. Behavioural framework for destination recommendation systems.

it depend on the decision frame that guides the decision-making process. Decision frames can be characterized by the specificity of the destination decision to be taken, the extent to which the trip is planned in advance, as well as the nature, number and importance of criteria and decision-making strategies taken into account when making a destination decision. The nature of the trip will depend on the situational needs to be satisfied by the trip and the constraints that have to be considered. Although destination decisions are generally high-level decisions and are typically made when most other aspects of the trip are still undefined, individuals who use a DRS are expected to have at least some idea of when they would like to travel (e.g. winter vs summer vacation), how long they would like to stay (e.g. week-long vacation vs getaway trip), who they would like to take along (e.g. spouse vs entire family), what the purpose of the trip is (e.g. relaxation vs adventure), what main activity they will engage in (e.g. beach vacation vs skiing trip), what the main mode of transportation will be (e.g. car vs airplane) and from which point of origin the trip will start. If the main destination has been selected and the search effort focuses on secondary destinations or attractions within destinations, the situational needs and constraints can be assumed to have been established in greater detail. The specific decision task is shaped by the decision frame selected, which is, of course, also a priori adjusted to accommodate the specific trip situation. Thus, the needs and constraints that drive the nature of the trip are important indicators of the particular decision task to be accomplished as they directly influence the nature of the trip and also have an impact on the way the destination decision is framed and executed.

However, information search and decision-making behaviour is not only determined by situational variables. Both the decision frame and situational needs or constraints selected depend on personal characteristics of the individual decision-maker. Personal characteristics include sociodemographics but also values, personality and attitudes, involvement in travel and travel-related decision-making, and personal knowledge and experience regarding travel in general, and various destinations in particular. Personal characteristics have a great impact on the destination decision to be taken. A high tendency towards sensation-seeking, for instance, will influence travel needs as well as the extent to which a trip is planned and what criteria are considered during the decision-making process. In addition to their influence on the nature of the trip and the specific decision task, personal characteristics directly influence information search and processing behaviour; e.g. personal knowledge has been found to positively influence processing ability. Further, an individual's skills, involvement, personality, etc. appear to have direct impact on the individual's interaction with an intelligent information environment such as a DRS (Hoffman and Novak, 1996).

Following from this behavioural model, interaction with the system is driven by personal characteristics, situational factors and the resulting nature of the trip to be planned, the decision frame applied and the specific decision(s) to be taken, which all result in particular information needs and search strategies. In addition, a user's interaction with a DRS is shaped by the characteristics of the recommendation system itself. The proposed model is dynamic in the sense that it recognizes the importance of feedback resulting from a user's interaction with the system. Based on the processing and evaluation of the recommendations obtained, the user might decide that more or better information is needed, and therefore might engage in additional information search processes until a satisfactory level is reached. In a different case, the information obtained from the system could expose additional situational constraints and make changes in the decision frame and/or the nature of the trip necessary. For instance, destinations could be recommended and perceived as being optimal in terms of the activities they provide, and the way in which they cater to the needs of the members of the travel party. However, they could be seen as offering too many interesting things for just a day trip and lead to a revision of the 'length of travel' constraint. Similarly, a user could be given the options of loosely specifying trip characteristics in the beginning of the search process and would subsequently be encouraged to refine them as more information is being taken into account. Ideally, the process ends when all necessary information has been collected and processed, and an informed destination decision can be made. The time and number of iterations necessary to reach this point will vary, depending on the number of potential alternatives under consideration, the quality of the recommendations and the changes in the decision frame as set by the user. The worst-case scenario in terms of behavioural outcomes is, of course, a situation whereby the user terminates the process without having reached a decision. Alternatively, use of the system could lead to a postponing of the decision, but at least with a narrowed-down set of alternatives.

3. Guidelines for Destination Recommendation Systems Design

The design elements of a DRS play a crucial role in shaping the user–system interaction process. Specifically, the amount and presentation of the DRS's content and the structure of its interface are key aspects determining the nature of the interaction (Dholakia *et al.*, 2000; Spiekermann and Paraschiv, 2002). Further, the intelligence built into the system through data storage and mining capabilities influences the level of interactivity and personalization that can be provided. System intelligence, therefore, is a core element in defining user interactions with a DRS. Thus, the model clearly supports the idea that DRSs should be highly interactive and adaptive in order to provide appropriate guidance in the travel-planning process. Another important capacity of a DRS that is rooted in its design is its ability to provide users with enjoyment and excitement as well as types of information exchanges that can convey the experiential aspects of travel and tourism products and services. Figure 5.2 summarizes these core DRS design components.

Each of these design components has to be informed by the behavioural foundations outlined above to truly support destination decision-related human behaviour. The proposed behavioural model provides the basis for general guidelines with respect to the design of user-centred destination recommendation systems. The ultimate goal of these guidelines is to provide directions regarding issues that need to be addressed in order to be able to provide travellers with a list of destination alternatives they would find appealing and useful with respect to their specific decision-related needs. The following sections briefly introduces and discusses guidelines for each of the design components.

Destination recommendation systems design			
Content	Structure	System intelligence	Experience

Fig. 5.2. Design components of destination recommendation systems.

3.1 Content

Content refers to the information about destinations that resides within the DRS and also the content of the recommendations provided to a DRS user.

Guideline 1: Destination recommendations should vary in their content based upon the nature of each trip, the specific decision task and the personal characteristics of the user.

Recommended destinations need to reflect the meaningful differences that define each trip. These meaningful differences emerge from the needs/ benefits sought and constraints encountered for each trip. In addition, the information provided about a destination should reflect the specific stage of the decision-making process, recognizing differences in the nature of the information sought and the style with which the obtained information is processed. Travellers are interested in different information depending on the specificity of their destination decision at the time of the information search (Um and Crompton, 1990; Fesenmaier and Jeng, 2000; Jeng and Fesenmaier, 2002). For instance, travellers in different stages of the decision-making process require different types of information in terms of focus and level of detail (Bloch *et al.*, 1986). Some travellers may be more interested in attractions within a specific destination and look for prices or opening hours, while others may seek brand or image information to be able to construct ideas about potential travel destinations. Furthermore, information search means different things to different people (Vogt and Fesenmaier, 1998). Based on individual risk avoidance needs, the amount of information required about a destination or attraction may vary. This implies that a DRS needs a comprehensive database of information available and retrievable in multiple ways. Such a need for varying contents and levels of content suggests that DRSs might be more feasible for larger geographical areas such as regions or states and only make sense if the destinations, attractions or activities available are rather heterogeneous.

Guideline 2: The number of recommendations should be limited to a reasonably small set of destinations, attractions and/or activities but large enough to convey variety or choice.

Users have constraints regarding the amount of information that can be effortlessly processed (Miller, 1956). Also, recent research clearly suggests that the attention of web users is rather limited and that the user would prefer a list of 'high-quality' recommendations rather than a long list (Jansen *et al.*, 2000). Thus, a DRS should focus on providing a brief list of recommendations, possibly enabling the user to define the number and range of destinations to be displayed as users may vary in need for cognition (Cacioppo and Petty, 1982). According to the proposed model a 'high quality' of recommendations can only be achieved if the decision task at hand within the context of a specific trip can be identified. However, decisions regarding the number of recommendations presented to the user also have to take individual variety-seeking tendencies and the persuasiveness of choice into account. Variety seeking is rather pronounced in the context of tourism (Jeng and Fesenmaier, 1998) and, thus, variety has to be displayed not only within a set of recommendations but also across a user's history with a DRS. Actual choice as well as perceived choice have been found to favourably affect attitudes (Schlosser and Shavitt, 1999; Flowerday and Schraw, 2003) and confidence in judgement (Sniezek *et al.*, 1990). Therefore, providing only one or two recommendations will deprive a user of the important opportunity to choose. Last, the logic for deriving the 'best' set of recommendations out of the many alternative destinations should be well articulated. This is important not only as transparency has been found to be a vital factor in the evaluation of recommendations (Kramer, 2003), but also because the behavioural framework assumes that users should be provided with feedback so that they could revise their specifications if necessary.

3.2 Structure

The structure of a DRS encompasses the navigational properties that determine the ways in which users can and should move through the system.

Guideline 1:   A DRS should support interactions with many types of users.

User interactions with a DRS are directly influenced by personal characteristics of the user. For instance, users may differ in their navigational needs or preferences based on previous knowledge and skills (Tabatabai and Luconi, 1998; Novak *et al.*, 2000) or their state of mind at the time they seek recommendations (Dholakia and Bagozzi, 2001; Novak *et al.*, 2003), i.e. they can be experts or novices, goal-directed or playful, etc. This implies that a DRS should offer many different entry ways into the recommendation process. Travel personality categories, as discussed in a later chapter of this book, could serve as such an alternative way to structure the process used to gather user information. Users also differ in terms of their decision-making styles (Grabler and Zins, 2002). This could be recognized by a DRS through adjustment of the preference elicitation process through which the user is led before recommendations are made, for instance, by varying the type and number of questions asked if the input is gathered through explicit input.

Guideline 2:   A DRS should provide opportunities for interative recommendation processes.

One of the important assumptions made by the above-described behavioural foundations framework is that users may revise certain trip specifications based on feedback in the form of recommendations provided by the system. The feedback loop can only be successfully closed if the system allows users to easily change previously specified input and effortlessly switch back and forth between the specification and recommendation components of the DRS. This constitutes an especially difficult challenge for systems that gather user input implicitly, e.g. through tracking user behaviours. It is believed that the evaluation of the information provided by the system should still be part of the interaction with the DRS rather than a step that occurs after the interaction has been terminated, as it provides invaluable opportunities for persuasion of the user and also for data gathering and learning on behalf of the system.

3.3 System intelligence

System intelligence describes the ability of the system to learn and remember user and/or trip characteristics and adjust the content, type, number and/or presentation of recommendations accordingly.

Guideline 1: A DRS should be user- as well as context-aware in all phases of the recommendation process.

Recommendation systems have traditionally focused on making recommendations based on matching users or matching the decision context with the space of possible recommendations. The behavioural foundations framework presented in this chapter indicates that user and situational variables are equally important in determining high-quality recommendations. However, it also illustrates that the importance of taking user and situational needs into account goes beyond the selection of the recommendations to be presented to the user; rather, it has critical implications for the data-gathering process, the presentation of the recommendations and the feedback solicited from the user after a recommendation is made.

Guideline 2: A DRS should incorporate different strategies for obtaining data necessary for the provision of dynamic and personalized recommendations.

Data-mining strategies to obtain travel behaviour information are well documented in the literature (Hwang and Fesenmaier, 2001; Delgado and Davidson, 2002; Ricci, 2002). However, not every strategy available to obtain user or trip data is equally effective in every context and for every user. Hybrid systems have recently been promoted as ways to overcome the limitations of certain mining strategies (Burke, 2002). It is argued here that hybrid approaches also provide the possibility of increasing the flexibility of the DRS and its adaptability to specific user and/or situational needs. New users, for instance, might be willing to provide additional input to improve their recommendations if the system cannot fall back on any previous user history or profile, but might not be willing to answer such questions every time they use the DRS. Also, users might differ in their general preference for explicit vs implicit methods of data gathering. Finally, for certain trips users may prefer an easy and fast recommendation process, whereas destination decisions in other trip contexts may warrant the creation of extensive profiles.

3.4 Experience

Experience denotes the ability of the system to create and convey enjoyable experiences.

Guideline 1:   Destination recommendation systems need to exploit the experiential aspects of travel in order to provide more convincing and persuasive results.

Depending on personal and situational needs, users may require more information about the actual experience they can expect at a certain destination. There are a number of potential strategies for making a DRS more experiential. At the most basic level, photos that convey the specific image(s) promoted by the destination can be easily integrated into a system, enabling potential visitors to quickly judge whether they would enjoy the experience provided by a place. However, real-world destination experiences are not just visual but encompass a variety of sensory and emotional aspects. This variety of sensations and emotions needs to be included in recommendations through sounds, emotional appeals, lively descriptions of smells and tastes, etc. (Gretzel and Fesenmaier, 2003). Experiences can be further enhanced using a variety of animated and interactive tools such as virtual reality, which enables visitors to become 'players' who actively participate in creating their own personal virtual experience (Cho *et al.*, 2002; Teo *et al.*, 2003). Studies in this area clearly demonstrate the potential impact that interactive technology has on influencing one's image of a destination. Virtual communities also offer the opportunity to enhance one's 'experience' of a destination by creating more realistic expectations through conversations with people who wish to share their experiences of the destination under consideration. A number of virtual communities now exist and are used to actively support and encourage travel decision-making (Wang and Fesenmaier, 2003). This area of system design continues to grow by rethinking the basic structure of online communication systems and the ways in which human beings learn, arguing that information presented in an impersonal list or under separate categories makes it difficult for consumers to construct a cohesive picture of a travel experience. Gretzel and Fesenmaier (2002a,b) argue, for example, that narrative design (storytelling) may be much more effective in conveying the potential range of experiences one may have at a destination.

Guideline 2:   A DRS needs to transform the search process into an enjoyable experience.

The behavioural foundations framework illustrates how users' interactions with the DRS can have an influence on their evaluations of the recommendations provided by the system. Considering the fact that the 'costliest' process of destination recommendation systems is to ask the user to provide a considerable amount of information necessary to optimize the recommendation results, experiential searches would provide a win–win solution by allowing the system to get all the necessary information while the user is enjoying the query process. There is increasing evidence that enjoyment of one's interactions with technology has important consequences on perceptions of the technology and subsequent evaluations (Hoffman and Novak, 1996; Chen *et al.*, 1999; Agarwal and Karahanna, 2000; Venkatesh and Davis, 2000; Woszcynski *et al.*, 2002; Blythe *et al.*, 2003), and that such enjoyment can be manipulated through design (Shedroff, 2001; Huang, 2003).

4. Conclusions

Incorporating the rich information search and decision-making literatures presented in the previous chapters offers a tourism-specific behavioural framework that can be used as a basis for the design of human-centric destination recommendation systems. The outcome of this effort is a series of principles for each of the four system components which we believe should guide system development and which emphasize the diversity of factors that make destination decisions unique, the experiential nature of tourism information and the importance of interactivity. Importantly, these guidelines simultaneously represent the starting point in the development of an effective travel recommendation system and a road map for future research. There is much evidence that online recommendation systems can effectively guide consumer decision-making. Amazon.com is one of the most popular examples of an effective online recommendation system as it offers a variety of entry points, multiple formats with which to evaluate potential products, easy purchasing through the patented One Click system and intelligent mining approaches that help to track consumer purchasing behaviours and interests. Triplehop's Tripmaker is an example of a travel-related recommendation system that addresses many of the guidelines set out in this chapter. More recently, Fesenmaier *et al.* (2003) proposed a system called DieToRecs, which represents a new generation of travel recommendation systems that are significantly more responsive to individual decision styles. In addition, Gretzel and Fesenmaier (2002b), Picard (1997) and Dittenbach *et al.* (2003), among others, clearly document ways in which these systems can be enhanced by integrating sensory and emotional cues necessary for the conceptualization and evaluation of vacation experiences and by offering natural language processing.

Successful implementation of destination recommendation systems will depend in large part upon the extent to which system designs can address the issues discussed above. An interesting issue is the impact of such systems on consumer behaviour and the evolution of these systems as a form of persuasive technology (Fogg, 2003). The first applications of recommendation systems in the tourism industry were developed primarily to simplify the process of booking flights by allowing travel agents to find relevant flight information and to make reservations directly from their terminals. These systems now enable consumers to directly access this data, providing them with a variety of offers. The operators of these systems have clearly recognized the potential impact of these technologies on the consumer. Recently, a number of scholars have begun to consider the potential impact of recommendation systems, providing considerable insight into current and potential relationship(s) between computers and their users. Dholakia and Bagozzi (2001) provide an excellent discussion of the various roles of online technologies and consumer behaviour. They argue, for instance, that web-based systems can effectively reduce cognitive effort, transfer control from self to the system and positively affect the quality of actual decisions.

In a more comprehensive examination of persuasive computing, Fogg (2003) argues that online systems provide an exceptional basis for e-commerce in that they offer the necessary tools to effectively encourage consumer behaviour through a variety of different strategies. However, there are a number of concerns regarding the use of these systems including the ease with which one can mask the true intent of the system, the degree to which systems can manipulate the set of alternatives under consideration as well as the ability of these systems to affect emotions. Clearly, the nature and extent to which such technologies can be used to manage consumer behaviour should be discussed and guidelines need to be established.

Another important issue focuses on the emergence of the 'new consumer' and related implications concerning the next generation of online destination recommendation systems. Many authors including Poon (1993) and Werthner and Klein (1999) have suggested the emergence of technology-induced key trends in the travel and tourism industries:

- The Internet and alternative access devices will continue to increase the number of electronic connections between customers and the tourism industry and these new technologies will continue to provide an environment for creating relationships, allowing consumers to access information more efficiently, conducting transactions, and interacting electronically with businesses and suppliers.
- The changing demographic profiles of Internet users over the last decade suggest that the evolving Internet and related systems will ultimately be adopted by the large majority of the travelling public and, therefore, the Internet will be considered the primary source for travel information.
- The demands of travellers, in particular the purchase process(es) they use, will continue to evolve as consumers of travel products gain more experience and confidence in product purchasing over the Internet. Importantly, conversations among travellers (through travel clubs, virtual communities, etc.) will continue to grow and will increasingly be mediated through Internet technologies.

These changes have (and continue to) set the stage for an interesting and challenging future for the travel and tourism industry in which destination recommendation systems are expected to play a critical role. However, given the changing nature of travel consumers' behaviour, the success of a specific DRS will largely depend on its ability to anticipate and creatively respond to transformations in the personal and situational needs of its users.

Chapter Summary

In order to evolve into more helpful and successful decision-making support tools, destination recommendation systems need to become truly human-centric in their design and functionality. This requires a profound understanding of human interactions with technology as well as human behaviour related to information search and decision-making in the context of travel and tourism. Based upon the literature discussed in the previous chapters, a behavioural framework for the development of destination recommendation systems is proposed that takes into account the specific characteristics of travel information search and decision-making. Specifically, it outlines several design guidelines for destination recommendation systems that follow from the discussion of the various behavioural components. This chapter concludes that the success of a specific DRS will largely depend on its ability to anticipate and creatively respond to transformations in the personal and situational needs of its users.

Acknowledgement

This work has been partially funded by the European Union's Fifth RTD Framework Programme (under contract DIETORECS IST-2000-29474). The authors would like to thank all other colleagues of the DieToRecs (http://dietorecs.itc.it/) team for their valuable contribution to this chapter.

II Design of Destination Recommendation Systems

6 Case-based Travel Recommendations

Francesco Ricci, Dario Cavada, Nader Mirzadeh and Adriano Venturini

1. Introduction

Searching for travel-related information and services is one of the top web activities and there is a fast-growing number of websites that support a traveller in the selection of a travel destination or a travel service (e.g. flight or hotel). Users search for destination-related information such as point of interest, historical data, weather conditions and for products and services such as travel packages, flights and hotels. The wide spectrum of information currently provided by a number of web actors includes: online travel agency, tour operators, cruise operators, destination management organizations (multidestination, regional, city), airlines, hotel chains, convention and visitors' bureau (Werthner and Klein, 1999; Buhalis, 2003).

Basically, the websites maintained by the various tourism organizations offer search tools and content browsing. In the first case, mostly exploited to select a product or service, the user is required to input some product constraints or preferences that are matched by the system in its electronic catalogue. In the second case, the user is offered to navigate the website and browse the structured multimedia content. Hence, the technology largely exploited in the above-mentioned websites is not much different from those found in any other e-commerce site.

Trip planning is a complex problem-solving activity (Moutinho, 1987; Ankomah *et al.*, 1996; Fesenmaier and Jeng, 2000; Hwang *et al.*, 2002). The terms 'travel plan' and 'destination' lack a precise definition; indeed, even the destination spatial extension is known to be a function of the travellers' distance from, and knowledge about, the destination. Importantly, travel plans may vary greatly in structure and content. For instance, some search for pre-packaged solutions (all included), while other 'free riders' want to select each single travel detail independently. Because of this, the straightforward implementation of general decision aid and recommendation technologies often fail when applied to travel planning and destination choice (Ricci, 2002). Case-based reasoning (CBR), a problem-solving methodology that has been recently exploited to build a number of product recommender systems (Cunningham *et al.*, 2001; Shimazu, 2001; Bridge and Ferguson, 2002; McGinty and Smyth, 2002, 2003; McSherry, 2002, 2003) must be reshaped to fit the requirements of the travel domain. A CBR recommender is a knowledge-based system that exploites a 'search and reuse' approach. The search is performed on the catalogue of items (to be suggested), and the reuse of retrieved items could be implemented in different ways, from a simple display of the retrieved items to a more complex adaptation of the items to fit to the peculiar preferences of the user.

We describe Trip@dvice, a travel recommendation methodology that supports the selection of travel products (e.g. a hotel or a visit to a museum or a climbing school) and building a *travel plan*, which is a coherent (from the user point of view) bundling of products. In this approach the case base is composed of travel plans built by a community of users. A case is structured hierarchically (Smyth and Keane, 1996; Stahl and Bergman, 2000) including components that represent the search and/or decision problem definition, i.e. the travel's and the travellers' characteristics, and the problem solution. Trip@dvice extends case-based reasoning with interactive query management (Gaasterland *et al.*, 1992). This system attempts to understand the gist of a user request in order to suggest or answer related questions, to infer an answer from data that are accessible or to give an approximate response. Trip@dvice tries first to cope with user needs satisfying the logical conditions expressed in the user's query and, if this is not possible, it suggests query changes (relaxation and tightening) that will produce acceptable results. In Trip@dvice failures to satisfy all user needs are not solved relying on similarity-based retrieval, as is usual in CBR. Instead, (case) similarity is exploited, first, to retrieve relevant old recommendation sessions and, second, to rank the items in the result set of the user's given logical query.

2. Case-based Reasoning

CBR is a multidisciplinary subject that focuses on the reuse of experience, which is modelled as a case (Aamodt and Plaza, 1994; Aha, 1998). There are at least a couple of interpretations of CBR: a plausible high-level model for cognitive processing (Schank, 1982; Kolodner, 1993) and as a computational paradigm for problem solving (Aamodt and Plaza, 1994). We shall focus on the second interpretation only. Aamodt and Plaza refer to CBR as a problem-solving paradigm that uses the *specific* knowledge gathered solving concrete problem situations. This is in opposition with more classical approaches based on *general* knowledge about the problem domain (domain theory), which can be expressed using a knowledge representation language such as those based on rules, frames, semantic networks and first-order logic.

The first fundamental issue in CBR is the case representation language (case model) and therefore the scope of the case concept itself. In any CBR application the designer must decide: (i) what to store in a case (content); (ii) the appropriate structure for describing the case contents; and (iii) deciding how the case memory must be organized. What to store in a case is typically application-dependent and therefore we shall not comment on this now (see Section 5 for details on the Trip@dvice model). There are three major ways to basically represent (implement) a case: as a linear vector of features (or more in general a set of features); as a text, eventually semistructured and with mixed content; and as a complex structured object such as a labelled graph or a pattern of objects in an Object-Oriented language. There are also 'mixed' approaches that merge, for instance, text-based and vector-based representations but as a first classification this is quite adherent with the current reality of CBR applications.

In a vector-based representation a case is described as a fixed list of heterogeneous features (nominal-string, real numbers, integer numbers, Boolean, etc.). The CBR systems that adopt this representation language are usually derived from, or strongly influenced by, Machine Learning and Pattern Recognition, and are defined as exemplar-, instance- or memory-based (Aha *et al.*, 1991). Often, these approaches view problem solving as automatic classification or function approximation tasks (Witten and Frank, 2000). In a text-based CBR system the major input for case content is considered to be the information contained in a text. The text itself is typically processed in order to come up with the final case object. In this 'compilation' step, indexes are built, part of the text is tagged with meta-data information and possibly the text is summarized. This approach usually integrates CBR with Information Retrieval (Börner *et al.*, 1996; Burke *et al.*, 1997; Daniels and Rissland, 1997; Lenz and Burkhard, 1997) and is now again raising a lot of interest because of the Web and semi-structured languages like hypertext mark-up language (HTML) and extensible mark-up language (XML) (Shimazu, 1998).

In the complex structured approaches, cases are modelled as combinations of the previous approaches or using graph-based data models (Bunke and Messmer, 1994; Plaza, 1995; Gebhardt *et al.*, 1997; Macedo and Cardoso, 1998; Ricci and Senter, 1998; Stahl and Bergman, 2000). Complex structured case representation languages are often used in planning and design applications where the structure of the case reflects the task–subtask or component–subcomponent hierarchy. The approach, described in this report, belongs to this last category and exploits XML as target implementation data model (see Arslan *et al.*, 2002) for a detailed description of the XML model used in the DieToRecs prototype, shown in Section 8.2).

Independent from these approaches, a case is usually decomposed into three subcomponents: the problem description, the solution and the outcome. The first refers to the part that is matched when a new problem arises. This must include all the information needed to first guess that a case can be fruitfully reused for solving a similar problem. Considering problem solving as function approximation, the problem description becomes the domain of the function, where the co-domain is given by the solution and outcome.

The solution models the chunk of information that is searched for, e.g. the diagnosis of a malfunction or the plan to reach a destination. Finally, the outcome provides an evaluation of the applicability or goodness of the solution to the given problem. Our case model further extends this model, as there is no sharp separation between problem and solution components. In a stage of the decision process a case component must be defined or selected (e.g. the destination) and in a successive stage this can be used as part of the problem description when, for instance, the user is searching for attractions. The CBR problem-solving cycle is universally recognized as the basic common denominator of all CBR approaches and is summarized in Fig. 6.1 and discussed more fully below.

1. **Retrieve.** Given a problem description, retrieve a set of cases stored in the case base, whose problems are evaluated as similar. A similarity metric is used to compare the problem component of the new case being built with the problem description of the cases in the base. Indexes, case base partitions, case clusters or other similar tools can be used to speed up this stage.
2. **Reuse.** The retrieved cases are reused to build the solution. This stage could be very simple, e.g. only extract the 'solution' component from one retrieved case, or much more complex, e.g. to integrate all the solutions extracted from the retrieved cases to build a new candidate solution.
3. **Revise.** The solution is then adapted to fit the specific constraint of the current situation. For instance, a reused therapy for a patient suffering for similar disease must be adapted to the current patient (e.g. considering differences in the weight or age of the two patients).
4. **Review.** The constructed solution is evaluated applying it (or simulating the application) to the current problem. If a failure is detected, backtracking to a previous stage might be necessary. The 'reuse', 'revise' and 'review' stages are also called case adaptation.

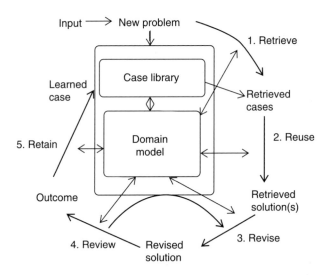

Fig. 6.1. The CBR problem-solving process (from Aha and Breslow, 1997).

5. Retain. The new case is possibly added to the case base. Not all the cases built following this process must be added to the case base. There could be poorly evaluated cases or cases too similar to previous situations, and therefore not bringing new knowledge.

3. CBR and Travel Planning

CBR may be used to build recommender systems, and a number of proto-types have proved the effectiveness of this methodology (Aimeur and Vézeau, 2000; Burke, 2000b; Doyle and Cunningham, 2000; Göker and Thomson, 2000; Smyth and Cotter, 2000; Bridge, 2001; Cunningham *et al.*, 2001). When CBR is applied to recommender systems, the user needs and wants basically define the problem to be solved and a product suggested is considered as the solution. Hence, CBR recommender systems typically provide sugges-tions for a product, first asking the user to specify some personal data and preferences related to the product for which a suggestion is searched, and then retrieving from the case base a subset of cases that best match the input description. A case in the memory, in order to adhere to the CBR problem-solving loop described in Section 2, should represent a problem together with its solution; hence the product recommended (solution) together with the motivations for such a recommendation, i.e. a description of the situation in which the user asks for a recommendation. Actually, almost all the CBR recommender systems take a simpler approach: they simply define the case base as the full list of available products. In other words, they assume that the product description, i.e. basically a set of attributes of the product, can even play the role of problem description. We shall comment on this issue by referring to an example.

Lenz was among the first to apply CBR to travel and tourism in the CABATA system (Lenz, 1996, 1999). In these studies, CBR was exploited as a tool to issue similarity-based queries to a catalogue. The user is supposed to enter the partial specification of a hotel and the system responds with the most similar ones in the catalogue. So, for instance, if the user enters a partial description of a hotel such as 'cost = 100 and location = Rome', the system would retrieve all the hotels that satisfy those conditions (if any) and also those that do not match all these requirements but are similar, e.g. a hotel that costs 110 and whose location is Rome. In this example, the user needs and wants are modelled by two attributes of the hotel (cost and location). One first observation relates to the retain stage of the CBR problem-solving loop. If, for instance, the user selects the hotel 'Gladiator', among those shown by CABATA, the system does not store in the case base that a given problem, i.e. 'cost = 100 and location = Rome' was solved by the hotel 'Gladiator'. In that respect CABATA, and similarly many other CBR recommender systems, do not close the CBR learning loop, retaining the newly acquired experi-ences. Another major limitation of all the CBR recommenders that identify a product with a case is that users can query the case base only referring to attributes of the product. Hence, if, for instance, the user would like a hotel with 'cost = 100 and location = Rome' and 'suited for a family with children', and this 'suited for' attribute is not part of the hotel description, the system will never learn the association of some hotels to this attribute. Conversely, if the system would store the full list of user needs and wants, even those that are not explicitly represented as attribute of the product, together with the product chosen at the end of the problem-solving process, the case base could be mined to discover this kind of implicit associations.

Another consequence of the limitation of modelling a case as a product to be recommended is that it is impossible to apply CBR for those products or services that are sold, only aggregating more elementary components. A travel plan is a typical example of a bundled product, it generally comprises some transportation services (flight, train or car), accommodations, attractions to visit and activities to do at the destination. Sometimes this is pre-packaged, but one of the main motivations for going online and searching for travel information is to build a tailor-made travel selecting from multiple suppliers and catalogues. To make possible such a bundling the user should be able to search in a range of catalogues but at the same time to compose a single plan where these elementary products fit well together. Once again, it is clear that in travel planning, the problem (user needs and wants) and the solution (tailor-made travel plan) cannot be described as predefined products in a catalogue. These issues motivate the methodology we shall describe in the following sections.

4. Trip@dvice Methodology

We have designed a novel hybrid recommendation methodology called Trip@dvice that integrates CBR, interactive query management and collaborative-based filtering. Trip@dvice is motivated by some basic requirements:

- Tourism products and services typically have **complex structures**, where the final recommended item is an aggregation of more elementary components. For instance, a trip may bundle a flight, an accommodation and a rental car. Similarly, in other application domains, such as computers, a desktop computer may be sold together with a printer, a monitor and a scanner.
- The recommender systems based on Trip@dvice must allow the user to **bundle a mix-and-match travel plan**. This can either comprise a prepackaged offer or can be obtained by selecting travel components (items) such as locations to visit, accommodations, attractions and services.
- The recommendation methodology must support the implementation of advanced search functions that are still perceived by the user as conventional, and simple to use, as in **form-based information search engines**. This would make the methodology simple to integrate into existing systems. A recommender system, exploiting the methodology, must provide a range of query-forms: for elementary products and services and for predefined combinations (e.g. a complete travel package).

- The recommendation methodology must support **dialogues between the user and the recommender system**. A user should be allowed to criticize, or comment on, a query result or to refine the query definition. On the other hand, the system should actively support this query-refinement process by suggesting the most reasonable and minimal changes either for relaxing or tightening the user preferences. The final goal is to present the user with a manageable set of options in few interactions.
- Both **short-term (goal-oriented) and long-term (stable) preferences** must influence the recommendation. Short-term preferences are highly situation-dependent, tend to be hard constraints and should dominate long-term preferences. For instance, if the user searches for a business flight, the system must shade the influence of a previous history of 'no frills' flights bought by the user for a leisure travel.
- **The system should bootstrap without an initial memory of user interactions**, i.e. the Trip@dvice methodology should support the user even when not enough cases are collected. If the system has not learned 'enough', then more straightforward search functions should be available.
- **Unregistered users should be allowed to get recommendations** without being identified, if they do not want to. The methodology must exploit in this case only knowledge acquired during the current recommendation session.
- The methodology should **support a large number of user typologies with their preferred decision styles**. Hence, users should be allowed to provide in whatever order and amount they like general and detailed travel needs and wants. Users with a clear picture of what they are looking for should find immediately the searched product or understand why this is not attainable and what compromises they must accept. Conversely, users with a less clear goal should be supported in a more explorative browsing of the options.
- **The system should not assume that products and users' needs and wants completely overlap in their definition.** The methodology must exploit the characterization of the traveller needs and wants that are known, according to the literature on travel decision choice, to influence or determine their choices.

Trip@dvice bases its recommendations on a case model that capture a unique human–machine interaction session. A case collects information provided by the user during the session, the products selected and some stable user-related preferences and demographic data if it is registered. Recommendation sessions are stored as cases in a repository (case base). In addition to the case base, catalogues of products (databases) described according to the supplier view are also exploited.

Input information provided by the user during an interaction session fall into two categories: content queries and collaborative features. Content queries constrain attributes of the products in the catalogues. For instance, 'cost = 100 and location = Rome' is a content query on the Hotel catalogue. Collaborative features may not be descriptors of the products, are acquired from the user and are meant to describe the recommendation problem. For instance, the nationality of the user or the travel purpose could be used to describe a travel, and specify the context in which a travel is built. These in general are not part of the description of the products found in the catalogue. Collaborative features, as the name suggests, are exploited in Trip@dvice to identify similar past recommendation sessions, e.g. human–machine interactions took place with similar user with similar needs and wants.

The recommendation process is basically initiated by the system with a request for some collaborative features. Users can either input some of these or completely skip this stage and ask for suggestions. In the first case, users are forwarded to a search step where they can query the catalogues (for elementary and already bundled products) and get some ranked recommendations with their corresponding rationale. In the second case, users are immediately presented with a limited set of alternative travel options and they are only requested to provide a feedback ('I like it') about the shown options. This initiates a 'conversation' that after some iteration is supposed to terminate with a selection.

In both situations the collaborative features provided by the user during the interaction and the current case (the products and services selected in the interaction) are exploited to retrieve similar cases from the case base. This means that the similarity measure uses only the collaborative features and the cart composition to estimate what the other cases in the case base are that could provide useful knowledge for personalizing the interaction and the results. The exact definition of the recommendation procedure and in particular of the similarity function is described in the following sections. The idea is that what has been selected by other users, and was put in the carts, can provide useful knowledge to personalize the interaction. But to be effective this mechanism requires that only those cases that are pertinent in the current recommendation session be reused; hence, there is an evaluation of similarity that takes into account the traveller and travel characteristics (collaborative features) and products selected (those in the cart).

5. Case Model

In Trip@dvice, a case represents a user interaction with the system, and therefore is built incrementally during the recommendation session. A case comprises the following main components:

- **Collaborative Features (clf)** are features that describe general users' characteristics, wishes, constraints or goals (e.g. desire to relax or to practice sports). They capture preferences relevant to the users' decision-making process, which cannot generally be mapped into the features of products in the electronic catalogues. These features are used to measure case (session) similarity. Knowledge of the domain and the decision process is essential to select the right collaborative features (Ricci *et al.*, 2002a).

- **Content Queries (cnq)** are queries posed over the catalogues of products. Content queries are built by constraining (content) features, i.e. descriptors of the products listed in the catalogues. Some content features can also be exploited as collaborative features; hence, in general collaborative features and content features have a non-void intersection. For instance, a constraint on the budget for a Hotel search is also exploited as a collaborative feature.
- **Cart** contains the set of products chosen by the user during the recommendation session represented by the case. A cart represents a meaningful (from the user's point of view) bundling of different products. For instance, a travel cart may contain some destinations, some accommodations and some additional attractions. A product in the cart may be rated by the user, and this typically occurs after the travel is done.

Figure 6.2 shows an example in the tourism domain. It represents a user, who is single, has a medium budget (between €20 and €40) and is looking for a vacation (destinations and accommodation) where he can practice some sports and have some eno-gastronomic 'experience'. These are the collaborative features. Then there are a couple of queries (over the product catalogues) that constrain content features of the products. He wants to stay in a three-star hotel, which has a private parking lot and has a cost per night of less than €40. The destination should be a resort suitable for rock climbing and

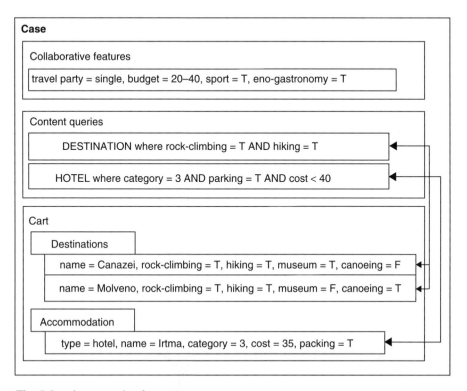

Fig. 6.2. An example of a case.

hiking. Given these preferences, the user is supposed to have selected and added to his cart the Irma Hotel, and Molveno and Canazei resorts. In this example, the user has selected two destinations by querying the destination catalogue.

More formally, the Case Base (CB) is defined as follows: $CB \subseteq CLF \times \wp(CNQ) \times CART$, where $\wp(X)$ is the power set of X, i.e. the set of all subsets of X. The detailed description of a case will be discussed in Section 7, where we shall see how the similarity between two cases is computed. Here we provide a simpler presentation in order to focus on the recommendation methodology (process) and its main elements.

The **Collaborative Features (CLF)** can be modelled as a vector space $CLF = \prod_{i=1}^{l} CLF_i$, where CLF_i could be a set of symbols, a finite subset of the integers or a real interval. In the example shown in Fig. 6.2, we have $CLF = TravelParty \times MinBudget \times MaxBudget \times Sports \times EnoGastronomy$, where $TravelParty = \{single, family, friends, couple, group\}$, $MinBudget = [0, 80]$, $MaxBudget = [10, \infty]$ and $Sports = Relax = \{T, F\}$. In the example shown, the collaborative features are $clf = (single, 20, 40, T, T)$. Please note that this is a simplified example. In real systems (such as those discussed in Section 8) a case can contain dozens of collaborative features. Moreover, we observe that real systems exploiting Trip@dvice may adopt a structured representation of CLF, i.e. subsets of features in CLF may be grouped together to form a composite feature. For instance, the MaxCost and MinCost may be grouped to define the Cost (structured) feature (cf. also Section 7 where this topic is further described).

Content Queries (CNQ) is the space of all the queries that the user can specify over products in the catalogues. We assume that each product can be represented as a vector of features $CNF = \prod_{i=1}^{n} CNF_i$. CNF_i can be (as above for CLF_i) a set of symbols, a finite subset of the integers or a real interval. A catalogue $CAT \subset CNF$ is said to be of type CNF. A query q over a catalogue CAT is a conjunction of simple constraints, where each constraint involves only one feature. More formally, $q = (c_1, \ldots, c_m)$, where $m \leq n$, and c_k is an equality constraint $(x = v)$ in case it refers to a feature that takes values in symbolic space CNF_i, and c_k is a range constraint $(v \leq x \leq u)$ in case it refers to a feature that takes values in numeric space CNF_j.

Let $Q(CNF)$ be the space of all the queries over CNF. Furthermore, let us assume that there are N product types $CNF^1, \ldots, CNF^N$. Then we denote by $CNQ = \bigcup_{i=1}^{N} Q(CNF^i)$ the space of all the queries on the catalogues. We finally denote with $\wp(CNQ)$ the set of all subsets of queries over the catalogues, i.e.

$$\wp(CNQ) = \{cnq = \{q_1, \ldots, q_k\} \mid q_i = Q(CNF^{j_i})\}$$

In the example shown in Fig. 6.2, cnq = {(rock climbing = T AND hiking = T), (category = 3 AND parking = T AND cost ≤ 40)}.

CART is defined as $CART = \wp(\bigcup_{i=1}^{N} CNF^i)$, i.e. an element cart ∈ CART is subsets of products: cart = $\{p_1, \ldots, p_k\}$ such that $\big| p_i \in CNF^{j_i}$. In the quoted example, cart = {(Canazei, T, T, T, F), (Molveno, T, T, F, T), (hotel, Irma, 3, 35, T)}.

6. Product Recommendation

As discussed previously, Trip@dvice supports a range of decision styles. In this section we describe two of them: the single-item iterative selection and 'seeking for inspiration'. The first is designed for a user who has some rather precise needs and wants, and who wants to search the available options driven by these requirements. The second is designed for users who would rather browse the options and get inspired by the alternatives before taking some decision and focus on some particular products. A third recommendation functionality, named travel completion, which is aimed at completing a partial travel plan, is not shown here for lack of space.

6.1 Single-item iterative selection

The overall process supported by Trip@dvice, for the single-item iterative selection, is shown in Fig. 6.3. The user interacts with the recommender system by asking for recommendations about a product type (e.g. a destination). To simplify the notation, we will consider just one product space CNF, and q will denote the user's query on this catalogue (1: AskRecommendation(q) in Fig. 6.3). The system replies to this query q either by recommending some products or, in case the query fails, by suggesting some query refinements. The RecEngine module manages the request. First, it invokes the Evaluate-Query function (2) of the Intelligent Query Manager module (IQM), by passing the query. This function searches the catalogue for products matching the

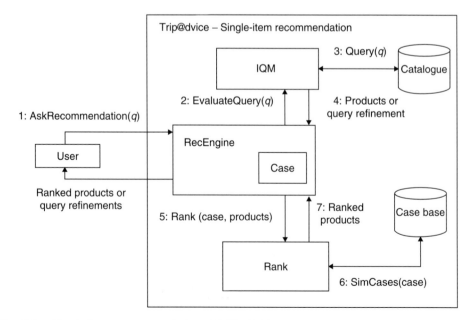

Fig. 6.3. Single-item recommendation with Trip@dvice.

```
CAT is the product catalog
q is the user's query
P = {p₁, ..., pₖ} the products selected by the user query q.
R = {(f₁, c₁, op₁), ..., (fₘ, cₘ, opₘ)}, opⱼ ∈ {add, modify, remove}, cⱼ is a
constraint on feature fⱼ to be: added, modified or removed (opⱼ)

EvaluateQuery(q, CX)
1  P ← SearchCatalog(q, CX)
2  if Size(P) > threshold
3          R ← TightenQuery(q, CX)
4          return R
5  else if Size(P) = 0
6          R ← RelaxQuery(q, CX)
7          return R
8      else
9          return P
```

Fig. 6.4. The EvaluateQuery algorithm.

query. If too many or no product matches the input query q, then IQM analyses q and determines a set of query refinements for suggestion (Ricci *et al.*, 2002b). If there are too many results, three features, not already constrained in q, are selected and the user is asked to provide a value for one of them to narrow down the search result. Conversely, if no result can be found, the system explains to the user the cause of the failure, i.e. it lists those constraints that, if relaxed, would allow the query to return some results.

The EvaluateQuery algorithm is described in Fig. 6.4. It receives as input a query q, over a product catalog CAT. It returns the products P matching the query q or a set of query-refinement suggestions R. R is a set of triples, each containing a feature f_k, a constraint c_k over the feature f_k and the suggested operation op_k (add, modify or remove from q). In line 1, the SearchCatalog function is invoked, passing the q query as parameter. The function searches through the catalogue for products matching q, and returns the set of matching products. Line 2 evaluates the size of the result set. If the number of selected products is above a certain threshold, the TightenQuery function is invoked (line 3). This function, using information related to the product catalogue data distribution (entropy and mutual information), returns a set of features (three) suggested to the user to further constrain the search. The user can choose one (or more) and provide a value (symbolic feature) or a range of values (numeric feature). Actually, TightenQuery returns a set of triples (f_i, *null*, *add*), where f_i is a feature and $c_i = null$, since the TightenQuery function cannot guess the exact value (or range of values) the user may want to specify for a suggested feature. Line 5 tests the empty result set condition. If the result set is empty, the RelaxQuery function is called (line 6). This function searches for those q modifications (constraint relaxation) that will allow q to retrieve some results. The suggested modifications are again returned as a set of triples (f_i, c_i, op_i), where $op_i = remove$ for symbolic features and $op_i = modify$ for finite integers or real features, and c_i represents the new (larger) range to be set. If neither relaxation nor tightening is invoked, the result set P is returned (line 9).

$RC = \{rc_1, \ldots, rc_{10}\}$ retrieved cases
$RP = \{rp_1, \ldots, rp_{10}\}$ products inside the reference cases
c is the current case
CB is the case base
$P = \{p_1, \ldots, p_k\}$ the products selected by the user query

Rank(c, p, CB)
1 $RC \leftarrow FindSimilarCases(c, CB)$
2 $RP \leftarrow ExtractReferenceProducts(RC)$
3 **for each** $p_i \in \{p_1, \ldots, p_k\} = P$
4        $Score(p_i) \leftarrow max_{j} = 1 \ldots 10 \{Sim(c, rc_j)^*Sim(p_i, rp_j)\}$
5        $P \leftarrow Sort\{p_1, \ldots, p_k\}$ according to $Score(p_i)$
6 *return P*

Fig. 6.5. The Rank algorithm.

When the number of items retrieved is satisfactory, the products are ranked by invoking the Rank method (Fig. 6.5). Rank receives the current case and the set of products selected by the EvaluateQuery function (the set P in Fig. 6.4). The current case is used to retrieve the set of K most similar cases, and the products contained in these retrieved cases are then used to rank the user-selected products. Finally, the ranked products are returned to the user. The RankProducts algorithm ranks the products retrieved by EvaluateQuery. Ranking is computed exploiting two similarity metrics: first, the case base is accessed to retrieve the K most similar cases (reference cases) to the current one. This similarity-based retrieval in principle can exploit all the case content, but an empirical evaluation has shown that it is more convenient to focus on the collaborative features and the cart content (cf. Section 7 for more details). Then, the products contained in the carts of the retrieved reference cases (reference products) are used to sort the products selected by the user's query. The basic idea is that among the products in the result set of the query one will get a better score if it is similar or equal to a product (of the same type) bought by a user with similar needs and wants. Figure 6.5 describes the algorithm in detail.

The Rank function receives the current case c, the set of products P retrieved by the function EvaluateQuery and the case base CB. It returns the products P ranked. First, it retrieves from CB the reference cases RC (line 1). In line 3, RP is defined as the products contained in the reference cases RC, having the same type of those in P.[2] In line 4, the $Score$ of each product $p_i \in P$ is computed as the maximum value of $Sim(c, rc_j)^*Sim(p_i, rp_j)$ over all the reference products rp_j (the similarity functions are described in Section 7).

Computing the final product score as the multiplication of cases and products similarity mimics the collaborative-filtering (CF) approach, but there are some notable differences. First, differently from a standard CF approach, only the first nearest neighbour case is considered, i.e. the case

---

[2] For sake of simplicity we assume that each reference case rc_j contains just one product rp_i of the same type of the products to be ranked, but the same approach applies also when more products are contained in a case.

that yields the maximum value for $Sim(c, rc_j)*Sim(p_i, rp_j)$. The rationale for this choice is that we can use the retrieved case to explain the score value to the user. Conversely, if we had used the classical CF approach (Breese *et al.*, 1998), we would have described a weighted average score without any possibility to refer to the 'collaborating' cases. Second, we do not consider the votes given by other users to the product to be scored, as is common in CF. Conversely, we use the similarity of the product to be scored with products selected in a similar case (user session) as a sort of implicit vote: if another user in a similar session has chosen that product or a similar one, this is an indication that this product fits the needs that are shared by the current user and the previous user.

Let us consider the following simple example. Let us assume that the collaborative features in *CLF* are *TravelParty* (symbolic), *MinBudget* (numeric), *MaxBudget* (numeric), *Sports* (Boolean), *Relax* (Boolean), that the product features in *CNF* are *DestName* (symbolic), *RockClimbing* (Boolean), *Hiking* (Boolean) and that the collaborative feature values of the current case c are: $clf = (single, 10, 40, T, T)$. Assume that a user query q has retrieved the products: $p_1 = (Predazzo, T, T)$ and $p_2 = (Cavalese, T, T)$. Then FindSimilarCases retrieves two cases rc_1 and rc_2, whose similarities with the current case c are $Sim(c, rc_1) = 0.75$ and $Sim(c, rc_2) = 1$. Let us further assume that rc_1 and rc_2 contain the product $rp_1 = (Campiglio, T, T)$ and $rp_2 = (Cavalese, T, T)$, respectively. Moreover, the product similarities are (see Section 7 for the similarity definition): $Sim(p_1, rp_1) = 0.66$, $Sim(p_1, rp_2) = 0.66$, $Sim(p_2, rp_1) = 0.66$, $Sim(p_2, rp_2) = 1$. The score of each p_i is computed as the maximum of $Sim(cc, c_j)*Sim(p_i, rp_j)$; thus: $Score(p_1) = max\{0.75*0.66, 1*0.66\} = 0.66$, and $Score(p_2) = max\{0.75*0.66, 1*1\} = 1$. Finally, p_2 is scored higher than p_1. The user, after having selected a first item (e.g. a destination) and added it to the cart, can iterate the process selecting another destination or another product or service among those offered in the supplier catalogues. It is worth noting that in these next iterations even the content of the cart (the products selected at that point) are used to compute the similarity with past cases. In this way the decisions taken by the user, at a certain point, impact on the computation of similar cases and in turn on the ranking of the products recommended in the next stages.

6.2 Seeking for inspiration

The second decision style supported by Trip@dvice is seeking for inspiration. This is designed for users who would rather 'look at' the options and get inspired by the alternatives before taking some decision and focus on some particular products. The recommendation proceeds according to the following loop (see Fig. 6.6):

- **First Retrieval.** The process starts with a seed case c, which could be either the current case or a random case taken from the case base. It is the current case if the user has already created one case in the previous stages of the interaction, for instance by selecting a destination and adding it

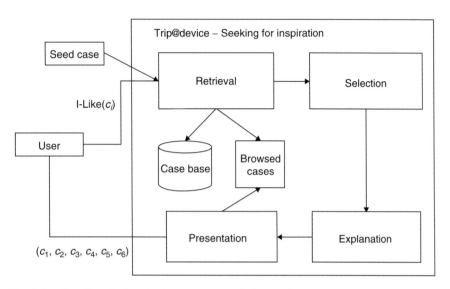

Fig. 6.6. Seeking for inspiration recommendation cycle.

to the cart using the single-item recommendation function. Conversely, if the interaction with the recommender starts with this first retrieval, the recommender does not know anything about the user and can only make an initial random guess of what could be a good travel for the user. The retrieval module searches for the M most similar cases in the case base and passes this set to the next module, the Selection. We call $Ret(1, M)$ this retrieval set to stress that this is the first retrieval set and its cardinality is M. The parameter M is typically a large number, possibly equal to the cardinality of the underlying case base. The Retrieval module is aimed at selecting past cases (travel plans) that are similar to the current one, hence potentially applicable even in the current situation.

- **Case Selection.** In the second step the M cases retrieved from the memory are analysed to select a very small subset of candidates to be presented to the user. In the DieToRecs system, for instance (see Section 8), six cases are selected. The selection is accomplished by a greedy algorithm that iteratively chooses the six cases starting from the seed case and puts them in the result set. The case added at each iteration is the one that minimizes the sum of the similarities between itself and the cases already in the result set. For instance, the second case added to the result set is $c_2 = argmin_{c_2 \in Ret(1, M)} \{Sim(c_1, c_2)\}$. Similarly, the third case is defined as $c_3 = argmin_{c_3 \in Ret(1, M)} \{Sim(c_1, c_3) + Sim(c_2, c_3)\}$. The selected cases $\{c_1, ..., c_6\}$ are then passed to the explanation module.

- **Explanation.** This module is aimed at providing a rationale for the selected cases. The explanation computed in this module stresses the differences of the selected cases, i.e. identifies the attributes that are peculiar to one case and are not common among the six selected cases. The algorithm considers each case and computes, for each feature f in a subset of all the case features (the most relevant for the explanation), a diversity count value $dc(f, c)$. This is the number of times the feature f has a different value in the other five cases. For instance, if $f_1 = accommodation\text{-}type$ feature, has value 'hotel' in c_1 and 'apartment' in the others, then $dc(f_1, c_1) = 5$, and $dc(f_1, c_i) = 1$ for $i = 2, 3, 4, 5, 6$. Having repeated this for all the explanation-relevant features, for each case the three most peculiar features, i.e. those with higher diversity count, are selected. The explanation module then passes the six cases and the selected features to the presentation module.

- **Presentation.** The goal of this module is to present the six selected cases along with an explanation of their peculiarities. The explanation basically argues that a travel case is potentially interesting because it possesses some characteristics (features) that are not shared by other cases. Referring to the example above, the first case will be described, together with other descriptors, as a travel with a Hotel accommodation. Moreover, the presentation component selects some images, taken from the products or services included in the travel, to illustrate pictorially the case content. At this point the user is supposed to browse the offers, and eventually provide a positive feedback on one of these cases. This feedback, i.e. the selected case, is given as input for a possible successive retrieval.

- **Retrieval.** The second time the retrieval is called, the procedure described above is repeated, with some notable changes. The seed case is now the case that received positive feedback from the user, and the number of cases retrieved from the case base, M in the first retrieval, is decreased by a factor $0 < \lambda < 1$, i.e. the new retrieval set is $Ret(2, \lambda M)$. The rationale for decreasing the number of retrieved cases is to better focus the retrieval around the input case, since at this new stage we must count on the positive evaluation of the user on the selected case. This λ parameter is tuned in such a way that $M\lambda^{l+2\sigma} < 6$, where l is the average interaction length (as observed in the experiments with real users) and σ is the standard deviation. In this way there is no further diversity selection after a typically maximal number of iterations $(l + 2\sigma)$.

7. Similarity Measures

The recommendation functions described above heavily exploit similarity-based computation and similarity-based retrieval. The first refers to the computation of a similarity measure for two objects, either cases or products. The second refers to the extraction from the case base of a set of cases similar to a given one. In this section we shall focus on the similarity computation and will describe the general similarity metric defined in Trip@dvice. In this chapter we do not discuss the particular implementation of the similarity-based retrieval. The reader can assume that a standard linear scan of the case base is implemented (see Arslan *et al.*, 2002) for further details on this topic). As we observed in Section 5, a case is a structured object, i.e. a case c can be decomposed into three subcomponents: the collaborative features, the content queries and the cart. In this section, to make the discussion more general, we shall simply assume that a case c is a rooted and ordered tree $G_c(V_c, E_c)$, which we denote with V_c, the nodes, i.e. the set of all subcomponents of c, and with E_c, the set of edges. An edge (p, q) is in E_c if the component p contains the component q. In this case, we say that q is an out-neighbour of p and we shall denote with $O(v)$ the set of out-neighbours. The out-neighbours of a node are ordered, hence we shall indicate with $v = (v_1, ..., v_n)$ the out-neighbours of v, instead of using the notation $O(v) = \{v_1, ..., v_n\}$. For instance, considering the case $c = (clf, cnq, cart)$, we have $(c, clf) \in E_c$ and clf is an out-neighbour of c. Moreover, each node v is labelled by a type information $\tau(v)$, which describes the type (with a name) of the case component represented by the node. For instance, in the case c as above, $\tau(clf) = $ *collaborative features*.

In addition to the type $\tau(v)$ of a node v, it is defined by the metric-type $\mu(v)$ of the node. The metric-type determines how the metric is computed at the node and depends on: (i) the type of the node; and (ii) the metric-type of the out-neighbours. First of all, let us define a leaf node as a node that cannot have any out-neighbour; then we have the following cases:

- $\mu(v) = $ *vector* means that if $O(v)$ is not empty, then it is an ordered list of nodes with fixed length.
- $\mu(v) = $ *set* means that if $O(v)$ is not empty, then it is an unordered set of nodes.
- $\mu(v) = $ *heterogeneous* if and only if $O(v)$ contains leaf nodes (i.e. nodes that have no out-neighbours).

Leaf nodes can have the following metric-type: hierarchical, numeric, jaccard, modular, symbol, and range as explained below:

- $\mu(v) = $ *hierarchical* means that v is a vector of features with a precise hierarchical relationship. For instance, a node of type 'geo-area' is a vector of four symbols (country, region, area, village).
- $\mu(v) = $ *numeric* means that v is a numeric feature (float or integer).
- $\mu(v) = $ *jaccard* means that v is a vector of Boolean features.
- $\mu(v) = $ *modular* means that v is a modulo. For instance, the hours are integer modulo 24 (e.g. $23 + 3 = 2$).
- $\mu(v) = $ *symbol* means that the value of v is an arbitrary symbol in a given symbol set (e.g. a Boolean feature).
- $\mu(v) = $ *range* means that v is a range of numbers, e.g. (minPrice, maxPrice) constraints in a hotel query constraint.

Before explaining how the distance metric is computed, let us extend our case example $c = (clf, cnq, cart)$ to describe the above-mentioned node metric-types. For sake of simplicity let us describe a simpler case $c = (clf, cart)$, i.e. where the content queries are not considered. Then let us assume that $clf = (single, 1, \quad [20, 40], \quad [0, 1, 0], \quad [italy, trentino, fassa, null])$, $cart = (ds, as)$, $ds = (de_1, de_2)$, $as = null$ $de_1 = vigo, de_2 = pozza$. Then c has type *case* and metric-type *vector*. clf has type *collaborative features* and metric-type *vector*. $cart$ has type *cart* and metric-type *vector*, ds and as have type *destinations* and *accommodations* and metric-type *set*, de_1 and de_2 have type *destination* and metric-type *symbol*. The first out-neighbour of *clf* (*single*) has type *travel party* and metric-type *symbol*; the second (1, i.e. January) has type *month period* and metric-type *modulo*; the third ([20, 40]) has type *budget* and metric-type *range*; the fourth ([0, 1, 0]) has type *interests* and metric-type *jaccard* (represents the presence or absence of three interests, e.g. *sport, culture, wellness*); the fifth ([*italy, trentino, fassa, ?*]) has type *geo-area* and metric type *hierarchical*.

The cases contained in a cases base all share the same structure, i.e. the out-neighbours of a node with given type have always the same type. In more formal way, if $c = G_c(V_c, E_c)$ and $c' = G'_c(V'_c, E'_c)$, then $c = (v_1, ..., v_n)$, $c' = (v'_1, ..., v'_n)$ and $\tau(v_1) = \tau(v'_1), ..., \tau(v_n) = \tau(v'_n)$ and then recursively down to the leaves of the case. Moreover, if v is a node of c and its metric-type is *set* (i.e. $\mu(v) = set$), then $v = (v_1, ..., v_{n(v,c)})$, all the v_i have the same type and metric-type and we denote with $n(v, c)$ the fact that the number of out-neighbours of v is case-dependent. A typical example is the node representing the activities contained in a case. All the out-neighbours are activities, represented in the same way (metric-type), but the number of activities varies case by case.

We can now define the case metric $d(c, c')$ by recursively applying the distance computation on the subcomponents of the given nodes. It starts from the two nodes c, c' and applies a different computation according to the node metric-type. More formally, if $v = (v_1, ..., v_n) \in V_c$ and $v' = (v'_1, ..., v'_m) \in V'_c$, then

- If $\mu(v) = \mu(v') = vector$, then $n = m$ and

$$d(v, v') = \frac{1}{\sum_{i=1}^{n} w_i(\tau(v))} \sum_{i=1}^{n} w_i(\tau(v))d(v_i, v'_i)$$

where $0 \geq w_i(\tau(v)) \geq 1$ are weights depending on the type of node.

- If $\mu(v) = \mu(v') = set$, then

$$d(v, v') = \frac{1}{n*m} \sum_{i=1}^{n} \sum_{j=1}^{m} d(v_i, v'_j)$$

- If $\mu(v) = \mu(v') = heterogeneous$, then $n = m$ and

$$d(v, v') = \frac{1}{\sqrt{\sum_{i=1}^{n} w_i(\tau(v))}} \sqrt{\sum_{i=1}^{n} w_i(\tau(v))d(v_i, v'_i)^2}$$

- If $\mu(v) = \mu(v') = hierarchical$, then $n = m$ and

$$d(v, v') = 1 - (\max_i \{i : v_i = v'_i\}/n)$$

- If $\mu(v) = \mu(v') = numeric$, then $v, v' \in R$ and

$$d(v, v') = \begin{cases} \dfrac{||v-v'||}{4\sigma} & if \quad \dfrac{|v-v'|}{4\sigma} \leq 1 \\ 1 & else \end{cases}$$

where σ is the standard deviation of the values of all the nodes x of type $\tau(v)$ in the case base (or in the catalogue).

- If $\mu(v) = \mu(v') = jaccard$, then $n = m$ and

$$d(v, v') = \frac{N_{01} + N_{10}}{N_{01} + N_{10} + N_{11}}$$

where N_{01} is the number of times $v_i = 0$ and $v'_i = 1$. The other numbers are defined similarly.

- If $\mu(v) = \mu(v') = modular$, then $v, v' \in R$ and
  $d(v, v') = (arg_x \min \{v + x = v' \ (mod \ k), \ in \ v' + x = v \ (mod \ k)\})/k$

where k is the modulo of the nodes v, v'. Hence, for instance, if $k = 12$ (12 months), then the distance between 11 (November) and 1 (January) is the minimum $x/12$ s.t. $11 + x = 1 \ (mod \ 12)$ and $1 + x = 11 \ (mod \ 12)$, therefore $x = 2$ and the distance is $2/12$.

- If $\mu(v) = \mu(v') = symbol$, then

$$d(v, v') = \begin{cases} 0 & if \ v = v' \\ 1 & if \ v \neq v' \end{cases}$$

- If $\mu(v) = \mu(v') = range$, then $v = [v_1, v_2]$ and $v' = [v'_1, v'_2]$

$$d(v, v') = \frac{|v_1 - v'_1| + |v_2 - v'_2|}{2 * 4\sigma}$$

where σ is the standard deviation of the values of all the nodes x of type $\tau(v)$ in the case base and in the catalogue.

It must be noted that if a node v is null, i.e. it is not defined in the case (e.g. it is unknown), then the distance of that node with any other node is the maximal distance, i.e. 1.

Let us now take an example to illustrate how the case distance is computed. Referring to the previously mentioned example, let us imagine that:

$c = (clf, cart)$
$clf = (single, 1, [20, 40], [0, 1, 0], [italy, trentino, fassa, ?])$
$cart \ (ds, as), \ ds = (de_1, de_2), \ as = null, \ de_1 = vigo, \ de_2 = pozza$
$c' = (clf', cart')$

$clf' = (couple, 2, [30, 40], [1, 1, 0], [italy, trentino, fassa, campitello])$
$cart'(ds', as'), ds = (de'_1), as = null, de'_1 = mazzin.$

Then we have:

$d(c, c') = [1/(w(clf) + w(cart))] (w(clf) d(clf, clf') + w(cart) d(cart, cart'))$
$d(clf, clf') = [1/(\sqrt{\{\sum_{i=1}^{5} w_i(\tau(clf))\}})]\sqrt{\{\sum_{i=1}^{5} w_i(\tau(clf)) d(clf_i, clf'_i)^2\}}$
$d(clf_1, clf'_1) = 1$
$d(clf_2, clf'_2) = 1/12$
$d(clf_3, clf'_3) = 10/(8\sigma)$
$d(clf_4, clf'_4) = 1/2$
$d(clf_5, clf'_5) = 1 - 3/4$
$d(cart, cart') = [1/(w(des) + w(acc))] (w(des) d(ds, ds') + w(acc) d(acc, acc'))$
$d(des, des') = 1/2 (d(de_1, de'_1) + d(de_2, de'_1)) = 1/2 (1 + 1)$
$d(as, as') = 1$

Using the same approach the metric can compute the distance of two items in a catalogue. Hence, if, for instance, the destination is modelled as a heterogeneous vector of the features (nodes) $de = ([italy, trentino, fassa, campitello],$ 1448, [1, 1, 0]), then in computing the distance between this destination and another destination the same rules as above apply. Finally, the similarity of two cases c, c' (or two items) is defined as

$$Sim(c, c') = exp(-d(c, c'))$$

8. Prototypes

8.1 NutKing

In the NutKing prototype, Trip@dvice supports the interaction mimicking a typical counselling session in a real travel agency. The user initially defines the major trip goals and constraints entering some preferences as shown in Fig. 6.7. These are general features of the proposed trip including travel companions, budget and means of transportation. These wishes are used both to recommend products, exploiting other users' trips, and to set some default constraints in successive query-forms. After this initial step, the user can start building his or her itinerary by searching for travel products, as required. This could be a destination, an accommodation, an event or an attraction (available catalogues).

Assume that the user is looking for a destination; the system offers the user a classical Query-By-Example interface (left side of Fig. 6.8), where he or she can set constraints on the product features. If the query retrieves too many products to be examined, Trip@dvice asks the user to provide some additional (alternative) constraints. Another possible situation may occur when no products satisfy the query; in this case the system proposes some alternative query's relaxations, which, if applied, would provide the user with a suitable result set (Fig. 6.8).

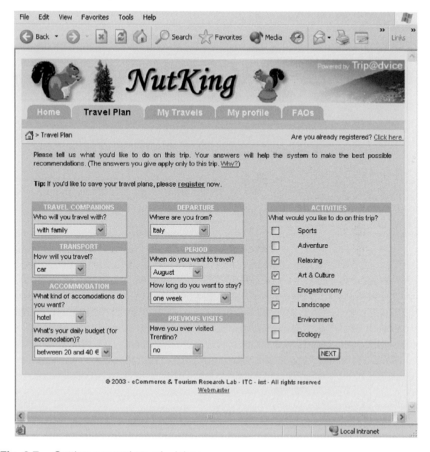

Fig. 6.7. Setting general travel wishes.

At the end of this interaction a list of recommended products is shown (Fig. 6.9). All of these satisfy the (explicit) user constraints, but furthermore the products most similar to those selected by other users with similar general wishes are ranked first. By clicking on the small trees icon on the right side of the product, the user can obtain an explanation of the recommendation. Then the user can add the selected product to his or her travel bag and proceed by adding other items to the trip. Finally, the user can print the complete itinerary in a brochure-like style.

8.2 DieToRecs

DieToRecs recommender system extends in many ways the NutKing prototype described above. In addition to the single-item iterative recommendation function, which has been illustrated in Section 8.1, DieToRecs includes the travel completion and seeking for inspiration functions. The seeking for

Fig. 6.8. Suggesting query relaxations.

inspiration recommendation function is designed for a tourist who is less constrained by precise needs and wants and is more prone to consider 'good proposals'. Hence, the selection process is more system-driven in the form of pictorial representations of former trips. In seeking for inspiration, users are not requested to specify general travel or travel item preferences to get some recommendations, but they immediately get some travel recommendations by the systems (see Fig. 6.10). The system proposes six complete travels, represented by images about the destination and the accommodation and the two most important and characterizing features. Users can then access detailed information about each proposal and the included tourist products, like details about the suggested accommodations, descriptions about the destinations and attractions. After examining the proposals or, just being inspired by the shown images, the users can get six new different proposals simply by expressing their interest about one of them; the system, exploiting the fact that the users are interested in that particular alternative, proposes six other alternatives that are more focused on the user wishes. In this way, the users can browse the catalogue space without explicitly specifying constraints and

Fig. 6.9. Showing the final recommendation.

wishes. When the users find the proposal that suits their needs, they can add the suggested products to their personal travel bag.

9. Discussion and Conclusion

In this chapter we have presented Trip@dvice, an approach to products and services recommendation that exploits in a novel way the classical CBR learning loop. Trip@dvice integrates CBR and interactive query management to support a number of decision styles. The proposed methodology can help the user to specify a query that filters out unwanted products in electronic catalogues (content-based) and can as well serve less structured search process that are mostly driven by browsing options rather than imposing restrictions on options. The approach has been applied to a couple of web travel applications and it has been empirically evaluated with real users. We have shown that the proposed approach: (i) reduces the number of user queries; (ii) reduces the number of browsed products; (iii) increases user satisfaction;

Fig. 6.10. Seeking for inspiration user interface in DieToRecs.

(iv) produces good recommendations; and that (v) the selected items are found first on the ranked list.

We have already talked about the general flow of the CBR cycle in Section 2 and explained why the classical approach has some limitations when applied to complex products recommendation. To tackle these problems we designed the Trip@dvice methodology. This yields a change in the CBR loop, which is described below. The description here refers to the single-item recommendation only. A similar description would be necessary for the other decision styles, but it is here omitted for lack of space.

The left part of Fig. 6.11, i.e. (a), covers the mentioned classical CBR cycle, plus an extra step '6. Iterate', which is particular to our approach. The boxes are the points where we have introduced some changes to the classical framework. The separation between the left and right parts of Fig. 6.11, i.e. (a) and (b), underlines one of the main differences between the Trip@dvice methodology and the basic CBR cycle.

The travel items selected in a recommendation session, i.e. the items that form the travel cart, are contained in electronic catalogues (products database). The case base provides information about good bundling of products and is therefore used for acquiring this knowledge and for ranking items selected in the catalogues as we have explained throughout this document. The catalogues are exploited for obtaining up-to-date information about currently available products and services.

- **Retrieve.** Retrieval is done considering also similarities between sub-components of cases. Section 7 explains how we obtain the set of retrieved

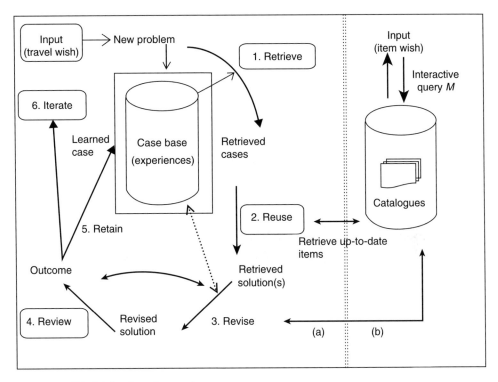

Fig. 6.11. Trip@dvice learning cycle.

cases that are called 'Reference Set' to stress their importance in all the recommendation stages.

- **Reuse and Revise.** We do reuse the previously experienced cases, but in a different fashion. Mainly we use the past experiences to get the required knowledge for aggregations of travel items. Instead of re-using exactly the same recommendations as in the past (solutions to the previously stated problems), we always recommend up-to-date items to the user. Therefore we deliver to the user already revised (updated) recommendations.

- **Review.** The last decision is always made by the user. Trip@dvice users are always allowed to reconfigure the recommended bundles. Using the experienced successful cases, the system opens a new door to the user. Having adapted and updated versions of these templates, the user may replace, add or remove one (or more) of the items in the recommended travel. In this view, we manage the Review step in a mixed-initiative way, in collaboration with the user.

- **Retain and Iterate.** When the user accepts the outcome (the final version of the recommendation delivered to the user), this action forms a new learned case, i.e. a complex problem and its solution to be used for further recommendations, which is the point at which a standard CBR cycle completes the loop. But we need to underline that Trip@dvice CBR cycle may not be completed at this stage, if the user does not think that the travel bag is completed yet.

- **Input.** The first remark here is that in Trip@dvice, the user input is gathered in a structural way (Travel Wish and Item Wish). One can say that the 'Input' is the problem description for a classical CBR application. But, as the 'Iterate' step states, the underlined loop in Fig. 6.11 may take place repeatedly. Each time the user starts a new loop, what he already has in his travel bag defines a part of the new problem. Therefore, the notion of complete travel bag makes the problem description (i.e. input) a little fuzzy and a cloudy concept.

Our framework extends the basic CBR model presented in Section 2. First, the scoring and ranking mechanism is determined not only by the user input conditions and the product catalogues but also on the memory of past interaction sessions (case base). Therefore, referring to the example quoted above, we can rank and differentiate even the hotels that satisfy the query conditions ('cost = 100 and location = Rome') by measuring the similarity of the hotels that satisfy the user query with those chosen in the past for similar travels. In CABATA all the hotels that logically satisfy the query conditions have maximal similarity with the query and therefore are not differentiated in the recommendation.

The second major aspect that differentiates our system from standard CBR recommender systems refers to the case structure itself. Our case base is made up of complex structures of more elementary components (travel products). This case base is used both when the elementary components retrieved from a catalogue must be ranked and when similarity-based retrieval is performed at the case level itself. Standard CBR recommenders only perform this last function, i.e. similarity-based retrieval on the case base.

That points out a third element, i.e. the usage of both a case base and catalogues. The case base provides complex knowledge about travel products bundling and user navigation preferences, whereas the catalogues of products, accessed as external systems, provide up-to-date information on the available travel products.

A number of open issues are still to be addressed. We would like to mention first the adaptation of the similarity metric. This depends on a number of parameters (weights) and it is applied in a range of recommendation functions and, more internally, in steps of the recommendation process. General knowledge can be exploited to design a default weighting scheme but a finer tuning is necessary to improve the recommendation quality. Another major issue is related to the case base management. Currently the methodology has been tested with small case bases. An operational system that includes Trip@dvice will produce a large case base in a few days of proper usage. Hence, the problem of discarding unnecessary cases will become more and more relevant. Even if this is not a new problem in CBR, the customization of general techniques to the peculiar case structure and CBR application poses interesting and unsolved issues.

Chapter Summary

In this chapter we provided the methodological foundations and the rationale for approaching travel destination recommendation as a problem-solving activity. The CBR was presented both as a cognitive plausible approach and as an integrated paradigm to build advisory systems. We then described an integrated solution called Trip@dvice that employs CBR. Finally, we discussed the most important findings of various validation activities and future research.

Acknowledgements

This work has been partially funded by CARITRO foundation (under contract 'eCommerce e Turismo') and by the European Union's Fifth RTD Framework Programme (under contract DIETORECS IST-2000-29474). The authors would like to thank all the partners of the DieToRecs (http://DieToRecs.itc.it/) project for their original ideas and comments on the Trip@dvice methodology.

7 Destination Recommendations Based on Travel Decision Styles

ANDREAS H. ZINS AND KLAUS GRABLER

1. Introduction

What is the motivation for a potential traveller to consult some web-based resources instead of picking the phone or entering the nearby travel agency to get some useful information for making the next trip planning? After two decades of the rapid diffusion of personal computers (PCs) in both working and home environments and a substantial adoption of Internet usage, the advantages of information have been widely acknowledged. However, it is obvious that all these benefits cannot outweigh the restrictions imposed by the shift from human-to-human or paper-to-human to the machine-to-human interface. While the area of data storage, data retrieval, information processing and data presentation has progressed considerably in terms of effectiveness and efficiency, the area of problem solving in an adaptive way is a major challenge of this decade. In order to build useful recommender systems for tourism purposes (Ricci, 2002) it may be helpful to consider the characteristics of a good salesperson; they are:

- helping the customers in making a good decision;
- giving an overview of the available supply side;
- finding a good match between someone's interests, preferences, wishes and the offered products and services;
- reducing the everlasting and varied risks for experiential goods; and
- listening, recommending, interpreting, translating, explaining, delivering inspirations, imagining and making dreams come true.

How can sales representatives achieve a good or even excellent service quality? Basically, the resources are multidimensional covering at least the following:

©CAB International 2006. *Destination Recommendation Systems: Behavioural Foundations and Applications* (eds D.R. Fesenmaier, K.W. Wöber and H. Werthner)

- to be able to ask questions to learn efficiently about the customer's wishes and preferences;
- to share a comprehensive knowledge about the supply side or enabling access to the relevant information; and
- to be adaptive and responsive to the customer's response to the ongoing recommendation process.

Travel agents or destination sales representatives have to be trained to gain the necessary competence. Similarly, computer systems need to be equipped with structures and elements empowering them to learn as fast as possible and to adapt to the user's needs. From communication science it is clear that, for example, a sales relationship is not unidirectional. Hence, it is equally important to recognize that the user (= consumer) has limited motivation and capabilities to learn and adapt to the prevailing interface, which should help to solve an information or decision problem. Consequently, the best possible approach is to build recommender systems incorporating all knowledge about information behaviour and travel decision-making, and to find how these insights can be represented and applied dynamically.

Section 2 provides a discussion on this framing task. A methodology is introduced that allows more detailed insights into the decision process of travellers. After presenting the results emerging from this study the usefulness and the further development of travel decision styles will be discussed.

2. The Role of Decision Styles in Marketing

For more than 20 years marketing literature has applied different concepts to predict consumption activities. They can be summarized as consumer styles and comprise: (i) psychographics or lifestyle approaches (e.g. Wells, 1974; Lastovicka, 1982); (ii) consumer typology approaches (e.g. Stone, 1954; Darden and Ashton, 1974–1975; Moschis, 1976); and (iii) consumer characteristics approaches (e.g. Sproles, 1985; Westbrook and Black, 1985).

The latter approach relied on cognitive and affective characteristics of consumer decision-making. Sproles and Kendall (1986) proposed an eight-dimensional inventory of consumer decision-making styles. They purported that such a style characteristic or consumer personality is analogous to the concept of psychology in psychology with a stable and lasting effect on consumer decision-making. In a more recent appraisal the value of this instrument was stated to go far beyond a unidimensional attribution of being either 'economic, apathetic, quality conscious, choosy, information seeking, price conscious, variety seeking or brand loyal' (Walsh *et al.*, 2001, 117 ff.). By its multidimensional structure it should be much more apt to grasp the so-called hybrid consumer of the post-modern era. 'A consumer decision-making style is defined as a mental orientation characterizing a consumer's approach to making choices' (Sproles and Kendall, 1986, p. 268). Walsh *et al.* (2001, p. 121) correctly identify that they can be acknowledged 'as basic buying-decision-making attitudes that consumers adhere to, even when they are applied to different goods, services or purchasing situations'. The following eight 'most basic mental characteristics' are the basis for the style inventory:

- perfectionism or high quality-consciousness;
- brand-consciousness;
- novelty fashion-consciousness;
- recreational, hedonistic shopping-consciousness;
- price-value consciousness;
- impulsiveness;
- confusion from overchoice; and
- habitual, brand-loyal orientation towards consumption.

Meanwhile, the instrument for identifying consumers' decision-making styles, Consumer Styles Inventory (CSI), has been tested and partly adapted in different cultures and countries (South Korea, New Zealand, India, Great Britain, China, Germany, mentioned in Walsh *et al.*, 2001) with a varying degree of reliability and validity of dimensions. In the German study the authors used these styles as a basis for market segmentation (McDonald, 1993), which resulted in a six-segment solution (Walsh *et al.*, 2001, 125 ff.). Segment 1 represented consumers whose buying behaviour was factual and value-oriented. Only the dimension 'perfectionism' had a high average mean, while all the other dimensions had a low mean, particularly 'impulsiveness'. Segment 2, labelled 'demanding comparison shoppers', comprised 30% of the sample, which was the largest group in the survey. The consumers in this group had high demands with regard to products they purchased and enjoyed searching for and choosing products. Segment 3 represented very impulsive consumers who tend to be rather indifferent with regard to brand and shopping experiences. The buying decisions of consumers in Segment 4 were strongly emotionally dominated. These consumers, however, turned out to be 'hedonistic' and more likely to perceive 'confusion by overchoice'. Segment 5 represented brand-oriented and shopping-enthusiastic consumers. They had keen interest in new products, which caused them to alter their buying decisions. Finally, the fashion-conscious result-oriented consumers in Segment 6 were less interested in the buying process itself than in the (branded) products they purchased.

While the early research on consumer decision-making styles had their merits on a descriptive level explaining how these prominent generic buying attitudes play together, the later research turned more to a prescriptive concern for marketing goods and services. For instance, questions about how to serve and communicate best with emotionally dominated consumers or brand-oriented enthusiasts or result-oriented shoppers were discussed with greater emphasis.

Another contribution shows evidence for moving away from the concern about the outcome of the consumer's decision-making towards the process itself. This effort goes back to the authors of the consumer decision-making styles inventory: Kendall and Sproles (1990). They investigated the relationship between consumer decision-making styles and individuals' learning behaviour. For this reason the authors first adapted Kolb's inventory base on his experiential learning theory (Kolb, 1984) into a Secondary Learning Style Inventory (Kendall and Sproles, 1986). As a next step they identified six characteristics of learning style:

1. Serious, analytical learner (enjoys thinking through difficult material in a serious and abstract manner);
2. Active, practical learner (experience-oriented, enjoys learning by doing practical learning activities);
3. Observation-centred learner (enjoys first seeing and then doing in his or her learning experiences);
4. Passive, accepting learner (quiet, basically uninvolved learner who prefers to absorb passively or reflectively what is seen and heard);
5. Concrete, detailed, fact-oriented learner (enjoys the 'nitty-gritty', meticulous details of the learning experience); and
6. Non-adaptive, struggling learner (feels uncertain while learning and perceives learning as a difficult experience).

Finally, they analysed the correlations between both the style inventories, which resulted in highly interesting findings summarized in Table 7.1. This research provides the overall frame for a better understanding of how consumers learn about their alternatives and by what elementary attitudes they are guided through the decision-making process. However, these insights are not sufficient for building efficient recommender systems for a particular product class.

Table 7.1. Correlation of consumer style and learning style characteristics (from Kendall and Sproles, 1990, p. 139).

Consumer style characteristics	Learning style characteristics						
	Serious, analytical learner	Active, practical learner	Observation-centred learner	Passive, accepting learner	Concrete, detail, fact learner	Non-adaptive, struggling learner	Multiple R^2
Perfectionistic	0.25**	0.15**	0.15**	−0.14**	−	−	0.36**
Brand-conscious	−	−	−	−	−	0.10*	−
Novelty-fashion-conscious	0.16**	−	0.16**	0.14**	−	−	0.26**
Recreational shopping-conscious	−	−	−	−	−	− 0.12*	−
Price-value-conscious	0.14**	0.21**	0.10*	0.14**	0.17**	−	0.35**
Impulsive	− 0.13**	0.11*	−	−	−	0.29**	0.34**
Confused by overchoice	−	−	−	0.15**	0.14**	0.14**	0.25**
Habitual, brand-loyal	0.11*	−	−	−	−	−	−

Levels of significance: * $p < 0.05$; ** $p < 0.01$; − not significant.

Decision-making relies on learning and adaptation processes. This perspective encompasses the possibility that consumers apply different rules in different stages of the decision-making process. The problem of deciding how to decide is not new (Einhorn *et al.*, 1979). The identification of different dimensions, rejection-inducing, relative preference, and trade-off, emerges from the same line of thought (Park and Lutz, 1982). Payne *et al.* (1992) brought more detailed assumptions into the array of set theories (e.g. Crompton, 1992; Um and Crompton, 1992). They combined the economics of information processing (trade-off between accuracy and cognitive effort) with the way sets of alternatives are subsequently reduced by using either non-compensatory or compensatory decision rules. The same basic structure of the decision-making process by filtering first and comparing alternatives subsequently was proposed for an online decision environment (Häubl and Trifts, 2000).

For both situations, single-item or multiple- (or bundled-) item decision-making, the same questions arise: Do specific decision heuristics appear for particular travel items? Are they applied in a uniform way across different consumers? Are they applied differently by one consumer for different items or triggered by specific decision contexts? Are these contingent factors stable along a limited time or subject to change from one decision-making task to the next? And, finally, are heuristics for decisions applied by retrieving evaluation and selection schemata or are they generated or constructed simultaneously with the emergence of a particular decision problem? (Bettman *et al.*, 1998). Again, the question comes up as to how destination recommender systems can accommodate this wide array of decision heuristics and contexts. Many researchers in the field acknowledge that decision-making in the tourism context is highly complex and sensitive to many situational and environmental influences. Consequently, for a recommender system it is important to anticipate the 'interdependence and coordination of these processes' (Einhorn and Hogarth, 1981, p. 83). Even if a recommender system could immediately deliver proposals with a high degree of matching with consumers' needs and preferences, the customer requires an explanation afterwards to defend and justify his or her choice. So, a high prognostic ability alone would not be a sufficient condition for a good recommender.

The practical relevance of this kind of knowledge is easily grasped. If there would be some stable patterns and interdependencies across trip elements and travel experiences over time, recommender systems should learn about these general structures and, where too much individualized and varied, they should store and administer the users' personal profiles in order to better support and predict future decision-making.

In a generalized mode, Jeng and Fesenmaier (2002, see Part I) reframed the decision-net approach to an extended conceptual model of travel decision-making. The key principles are: (i) multidimensionality (i.e. multiple sub-decisions and facets); (ii) multistaged based on centrality (i.e. importance), rigidity (i.e. flexibility) and sequentiality (i.e. decision order); and (iii) adaptivity to the decision context. Obviously, there are parallels to the information behaviour literature bridging the modelling objectives for a broader perspective (e.g. considering the whole travel experience) with the micro-view of highlighting the cognitive processes necessary for problem solving. It is not surprising that Fesenmaier and Jeng (2000) recommended to apply a longitudinal approach to better track the dynamics of the trip-planning process and to possibly identify trip-planning styles. They concluded by hypothesizing:

> that travellers develop certain approaches or 'styles' to handling or simplifying the trip planning processing order to reduce the burden implicit in the solution of 14 (or more) subdecisions. Research in this area should focus on the pattern and extent of problem solving for each facet, the nature and extent of information search required for each facet, as well as assessing the contextual factors (i.e. household and travel party demographic and psychographic characteristics as well as aspects of the trip), which may impact this typology.
>
> (Fesenmaier and Jeng, 2000, p. 24)

The following sections discuss the mechanisms and contingencies potential travellers go through in order to plan their favoured vacation trip. The basic research question is whether one hierarchy of decision sequences and one pattern of decision heuristics are sufficient to be later implemented in a destination recommender system in order to optimally interact in a travel-counselling setting. The study and documentation referenced here is the outcome of a joint research project co-funded under the European Union's Fifth Research and Technology Development Framework Programme (contract DIETORECS IST-2000-29474). It represents the foundation for building an intelligent destination recommender system (See Fesenmaier *et al.*, 2002 for a more comprehensive report; and Fesenmaier *et al.*, 2003 for an overview).

3. Methodology for an Empirical Study on Decision Styles

3.1 Study design

The study was designed to evaluate the dynamics of the information retrieval and decision-making process. It was hypothesized that people vary in the way they come to a final travel decision and was based on different aspects: the travel experience, the trip purpose, the specificity of trip motivations and sub-decisions already taken, the information sources and media familiar with and/or available, the cognitive effort allocated to this problem-solving task, the information cues used to evaluate and select alternatives. From this list of criteria it was possible to assume a large number of various trip-planning styles. The research question was: Is it reasonable to accommodate different planning styles that can be used as a basic guideline for an automatic recommendation system? In order to find an answer to this question two steps had to be taken: it was necessary to investigate whether (i) the variability between, and homogeneity within, individual decision styles was large enough; and (ii) the commonalities justify to develop and implement different functions in a recommender system that will support users from different decision styles individually in their trip-planning process. The purpose of the following study was to give an answer to the first step, which could act as the basis for taking the second.

The initial study design implied a combined approach: on the one side, the cooperative evaluation was scheduled for a more experimental setting having travel-interested participants planning their preferred vacation trip by the means of web-based information and booking platforms (Study A, Table 7.2);

Table 7.2. Overview of methods applied for studying trip-planning processes.

Study label	Task	Setting	Method	Study material
Study A1	Trip planning for an alpine destination	Experimental, moderated	Cooperative evaluation, observational, computer-interactive exit survey	Observational video tape, transcript of think-aloud protocol, video protocol of screen interaction, post-experimental questionnaire
Study A2	Trip planning for a Mediterranean destination	Experimental, moderated	Cooperative evaluation, observational, computer-interactive exit survey	Observational video tape, transcript of think-aloud protocol, video protocol of screen interaction, post-experimental questionnaire
Study B1	Travel agency dialogues for trip planning in various stages for alpine or sun-and-beach destinations	Real-life travel counselling	Ethnographic, audio-taped, post-intervention self-administering survey	Audio tape, transcript of dialogues, post-intervention questionnaire
Study B2	Trip planning in various stages for alpine or sun-and-beach destinations	Simulated travel agency counselling, moderated	Cooperative evaluation, computer-interactive exit survey	Observational video tape, transcript of think-aloud protocol, post-experimental questionnaire

on the other side, there was a realistic setting in travel agencies applying an ethnographic method (Study B).

Study A applied a simulated travel decision process by inducing pre-selected participants to prepare a vacation trip they generally prefer or even plan or had already planned for the previous summer by the means of a particular travel-related website. By the means of a commercial website (44 cases with TISCover, 57 cases with Allesreise.com) respondents should assemble their preferred travel items to prepare a complete vacation trip. While retrieving and interpreting the appropriate information over the Web they were encouraged to think aloud about what they were thinking and doing. The whole process was moderated by a professional market researcher and respondents (singles and occasionally travel parties) were video recorded while surfing on the appropriate websites. The entire surf process was recorded digitally as well. After this simulated travel plan respondents were asked a predefined sequence of questions about their perceptions of the planning process and about travel decision-making in general (exit survey). The entire material for further analysis comprises: a CD-ROM archive containing a synchronized pair of the video and the screen clip for immediate play (Fig. 7.1) together with transcripts of each session; finally, a data file of the structured interviews that took place afterwards.

In contrast, the design of Study B followed the traditional human-to-human interaction approach of travel counselling. It used the above-mentioned mixture approach by contacting travel-interested people in a travel agency asking for travel information and preparing a particular leisure

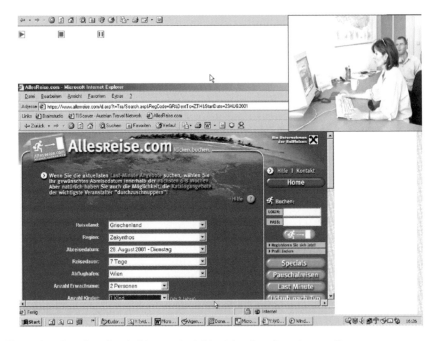

Fig. 7.1. Synchronized video material for trip-planning observation.

trip. It was supposed to encounter travellers at different stages of their planning process. These dialogues were planned to be voice-recorded with prior approval of the customers. Despite appealing incentives for both travel agents and customers, it was almost impossible to find cooperative agency employees. In addition, the timing of the fieldwork (August–September 2001) did not facilitate achieving the targeted quotas. Finally, after September 11 the scant commitment dropped to zero. Therefore, Study B was split into two sections, both taking place in Berlin (Germany):

- Study B1 followed the initial instructions and layout to collect conventional real-life counselling cases in travel agencies. The new target was at least 20 observations of a variety of demographics and destinations (alpine vs sun and beach).
- Study B2 invited potential travellers for a simulated trip-planning session using only printed travel information, predominantly travel catalogues. Again, the sessions were moderated to encourage participants to think aloud what they are doing and thinking; the sessions were video recorded and transcribed. After this simulated session the same structured interview as in Study A collected answers to perceptions of the trip-planning process and decision-making for vacation trips in general. Within this design 80 dialogues were recorded. The focus of interest remains the same for all four variations of the study: What is the concept of destination in the traveller's mind? What information is more or less important? How are different information pieces used to guide and support the consecutive interactions and evaluations? And, on which criteria do alternative filtering and evaluation takes place?

Tables 7.3 and 7.4 provide a detailed overview of the achieved sample structures. They signify the study objective to reveal maximum variation in travel planning. For Study A – the web-supported trip planning – individuals had been recruited and selected via telephone. If they had recent travel experiences about one of the predetermined geographical areas (either alpine or Mediterranean destinations), or were currently planning a vacation trip to these destinations, then they were assigned to one of the two split groups. City breaks had been excluded from the survey. In the laboratory the moderator asked the respondents to reveal their initial views (e.g. objectives, motives, sub-decisions already taken) about a much favoured vacation trip. According to these indications they were asked to use the appropriate website – either TIScover or Allesreisen.com – to plan, find and determine a trip they would like to book.

Quotas had been specified for balancing age, gender and Internet usage cohorts. Only individuals with a minimum of PC familiarity and Internet usage were accepted for this experiment. According to the average Internet usage distribution, about two-thirds of the invited respondents should have used the Internet for information retrieval, whereas the remaining third should have used the Internet for buying services (e.g. banking account, flight tickets, hotels) or goods (e.g. books, CDs, videos). It is evident that this usage pattern varies across the age cohorts, with a higher buying rate among

Table 7.3. Sample quotas for Study A – web-supported trip planning.

Structure of the sample		Male	Female	With partner/ family/friends
A1: alpine destinations (TISCover users): $n = 44$		$n = 19$	$n = 25$	$n = 18$
18–30 years: $n = 16$	Internet user	3	5	4
	Internet buyer	3	5	3
31–45 years: $n = 13$	Internet user	4	5	4
	Internet buyer	2	2	1
46–60 years: $n = 15$	Internet user	4	7	4
	Internet buyer	3	1	2
A2: Mediterranean destinations (Allesreisen.com users): $n = 57$		$n = 28$	$n = 29$	$n = 18$
18–30 years: $n = 19$	Internet user	4	4	4
	Internet buyer	6	5	4
31–45 years: $n = 21$	Internet user	7	7	5
	Internet buyer	4	3	3
46–60 years: $n = 17$	Internet user	5	8	4
	Internet buyer	2	2	2

Table 7.4. Sample quotas for Study B – travel agency-supported trip planning.

		Travel agency	Travel catalogues
		B1	B2
Structure of the sample	$n = 99$	18	81
Alpine destinations: Austria, Switzerland, South Tyrol, Germany	$n = 48$	8	40
Gender: female		71%	49%
18–30 years	$n = 16$	2	14
31–45 years	$n = 16$	3	13
46–60 years	$n = 16$	3	13
Mediterranean destinations: Italy, Spain, Portugal, Greece, Turkey, Tunesia, France, Egypt, Maroc, Croatia:	$n = 51$	10	41
Gender: female		64%	52%
18–30 years	$n = 11$		11
31–45 years	$n = 17$	3	14
46–60 years	$n = 23$	7	16

younger people. Another precaution had been taken: usually travel planning is a matter of the entire travel party including adults and children alike.
Hence, if a respondent would not plan to travel alone, the observed planning
process would not demonstrate a realistic perspective. Consequently, about
one-third of the invited individuals came in company and discussed the trip-
planning task with their partner.

Study B tried to enable contrasts between typical sun-and-beach and
alpine destinations, between age and gender cohorts. The prescription of
quotas was difficult to meet under the existing circumstances (e.g. seasonal,
personal and political situation) in the travel agency sector. However, a better balanced sample structure could be achieved among the B2 respondents.

3.2 Exit survey

In order to complement the observational approach of this study each test
person was invited to go through a couple of – predominantly – closed-format
questions. For A and B2 respondents, a moderated computer-interactive
interview was prepared following the planning task. B1 (travel agency dialogues) respondents were handed over a questionnaire in printed format,
which could be filled out immediately or be returned later via mail. Three
areas were identified to be covered in this survey: (i) perceptions and reflec-
tions about the planning process (e.g. degree of satisfaction with the entire
trip-planning process, with the sequence of information retrieval, with the
alternatives offered by the system; degree of familiarity with the process and
criteria; degree of involvement and entertainment); (ii) some characteristics of
the just-prepared trip (e.g. type of destination, timing of the destination decision, main purpose, travel budget, travel experience, travel organization);
and (iii) general travel decision-making (e.g. sources of information used,
scales for representing the information-processing mode and the affective
choice mode (Mittal, 1988, 1994; Zins, 2001)). Some special information about
the completeness of the trip planning and/or details available about the subjective flexibility in some main sub-decisions (country, region or community,
hotel) were collected.

3.3 Content and coding

The various trip-planning dialogues of Studies A and B were recorded at
least by voice and by video including voice for most of the cases. With the
exception of Study B1 the experimental setting was held constant throughout the whole investigation. A standardized introduction into the task was
given by the moderator, whose role was strictly reduced to encouraging the
think-aloud process. The respondents started with a brief verbal statement
about their travel plans and were invited to consult the Internet or travel
catalogues in order to select an offer that matches their preferences best. The
time limit for the travel-planning experiment was set to about 30 min. Hence,
different situations at the end of this experiment occurred: individuals who

were lucky to find a highly preferred offer; individuals who interrupted the search process because they were completely dissatisfied with the range of products; others who stopped with some alternatives in the choice set while wishing to continue the evaluation process or to discuss some interesting offers with other travel party members.

The study material (videos, audios, transcripts, catalogues, travel website clips) allowed to have the dialogues analysed from an observatory perspective. The authors identified 30 'trip-planning elements' to be analysed from the dialogues (Table 7.5). These information items on content, timing, and functional characters will later act as the constitutive dimensions for identifying different travel decision styles. Four areas of interest were identified to be coded in a quantitative way:

1. Which elements did the respondents use to verbalize their preferred vacation trip in the initial phase? Did they use negative clauses such as exclusions from the realistic set of alternatives? And, finally, which sub-decisions and specifications were finally decisive for the intended trip? In general, these and most of the other descriptors of the planning process are represented only in an abstract manner, capturing whether the particular element was mentioned or used by the respondent or not.

2. Whereas the previous variables cover static information, the second area of observations focused on the dialogue procedure. The character of the dialogue can be described generally by the way the various elements are used for retrieving and evaluating information about travel alternatives. For this purpose, the trip-planning elements were tracked if they were actively requested – either by the clicking behaviour or by verbal statements – by the respondents and/or if they were passively presented to the respondent. Sometimes respondents mentioned verbally that some aspects of trip-planning elements were completely irrelevant to them. This perspective was coded separately. In order to capture the timing of the occurrence of the various elements it was distinguished whether these elements had been used earlier in the trip-planning process or later. Finally, it was monitored whether the characteristics of these aspects were subject to intra-individual negotiations (→ flexible element) or not (→ fixed element).

3. A list of additional characteristics was developed in order to get an impression about the respondents and their travel needs. On the one hand, travel experience relative to the destination, the means of transportation, the mode of accommodation and catering, the main activity and the travel type was observed in a single-item manner as well as using Cohen's (1972) familiarity vs novelty-seeking dimensions; on the other hand, five benefit dimensions (nature, culture, entertainment, challenge, comfort) were identified in advance from the latest Austrian National Guest Survey data from the summer season 2000 ($n = 7000$) and used for categorizing the respondents accordingly.

4. Finally, a set of variables were related to the entire planning process or task. The length of the dialogue was registered as well as the previous experience with the travel website used. Approximations for the number of distinct products offered by the system (website or catalogues) and screened by the respondent were registered as well as the wish for more or less alternatives.

Table 7.5. Trip-planning elements by information integration aspects (frequencies in per cent of respondents).

Trip elements	What?		Who?		When?		How?	
	Start	End	User	System	Earlier	Later	Fixed	Variable
Destination: country	78	94	87	72	93	1	58	21
Type of accommodation	51	89	75	86	78	14	41	37
Destination: region	53	88	77	82	90	4	26	46
Travel party	60	88	63	59	66	15	70	5
Geographical area	71	84	73	62	81	0	70	6
Price	29	83	79	89	69	29	24	63
Destination: community	19	81	49	79	71	16	13	56
Travel type in general	40	81	72	59	81	3	60	18
Accommodation: place	26	81	55	75	45	34	47	21
Accommodation: catering	28	80	53	85	55	38	35	41
Natural factors	52	78	59	55	67	9	64	9
Type of transportation	42	77	51	56	54	22	55	10
Length of stay	29	77	60	64	62	22	39	27
Time of travel	45	77	70	70	76	12	40	42
Accommodation: equipment	15	74	47	77	47	40	22	52

Average

Accommodation: pictures	10	74	54	87	53	36	36	34
Accommodation: category	25	73	43	81	61	24	18	46
Additional geographic information	n.a.	64	35	30	31	18	22	14
Activities/facilities	47	63	59	54	53	18	46	20
Accessibility of the destination	13	48	39	43	30	28	35	13
Travel type: independent traveller	22	43	39	34	43	4	33	10
Additional information	n.a.	42	52	18	25	34	40	11
Travel type: tour operator product	15	33	34	38	42	4	22	17
Transfer to accommodation	11	30	19	23	9	24	13	11
Get in contact	n.a.	30	42	n.a.	9	22	35	8
Attractions	45	24	51	45	44	13	38	14
Travel type: low-budget	5	15	15	9	14	4	14	3
Travel type: all-inclusive	14	13	8	10	9	2	6	4
Travel type: last-minute	9	10	16	9	14	3	5	10
Travel type: special-offer	2	7	14	9	9	8	5	11
Number of elements	**8.5**	**17.9**	**14.6**	**15.6**	**14.8**	**5.0**	**10.3**	**6.8**

n.a. not applicable.

Dialogue problems (technical or conversational), disruption of the process together with the obvious reason (content or technical) were identified if occurring. Screening the whole experimental process should allow to qualify whether the respondents came close to a positive or negative decision (i.e. booking probability), whether they were more or less involved and satisfied with the task during the process, whether they had a clear concept or were driven by the various proposals of the system and whether they revealed a more holistic or a more criteria-related decision behaviour.

A team of 13 coders were instructed how to infer the classified observations described above from the study material. They had to screen the video sequences together with the written transcripts independently. Each dialogue was screened and analysed by at least two coders. After this procedure the two coders had to match their observations in a separate session. If ambiguous codes appeared, they had to go through the appropriate sequences once again (videos, transcripts) in order to find a compromise. Pairs of matching coders were rotated to avoid familiarization of negotiation strategies.

4. Results

4.1 Trip-planning observations in general

The observational study focused on illustrating various trip planning and decision styles and their underlying components. Taking the different situations of Studies A, B1 and B2 into consideration, the mixture of completely different information contexts serves one objective: to capture a maximum variety of retrieval and evaluation processes. In order to keep the systematic variance under control some critical factors outlined in the methodology section were matched. Interestingly, the implied success (outcome or end state) of the observed dialogues does not differ significantly across the types or mode of dialogues (A vs B1 vs B2). Overall, it was identified that two-thirds of the dialogues ended with a situation in which the coders attributed a medium to high booking probability. This means that the type of task or setting did not reveal a systematic influence in favour of finding an acceptable travel alternative.

The percentages in Table 7.5 give an insight into the observational elements' occurrences in the previously defined perspectives or decision style dimensions. The table is sorted in descending order by the trip-planning elements used and applied until the end of the observation. The numbers give frequency counts relative to the respondents who used or mentioned these elements during the dialogue. For example, only 78% mentioned at the beginning – before starting the information-gathering process – a particular country where they wanted to go. At the end of the dialogue 94% of the respondents had selected a definite country. As many as 87% of the individuals actively looked for a particular country. The dialogue medium provided information about country alternatives to a somewhat lower degree. Country selection or orientation processes are most liked early in the information-gathering process (93%). For 58% of the respondents the country decision (taken rather early if not even specified before the dialogue) cannot be negotiated (column: 'Fixed'). About 21% are more flexible on this issue. The rest of the respondents did not reveal clearly what they had in mind while retrieving and evaluating additional travel information. For this example it can be assumed that the remaining proportion of individuals had already taken the decision about the destination country; so it had not been subject to further discussion during the planning process. However, at least one-fifth of the sample population is not sure about the destination country at the beginning of the planning process, and needs therefore other cues to identify the most suitable travel offer in order to arrive at a specific country decision.

The geographical specification was split into four hierarchical levels: area (e.g. alpine region, Mediterranean region), country, region and community. For most of the respondents the area and country could be determined at the end. In contrast, at least one-fourth did not start with a verbal identification of their preferred destination. The specificity of the preferred region is even lower and is handled to a high degree in a flexible way.

Price perceptions are another interesting detail. They are revealed initially only by one-third of the respondents. Of course, they are important when evaluating and selecting alternatives. For two-thirds, price issues appear rather early in the decision and problem-solving process; 29% considers price aspects rather later. For one-fourth of the sample it seems to be a non-negotiable factor. Even when evaluating the importance of the trip-planning elements from the perspective of which of them is actively searched by the respondent (cf. column 'User' of Table 7.5), it turns out that area is not favoured to be specified by individual travellers. Besides type of accommodation, time of travel and trip party, other cues such as travel type (in terms of typical motivational bundles or trip organization), natural factors and activities are heavily used to find suitable travel opportunities.

Another measure of importance within the travel-planning process is reflected in the type and number of fixed travel elements. More precisely, the ratio between fixed and variable frequencies gives a clearer indication because not every element was relevant in each dialogue. Again, geographical area is not frequently changed. The travel party comes second in this list; natural setting combined with the preferred activities or the travel type show a high (fixed-to-variable) ratio.

The most flexible element appears to be the destination community followed by region, price, equipment details and accommodation categories. Where the ratio for one particular element is near 1, it can be assumed that at least two distinct decision profiles exist: one in which this element is treated more flexibly (e.g. in a compensatory way) and another in which this element is non-negotiable (e.g. type of accommodation, length of stay, time of trip, type of catering, tour operator travel and whether or not pictures about the destination are a must).

Overall, one out of two travel planners stated that some information details are missing. The most important single item is the description of the destination in order to get an overview of the facilities and the surrounding. Price details and price differentiation by target segments come next. The fourth prominent missing factor comprises pictures and videos about the accommodation and the place to go in general.

The bottom line of Table 7.5 allows some inferences on the number of elements used during the travel decision-making process. The average number of 8.5 elements that are used to make a brief initial statement is, of course, biased by the research setting: the time left for verbalizing before starting to look for additional information and the number of elements to be observed. However, one-third of the complete list is used on average at the beginning and doubles towards the end of the process. The respondent actively looks for 15 elements during decision-making. The same amount – not the identical items – of trip elements is delivered by the information medium during this information process. Out of the about 20 elements in this process, 14 are considered earlier. More than half of the qualified trip elements are not subject to change. This means that these items are used more or less to sort out acceptable choices from the total range of available alternatives. While other – flexible – trip elements are applied in a negotiable way, some of them are non-compensatory.

Once a trip element is specified by the traveller – either from the very beginning of, or during, the planning process – it should act as a filter for retrieving and offering only those products meeting the specified characteristics. However, several times it was observed that the respondents moved away from their initial trip specifications either because nothing convenient was offered or because other more attractive alternatives came up.

Part of the initial vision of a preferred trip is expressed by negative clauses (e.g. 'Wish to travel anywhere but Greece'). In 55% of the dialogues such initial clauses had been used. Most frequently they refer to some characteristics of the accommodation; otherwise for geographic exclusions. Only one-third of respondents mentioned at least one item to be irrelevant for their trip. This means that the respondent would not stress to inspect this part of information. Hence, the presentation does not contribute to making a better evaluation and selection. Accommodation details appear on top of all irrelevant items.

4.2 Successful dialogues

Each dialogue observation was accompanied by a post-intervention interview with the test person. For both studies of trip-planning dialogues it was important to identify the degree of success of the conversation. This concept was defined as the extent to which someone's trip preferences and travel wishes have found an acceptable counterpart among the mass of travel opportunities offered by the particular information source. The coders captured the verbalized intent to continue the dialogue with a booking or reservation procedure. However, not every respondent came to this point or expressed this intention explicitly. Therefore, the coding scheme considered a classification of the booking probability derived from the overall itinerary of the dialogue independently from a concrete booking or reservation wish. This measure ranged from no (16%) to low (14%) probability to medium (29%), and finally to high (41%).

In order to validate this derived or observed success measure it is possible to investigate the subjective perception and evaluation of the dialogues. For this purpose a list of statements in the post-study questionnaire was used to evaluate various facets of the dialogue (see Table 7.6). In general, 'ease of use' was rated rather favourably. The same degree of satisfaction was stated with respect to the criteria applied or requested for evaluating and selecting trip alternatives. The overall satisfaction with the planning process is ranked in the middle of the range of evaluative criteria. The same conclusion can be drawn for the support offered by the information medium, the impression of being empowered for making a good decision, the degree of familiarity and satisfaction with the whole process of information gathering and analysis. Less favourably rated are the delivered alternatives and the impression of the overview and completeness of the alternatives offered. Turning to the validation of the former (observed) success criteria of judged booking probability, it can be seen from Table 7.6 that each element of the perception measure correlates significantly with this rough ordinal classification measure. As the perception for 'ease of use' reveals the least correlation and the perceived overall satisfaction, the highest, the discriminant validity of the judges' success measure towards a matching indicator between trip preferences and fitting product alternatives has reasonable evidence. As the number of dialogues is quite limited, the lower and upper two categories of the booking probability measure were collapsed into an unsuccessful (30%) and a successful (70%) group of dialogues. The correlations with the perceptual measures are still significant and in a similar range.

Table 7.6. Perceptual measures about the counselling dialogue.

Statement	Average rating	Correlation with booking probability
Satisfaction with trip planning	3.1	0.78
Satisfaction with the course of information provision	3.2	0.44
Satisfaction with the overview of offerings	3.9	0.33
Ease of use	2.7	0.17
Good support by the medium	3.0	0.53
Perception of a good decision	3.0	0.49
Decision-making based on familiar criteria	2.7	0.32
Decision-making based on familiar course	2.9	0.45
Satisfaction with alternatives offered	3.4	0.39

Scale range: 1 = best evaluation; 7 = worst evaluation; correlations based on Spearman-Rho, all significant at $p < 0.01$.

4.3 Condensing into decision styles

From the think-aloud protocols and the records of the screen interactions and the catalogue browsing the type and number of elements used to plan a vacation trip could be extracted (see Table 7.5). A classification was done on the basis of the amount of trip elements used either at the beginning, during or at the end of the planning process. Such volume indicators are interpreted as the degree of elaboration or cognitive effort dedicated to the planning task. It is hypothesized that travellers differ in the way they arrive at an acceptable choice, incorporating that they differ in the importance they assign to various trip elements (Zins, 2001).

One heuristic to solve this complex task was to apply a similarity measure over the 'When' and 'How' perspective of the trip-planning process. It is clear that those two dimensions are strong reductions of the real contingencies about the use of more complex information. The 30 style variables from the user sessions were grouped for describing decision styles by a vector quantization procedure using the Topology Representing Network (TRN) which is based on the 'neural gas' algorithm developed by Martinetz and others (Martinetz *et al.*, 1993; see also Martinetz and Schulten, 1994; Mazanec, 1999b, 2001). Three alternative approaches differentiating by content had been tested and cross-validated:

1. Similarity among the fixed trip elements only (30 variables);
2. Similarity among the fixed and the variable trip elements (60 variables); and
3. Similarity among the fixed and variable as well as the earlier and later trip elements (118 variables).

When analysing solutions from 2 to 8 different profiles for each of the three alternatives the range 5–7 was considered more deeply following the suggestions based on the homogeneity measure. Using additional external validation criteria (e.g. trip characteristics, sociodemographic variables) the third alternative, surprisingly the most complex approach, with six different decision styles, turned out to be the most informative one. In terms of robustness (meaning that a certain pair of consumers falls into the same class of decision styles when replicating the analysis several times) the analysis of 30 replications revealed an acceptable proportion of stability, as more than 50% zero errors (mis-classifications) occurred. The following interpretation focuses on the differences among the decision styles revealed by the study.

4.3.1 Decision style 1: highly predefined users (14%)
This group of travellers, which accounts for approximately 14% of all respondents, has a well-elaborated picture in mind of what they are searching for. They are already quite sure about the destination in terms of country, which is highly influenced by the natural resources there as an absolute must. Their mental picture of the vacation trip comprises also very strict conceptions of the accommodation, which includes type, location, category and even details such as the visual appearance and other special features. The highest number

of attributes mentioned at the beginning of their recommendation process proves the highly elaborated mental mode. They rather tend to all-inclusive offers but are not looking for last-minute offers. This does not mean that price is not important – they also start with very concise price considerations. But they do not search for cheap deals and are willing to raise their price levels when suitable offers are presented. Throughout the process of getting recommendations they try to get the optimal offer for their very closely defined needs. And these recommendations should include details such as transfer to the accommodation, attractions and other information about the destination. In this way the recommender optimally helps them to arrange and plan their total vacation trip in advance.

4.3.2 Decision style 2: accommodation-oriented users (9%)

For this smallest subgroup of users accommodation is a very important feature of the trip they plan. The type of accommodation, the location and sometimes even more details are the focal points at the beginning of their recommendation process. From a geographical point of view, they rather have the idea of spending their holiday in a certain geographic area than in a certain village. Right from the country level they fall below average regarding geographical conceptions. They prefer to trade off good accommodations against destinations. Compared to others, price is less important and is considered relatively late in the decision process. It appears that they are looking for a high-quality accommodation and put less value to a specific destination. They have no interest in special offers at all.

In the recommendation process they look for very specific information about possible destinations. Thus the destination is not unimportant, but the set of possible destinations is much larger than for others. The final decision then is not possible without specific information about attractions the destination offers. They want as much information as possible about geographical aspects and even more detailed information about the recommended destinations.

4.3.3 Decision style 3: recommendation-oriented users (14%)

The most typical characteristic of this group is that there is no typical fixed feature of the trip they have in mind. The most positively deviating aspect from the others is their focus on the type of travel. They have a tendency to last-minute travels as well as completely individual travel arrangements. In comparison to others they do not feel bound to certain destinations or accommodation types. Generally, they show a high affinity to recommendations – they also state in the interview that personal recommendations from friends or travel agents are their primary source of information. One of the most typical pieces of information is the need for geographical information about the destination. In most cases their starting point is also constituted by a (geographical) destination concept or the date of their travel. But this information is just used for the sake of instigating the process and is not understood as an absolute, unchangeable must. Moreover, this type does not define too many things throughout the recommendation process. It still leaves many things unspecified pointing at a traveller type who makes sub-decisions on the spot.

The highly undefined mental mode may be due to fewer restrictions in their choice set. As an example, they appear to be flexible in terms of date and especially length of their planned trip. Also the travel type and the destination itself are used in a compensatory way throughout the recommendation process. In short, the mental mode can be described as 'look what is going to be offered'. Therefore, they heavily rely on pictures when evaluating different offers. The flexible mode has two exceptions: many respondents of this type are bound to a certain mode of transport. It can be argued that this mode of transport refers to car, which again serves as an explanation for their high 'degree of flexiblity' regarding many trip aspects, and the car proneness may be due to the second fixed aspect: the travel company that may in many cases be families.

4.3.4 Decision style 4: geography-oriented users (22%)

This group comes up with only few conceptions at the beginning of their recommendation process. Especially the type of accommodation is not pre-defined then. When they start their search for their next trip, they all include a certain country. So they appear to be heavily led by geographical aspects. The geographical area, one specific country and the possible activities and facilities there are typical outcomes of the recommendation session. Inter-estingly, they have rather fixed conceptions on a higher level of destination (country), but are flexible on lower levels (e.g. village). Very typical is their need for more detailed geographical information. The affinity for last-minute and special offers is not that strong as in the case of decision style 3; neverthe-less, they demonstrate a certain tendency to a certain trip type. However, this is not primarily caused by the price aspect, but seems to be evoked by con-venience: they like package tours – also in the form of last-minute packages. Information about accommodations is used rather passively and is not spe-cifically asked for. They rather like to see which accommodations are offered within a specific destination and then decide about the best one.

4.3.5 Decision style 5: price-oriented users (15%)

The set of defined attributes at the beginning of the recommendation session is rather similar to that of decision style 4: they come up with few specifica-tions regarding accommodation, destination and even the natural resources. However, the search process is completely different compared to style 4. They start especially with the type of travel and with price limits. Travel packages and special offers are of high interest for them. They clearly look for the best offer within a certain price range. As it is not so important for them to which place they travel, they like to get information about the recommended des-tinations – and here they require geographical information as well as other details about the destination (typically: climate, atmosphere, nightlife, etc.).

For them the destination is primarily made up of the natural resources and the activities offered. Therefore, natural resources show up as the most typi-cal fixed trip attribute, whereas the destination itself is changed throughout the process. At the end of the recommendation process the trip type together with a geographical area are mostly determined. Their spontaneity is documented by a clearly below-average rate of attractions fixed at the end.

4.3.6 Decision style 6: activity-driven, independent travellers (26%)

The most typical attribute that is verbalized at the beginning is a specific country destination. This geographical definition is used as a cue for specific natural resources. Beside the destination itself, price is used early in the decision process. However, price is used in a compensatory way. It is an important piece of information, but not typically used as a criterion for excluding offers. Consistently, this group is not strongly attracted by special offers. As with all types relying heavily on destination this group is searching for geographical information about the specific villages rather early in the recommendation process. Later on, they want to get more detailed information about the destination too. And the information about the villages is used for trading off different offers as they are not bound to a certain village. To the contrary, there are a very high percentage of travellers willing to trade off villages and even regions. However, the type of trip (mostly individual) remains fixed throughout the process. From the timing of the process they come closest to classical decision models: they first search for destinations, later on for accommodation type and price, and even later on for details of the accommodation.

During the search process they try to find a good accommodation for their needs. Referring to the characteristics of the accommodation, they are rather flexible, with the exception of the location. This fact, together with a high percentage of activities and facilities asked for, demonstrates that they actually look for some benefits – and these benefits can be satisfied by a certain location and some specific activities and facilities. It appears that the geographic concept of destination rather works as a cue for these benefits than being a benefit itself.

4.4 Recommendations regarding decision styles

The (few) observations in the real travel agency setting belong to styles 1 and 2. This is partly due to the later phase in the decision process coinciding with more elaborated concepts than in the experimental settings. Maybe the human recommenders are also better able to find out what travellers are searching for. In any way, a real system has to cope with such decision styles too. A lot of the catalogue design observations fall in decision style 6 – the individual traveller. This explains the almost classical phases of the decision-making process as the catalogues are structured in this way.

To optimally serve different decision types the recommendation strategies should be varied. The most favourable way to reduce the set of possible offers to a feasible number differs according to the decision style being recommended. Table 7.7 gives some ideas how an appropriate way may be organized. It shows prototypical ways of leading them efficiently through a

Table 7.7. Decision styles and possible recommendation strategies.

Number and name	Decision style characteristics	Recommendation/reduction strategy
1: Highly predefined	Many trip attributes predefined Natural resources very important	Let user specify many attributes, maybe phased: first destination, then accommodation and price, then further details
2: Accommodation-oriented	Highest importance on accommodation; high quality, not price sensitive	Only broad geographical area, then ask for characteristics of accommodation; list attributes of recommended destinations for comparison
3: Recommendation-oriented	Few trip attributes predefined; affinity for certain travel types	Come up quickly with pictures, let user 'feel' recommendations
4: Geography-oriented	Clear conception of geographical area and region	Let user search by map (giving detailed information about the areas clicked); concrete accommodation offers not given before village is determined
5: Price-oriented	Price as most important feature, searching for benefits within a certain price range	Ask for price range and natural resources sought; begin list from cheapest
6: Activity-driven traveller	Destination as cue for benefits and activities sought	Ask for benefits and activities sought; determine travel typology; describe offers detailed

counselling system. It has been demonstrated in the experiments that asking too many questions causes annoyance and dissatisfaction. Thus, there is a need for an efficient way through a recommender system. There is also no difference in the success rate among the different decision styles. Hence, various strategies cannot be classified as more or less successful. A good recommender system obviously has to cope with different styles.

5. Discussion and Implications

The design of the two observational studies allowed to describe and to elucidate more on the content and its dynamics of the information behaviour and trip-planning process. Contingent factors such as different motivations, travel distances, type of trip organization, structure of the information sources, gender, age, family life cycle and familiarity with the Internet had been considered when constructing the study design. In this respect, the findings on travel decision styles coincide partly with the more generic style inventory. Hence, it can be argued that style 1 'highly predefined' has much in common with the 'perfectionist' (Sproles and Kendall, 1986; Walsh *et al.*, 2001); that style 2 'accommodation-oriented' shares common values and habits with the 'demanding comparison shopper' and the 'brand-loyal habitual buyer'; that style 3 'recommendation-oriented' can be reidentified with the 'recreational shopping conscious'; that style 5 'price-oriented' is a relative to the 'price-value conscious', or finally that style 6 'activity-driven traveller' has something in common with the 'impulsive buyer'. However, the travel decision styles go far beyond since they incorporate much more processing and product class details that are quite specific to the travel domain.

5.1 Sub-decisions and phasing

The complex process of selecting a travel destination and particular travel products is in fact a series of sub-decisions comprising amongst others destination, accommodation, timing, transport, attractions and activities. These sub-decisions are known to be interrelated and should not be treated as independent sub-decisions that jointly generate the final travel plan. In fact, they follow some hierarchy and are classified as core, secondary and en route decisions in the literature. The empirical study demonstrated that there are substantial differences in the hierarchy of these sub-decisions amongst travellers. This leads to the following conclusion:

- A destination recommendation system should offer different hierarchies of going through the search and decision-making process.

The decision style typology centres on the individual differences in the search and planning process and asserts the existence of a multiphase process. However, some commonalities can be identified and integrated in the general outline of a recommender system. The initial phase can be identified as a filtering stage where the system can turn the focus of products and services to what the user has revealed previously to any kind of specification or interaction. Induced by some rough proposals delivered by the system, the user can fine-tune his or her preferences and wishes. At this stage, it is a must to come up with specific alternatives to support an efficient problem-solving process. During the final stage of sorting, comparing, evaluating and selecting alternatives the user can be supported by various techniques and functions to decide on the best-fitting alternatives. The empirical study also revealed differences in the usage of travel search or recommender systems regarding the functionality of the system.

- Different usage situations have to be taken into consideration in a recommender system. In fact, the final decision style typology includes this aspect, e.g. the predefined user who searches for the exact fit of his predefined needs, whereas the recommendation-oriented user or the activity-driven one who is looking for experiences and matching travel products.

Information may be exploited holistically (alternative and benefit- or consequence-based) or analytically (attribute-based). In the empirical setting the information-processing mode was rather difficult to observe and to identify. Nevertheless, there is a tendency in different decision styles applying different processing strategies. In the case of analytical processing, the literature differentiates between compensatory and non-compensatory rules. This corresponds also to the term rigidity or flexibility of travel plan characteristics. In the observational study this was captured by the fact that respondents changed some criteria in the course of the process, whereas others remained fixed. The decision style typology is also strongly based on the flexibility of certain characteristics.

- A recommendation system has to cope with the fact that users may relax or change various constraints (specifications of trip characteristics and/or requirements). Hence, it has to offer convenient and transparent mechanisms to track and identify the consequences of such changes or inflexibilities.

Analogously to the findings reported by Kendall and Sproles (1990), it can be concluded here that the different paths through the problem-solving process of a trip-planning task ground on different learning styles consumers are attached to. More specifically, another consequence of the different general information-processing modes aims at different styles of product descriptions (Rumetshofer *et al.*, 2003).

- If a recommendation system identifies a user as being more prone to visual information, the proportion of pictorial representation should be raised dynamically.

5.2 Information sources

Concerning the information sources, it has been shown that most travellers tend to use a variety of information sources of different kinds: personal experiences, marketeer-oriented information (catalogues, brochures), neutral information (community, travel guides, maps) or experiential sources. The observational study design did not emphasize the importance and influence of different available information sources. However, quite a substantial share of respondents mentioned verbally that they are missing, for example, evaluations from others (neutral sources) or complementary information via pictures and videos (experiential). Consequently, a comprehensive recommendation system has to provide information from multiple sources (e.g. suppliers, agents, customers) offering the user different means to improve credibility and reliability.

5.3 Personality

There is a huge amount of literature exhibiting the influence of personality characteristics on the destination decision. The empirical study also showed some correlation of personal characteristics with the decision styles typology, but it is rather weak. This may be due to the focus of the empirical study and the decision styles, which are based on the decision process and not the final outcome (destination chosen). The problem of applying personality filters within a recommendation system lies in the difficulty of measuring personality efficiently. Most studies are using elaborate lists of personality measurement scales, making it almost impossible for the use in an online system. Thus, the recommendation resulted in the use of Plog's allocentric–psychocentric typology, which may be identified by only one or two questions.

5.4 Personalization

Generally personal characteristics such as personality as well as travel characteristics such as party composition influence the optimal decision (process). The strong influence of travel characteristics results in the fact that even for the same person the needs and benefits sought may vary from one planning task to another. Thus, personalized information (experience) may be useful for supporting a concrete travel decision process but cannot replace information on each trip planned. The observations also showed that personal experience is a rather weak predictor of the actual wishes in a given situation. The phenomenon of variety seeking makes it even more difficult to make use of the personal experiences and the individual consumption history. It is therefore recommended to integrate personalization in terms of user profiles addressing personal characteristics as well as travel wishes and travel plans. This will facilitate the saving and retrieval of different travel settings, specified needs and selected travel products. Together with evaluative responses from the user, this part of information could be useful for collaborative filtering processes. It also may help to identify travel products for different occasions to be used for specifying recommendations (e.g. 'best for camping').

5.5 Designing a consumer-oriented destination recommender system

The consumer perspective generally suggested that a recommender system should be made up of some elements that adapt to the individual user and travel characteristics. In order to efficiently match travellers' needs with the offers in the databases such a system should adapt itself to the user in terms of:

- hierarchy of questions (sequence of sub-decisions);
- mode of representation (information search vs experiential); and
- degree of recommendation vs search functions (user- or system-driven sessions).

This implies that a (new) user entering the system has to be classified quickly in order to provide him or her with the optimal way and mode of presentation. Other, more general, guidelines for developing recommender systems that emerged from the study include:

- Recommendations should appear quickly in a session, without asking too many questions in advance.
- Reliability, credibility and transparency are of utmost importance for the acceptance of the system. Thus, the amount of product alternatives should be shown to the user at any time by counting the possible travel products dynamically. The logic and arguments for recommendations should be revealed to the user.
- Presentation of a reasonable number of recommendations (about five), optimally presenting the logic behind, appears important.
- Integration of as many sources of information as possible, e.g. supply-side descriptions, maps, pictures, videos and community feedback, is appreciated by most users.

Chapter Summary

Destination recommender systems have to simulate the human-to-human dialogue and counselling process while exploiting the additional benefits of the almost unlimited processing and storage potential that information technology offers. Consumer behaviour theorists, selling agents and consumers are getting more aware that the process, from identifying needs and wants to gathering appropriate information, filtering available opportunities and assembling an optimal travel product, cannot be standardized so that it fits for all users. In finding a sustainable compromise between efficient resource allocation and completely individualized treatments (concept of one-to-one marketing), the marketing literature has started already some decades ago to profile consumers along their decision-making attitudes and habits. Following this line of research and considering the insights on cognitive information processing generated during the last 15 years, this chapter reports on the development of travel decision styles. In a comprehensive study various trip-planning elements were proposed and evaluated and, finally, condensed into six decision styles. Implications for the construction of travel recommender systems were discussed.

Acknowledgement

This work has been partially funded by the European Union's Fifth RTD Framework Programme (under contract DIETORECS IST-2000-29474). The authors would like to thank all other colleagues of the DieToRecs team for their valuable contribution to this chapter.

8 Travel Personality Testing for Destination Recommendation Systems

ULRIKE GRETZEL, NICOLE MITSCHE, YEONG-HYEON HWANG AND DANIEL R. FESENMAIER

1. Introduction

The lack of purchase information, infrequent use and the pronounced variety-seeking tendencies of its users constitute serious problems for a destination recommendation system (DRS) that seeks to provide personalized and situation-specific recommendations. Although collaborative filtering and case-based reasoning approaches have been developed to provide more suitable destination recommendations (Ricci *et al.*, 2002b), there seems to be a need for more explicit ways of capturing user preferences so that the resulting recommendation can reflect personal and trip-related needs for a specific point in time. Leading the user through a series of questions in a sort of self-assessment process as suggested by Franke (2002) and Rumetshofer *et al.* (2003) is a possible way of establishing more sophisticated user profiles. However, such self-assessment modules are typically very cumbersome and time-consuming for the user to complete. They are, consequently, more suitable to capture user characteristics that are relatively stable. For recommendations based on frequently changing preferences and/or situation-specific variables, however, approaches that can quickly and rather effortlessly capture the necessary information are needed. A potential solution to this problem is providing users with a choice among predefined travel types or decision-making styles (Delgado and Davidson, 2002; Grabler and Zins, 2002; Zins, 2003). This idea of predefined categories has been implemented most frequently by inviting users to select a product-related personality category and providing recommendations based upon predetermined preferences that characterize the selected personality type. The aim of this chapter is to investigate the extent to which such predefined personality types can be used to enhance the personal relevancy of recommendations provided in a DRS.

2. Background

Personality traits are believed to be able to accurately predict behaviour over time and across situations (Woszczynski *et al.*, 2002). Most importantly, consumer behaviour research has found a linkage between individuals' personality and their preferences for certain brands, suggesting that personality type is an important indicator for product choice (Malhotra, 1988; Aaker, 1997). In tourism research, personality has often been used as a basis for market segmentation purposes, with Plog's delineation of travel personality types along an allocentrism–psychocentrism continuum having received substantial attention (Plog, 1974). Personality has also been related to the selection of vacation destinations, the choice of leisure activities engaged in while on vacation, as well as other travel-related decisions (Nickerson and Ellis, 1991; Madrigal, 1995). In addition, identifying a customer's personality has been proposed as a suitable tool for directing a customer to a preferable destination in the course of a travel agent–client interaction (Griffith and Albanese, 1996).

Existing personality research focuses on personality identification and subsequent personality-type classification through sophisticated measurement scales that have only limited applicability in the realm of a DRS. Only very recently has personality-related research started to investigate the possibility of developing very brief measures of personality (see Gosling *et al.*, 2003). However, such short diagnostic tests are believed to have several shortcomings, including inferior reliability and a restricted ability to capture specific personality facets. In addition, it is not clear how easy it is for individuals to select and identify with an existing topology of personality types (whether these are based on rigorously tested psychological measurement or the assumptions of marketing managers, as in the case of most personality categories found on the Web). Also, no evidence was found in the existing literature with respect to the power of such predefined personality categories to predict actual behaviour.

Within the context of recommendation systems, personality is sometimes used in a very colloquial sense, referring to the user preference models or the user classes on the basis of which recommendations are made. For instance, given certain preferences for some items, the probability that the user has the same 'personality' as other users is calculated (Pennock *et al.*, 2000). Also, particularly in the case of destination recommendations, these categories are often based on preferences for certain travel-related activities (e.g. hiking, sightseeing) rather than preferences directly linked to any personality traits. Thus, what is referred to as a 'personality type' in travel recommendation systems is often a preference structure that is assumed to result from, rather than directly describe, specific personality characteristics. One of the apparent advantages of such an 'interest'- or preference-based categorization is the ability to easily accommodate different travel needs based on situational changes, which would be harder to achieve in a classification model that emphasizes stable personality traits.

Examples of personality categories found on the Web suggest that certain linkages between personality and consumption patterns have been recognized by system developers; however, it seems that such approaches have been implemented without thorough consideration of the ability of such predefined travel personality categories to serve as substitutes for lengthy personality or travel needs assessment tests. The ultimate question that needs to be answered is whether these personality types can be used as the foundation for destination recommendations. This chapter looks at the most commonly implemented typology on travel websites (i.e. activity-related personality types), and investigates whether or not sophisticated measurement is, indeed, necessary to enhance a recommendation process, or whether letting a user choose among predefined categories provides a valid short cut to more personalized and, therefore, more relevant destination recommendations.

3. Methodology

The findings presented in this chapter are based upon a survey of 3525 randomly selected persons who had requested travel information from a Northern Indiana tourism office during summer and fall 2001. The data collection took place during a 2-month period (November–December 2001). The survey methodology followed a three-step process designed to maximize the return rate. The initial mailing consisted of a cover letter, a survey, a postage-paid return envelope and a description of the incentive. One week later, postcards were sent out to remind those who had not completed the survey and to thank all respondents for participating in the study. All non-respondents were sent a survey kit 2 weeks later. The survey effort resulted in 1436 completed responses for a 42.1% response rate (113 letters were undeliverable).

The survey comprised a series of questions related to travel style, psychographic characteristics and actual travel behaviour. In one section respondents were asked to indicate the travel personality that described them 'best' and the one that described them 'least'. Respondents were provided with a total of 12 travel personalities from which to choose. Each personality type was described by a short paragraph (Fig. 8.1). The descriptions were initially adapted from examples found on the Web such as the travel personality feature Travelocity.com used to have in its Guides & Advice section. However, the descriptions were further adjusted and specific travel personalities were added to reflect personality types that could be attracted to visiting destinations in the Midwest.

Travel motivations and travel styles were measured using 5-point Likert scales and values were measured using semantic differential scales. Respondents were asked to rate the importance of certain motivations (escapism, social contact, relaxation, excitement, physical activity, etc.) as well as the importance of certain destination features (scenery, good value for money, diversity, quaintness, etc.). Travel style questions focused on variety seeking and multidestination travel patterns. Travel values examined the emphasis

Below are 12 different travel personalities. Pick a travel personality that 'best' describes you as you travel in the Midwest; then, choose one that does not describe your personal travel style at all. Please select only one for each category.

A. Culture Creature
Loves everything cultural – theatre, shows, museums, festivals and fairs and local culture, too!

E. Beach Bum
Somebody who has to lie around on the beach with little umbrellas pitched in their drinks.

I. Trail Trekker
If it's outdoors – you are there. Hiking, walking, parks, forests, mountains, birdwatching, etc.

B. City Slicker
An urban creature who goes where the action is. Loves clubs, meeting people and needs the pulse of the city.

F. Avid Athlete
Always on the court or the course. Always in the game … whatever game it is.

J. History Buff
Travels back in time. Your vacation is a learning experience that focuses on historic facts and sites.

C. Sight Seeker
Always ready to stop for that landmark, event or attraction.

G. Shopping Shark
Stopped looking for a cure for your shopaholism?

K. Boater
Your world is the lake and your boat is your home. Feeling the breeze is what you really care about.

D. Family Guy
The destination is not what counts, it is the time you spend with your family that makes your vacation.

H. All Arounder
You need to have it all. You go where there is lots to do and see.

L. Gamer
Electrifying slots and skill-testing table games, fantastic fare and nightly entertainment are a crucial part of your trip.

Travel personality that 'best' describes you (A–L): _____

Travel personality that does not describe you at all (A–L): _____

Fig. 8.1. Travel-related personality types.

placed on stability vs excitement, family vs self, being passive vs being active, learning vs dropping out and following tradition vs trying new things.

Actual travel behaviour was elicited by asking survey respondents to indicate which destinations they had visited and which activities they had participated in during their most recent visit to Northern Indiana. A map of Northern Indiana was included in the survey to facilitate recall of the destinations that belong to this specific region. Respondents were asked to list up to 10 different destinations visited during their most recent trip; however, only the 20 most frequently mentioned destinations across all respondents were included in the subsequent analyses. Also, they were asked to choose among a list of 21 activities provided in the survey. Four of these activities (overnight stay, restroom stop, visiting friends or relatives and other) were excluded from further analyses. Table 8.1 lists the travel personality types, destinations and activities on which the analyses presented in this chapter are based.

Table 8.1. Travel personalities, destinations and travel activities included in analyses.

Travel personalities		Destinations		Travel activities	
1	Culture Creature	1	Shipshewana	1	Antique shopping
2	City Slicker	2	Michigan City	2	Beach/waterfront
3	Sight Seeker	3	South Bend	3	Biking
4	Family Guy	4	Nappanee	4	Birdwatching
5	Beach Bum	5	Middlebury	5	Boat/auto/antique show
6	Avid Athlete	6	Goshen	6	Boating
7	Shopping Shark	7	Merrillville	7	Dining
8	All Arounder	8	Elkhart	8	Festival/special event
9	Trail Trekker	9	Chesterton	9	Gambling
10	History Buff	10	Valparaiso	10	Golfing
11	Boater	11	La Porte	11	Hiking
12	Gamer	12	Hammond	12	Hunting/fishing
		13	Crown Point	13	Museum/play/concert
		14	Angola	14	Nightlife
		15	Warsaw	15	Shopping
		16	Mishawaka	16	Sightseeing
		17	Plymouth	17	Visit historic site
		18	Portage		
		19	Lagrange		
		20	Ft Wayne		

Additional data was collected in the course of four focus groups that were conducted in Chicago, Illinois, in the fall of 2002. A total of 43 participants from the Northern Chicago suburbs were recruited based on age, gender and income level so that the structure of the groups represented the major target markets of the destination under consideration. An additional criterion for selection was that the participants were to have travelled in the Midwest within the last 18 months and were to have stayed in paid lodging. The groups were also screened to obtain respondents that were actively involved in travel decision-making. All names for recruitment were taken from the inquiry database of the Northern Indiana tourism office used in the previous survey effort. The focus group members were presented with a sheet of paper that featured the same 12 personality types used in the survey questionnaire. However, in contrast to the mail survey, the personality type descriptions were enhanced with small graphics and the focus group participants were allowed to choose more than one personality type if necessary.

A series of analyses were conducted to investigate the potential contribution of such travel personality categories to the recommendation process. First, the 12 travel personality categories were analysed with respect to how much overlap exists between them and how easy it was for respondents to identify themselves with any of the personality types. Frequencies and cross-tabulation were used to explore the choice patterns of the survey and focus group participants. Discriminant analysis with personality types as the grouping variable and several psychographic and travel-related variables (travel needs or motivations, travel styles, desired activities, desired destination features, personal values) as independent variables was then conducted to assess the distinctiveness of the travel personality categories. Second, the personality types were described in terms of the personality profiles gained from the numerous personality and travel style–related questions asked in the survey to examine the specific personality traits underlying each predefined personality category. Finally, correspondence analyses were conducted to assess the degree to which personality types, activities and destinations could be matched.

4. Results

Table 8.2 shows the frequency distributions for both choice settings: travel personality that describes best and travel personality that describes least. The top three travel personalities selected as being most appropriate were All Arounder (24.6%), Sight Seeker (21.6%) and Culture Creature (14.6%). This finding largely corresponds to market segmentation results found in previous studies for the area. The travel personalities selected most often as being not applicable were Gamer (38.8%), Avid Athlete (17.1%) and City Slicker (12.6%). In general, the least frequently selected categories in one choice setting are the most frequently selected in the other, indicating that respondents were consistent in their choices. Several interesting choice patterns emerged from the crosstabulation between 'best' and 'least applicable' travel personality. For instance, individuals who identified themselves with the Trail Trekker personality type were significantly more likely to select City Slicker, Shopping Shark or Gamer as the least applicable travel personality than one would expect from the overall frequency distribution of those categories. Similarly, Family Guy and Gamer seemed to be mutually exclusive

Table 8.2. Frequency distribution of travel personality categories.

Travel personality that describes best	Percent of respondents	Travel personality that describes least	Percent of respondents
All Arounder	24.6	Gamer	38.8
Sight Seeker	21.6	Avid Athlete	17.1
Culture Creature	14.6	City Slicker	12.6
Family Guy	10.6	Beach Bum	9.3
Trail Trekker	9.5	Boater	8.1
History Buff	7.7	Trail Trekker	4.6
Shopping Shark	4.1	Shopping Shark	3.3
Beach Bum	3.0	Culture Creature	2.3
Gamer	2.2	History Buff	2.0
Boater	1.3	Family Guy	1.1
Avid Athlete	0.6	All Arounder	0.5
City Slicker	0.3	Sight Seeker	0.2

categories. Other examples are Boaters, describing themselves as not being Sight Seekers, and Beach Bums, declaring themselves as not falling into the History Buff category. These patterns intuitively make sense and suggest that many respondents were not only able to easily identify with particular travel personality categories but also were able to clearly distinguish between who they are and who they are not when they travel to Northern Indiana destinations.

Interestingly, the prevalence of the All Arounder category seems to indicate that many travellers have multifaceted personalities and pursue a diversity of interests when they travel. The focus group results are consistent with this survey finding, indicating that individuals tend to select more than one travel personality if provided with the opportunity to do so. On average, the focus group members selected 3.9 travel personalities to describe who they are when they travel. Importantly, the All Arounder category was less frequently selected by focus group members (ranking fourth after Culture Creature, Family Guy and Sight Seeker). This finding suggests that choosing multiple specific personality types was preferred over selecting one category that subsumes many interests. Also, the focus group participants reported that it was easier to indicate which personality type was not applicable than to select the one(s) that best described one's travel personality. Specifically, some focus group members were hesitant when asked to pick a travel personality and stressed that their travel personalities depended on the travel situation, especially the composition of the travel party. However, all of them were quick to select the personality type they were 'definitely not'. For instance, one focus group member stated: 'I guess I am a Family Guy, but the only one I am really not is Avid Athlete.'

Table 8.3 presents the top 20 destinations visited in Northern Indiana. As can be seen, Shipshewana (41.4%), Michigan City (22.2%) and South Bend (20.9%) were the three most popular destinations. However, smaller Amish villages including Nappanee and towns with natural environments including Middlebury were also popular places to visit. In general, Northern Indiana visitors explored 2–3 cities or towns during their stay (mean = 2.5 places). The top three activities were dining (65.5%), shopping (65.1%) and sightseeing (51.3%). In addition, antique shopping, visiting a festival or special event, beach or waterfront and historic sites were common activities of visitors to Northern Indiana. Overall, respondents participated in 4–5 activities up to a maximum of 13 (mean = 4.4 activities).

4.1 Results of discriminant analyses

The second phase of the study examined the degree to which travel needs and/or motivations, travel styles, desired activities, desired destination features and personal values could be used to discriminate the 12 travel personality types. Two analyses were conducted based upon the 'best fitting' and 'worst fitting' personality types selected by the respondents. The results of the analyses suggest that the travel personality categories are distinct with

Table 8.3. Frequency distribution.

Destinations	Percent of respondents	Travel activities	Percent of respondents
Shipshewana	41.4	Dining	65.5
Michigan City	22.2	Shopping	65.1
South Bend	20.9	Sightseeing	51.3
Nappanee	19.9	Antique shopping	39.0
Middlebury	19.2	Festival/special event	29.2
Goshen	14.3	Beach/waterfront	25.4
Merrillville	12.0	Visit historic site	24.0
Elkhart	11.7	Museum/play/concert	14.0
Chesterton	11.3	Hiking	12.4
Valparaiso	11.2	Gambling	9.5
La Porte	10.0	Birdwatching	8.9
Hammond	7.8	Boating	5.9
Crown Point	7.4	Nightlife	5.8
Angola	7.1	Boat/auto/antique show	5.4
Warsaw	6.4	Hunting/fishing	5.1
Mishawaka	6.1	Golfing	3.1
Plymouth	5.4	Biking	2.8
Portage	5.4		
Lagrange	4.8		
Ft Wayne	4.2		

respect to their underlying travel motivations, styles and values. Specifically, the results for the analysis using 'best fitting' travel personalities indicate that 45.9% of the cases were correctly classified. Given the many categories in the grouping variable, this result is significantly better than an assignment by chance. This finding suggests that travel personality could, indeed, be a useful strategy for classification purposes and could be used as a surrogate for various psychographic variables. Interestingly, the classification result for 'least applicable' travel personalities was somewhat inferior, with only 38.3% of the cases being correctly classified. Thus, although it seems to be easier for respondents to select a single 'least applicable' category, these categories appear to be less distinct with respect to underlying motivations. However, the difference might be due to the fact that survey questions were worded in a positive way, and that the motivations, styles and values one has do not automatically reflect the psychographic characteristics one does not have.

Cross-tabulations and chi-square tests were used to examine the personality traits and styles underlying each personality category. Avid Athlete and City Slicker had to be excluded from this analysis as the sample size for these categories was too small. The results confirm the distinctiveness of the travel personality categories with respect to all values, motivations, planning and travel style-related variables. Most importantly, the personality profiles obtained are consistent and make intuitive sense. Consequently, the results illustrate that the predefined travel categories serve as very good proxies for capturing user personality traits and preferences and can be used to make specific destination recommendations. The following provides a brief description of the personality types and their underlying extended personality profiles.

4.1.1 Culture Creature

This personality type values excitement, being active, learning and trying new things. Experiencing new things and learning a lot is also an important travel motivation for this type. Further, Culture Creatures are less likely to travel to the Midwest to relax and do nothing than all other personality types except for History Buffs. Culture Creatures tend to visit more than one destination during a trip and most often use a base camp strategy, i.e. they stay overnight at one destination to visit places nearby. They specifically look for destinations that offer cultural sites or events as well as festivals and fairs. Historic sites are also frequently visited by this personality type. In general, travellers who identify with this personality type plan major aspects of a trip in advance but leave specifics open.

4.1.2 Sight Seeker

Sight Seekers value excitement, activity and learning. Trying new things is more important for them than following traditions. They enjoy taking chances by visiting new destinations and visit more than one destination during a trip. They are more likely than other personality types to visit destinations on the way to the main destination and also enjoy touring a region. Sight Seekers have a particular interest in destinations that offer historic sites and they also tend to keep their travel plans more flexible than most other personality types.

4.1.3 Family Guy

Family is a central value for this personality type and following traditions is more important for this type than for most other personalities. Visiting family and friends is an important motivation for Family Guys, as are spending more time with the children and relaxing and doing nothing. In comparison to other personality types, Family Guys are also more likely to seek out destinations that offer activities for children. Beautiful scenery matters less for this personality type than for other types, and convenience to home is more important when choosing a destination. This personality type tends to visit familiar destinations and plans vacations to a greater detail than others.

4.1.4 Beach Bum

Some Beach Bums value excitement; others, stability. The same is true for being passive vs being active; however, Beach Bums overall value being passive much more than other personality types and dropping out is more prominent as a value for this group than learning. Visiting friends and family is not an important travel motivation, whereas relaxing and doing nothing is. Beach Bums are also highly motivated by a desire to get away from work and daily life. In addition, Beach Bums are likely to stay at one destination and visit other places in the area. In general, they like to do different things when they travel. They most likely choose destinations that offer beaches or waterfronts, or destinations that have attractive lakes and rivers. Shopping and outdoor activities at the destination are also important and beautiful scenery is a must. Further, this travel personality type most often chooses destinations that are a nice quiet place and provide a unique experience. The Beach Bum category is the least likely to have flexible travel plans and most often plans everything in advance.

4.1.5 Shopping Shark

Shopping Sharks value stability and being passive. They also value the self much more than family. Dropping out is more important than learning for this personality type and following traditions is more central than trying new things. Meeting other people while travelling is not an important motivation and neither is experiencing new things and learning a lot. Spending more time with children is definitely not a high motivating factor for Shopping Sharks and being physically active and/or practising sports is a thought that rarely crosses Shopping Sharks' minds when they think of travel. Shopping Sharks keep going to destinations they know and do not enjoy touring a region. They do not like to do many different things while on vacation. This personality type visits destinations that offer festivals and craft fairs as well as general shopping opportunities. Shopping Sharks are thrifty travellers always looking for bargains. They most often choose destinations that offer reduced rates and seek out good value for time and money. This personality type is also drawn to destinations with lots or different kinds of food experiences. Shopping Sharks appear to have a wide variety of planning styles, ranging from total advance planning to en route planning.

4.1.6 All Arounder

All Arounders are thrill seekers. They value excitement more than any other personality type and being active is extremely important to them. Their desire for excitement is also reflected in the great emphasis they place on trying new things. Visiting family and friends is an important motivation and meeting people while on vacation is also a greater motivating factor for this group than for others. The thrill-seeking focus of this personality category is also apparent in their wish to travel in order to get more excitement into their lives. When on vacation, All Arounders do things they usually do not have time to do and they enjoy taking chances by visiting new destinations. All Arounders enjoy touring regions and, as their name suggests, do a lot of different things when they travel. They choose destinations that offer lots of things to do and see and prefer places that offer unique experiences. This personality type plans major aspects of a trip in advance, but is also to some extent open for changes.

4.1.7 Trail Trekker

Trail Trekkers seek a balance between stability and excitement. Importantly, they are the group that places the greatest value on being active, and learning is also an important aspect of their lives. They like trying new things but they do not necessarily travel to get more excitement into their lives. Being physically active and/or practising sports is their main travel motivation. They enjoy taking chances by visiting new destinations and especially like to explore places that are not typical vacation destinations. Trail Trekkers clearly like places where they can hike and bike and choose destinations that are great for outdoor activities. Destinations with attractive lakes and rivers and quiet places are also very important to them. Trail Trekkers are definitely not interested in gambling or shopping. In general, Trail Trekkers do a lot of different things when they travel and make many travel-related decisions while en route.

4.1.8 History Buff

History Buffs value both family and self, and being active is more important for them than being passive. Learning is a central value for this personality type and relaxing and doing nothing while on vacation is definitely not a motivating factor for this group. History Buffs travel to experience new things and learn a lot, as well as to do things for which they usually do not have time. History Buffs enjoy visiting new destinations instead of going to destinations they know. Further, History Buffs are highly likely to visit more than one destination when on a trip. They visit places on the way to the main destination and also like touring regions. When doing so they like to combine places that offer similar activities and experiences. History Buffs also like to explore places that are not typical vacation destinations. They most often choose destinations that have interesting historic sites, offer beautiful scenery, have quaint towns or villages and provide unique experiences. Most History Buffs plan major aspects of their trips but leave specific decisions open.

4.1.9 Boater

Boaters place equal value on family and self. Excitement is important for them; yet, a substantial number of boaters also value stability. Accordingly, they seek a middle path between following traditions and trying new things. Importantly, being active is definitely a core value that members of this personality category share; however, when Boaters travel, relaxing and doing nothing is an important motivation, as is getting away from work and daily life. Boaters also often travel to visit family and friends and to spend more time with their children. Boaters like to take chances by visiting new destinations; however, they typically select a single destination and do not like to tour regions or visit other destinations in the area while staying overnight at one place. They could not care less about historic or cultural sites and events at a destination, are also not interested in hiking or biking, but participate in outdoor activities as long as they have something to do with boating. They naturally seek destinations with beaches, waterfronts, lakes or rivers and choose places with beautiful scenery. Boaters also prefer destinations that are convenient to home and offer good value for time and money. Whether a destination offers lots to see or do does not matter for Boaters because they do not like to do a lot of different things when they travel. Importantly, Boaters tend to plan major aspects of a trip in advance.

4.1.10 Gamer

Gamers value excitement, dropping out and trying new things. Gamers do not travel to visit family and friends or to relax and do nothing. Meeting people or being physically active is definitely not on the Gamer's mind when travelling; instead, what drives Gamers to travel is the desire to get excitement into their lives. Gamers keep going to destinations they know and are clearly less likely to take chances by visiting new destinations than other personality types. They do not like touring regions but sometimes visit other destinations close to where they stay overnight. When doing so, they combine places or activities that offer the same kind of experience. Gamers do not enjoy visiting places that are not typical vacation destinations and, of course, they prefer destinations that offer gambling. Whether the destination has cultural sites, provides beautiful scenery or offers outdoor activities is irrelevant. Interestingly, this personality type wants to visit places that provide lots to see and do, quality accommodations and good value for time and money. Gamers have a clear preference for destinations that offer good and/or different kinds of food, which fits with the general indulgence theme that surrounds this travel personality. Gamers also like to gamble when it comes to travel by leaving their travel plans flexible and open.

4.2 Results of correspondence analyses

One of the most important questions to be answered within the context of a DRS is, of course, whether these travel personality categories can adequately predict the activities and/or places that might be recommended in the DRS. Correspondence analysis was used first to examine the relationship between personality types and activities. Again, Avid Athlete and City Slicker were excluded from this analysis as few respondents had selected either one of these personality types; also, they correspond little to the offerings of the Northern Indiana region. A correspondence map was created to visually assess the degree to which the personality types and activities are associated (see Fig. 8.2). The results indicate that the relationship between personality types and activities can be mapped into a two-dimensional space. The results are significant ($\alpha = 0.05$) and the two dimensions account for 59.2% of the inertia; adding a third dimension would not significantly improve the result. As illustrated in Fig. 8.3, dimension 1 is defined by Gamer and gambling on one end and History Buff and museum on the other. Thus, dimension 1 appears to reflect travel motives ranging from the desire to escape to engaging in learning while on vacation. Dimension 2 contrasts natural with man-made or constructed settings and is defined by Trail Trekker and hiking vs Culture Creature and museum.

The results reveal a close correspondence between travel personalities and respective activities. For instance, Boater and boating map almost

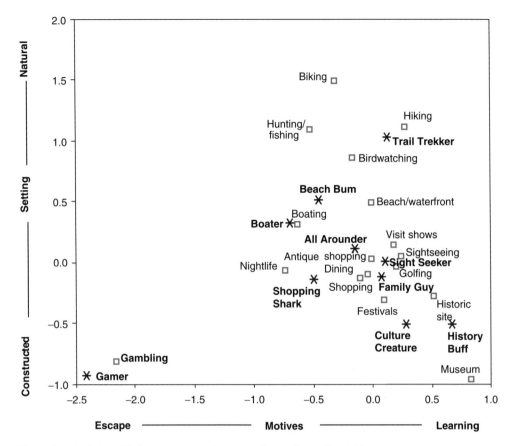

Fig. 8.2. Relationship between travel personality and travel activities.

perfectly onto each other, as do Sight Seeker and sightseeing. However, most travel personalities are related to more than one activity. For example, Culture Creatures seem to enjoy festivals, museums as well as historic sites, and Shopping Sharks engage in shopping but also nightlife and dining. As expected, the All Arounder personality is surrounded by many different activities. Similarly, the Family Guy personality seems to map onto several kinds of activities, but is definitely not related to gambling, hunting or fishing as well as biking.

A second correspondence analysis was conducted to directly assess the relationship between the personality types and the destinations visited in Northern Indiana. Interestingly, no significant relationship was found between travel personalities and travel destinations. It seems that many destinations in the Northern Indiana area offer a diversity of tourism products, thus catering to a variety of tourists. Also, they are, in comparison to each other, rather homogeneous. Further, certain destinations are very popular (e.g. Shipshewana) and are visited by many of the tourists who travel to the area (more than 41% of the survey respondents say they visited Shipshewana

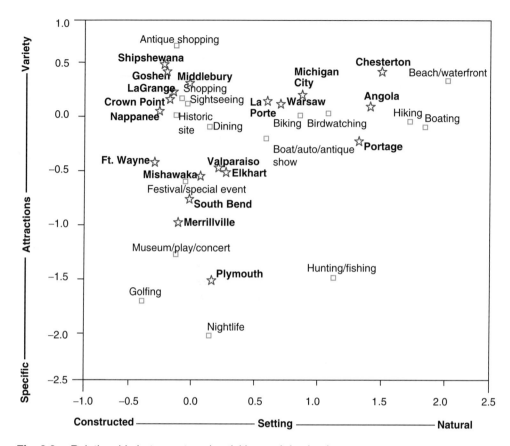

Fig. 8.3. Relationship between travel activities and destinations.

on their most recent trip to the Northern Indiana area). Although not significant, certain relationships are clear and consistent with a priori expectations; for example, the Boater personality is more closely related to destinations near Lake Michigan. In contrast, History Buffs seem to frequently visit destinations such as Nappanee, Indiana, which has a historic and cultural centre that explains the Amish way of life to visitors.

Since a direct matching of personality types with destinations was found to be difficult, a correspondence analysis of travel activities and destinations was conducted to potentially provide the 'missing link' in recommending destinations to different travel personality types. Gambling is a very distinct activity and was clearly associated with Hammond (nearly half of Hammond's visitors come to the destination to gamble) so that it dominated the correspondence plot and caused other places to appear extremely similar. For this reason, Gambling and Hammond were removed from the analysis (Bendixen, 1996). The resulting solution with two dimensions accounts for 58.5% of the inertia. A third dimension increases the value to 71.6%; however, only the two-dimensional solution is presented in this chapter as it is clearly easier to illustrate and interpret. Figure 8.3 shows that activities and destinations were matched based on constructed vs natural settings. The second dimension is less clear but seems to distinguish between destinations with specific offers and destinations like Shipshewana, which provide a greater variety of attractions that are being enjoyed by many types of visitors. In general, the destination and activity matches correspond to the product offerings of the destinations, e.g. Chesterton is the home of the Indiana Dunes State Park and was associated with beach or waterfront, whereas Shipshewana is known as an antique and shopping destination. Further, Plymouth has a renowned golf resort and Merrillville provides its visitors with an opportunity to enjoy entertainment in the Star Plaza Theatre.

5. Conclusions

The findings of this study suggest that travel personality categories can serve not only as a fun way to engage users in the recommendation process but, importantly, as a useful tool in a DRS to easily capture differences among users with respect to their preference for certain activities. The categories used in this study appear to be quite distinct in terms of underlying psychographic variables but not different with respect to actual destination choice behaviour. This could be seen as a potential problem for the design of the recommendation algorithm. However, from a marketing point of view, being able to suggest more than one destination can be seen as an advantage. Also, it is expected that there would be more variation in the data and consequently less ambiguous assignments if the travel personality approach were tested in the context of a less homogeneous area, e.g. destinations throughout a state, province or country. The results further suggest that for tourism regions with similar destinations, activities can serve as an efficient route for recommending potential places to visit.

Importantly, the study results indicate that specific system design decisions such as deciding whether the user is allowed to check more than one personality type and/or whether users can exclude certain types are all but trivial. Drawing on existing decision science and usability literature, further research is needed to investigate the implications of multiple-choice settings and 'exclude' options in the context of recommendation systems. In addition, the research presented in this chapter did not specifically address the effects of the way in which the personality types are represented, e.g. in text or pictorial form or a combination thereof. This appears to be an area in need of further exploration, as the ultimate goal of such a category approach is to provide users with the necessary cues for being able to quickly identify with, or discard, certain options.

The identified relationships between personality categories and activities participated in while on vacation look very promising. It is suggested that a simulation approach that compares predictions based on personality types to assignments based simply on probabilities derived from the frequency distribution of the activities could further enhance our understanding of the predictive power of category-based approaches. Also, although the mail survey used in this study provides some opportunities for comparing information derived from questions to user information derived from choices among predetermined categories, there is still a need for a more direct comparison of the two approaches in an actual DRS setting.

The increasing frequency with which category-based approaches appear on general consumer product as well as tourism-related websites indicates that marketeers see a need for innovative ways of customizing their offerings without forcing the user through lengthy registration-assessment processes or requiring a rich inventory of past search and/or purchasing behaviour. Personality types draw on users' needs for self-expression and personalization without imposing many constraints in terms of effort and time. In addition, they allow users to quickly revise their specifications if the recommendations do not match their interests. Thus, they point out that the ultimate goal of recommendation system design is not necessarily to find the most precise matching algorithms, but rather to simplify the decision-making process by offering a reasonable subset of alternatives. In addition, successful system design efforts need to focus on creating meaningful user experiences and travel personality categories which are fun to use and allow users to express their uniqueness. Most importantly, providing users with the opportunity to select a personality type implies choice and, consequently, makes subsequent destination recommendations more relevant and more persuasive.

Chapter Summary

Current efforts in destination recommendation systems research and design are based on the assumption that user preferences have to be captured in the most accurate way possible in order to be able to provide useful recommendations. However, leading the user through a series of mind-puzzling diagnostic questions is often cumbersome and, therefore, discourages use. This chapter has explored travel personality categories as a possible simple approach to classify users. The results of this study suggest that travel personality types can, indeed, be matched up with certain travel activities, and through these activities with specific destinations.

9 Building Adaptive Systems: A Neural Net Approach

Josef A. Mazanec

1. Introduction

This chapter introduces methodology that assists in making tourism coun-selling and recommender systems 'adaptive'. The kind of 'adaptivity' desired here is based on a system's capability of learning about changes in three respects: (i) macro patterns of consumer information acquisition and usage; (ii) correspondence between the (rather fuzzy) user language and the (more technical) jargon of product descriptions; and (iii) the way of exploiting the users' choice decisions to make inferences about the deci-sion relevance ('weights') of tourism and leisure product attributes. The DieToRecs system prototype discussed in several chapters of this book serves as a practical and empirical example. The DieToRecs project tried to recognize different macro patterns (named user 'decision styles') that are likely to require particular versions of system functionality. Neural network (NNW) techniques were used to provide the various learning capacities and to complement the Case-based reasoning (CBR) approach adopted for the DieToRecs project.

1.1 The matching paradigm of basic marketing

It is the overall purpose of the suggestions discussed in this chapter to facil-itate tourist life when confronted with an automated trip counselling and recommender system. To serve this purpose well, one must highlight some advanced features that a 'second-generation' counselling system ought to exhibit. These features have not yet been implemented in the current versions of recommender system prototypes (henceforth referred to as a 'system'). However, it is important to highlight some aspects of a vision of counselling intelligence independently from what may be realistic given the budget and time constraints in contemporary development projects.

In the following discussion, the terms *counselling* and *recommender* system will be used synonymously with a slight preference for *counselling*. Both concepts are used ambiguously in the literature. *Counselling* stresses the interrogative aspects, i.e. those responsibilities of a system that deal with the intelligent eliciting of the user's consumption goals. *Recommender* emphasizes the exploitation of past user sessions and the observed similarity of user profiles (via screening tools such as collaborative filtering).

The concept of adaptivity conforms with the basic matching paradigm of marketing thought. The matching paradigm has been outlined most convincingly by Malcolm McDonald in his introduction to 'Marketing Plans' (1995, 1 ff.; 1st edn, 1984). In short, it urges the product or service provider to align his own competences with the desires of demand, whether apparent or latent. The matching process is meant as a proactive endeavor rather than a pure adjustment exercise. For any counselling or recommender system this implies that the system designer cannot uncritically trust that the user is a mature consumer who is fully aware of the benefits sought in the forthcoming consumption experience. There are logical consequences flowing from this finding.

An advanced system is expected to:

- enhance its adaptivity by acquiring a fair amount of learning capabilities and real-time personalization capacity; thus,
- reducing the user's effort; and
- arousing excitement.

Therefore, one must not be satisfied with a solution that avoids prompting redundant and boring user input. It is even more important to have the system mediate between the two language levels involved in the producer–consumer interaction, i.e. the consumption goal and experience-oriented language, and the experts' jargon of trip package production.

Any long-term vision of a viable travel counselling system must be based on assumptions regarding the development of the tourism and leisure sector in the network economy. Among others the most radical alternative has been outlined by Achrol and Kotler (1999). In an advanced stage of evolution these authors expect the advent of what they termed the *consumer opportunity networks* (CON) (pp. 158–161). Within such a CON a 'marketing company' plays the central role. It maintains a database of products and suppliers and a second one of consumer information and content. Access providers and search engines, manufacturer stand-alone sites, consolidators and auction sites, individual consumers and consumer communities specializing in various lifestyle facets such as travel, investing, gardening and romance are the other interconnected partners. Real-world predecessors of some of these components are Infoseek, GeoCities, SuperProfile, Privaseek, Citigroup and First USA. The major marketing challenges refer to infomediary functions, brand mediation and consolidating consumer demand, and the management of customer communities. In this scenario of dramatic change marketing will become 'more a consumer-consulting function than a marketeer of goods and services' (Achrol and Kotler, 1999, p. 162), and, what the consumerists of the 1970s have been dreaming about may be impending now.

1.2 Levels of counselling intelligence

Coming back to the down-to-earth customizing of a counselling system prototype, how can the system learn to contemplate the world from the consumer's perspective? A first and not too surprising result may be that the users' mindsets are not static. The minimum requirements for adaptivity include the updating of the user 'decision styles' (as outlined in another chapter of this book). The user decision styles represent fundamentally different ways of processing information and arriving at conclusions. As a first step it is sufficient to perform a regular off-line update. To achieve this objective one will have to accumulate a database of counselling sessions and to extract the most significant decision style variables. An operational procedure will be suggested later in this chapter. For further improvement it is desirable to replace the predetermined and comparatively static decision styles by a continuous online tailoring of the counselling dialogue to the individual user's progress in information gathering and decision-making. As a consequence the system must become sensitive to:

- the degree of precision gained of the user's consumption goals during the individual counselling interaction;
- the fulfilment of the user's aspiration level regarding the volume of information needed;
- the ability to articulate owing to the user's active or passive response style; and
- the situation-specific importance rank order of the benefits and product attributes sought.

The last item is crucial for the system to demonstrate intelligence; the principles of a technical solution will be discussed in Section 3.

The objectives of introducing some advanced features of adaptivity into automated counselling and recommender systems are arranged in a stepwise manner (see Fig. 9.1). From bottom up, the systems currently available seem to reach the second level. A fairly adaptive system aims at stepping up further towards the third level. More precisely, such a system should be able to provide the data necessary for estimating trip attribute weights. This chapter will select and evaluate an appropriate methodology to cope with this computation task. The fourth and last level shown in Fig. 9.1 is somewhat visionary, as it needs a multiple of the funds and time usually invested into system development and prototyping.

Levels 1 and 2 pertain to a user-driven dialogue, where the consumer bears a clear specification of the desired product components in mind. The user either looks for one or a few products or services (level 1) or goes ahead specifying his or her desired product bundle in a straightforward manner

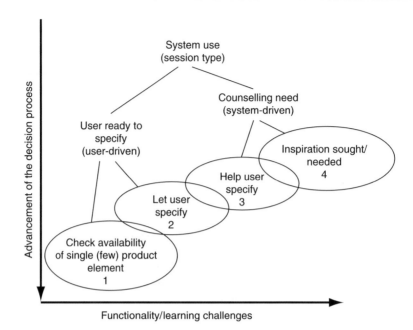

Fig. 9.1. The 'ladder of intelligence' for counselling systems.

(level 2). Levels 3 and 4 are system-driven as the user also receives unsolicited assistance while specifying the product components (level 3); if the desired consumption experience is still highly ambiguous, partly latent and flexible, the user is lingering in the pre-specification phase (level 4). Any system endowed with a fair amount of adaptivity and intelligence will have to recognize this fact, provide the inspiring stimuli and arouse the consumer's creative thinking.

2. Building Blocks of Adaptivity

2.1 Learning from the 'trip desired' and 'trip offered' (mis)match

Some of the fundamental concepts need not be reinvented here. The matching paradigm underlying an early example of a travel counselling system (Hruschka and Mazanec, 1990; Mazanec, 1990) introduced the concepts of the 'trip desired' and the 'trip offered'. At that time the Internet was still in its infancy, an expert tool for academics and research networks. However, the research on expert systems already had a two-decade history, and PC-assisted travel counselling in a travel agency did not seem to differ much from the problem of diagnosing patients in a medical consultation. In an expert system of the ordinary taxonomy or rule-base type, the user dialogue aims at diagnosing the 'problem' (i.e. the 'trip desired'), which may be cured by a 'therapy' (i.e. the 'trip offered'). When using this terminology one has to be aware of the fact that the recommendation process does not necessarily refer to a product bundle that makes up a 'complete' trip. Trips desired and offered are seen as bundles of leisure and travel-related products and services or packages of any degree of complexity.

Both concepts are not static but time-varying mixtures of perceived product and service elements subject to learning. Within a counselling session the 'problem' and the 'therapy' may even overlap and become interdependent as an intelligent system exploits the items offered and accepted for gradually improving the system's knowledge of the user's 'problem' definition.

Note that the 'trip desired' and the 'trip offered' are *behavioural concepts* that are given only a rough correspondence in the set-up of a system. A theoretical construct such as 'trip desired' carries the surplus meaning typical for behavioural variables. A concept such as the *TravelWish* defined in the newly developed DieToRecs System Prototype is hooked on a particular system implementation (see http://dietorecs.itc.it/). In other words, the *TravelWish* collects a number of items that must be directly comparable to the user's shopping list accumulated in the *TravelBag* (the equivalent to the 'trip offered'). These concepts operate on a manifest language level of user–system interaction. The same is not true for the 'trip desired' and 'trip offered'. The *TravelWish* is the system's approximation to the user's 'trip desired'. The *TravelBag* results from the user's response to the items suggested by the system. Its cumulative volume of items is the user's interpretation of the system's current 'trip offered'.

To elucidate the subtle differences take travel motives as an example and, for the sake of simplicity, assume that the user is driven by just one dominant motive. The user interacts with the system, looking for a long-haul trip. If the user were to state his or her motivation, he or she would answer with something like: 'I want to experience foreign cultures and enhance my knowledge of the world.' This is a false revelation because the 'actual' motivation is 'keeping up with the Jones', as his neighbours have visited a place equally far away last year. Even this 'prestige' motive may be wrong for those researchers who believe in the tourists' subconscious minds and may succeed in extracting an *escapism* motive (flee the nasty normal environment) with some odd means of psychotherapy.

A travel consumer develops the size and contents of the trip desired and the counter clerk (or the automated counselling system) adjusts and fine-tunes the composition of the trip offered. Unlike the counselor, recommender or seller, the consumer cannot be forced into precise specification; if he or she is compelled to do so, the results may be spurious and deceiving. In other words, the system must not rely on an interrogation scheme always leading to a sufficiently complete trip desired. Frequently, it will be more appropriate to watch the user's selection and rejection behaviour and to judge the importance of the various trip attributes indirectly.

Finally, in those instances where the user–system interaction progresses up to placing an order the user decides on a *trip chosen* or *accepted*. This may be (sometimes even a bad) compromise conveying limited information about the consumer's 'real' preferences. Nevertheless, a dynamic system will have to make inferences on the importance of the trip attributes that are fully or partly met or not at all. One of the principles that is instrumental in improving the quality of the system's conclusions is *reinforcement learning*. It is applicable in those situations where there is no actually desired trip target profile, but just a success–failure response.

Counselling or recommendation success is operationalized in a stepwise manner. There are a number of intermediate criteria other than reservations and bookings. For the system's reinforcement learning consider the following success criteria:

1. Pan and Fesenmaier (Chapter 4, this volume) distinguish three successive stages in the recommendation process: *filtering*, *specification* and *selection or sorting*. A counselling session is more successful the longer it survives through these stages.

2. The user's willingness to examine the details of a trip offered is a further success signal. The advice gained from the system has increased the user's trust to a level that warrants the effort to inspect a concrete offer. Actually, the trip offered corresponds to what has been termed the *TravelBag* in the DieToRecs system prototype. The user adding a trip item to his or her *TravelBag* signals acceptance and partial counselling success.

3. The next success level is reached if the user's satisfaction with the items offered induces him or her to save the trip profile for later retrieval. Each trip profile resulting in a permanent *TravelBag* functions as an input vector for later analysis.

4. Given the neurocomputing learning approach introduced in Section 3, the strength of the user's intention to choose (or book) is required. On the decision to save a trip profile the user may be offered a slide bar and invited to fix its value. The left and right ends of the bar are verbalized with the phrasing 'very unlikely' and 'almost certain'. The instruction runs: 'My later booking of the trip I have configured is …'

5. Asking for brochure(s) is another step towards the decision to choose a trip offered.

6. Making a reservation or booking is the most obvious success criterion.

7. Before ending a session the system may explicitly ask the user to express his or her degree of satisfaction with the counselling performance.

8. Returning to the system to enter a positive and assuring credential (triggering off some 'electronic' word of mouth) is a strong indicator of the user's product satisfaction and commitment.

As a general principle, one should favour implicit, indirect and unobtrusive measures such as (3) or (5) over direct questioning about the user's satisfaction with the counselling result such as (4) or (7). As a minimum for a system aiming at adaptivity, however, measures (3) and (4) are needed.

2.3 How to treat different types of trip attributes

Figure 9.2 highlights the various types of ingredients that make up the trip desired and the trips offered. Consider each of them. They are first discussed

Learning to improve the trip matching

Trip desired	Trips offered
• explicit constraints and conditions	• constraints and conditions
	– explicit (throughput)
• classes of trip product elements	– implicit (inferred)
	• concrete values and levels for the
• objective attributes (directly observable)	– product element classes
• abstract features	– abstract features

Fig. 9.2. The set-up of the trip desired and the trips offered.

from the tourist behaviour perspective and then connected to counselling system terminology. 'Attributes' is used here as the most general term for characterizing a multifaceted entity like a trip. Some of the attributes are equivalent to physical, functional or organizational trip components. Other attributes relate to a property of the entire trip. A travel consumer uses 'attributes' to characterize his trip desired. Depending on the prevailing evaluative mechanism these attributes may convey a more denotative meaning linked to the goal-satisfying capabilities of the items offered. Or they may impart a rather connotative and emotional response. The unavoidable ambiguity of this general notion of attributes is incompatible with the precision requirements of automated trip counselling. It is, therefore, preferable to permit only *features* that describe particular trip (product) items and can be given integer, real or symbolic values.

The trip desired may not be deliberately variable according to the user's discretion. Quite frequently it contains a number of predetermined constraints and conditions. Think of elementary trip data such as:

- the location of departure;
- the time and season dependent on the vacation schedules of the family or party;
- the duration (length of stay);
- the size and the composition of the travel party; and
- the mode of transport.

If the system behaves in an adaptive manner, it lets the user decide when and how to specify these restrictions. Although the user may not be able to relax all of the restrictions, he or she expects an immediate update of the number of trip options left in the 'solution space' after fixing these attributes.

Under the matching paradigm there are three more types of trip attributes. They emerge from the different languages practised by product designers and tourist consumers.

2.3.1 Type 1

The first type is called *trip product elements* (TPE). It is supply-oriented, focused on the service production jargon and expressed in 'expert' language. There are various classes of these 'technical' product elements. The most relevant examples relate to the:

- type of accommodation;
- catering or food arrangements (meals);
- transport and ancillary transfer services;
- events and excursions; and
- travel insurance services.

Type 1 elements require a minimum experience in travel. For the inexperienced user seemingly familiar notions such as 'hotel category', 'transfer' or 'extended breakfast' may not be readily decodable.[3] It is one of the conclusions from the comprehensive review of tourist decision-making in Part I that a counselling system should capture the desired values for these TPEs step by step while navigating through the three phases entitled filtering, specification and selection or sorting. Note that the decision styles postulated in Chapter 11 attach a different weight to these criteria and thus prefer a different specification sequence.

2.3.2 Type 2

The second type of product ingredients consists of concrete and objective attributes, which need not be translated when bridging the consumers and experts' language levels. They are operational, self-evident and can be checked and verified by considering the observable properties of the destination, resort or city, micro location, or hotel. Illustrative examples are:

- objective properties of the natural surroundings (e.g. an altitude >3000 feet);
- access and reachability by public transport;
- geographical location qualities (downtown, suburban, etc.); and
- distance to the major attractions.

The system is expected to 'put them through' (i.e. take them from the user dialogue and apply them to determine a trip desired–trip offered match). It is also expected to learn their importance weight for the tourists' choice decisions. Type 2 attributes are covered in all reasonable counselling system implementations as they always relate to specific *feature* values for, say, destination or location, or accommodation.

2.3.3 Type 3

The third ingredient that makes up a trip concoction comprises the abstract features, which are customer-oriented, experiental, *motive-* or *benefit*-driven,

---

[3] Consumer researchers are reminded of the *stimulus ambiguity* construct in the information panel of the Howard and Sheth model (1969).

expressed in layman's language and more easily comprehended if pictorially represented. Typical examples are:

- comfort and luxury, adventure and novelty, change pace;
- experience unspoiled nature;
- enjoy entertainment facilities; and
- train physical and mental fitness.

Type 3 attributes are most difficult to capture by machine learning in any automated counselling exercise. At the minimum, a system should allow for rough and directly specified areas of consumer *interest* such as 'culture and art' or 'sports'.

An intelligent system is expected to learn the strength of correspondence between these motivational and emotional items and the physical and functional attributes of a specific trip profile. Incorporating Type 3 items implies that the destinations, products or packages administered in the system are evaluated and rated by tour-operating specialists. This requirement is clearly stated in the TripMatcher description and its prerequisites outlined by Delgado and Davidson (2002). These authors also argue that – at least for activities, attractions and events – human judgement has been successfully replaced by semantic web-mining methodology. The technique still seems to be error-prone and subject to overruling by the user. Actually, the unwillingness of the tour operators to provide the 'man-made' evaluations in machine-readable format was the reason why the expert system prototypes developed in Hruschka and Mazanec (1990) were never brought to practice in a real-world travel agency. Type 3 counselling and learning capabilities are crucial for a recommender system to reach maturity level 4 in Fig. 9.1.

A CBR architecture as implemented in the DieToRecs prototype tries to avoid the tedious work of prefabricating trip descriptions by letting the user do the job. If the user dialogue succeeds in eliciting Type 3 attributes and incorporating them into the case base, these criteria serve as matching and filtering criteria for serving subsequent users later on. There are two ways of enhancing such a case base with new Type 3 attributes:

- The user indicates them as indicative of his trip desired. The system records them as a part of the trip desired. Then, within the respective case, they get automatically connected to a trip offered, thus establishing the desire–offer link; and
- The user reacts with a Type 3 response when invited to evaluate a fairly complete trip offered.

Future users roaming through similar regions of the case space benefit from this additional case description in terms of Type 3 attributes.

A trip offered includes constraints and conditions, which are either:

- explicit and thus put through or
- implicit, i.e. inferred by the system.

The second variant is important as it avoids redundant input and unnecessary user queries. If, for example, a user looking for a weekend city trip has entered 3 days for the length of stay, he or she will not be bothered with 1½ days duration of transport. The conditions are conjunctive decision criteria; they provide either a *min* or a *max* threshold, making them non-tradable requirements for the trips offered. As the constraints tend to lie outside the control of the user, they get the least priority when the system starts relaxing package selection criteria to overcome an empty basket of trip alternatives.

While the user may leave some slots of the trip desired open, the trips offered always suggest concrete levels for the TPE. By means of pictorial or promotional items the trip offered also conveys realizations of abstract motivational and emotional features ('fun', 'adventure', 'activity', 'coziness'). This may be a purposeful part of the matching (recall level 4 systems in Fig. 9.1) or incidental (lower levels) process. For example, for a TPE such as type of accommodation the trip offered includes one of the alternatives: hotel or category, apartment, bed and breakfast, camping site; or for meal arrangements it specifies one of these: full or half board, breakfast, none or self-catering. At the same time the system exhibits pictures, maps and other non-verbal material that arouses emotional responses. A level 4 system also learns the strength of association of the TPE values with the abstract features to reduce redundant and superfluous user input.

Learning from the user–system interaction is a standard property of any moderately intelligent counselling or recommender system. The precise scope and contents of the learning capability, however, vary considerably. It is useful to distinguish between two sorts of tourist information processing. Actually, there are two separable submodels:

1.   The *submodel for language bridging*: it assists the user in bridging the gap between two levels of languages by learning the relationship between the (fuzzy and redundant) user language and the 'technical' trip production terminology.
2.   The *choice submodel*: it helps tracing the tourist decision-making by learning the weights of the product attributes (or *features* in CBR terminology) in the tourists' choice decisions.

3. Updating and Optimization

3.1 Updating the user decision styles

The decision styles elaborated in Chapter 11 fulfil a double function. On the one hand, they demonstrate that a counselling system need not necessarily be customized to the individual user; it is sufficient to consider user types with a reasonably homogeneous search and navigation behaviour. On the other hand, they serve the purpose of initializing the system with a starting set of styles. User preferences and system usage patterns, however, are far from being constant. Hence, even the simplest form of adaptivity requires the user decision styles to be updated. Reanalysing the decision styles and updating their profiles is a continuing task. The number of styles initially adopted for a new system may vary according to changes in system usage behaviour. An adaptive system is expected to provide the methodology for monitoring the styles, for checking their temporal stability and for redesigning style-specific user interfaces.

Chapter 11 discusses the decision styles empirically analysed in the course of planning the DieToRecs system. The authors indicate that the small sample size and the sampling procedure for the respondents surveyed do not supply the reliable proportion of each of the styles, namely:

Decision style 1: highly predefined users   *15%*
Decision style 2: accommodation-oriented users   *18%*
Decision style 3: recommendation-oriented users   *10%*
Decision style 4: geography-oriented users   *18%*
Decision style 5: price-oriented users   *18%*
Decision style 6: individual travellers   *32%*

This is not a serious problem as the percentages may vary substantially once the system begins to collect the real-world data from actual user sessions.

Despite the impressive progress made in computational intelligence and web technology, it is unrealistic to implement an online updating mechanism that adjusts the set of decision styles in real-time and reorients the user interface accordingly. Rather, one has to rely on updating the styles in regular intervals depending on the number of usable counselling cases. 'Usable' means that the counselling session has advanced to a stage where at least one of the success criteria itemized in Section 2 becomes available.

Conceiving the update runs for the user decision styles demands a number of prerequisites. Consider the empirical results detailed in Chapter 11 as a real-world example. To capture the variety of user decision styles the DieToRecs project analysed a large number of style variables. For updating the styles routinely this number is reduced as a substantial amount of redundancy is expected in such a data-set. The following steps are appropriate:

1. The most significant variables determining the decision styles must be identified (see Table 9.1). Selecting 'significant' variables means that:

- one takes care of the redundancies in the original variable set;
- the percentage of unspecified (missing) values for the respective variable is small; and
- if there are more than one options, the variables corresponding with features that are defined in the trip desired and/or trip offered (*TravelWish* and/or *TravelBag* in the DieToRecs terminology) are preferred.

2. The values of the variables (e.g. 'earlier or later' and 'fixed or variable' describing two characteristics measured during a counselling session) must be operationalized in order to extract them later from the session log. The sequence of user actions transferring a new or a modified trip item to a user's consideration set (*TravelBag*) provides the relevant information.

3. Every counselling or recommender session ought to keep records of the user–system events that define each style variable. For batch updating, the

Table 9.1. The variables selected and corresponding with the DieToRecs *TravelWish* and *TravelBag* features for updating the decision styles (cf. Chapter 11, this volume for a full explanation of the style variables).

Style variables, i.e. the trip attributes of the travel styles study	Earlier/later series (1)		Fixed/variable series (2)		Features of the system prototype
	#	%*	#	%*	
Destination: country	**V5**	7	**V34**	09	**Country****
Destination: region	**V7**	07	**V36**	10	**Region**
Type of accommodation	**V27**	09	**V56**	21	**AccommodationType**
Geographical area	V9	20	V38	22	—
Travel party	**V13**	20	**V42**	23	**TravelParty**
Price	**V12**	04	**V41**	12	**BudgetRange**
Travel type in general	V14	17	**V43**	22	?***
Destination: community	**V6**	14	V35	15	**City**
Accommodation: place	**V25**	22	**V54**	31	**NearTo**
Accommodation: catering	**V26**	09	**V55**	21	**Catering**
Length of stay	**V4**	18	**V33**	32	**BeginDate & EndDate**
Natural factors	**V11**	24	**V40**	28	At least one out of **NaturalFactors**
Time of travel	V28	13	V57	17	—
Type of transportation	**V2**	25	**V31**	34	**TypeOfTransportation**
Accommodation: category	V24	17	**V53**	32	**Accommodation-Category**
Accommodation: equipment	V22	16	**V51**	27	—
Accommodation: pictures	V23	13	V52	29	—
Attractions	V3	44	V32	48	At least one out of Attractions/events
Additional geographic information	V29	53	V58	65	—
Activities/facilities	**V1**	30	**V30**	35	At least one out of **SportAdventure, ArtCulture or LeisureRelax**
Accessibility of the destination	**V8**	43	V37	52	?
Additional information	—	—	V59	50	—
Want to contact	**V10**	55	V39	59	?
Travel type: independent traveller	V16	54	V45	56	TripOrganization
Travel type: tour operator product	V19	54	**V48**	58	**TripOrganization**
Transfer to accommodation	V21	69	V50	74	—
Travel type: all-inclusive	**V15**	89	V44	91	?
Travel type: low-budget	V18	83	V47	84	—
Travel type: last-minute	V17	84	V46	85	—
Travel type: special offer	**V20**	84	V49	85	?

* Percentage remaining unspecified during the user sessions observed.
** Variables selected are in **bold**.
*** Equivalent needed in the *TravelWish/Bag*.

values of the style variables are generated off-line by analysing the log files later.

4. If an online version of updating were to be implemented, the measurement would have to be operationalized with respect to a current recommender session and generated dynamically. This entails much more computing effort than fixing the variable values in retrospect – as with mining the session logs or as has been done in the DieToRecs system usage study – and is unrealistic for making an initial system prototype operational.

5. The update cycle must be made dependent on the amount of change expected in the system environment. A minimum number of sessions completed is one criterion for closing a training interval. It should be complemented by others such as seasonal change or major alterations in the supply data repositories ('catalogues').

Before discussing the suggestions in Table 9.1 it is instructive to demonstrate the amount of redundancy in the original data-set of the decision style variables. Figure 9.3 exhibits the dendrogram of a hierarchical clustering, where the style variables are the clustered objects. Each variable appears twice. The first series of measurements named 'earlier or later' is recoded compared to the original DieToRecs study, where 1 = earlier, 0 = remained unspecified and –1 = later. The second series 'fixed or variable' is also recoded into new values, where 1 = fixed, 0 = remained unspecified and –1 = variable. The dissimilarities (Euclidean distances; 'height' in Fig. 9.3) among the 59 variables are calculated over the 201 respondents available in the sample. The ultrametric of the complete-linkage clustering is very robust vis-à-vis the dissimilarity measure employed.[4] The hierarchy in Fig. 9.3 reveals that there are several pairs and groups of style variables with very similar behaviour over the respondents.

Table 9.1 draws a compromise between the aforementioned selection criteria. The variables selected are in bold; for some of them either the 'earlier or later' or the 'fixed or variable' versions, and for others both versions, are required. As many as 31 variables from the original set are suggested for the routine updating of the decision styles, while 28 variables can be discarded.

The variables selected in Table 9.1 should be measured as follows, where the values apply to one particular session log:

- Each series (1) style variable $^{(1)}S_i$ resulting from a feature F_i, $i = 1, \dots n$, specified during a session attains a rank number r_i. The r_i are initialized with zero and assigned rank values in increasing order according to the sequence of the user's specification of the F_i. Ties are admissible as simultaneous specifications may happen when an incomplete *TravelWish* gets complemented with the default values of a case from the reference set of similar cases.
- Compute the median m of the r_i.

---

[4] Alternatively, the Pearson correlations r transformed into $1 - r$ resulting in dissimilarities $0 \leq d \leq 2$ may be used.

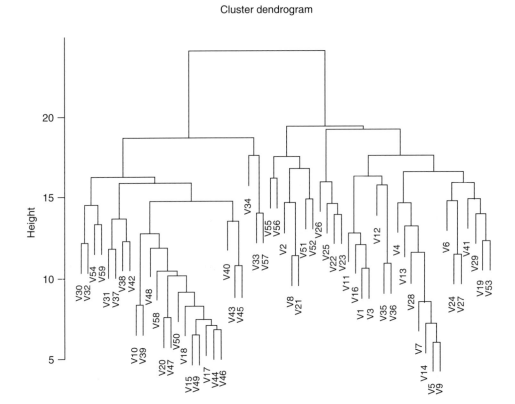

Fig. 9.3. Redundancy in the decision style variables.

$$
^{(1)}S_i = \begin{cases} 1, & \text{if } 0 < r_i < m \\ -1, & \text{if } r_i \geq m \\ 0, & \text{if } r_i = 0 \end{cases}
$$

The values of the style variables of the second series $^{(2)}S_i$ depend on the F_i having been specified and modified by the user during the session or not. Let the number of specifications and respecifications be s_i, then:

$$
^{(2)}S_i = \begin{cases} 1, & \text{if } s_i = 1 \\ -1, & \text{if } s_i > 1 \\ 0, & \text{else} \end{cases}
$$

$(^{(1)}S_1, \ldots, ^{(1)}S_n, {}^{(2)}S_1, \ldots, {}^{(2)}S_n)$ describes the session in terms of information-processing variables and is input to the vector quantization procedure suggested below for generating the user classes named 'decision styles'.

The 31 recommended style variables from the user sessions are input into a vector quantization procedure for classification. The method suggested for partitioning the respondents into decision styles is called Topology Representing Network (TRN) (Martinetz and Schulten, 1994; Mazanec, 1999, 2001). The TRN is based on the 'neural gas' algorithm by Martinetz *et al.* (1993), which is an efficient partitioning method capable of online learning. However, it is still subject to the old and intricate 'number of clusters' problem that cannot easily be solved automatically without a human interface for evaluating alternative solutions with differing number of subsets ('clusters'). This means that for every new update run a human analyst would have to go through several alternative solutions with a different number of decision styles and select the one with the highest face validity. This task may be automated by adopting one of the recent developments in adaptive partitioning. The Dynamic Topology Representing Network (DTRN) proposed by Si *et al.* (2000) also learns to increase the number of subsets if the need arises or shrink the number if some subsets prove to be superfluous. There is only one 'vigilance' parameter that governs the sensitivity of the partitioning process. Occasional recalibration will still be required for the DTRN. Readers interested in a more rigorous treatment of these new 'adaptive' procedures are referred to the outline of the DTRN in the Appendix.

In principle, the updating of the decision styles via the DTRN can take place online, processing each usable recommender session as soon as it arrives as input. The contextual interpretation, however, needs human judgement and evaluation. One may introduce a monitoring scheme as follows:

- to issue an early warning signal when the most recent style set has moved 'far' away from the styles underlying the current user interface; or
- to verify that the style set proves to be stable. 'Stable' does not allow for a trend, either in the number or in the profiles of the decision styles though they may oscillate around a long-term solution.

The analysts then will have to decide how to modify the sequencing and interrogation instruments of the system. Mere changes in the relative frequency of the decision styles and temporary changes in the composition of their characteristic attributes need not be reflected in the user interface.

3.2 Learning the trip attribute weights and optimizing the trip matching process

This chapter suggests employing neurocomputing methodology to carry out the learning operations of the two submodels of: (i) language bridging and matching; and (ii) choice. Two major NNW methods, which are instrumental in fulfilling these learning tasks, are Support Vector Machines (SVMs) and Multilayer Perceptrons (MLP). The SVMs are based on Statistical Learning Theory. They have proved to be valuable tools for preference learning (Herbrich *et al.*, 1999) and text categorization and information filtering (Christianini and Taylor, 2000, 150 ff.; see Raudys, 2000 for a criticism). MLP is the routine 'workhorse' of neural model builders for a wide area of applications (Bishop, 1995, 116 ff.). If the feedforward architecture of the MLP is combined with backpropagation learning, it forms a fairly risk-free learning machine. If there is something to learn, i.e. the users exhibit more than just random behaviour, a properly designed and data-fed MLP will learn it. In particular, the system should be able to estimate the importance weights of the trip attributes in determining the tourist's choice of a destination or trip product.

The adaptation procedures outlined in this section are not the only choice available from the neurocomputing tool kit.[5] The methods selected are intended to complement other methodology such as the learning principles foreseen in a CBR approach. The objective is to estimate the importance weights of the individual trip attributes (features) for the user's acceptance of a trip profile (*TravelBag*). Feature weights are also required in the CBR approach. But these are two different aspects of neurocomputing and CBR learning of product attribute or feature weights; more specifically:

1. CBR weights result from the feature value frequencies found in similar cases of the reference set. Network weights are derived from the users' response to a finalized trip offered in terms of choice or intention to choose; and

2. CBR weights only depend on the existence of an appropriate reference set of cases. The usability of the network weights depends on the users' prior assignment to a homogeneous user group such as a decision style. The assignment cannot be made unless a sufficient number of style variables have been collected during a session (or the session deals with a registered user); 'sufficient' means open to experimentation with real-world data.

Therefore, the network-gained weights are more closely connected to the promotional targets of a counselling system, but they are harder to get and retrieve.

The neurocomputing methodology is just an alternative and less common way of estimating parameters. One should be aware that the underlying consumer behaviour model does not differ from what is standard reasoning in marketing science. The most widespread 'user model' derived from the mainstream of consumer research is the binomial logit (BNL) or multinomial logit (MNL) specification. It relates the perceived product attributes to the probability of purchasing or choosing a particular buying alternative. The typical application comprises a number of rivalling product classes or brands, where the consumers have to decide whether to make a purchase in this class and what brand to choose. For a travel counselling system the range of choice alternatives is not as strictly defined as for branded products. Counselling and recommendation rather assist the user in gradually establishing a preferred trip profile, sometimes from scratch and sometimes by modifying partially acceptable offers. Normally, the user can never be certain

---

[5] Note that there are other NNW architectures that might be considered such as Grossberg's Adaptive Resonance Theory (see Carpenter and Grossberg, 1995) and an ART1 application to web user classification (Rangarajan *et al.*, 2004).

of the number and contents of further 'trips offered' the system is going to generate. Since the user tends to deal with one trip profile at a time, the multi-variate model is pointless and the much simpler BNL is appropriate. There-fore, if not buying ($c_j = 0$) is assumed to yield a utility v of zero, the choice probability $Pr(c_j = 1)$ of consumer j to buy or choose the trip offered is

$$Pr(c_j = 1 \mid a_j) = \frac{\exp(a'_j w)}{1 + \exp(a'_j w)} \tag{9.1}$$

where the weighted sum of n (compensatory) attributes $a'_j = (a_{j1}, ..., a_{jn})$ gives the utility v_j:

$$v_j = a'_j w = \sum_{i=1}^{n} w_i a_{ij} \tag{9.2}$$

Equation 9.2 assumes that the attributes a_{ij} are evaluative criteria and express some goal-satisfying capability. This is true for attitudinal items and other value-related criteria based on the consumers' product perceptions. Another behavioural interpretation of the a_{ij} is known as the ideal point of ideal vector model (Roberts and Lilien, 1993; Hruschka, 1996):

$$v_j = \left(\sum_{i=1}^{n} w_i \left| a_{ij \ offered} - a_{ij \ desired} \right|^d \right)^{1/d} \tag{9.2.1}$$

with Minkowski $d > 0$, or, more general,

$$v_j = g \left(h(w_i, a_{ij \ offered}, a_{ij \ desired}) \right) \tag{9.2.2}$$

Equation 9.2.2 has a special appeal for recommendation systems such as DieToRecs, as the CBR approach works on corresponding sets of feature values for the *TravelWish* and the *TravelBag*. The same similarity measures that are developed for the CBR procedure can be employed for computing the utility generating $a_{offered} - a_{desired}$ pairs of feature values. The weights w_i, of course, will still be subject to network learning, but no separate feature values have to be calculated for the NNW approach.

In real markets there is no error-free estimation of the deterministic utility v, so the observed utility u always includes a stochastic component such that

$$u_j = v_j + \varepsilon_j \tag{9.3}$$

where the ε values are independent and identically distributed and $f(\varepsilon)$ is double-exponential (extreme-valued) (Roberts and Lilien, 1993, p. 33). No such distribution assumptions are required for the NNW procedure.

The cognitive algebra of the traveller is likely to contain non-compensa-tory choice rules (Bettman *et al.*, 1998). This means that for some trip attributes travellers request minimum thresholds and thus are not prepared to trade off a highly satisfying value of one attribute against a less attractive one of another attribute. These non-compensatory decision rules are hard to capture with the usual linear utility functions, which make up the deterministic part in the choice modelling tradition of random utility theory (see Equation 9.2 above and Crouch and Louviere, 2001 and van Middelkoop, 2001, pp. 28–36 for an introduction and overview). NNWs have demonstrated that they are capable of managing threshold-based decision rules (West *et al.*, 1997). Hruschka (2001) has successfully combined the traditional MNL approach with an NNW model to account for non-linearity in the utility functions; he has also developed new interpretation tools for MLP networks that may replace the elasticities in conventional econometric modelling (Hruschka and Probst, 2001).

Consider the comprehensive model first. The lower part of Fig. 9.4 is the language bridging submodel (1), the upper part sketches the choice submodel (2). An MLP reads a number of input variables, weights and accumulates them into its 'hidden units' (transfer function), squashes the summed values in each hidden unit through a non-linear activation function (usually a sigmoid or a hyperbolic tangent) and forwards these activations to the output layer. By adapting the weights the MLP learns to map an input into a desired output pattern. Subnetwork (1) learns how to translate the trip desired described in colloquial language into an 'expert' trip profile that can be matched with various alternatives of a trip offered. Examples for the sort of variables involved in subnetwork (1) training are:

- 'luxury' or 'nature' as input items of the trip desired, corresponding to:
- Hotel Category 5-star or Farm House as output items of the trip offered.

Subnetwork (2) learns which trip attributes to what extent determine the acceptance or rejection of a trip offered, i.e. a choice probability depending on a weighted mixture of trip attributes. Examples of the sort of variables involved in the subnetwork (2) training are:

- the feature values of the standard items of the trip offered (i.e. location, accommodation, attractions or events and activities) as input, contributing to:
- the user's decision (choice) to save this combination of items as output.

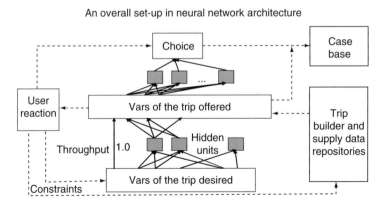

Fig. 9.4. The two submodels combined.

The input data for the network training would be taken from the trips offered collected in the case base. The most complete trip offered template defines the length of the trip offered vector. Symbolic features are transformed into dummy variables.

The interpretation of the output layer of the submodel (2) depends on how far the recommender system prototype advances in terms of booking options. *Choice* is a place-holder here. The *choice* variable may be a scalar or vector and may denote any counselling success criteria enumerated earlier. Choice = 1, for example, indicates an actual purchase if the system allows for selling trip products. Alternatively, if the system is limited to destination information (DIS) functions, choice is interpreted as a willingness-to-buy indicator or a height-of-preference value for a current trip offered approximating the trip desired.

The optimal number of hidden units in the network has to be determined by varying the size of the hidden layer and examining the network's ability to generalize, i.e. make predictions for previously unseen input data. Given a sample of session data the activation patterns of the hidden units assist in detecting symptomatic session profiles ('types') of the trip desired (submodel 1) or the trip offered (submodel 2). If, for example, only high and low activations are to be distinguished, a network with, say, five hidden units will reveal up to $2^5 = 32$ types of user–product interaction. Such taxonomy is highly relevant information for market segmentation and package planning in tourism marketing. Owing to the large number of weights to be estimated in such a network a sample size of about 5000 trip profiles will have to be extracted from user sessions before the network training can reasonably start.

Submodel (1) is indicative of a counselling or recommender prototype with the scope and flexibility required for a level 4 system (cf. Fig. 9.1). It moves one step towards understanding the inexperienced user. Improving the natural language-processing capabilities of the World Wide Web (WWW) is a highly topical issue and many research laboratories worldwide are focusing upon it. One of the promising approaches is the Semantic Web concept, based on domain-specific ontologies and machine-readable metadata (Maedche and Staab, 2002). In principle, the Semantic Web Mining tools tackle the same language-bridging problem as the mapping machine addressed in submodel (1) of Fig. 9.4. The rich functionality of a level 4 user interface is out of reach given the funds normally made available for system development. Submodel (1), therefore, is not treated further here.

Submodel (2) exploits the user reactions to learn about the importance of the individual product attributes. Any learning depends on the user feedback. The TripMatcher (Delgado and Davidson, 2002) is an example of a recommendation system that employs an incremental rating scheme to evaluate each individual trip item after the user has responded to it. The methodology preferred for submodel (2) determines the item weights indirectly by estimating their contribution to the user feedback prompted by a bundle of items. If the language-bridging submodel (1) is not part of the system, a simpler and direct access to the *desired–offered* problem comes to mind. It has already been indicated in the discussion about Equations 2.1 and 2.2. Before applying the NNW architecture, a number of processing issues must be covered first:

- The raw material for network training originates from the case base. In cases comprising the trip desired and trips offered, user and session data are preprocessed into training vectors. They consist of the distances between the trip desired and the trip offered feature values, which also contribute to measuring the trip desired–trip offered similarity in the CBR approach.
- Therefore, it is no longer necessary to construct separate network-usable trip attributes that are either dichotomous (e.g. domestic–abroad), binary-coded dummy variables (i.e. $\in \{0, 1\}$; consider, for example, meal arrangement), or real-valued and rescaled to the magnitude of the $[0, 1]$ interval (e.g. travel budget). Even the symbolic features defined in the CBR approach need not be transformed into dummy variables.
- The trip variables will be complemented by elementary user characteristics where they become known to the system (e.g. country of residence, age, gender). It is open to experimentation whether these criteria become network input or just remain external information for calibrating separate networks tailored to specific user groups.
- Separate networks may also be needed for each fundamentally different session (e.g. one seeking travel products for resort vs city trips, or summer vs winter vacation). Each decision style, too, may require a separate network to achieve acceptable prediction results. The usefulness of all these a priori segments cannot be judged theoretically and is open to analysis and experimentation with real-world data.
- In addition to experimenting with a priori segments advanced analytical tools are also capable of detecting response-based user segments during the parameter estimation (see the demonstration example in the Appendix to this chapter).
- Where prior hypotheses are readily available the full connectivity of a standard MLP may be replaced by selected relationships between the input variables, hidden units and output nodes of the network (see Davies *et al.*, 1999 for an application to travel research).
- The system builds the training data-sets from the user sessions surviving phases 1 and 2 (*filtering* and *specification*) and involving the judgement of items offered (filling the *TravelBag* in CBR terminology); i.e. the system has gained enough knowledge about the user's trip desired to retrieve promising trip profiles from reference cases.
- The system records the trip profile the user has accumulated in a session as part of his choice set. Each session leading to a trip offered worth of getting stored in the case base provides network training material.
- An additional similarity measure is suggested for analysing trip profiles (or cases) with numerical and dummy coded attributes:

$$s = \frac{x'y}{x'x + y'y - x'y}, \quad 0 \leq s \leq 1 \tag{9.4}$$

where x and y are the two attribute vectors $x' = (x_1, \ldots, x_n)$ and $y' = (y_1, \ldots, y_n)$ for a pair of trips. s works for binary and quantitative measurement levels and penalizes an increase in similarity just because of larger x and y values. It also ignores zero matching (i.e. both corresponding attributes are absent) as a source of similarity gain. Where attribute weights have already been learned they are easily incorporated into Equation 9.4.

Recommendations that proved to be successful for user i are likely to work for user j if i and j share the same or have a very similar profile. The raw material for calculating similarities may be the items selected by a user measured against the number of visits where the item could have been chosen. Delgado and Davidson (2002) give an example called the *attribute/interest ratio* v_k for attribute k and a similarity measure s_{ij} based on the normalized vector product of the ratios for a pair of users (p. 9). The attributes have a different weight h_k, which is considered to depend on the depth of the attribute in the domain tree. Details are not revealed, but it is obviously the underlying idea to attach higher weights to more specific attributes. That is, if two travellers choose a 'four-star hotel' as an accommodation, they are more similar than two others who choose 'hotel' without further hotel category specification.

The weighting principle in TripMatcher has face validity but it still originates from a production-oriented rationale. From the marketing perspective, there is only one legitimate source of determining attribute weights: the impact of attributes on consumer choice. That is exactly what the NNW approach for submodel (2) is aiming at. However, the NNW estimates of the attribute weights do not make much sense if they are derived from an undiscriminating selection of user sessions. Separate networks are likely to be necessary for homogeneous user subgroups. The precise meaning of 'homogeneous' is subject to experimentation with the decision styles being only one of the classification hypotheses. Other hypotheses relate to fundamentally different types of tourism submarkets with little competitive overlap (such as city vs resort tourism or short vs long trips). As the NNW training never starts before a session ends, there should be no problem in classifying the session prior to channelling its data into one of several specialized networks.

Within a priori defined user subgroups the cognitive processing of the trip attributes may still occur in a different manner. By monitoring the activations of the hidden units of the MLP the analyst may detect typical patterns of the users' cognitive algebra. The sample application in Section 3.4 demonstrates how sessions or user classes ('types') are derived from the activation patterns. One cannot yet predict whether and how this will also contribute to improving the dynamic deployment of information in advanced versions of a system.

In parallel, a second and parametric analysis of user heterogeneity is suggested. As it can be based on the BNL model (1)–(3), the extension to a generalized linear mixture (GLIM) model is straightforward (Fahrmeir and Tutz, 1997, 24 ff.). Under the GLIM philosophy the acceptance or rejection (choice c_j) of user j of a trip offered originates from a population mixture of segments $s = 1, \ldots, S$, where each segment emerges in proportion π_s (Wedel and Kamakura, 1998, 76 ff.), where π_s reflects the relative size of user segment s in the total user population:

$$\sum_{s=1}^{S} \pi_s = 1, \quad 0 \le \pi_s \le 1 \tag{9.5}$$

In a mixture choice model the density function of c_j results from the weighted sum of the conditional density functions for the individual segments $s = 1, \ldots, S$:

$$f(c_j \mid \pi, \theta) = \sum_{s=1}^{S} \pi_s \; f_s(c_j \mid \theta_s) \tag{9.6}$$

Vector θ_s contains the segment-specific parameters that govern the consumers' choice and includes the attribute weights w of Equation 9.2. These weights and the segment sizes π_s are simultaneously determined via maximum likelihood estimation. At the same time the mixture model estimates the *posterior probabilities* of belonging to each of the consumer segments (i.e. a *latent class*) for each individual. This is equivalent to *fuzzy clustering* results. A crisp clustering solution may be easily achieved by classifying the individuals according to their maximum posterior. The parameter estimates are *response-based* in a sense that a consumer's affiliation with a segment corresponds with the (segment-specific) weights he or she attaches to the various trip attributes while forming an acceptance or rejection reaction.

3.4 Prerequisites and usage of NNW results

The major difficulty in implementing learning is not the training algorithm itself, but the screening and preparation of the input data. First, the training relies on fairly advanced and complete sessions that led to trip offers in the selection or ordering phase. A couple of arguments regarding feature coding are offered here. They may also be worth considering for a CBR approach. A coding scheme that preserves as much information residing in the session data as possible is needed. As the NNW is a non-parametric mapping machine, it permits more parsimonious ways of coding than conventional estimators. If there is a meaningful ordering in a trip attribute it may be transformed in the following manner, which avoids abundant dummy variables:

Hotel category, accommodation quality level	Value
one or two stars, low level	0.20
three stars, medium level	0.40
four stars, high level	0.60
five stars, deluxe	0.80
not categorized, unspecified	0.00

For mutually exclusive and nominal variable values an ordinary dummy coding scheme serves the purpose. Consider an example for the trip product element 'meal arrangements':

Meal arrangements	SC	BO	HB	FB
Self-catering	1	0 (or −1)	0 (or −1)	0 (or −1)
Breakfast only	0 (or −1)	1	0 (or −1)	0 (or −1)
Half-board	0 (or −1)	0 (or −1)	1	0 (or −1)
Full-board	0 (or −1)	0 (or −1)	0 (or −1)	1
Unspecified	0	0	0	0

Most trip attributes are sufficiently abstract to let coding make sense. Some are not. Generalization does not function with individual resort or hotel entities described by their 'brand names'. Hence, the trip offered in the user interface does not fully correspond to the trip offered that qualifies as a training data vector for the network learning. This problem is not yet satisfactorily solved in the CBR methodology. If the destination feature were to convey any utility-related meaning, it would be imperative to suppress the 'brand' names (i.e. symbolic values) and to use classes of homogeneous destinations instead. In other words, the general implications of a 'brand' must be translated into specific image characteristics. Key criteria are high or low awareness or popularity and social status, or high or low price expectation. A workable approach to tackle this problem is to assign each destination or resort a prespecified image category such as: 'lower-class, low-priced, well-known or popular seaside resort', …, 'middle-class, medium-price, widely unknown alpine village', 'upper-class, cliquish or snobby, high-priced, well-known mountain resort'. The need for classification by an expert or consumer jury is not specific for preprocessing the data for network learning. It also arises in the semantic-based similarity search in advanced Vague Query Systems (see an illustrative example for event search with VQS reported by Palkoska *et al.*, 2002, 440 ff.).

Once an NNW has been trained, it may forecast the choice probability of the current trip offered to the user at any time. Its weight structure allows for *rule extraction*. This means that *if–then–else rules* may be inferred from the weight connections (Taha and Ghosh, 1999). These rules account for the mutual dependency found in the impact of the input variables on trip product choice. Such rules have a practical usage for trip package optimization and development. NNWs also fulfil a pattern completion function. In a recommender system context this would be a network that maps the trip profiles onto themselves. Such an auto-associative NNW serves to replace the missing values of a similar but poorly specified trip desired and complement the profile with the most likely attributes. By doing this the system may also calculate reasonable default values to speed up the user dialogue during the specification phase.

The attribute weights learned by the choice submodel assist the system in several ways. They point to the meaningful attributes to be used in the similarity calculation. Similarity values are indispensable for the system to choose suitable cases during the *selection/ordering* phase of a consulting session. They also contribute to the priority sequencing of the system queries; questions regarding more important product attributes are raised earlier than less important ones. The CBR approach also comprises learning about the users' importance weights of the trip features. An appropriate source of importance information is the frequencies of the features in the reference set of similar cases. While the network-generated weights exist explicitly for certain classes of users, the frequency-derived weights are created casewise once a partially filled trip desired and/or trip offered has become available in a session.

The knowledge of the network's associative memory also helps improving the system's personalization strategies. Web personalization may rely on simple content-based techniques or more sophisticated collaborative filtering techniques. Advanced methodology such as *partial evaluation* functions most effectively if a website is hierarchically organized (Ramakrishnan, 2000). The 'natural' levels of the hierarchy obviously correspond to the priority sequencing mentioned above.

Diagnosing the similarity of visiting patterns or counselling sessions for various users is a valid web-mining technique. It may be developed into a refined and automated procedure to detect information and decision styles. Order-sensitive measures such as the *sequence alignment method* has been proposed to determine the similarity of the web page sequences derived out of user log files (Hay *et al.*, 2003). Apparently, the results are more meaningful if the default sequence suggested by the system corresponds to the importance of the information needs felt by the majority of users. That is exactly what the NNW learns from analysing success and failure sessions.

4. A Demonstration Example of the NNW Learning of Trip Attribute Weights

A sample application of NNW learning[6] serves to illustrate the basic concepts and procedures. Consider a sample of 1000 tourist consumers with unknown preferences. The travellers' evaluations of four alternative trip packages are measured with 12 binary attributes (features) that are either present (which is good) or absent (which is bad). Each traveller chooses the trip package

---

[6] The model and data originate from the author's participation in the Special Research Program on 'Adaptive Systems and Modeling in Economics and Management Science' (SFB010). The programme started in 1997 and the responsibility has been the Research Initiative on Market Segmentation and Product Positioning. In particular, the author's group has been in charge of establishing an Artificial Consumer Market for agent-based simulation experiments (Buchta and Mazanec, 2001). A number of companies (managerial 'agents') compete on the artificial market with properties known to the experimental designer but unknown to the firms. The company agents perform analytical and strategic functions to survive and maximize accumulated profits.

that comes closest to their aspiration levels. So the challenge is to learn about the tourist preferences by watching their actual choices of trip profiles and by indirectly extracting the preferential patterns (preferred features). This is equivalent to the mystery to be solved by the submodel (2) of the travel recommender system, except the number of choice alternatives. There are always four alternatives in this example, while the recommender system will just need to differentiate between trip profiles liked or chosen and disliked or not chosen.

Figure 9.5 shows the neural architecture for a three-layer perceptron with 48 input variables for the features of four trip packages. There are four hidden units and the (output) choice probabilities for the four trip alternatives. The boxes denote the variables on the input layer ('In'), the hidden units ('Hidden1') and the output vars ('Out'). Unit 1 is a 'Bias' term comparable to the intercept in ordinary regression models. Each connecting line represents a weight to be estimated during network training. The left upper panel shows the reduction of the root mean squared error (RMS) over several thousand training iterations. Once trained, the net is expected to produce choice probabilities p_k for the trip options that sum up to unity. Therefore, it employs the normalized exponential activation function:

$$p_k = \frac{\exp(o_k)}{\sum_{k=1}^{4} \exp(o_k)} \qquad (9.7)$$

(also known as the *softmax* rule; Bishop, 1995, p. 238) to rescale the values of the units o_k in the output layer. High activations of the hidden units 51, 52 and 53 in Fig. 9.4 obviously lead to choosing trip alternative 3 (output unit 56). The activation pattern in the hidden layer in Fig. 9.5 (50 *lo*, 51–53 *hi*, or: <lo hi hi hi>) is one of $2^4 = 16$ possible combinations, if only low and high are to be distinguished. This means that a person perceiving the four trip profiles with all features present, except 6–9, 13, 23, 28, 29 and 40–44, belongs to a segment or tourist type <lo hi hi hi>. A cluster analysis based on the activation values classifies the tourists into homogeneous classes according to how they view the trip alternatives (see below). This is a response-based classification as the network's backpropagation learning algorithm adapts the weights top down, i.e. commencing with the errors produced in the output layer.

Figure 9.5 is for visualization only. The actual calculations for a more parsimonious 48-3-4 model are performed with the R system.[7] Out of five replication runs for the network training the one with the highest prediction rate of the actual choices is selected. $(490 + 29 + 296 + 32)/1000$ or 84.7% of

---

[7] *R* is the freeware equivalent of the *Splus* system (see http://www.r–project.org/). The interested reader may obtain the *R* script for the NaiveNeural agent applied here. It uses the *R nnet* function by Venables and Ripley (1994; see Ripley, 1996).

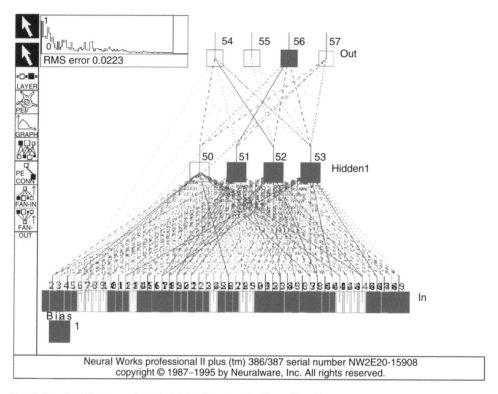

54 | 55 | 56 | 57 Out

50 | 51 | 52 | 53 Hidden1

RMS error 0.0223

LAYER
PE
GRAPH
PE CONN
FAN-IN
FAN-OUT

Bias 1

In

Fig. 9.5. Architecture of a 48-4-4 MLP network. Note: The NeuralWorks software (Neural-Ware, 1993) has been used for portraying the three-layer perceptron, not for the calculations.

correct choice predictions were attained.[8] Figure 9.6 exhibits the pairwise scatter plots of the output values of the choice variables for the four trip alternatives. There are $4 \times (4-1)/2 = 6$ bivariate scatterplots. The 'var' numbers in the panels of the main diagonal denote the row and column variables for each diagram. For example, in the lower diagonal part of the multipanel plot the var1 values increase from bottom to top and the var2–4 values grow from left to right. The data points neatly avoid the hi–hi (right upper) corners of the probability space, indicating a large majority of conclusive predictions.

```
          NNET predictions
          pct correct: 82.5
          pct correct: 84.7
          pct correct: 84.7
          pct correct: 84.7
          pct correct: 84.7
```

[8] The percentage correctly classified in a hold-out sample will be taken for a real-world application.

		Expected			
O		1	2	3	4
b					
s	1	490	4	6	0
e					
r	2	0	29	71	0
v					
e	3	3	0	296	1
d	4	65	0	3	32

In the next step one would like to check whether the activation patterns of the hidden units tell something about traveller types and how symptomatic or 'typical' these patterns are. To reiterate, such a traveller type is defined in terms of his or her perceptions of trip attributes and the way they affect his or her choice. Figure 9.7 shows the bivariate scatterplots of the activation values for the $4 \times (4 - 1)/2 = 6$ possible pairs constructed from the four hidden units.

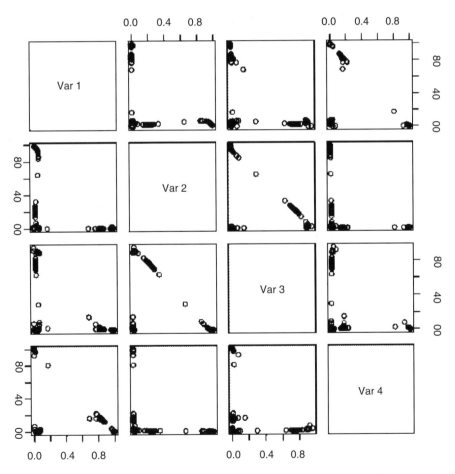

Fig. 9.6. Bivariate scatterplots for the NNW predictions of the four choice probabilities.

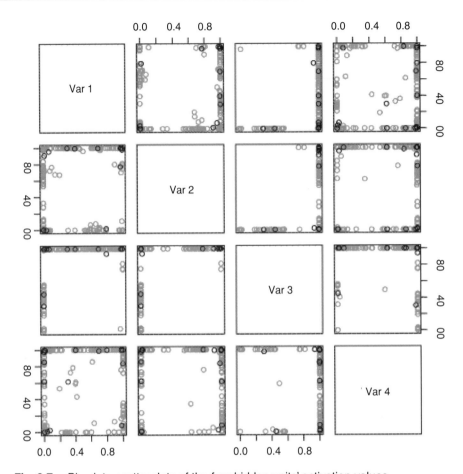

Fig. 9.7. Bivariate scatterplots of the four hidden units' activation values.

Owing to the logistic transformation applied to the output of the hidden units, the values are warped against the borders of the reduced space.[9] Only if low and high activations are distinguished, the four hidden units allow for $2^4 = 16$ different patterns. Not all of these combinations are needed as, for example, var1 = lo/var3 = hi or var2 = lo/var3 = hi do not really occur. On the other hand, intermediate values arise quite frequently, for example, for var2 or var3. To support a reasonable number of traveller types a distance matrix for the activation points and a subsequent hierarchical cluster solution are computed.

A complete linkage clustering generates the ultrametric shown in the dendrogram of Fig. 9.8. A number of 16 clusters make sense, so a K-means fixed point algorithm (Strasser, 2000) was used to compute the centroids to arrive at a traveller classification (typology). If the classification is meaningful, there must be a distinct association between the activation cluster membership 1–16 and the actual choice of a trip package 1–4. Indeed, the majority

---

[9] The four-dimensional 'hidden' space may be interpreted in analogy to a reduced space after a principal components compression of the 48-dimensional input data.

Cluster dendrogram

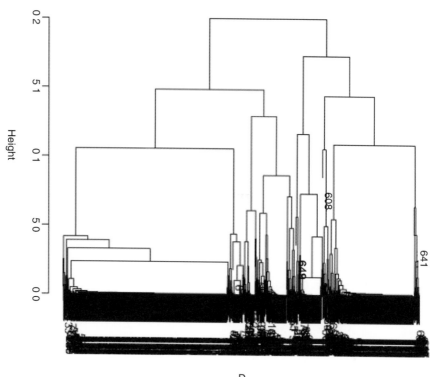

D
hclust (*,"complete")

Fig. 9.8. Hierarchical clustering of the activation patterns.

of certain trip choices happen within particular activation patterns, foremost 10 and 11 for the packages 1 and 3:

	1	2	3	4
1	0	10	0	0
2	1	2	0	39
3	7	0	0	0
4	0	19	0	1
5	53	0	27	1
6	0	30	34	0
7	15	1	19	1
8	10	0	0	1
9	0	0	7	0
10	393	1	1	51
11	0	20	204	1
12	0	0	8	0
13	13	0	0	0
14	0	17	0	0
15	0	0	0	5
16	8	0	0	0

A final step a manager would like to apply for any analysis of product or trip profiles refers to the weights of the attributes in determining choice. Given the full connectivity of the network one cannot simply interpret the individual weights or combine the weights along a sequence of network links. But the NNW, at least, permits the computation of pseudo-elasticities. Assume for a moment that all attributes were present (set to 1). For, say, trip package 3 a choice probability of 0.53 would result. Then, remove each of the attributes one by one (as if they were absent and hence set to 0). Clearly, the absence of the product attributes 12, 9, 11 and 10 damages the chance of getting purchased most dramatically. At least for this consumer target group it is desirable to include these attributes in a brand profile or trip offered:

```
Trip 3 average purchase prob: 0.5252902
if all attributes present.

Trip 3 average purchase prob | if attribute... were missing
        0.5794143                            1
        0.5637794                            2
        0.4790913                            3
        0.4410085                            4
        0.4022998                            5
        0.3961254                            6
        0.3368885                            7
        0.2309247                            8
        0.1384029                            9
        0.1649082                           10
        0.1520305                           11
        0.0851714                           12
```

5. Conclusions and Hints for Future Research

According to the basic marketing principle of uncompromising customer orientation a counselling system ought to serve its users by: (i) respecting their preferred styles of information acquisition and usage; and (ii) producing choice alternatives that match the users' desires in the important attributes. Varying information handling patterns and importance weights put the system under learning stress. The widely practised approach of providing personalized access for system-registered users is not considered a satisfying solution. The 'real' challenge arises for novel man–machine interactions where the user has not yet agreed (or will never agree) to get registered and to establish a personalized system account.

Fortunately, the world of consumers does not appear to be filled with entirely different and totally idiosyncratic individuals. Members of the consumer population tend to share some features with some of their fellow consumers, opening a road for efficient market segmentation strategies.

A counselling system may cash in on this user property by adapting to a limited number of 'decision styles' small enough to be monitored and correctly identified after a few interrogations. Pattern recognition procedures (e.g. DTRN detailed in the Appendix) help serve this purpose.

Bridging the gap between the user and travel expert languages is the toughest and largely unresolved of all the learning tasks. While neural classifiers are likely to have a stance in this problem area, workable prototypes are not yet available. However, the 'semantic web' is a field of lively research activities and seems to be making progress.

Also, a counselling system cannot compile recommendations efficiently unless it 'knows' about the likely importance of the trip attributes for a user. Updating the importance weights of the travel product attributes turns out to be a straightforward task for online learning with NNW methods. Although the functioning has been demonstrated in principle, there is still a lack of large-scale field experience. One may hope for conclusive results when some of the recommender system providers begin to offer system sites that are – though experimental – fed with real-world product data.

More than once an unresolved problem arose during the foregoing exposition of learning functions and the ways of getting them implemented. There is plenty of work for subsequent research projects; for example, the system designers are in urgent need of further empirical analyses such as:

- examining the usefulness of alternative computation schemes for trip attribute (feature) weights, e.g. comparing the NNW and CBR rooted techniques;
- extracting the reduced set of variables for determining the user decision styles and monitoring the size and composition of the styles by DTRN techniques;
- relating the *offered-desired* discrepancies of a trip profile to its chance of being selected for a successful response such as saving or retrieval, ordering further information, reservation or booking;
- using off-line updating to calibrate an NNW model that may be adopted for later online training;
- experimenting with alternative NNW specifications and user segment-specific samples of training data-sets;
- applying both a priori defined categories of user sessions and user types as well as response-based user segmentation with the activation patterns aroused by the trip profiles; and
- making comparisons with parametric BNL models including mixture regression models to detect group-specific user judgements.

Discussants in a debate on automated counselling often raise the question whether such systems are intended to, or actually will, replace a human adviser. This is equivalent to asking whether school children still need to be taught mental arithmetic while using computers and pocket calculators. The ideas presented here with regard to increasing adaptivity may contribute to making future counselling systems a little smarter than they appear today. This amount of self-adaptation is yet unspectacular compared with a trained human consultant with the appropriate product data repositories at his or her fingertips.

Chapter Summary

Adaptivity is an intricate concept operationally defined by specifying a sequence of learning capabilities. Advanced versions of adaptive counselling systems ought to serve even users only faintly aware of what they are actually looking for. This chapter introduces methodology instrumental in developing systems that adapt to the users' information acquisition and processing patterns. Judging from several decades of market segmentation research, these patterns are expected to be group-specific, though varying over time. Thus, the task turns out to require mechanisms for monitoring these user 'decision styles', for learning their fuzzy language and for updating the weights of their decision criteria.

Appendix: Brief Outline of the Dynamic Topology Representing Network

The DTRN was proposed by Si *et al.* (2000). A simplified explanation of its working principles is elaborated here. Like its non-dynamic counterpart, the TRN, the DTRN encodes a data manifold $\mathbf{X}$ with probability distribution $P(x)$ into a finite set of reference vectors ('prototypes', centroids) while respecting the topological properties of the observed data. The quantization techniques that are topologically sensitive are characterized by monitoring the neighbourhood structure of their prototypes. This information is stored in an adjacency matrix with zero/one entries and gets updated in each training iteration. Unlike the popular K-means cluster procedure, the neighbourhood structure in the (D)TRN permits indirect updates of the centroids. In analogy to the fuzzy K-means or overlapping K-centroids clustering (Chaturvedi *et al.*, 1997) this increases the robustness of the quantization results.

The similarity between a data point and a prototype is measured by the Euclidean distance d between the *i*th prototype's coordinates ('weights'), vector $\mathbf{w}_i$ and an input data vector $\mathbf{x}$ with values $x_1, \ldots, x_V$

$$d_i = \|\mathbf{x} - \mathbf{w}_i\| = \left(\sum_{v=1}^{V} (x_v - w_{iv})^2 \right)^{1/2} \tag{A.1}$$

The TRN and DTRN were inspired by the Self-Organizing Map (Kohonen, 1982), which employs stochastic approximation ('training') to adapt its weight structure according to the distribution pattern of the input data. Each of the prototypes thus learns to represent a homogeneous subset of data vectors. In the DTRN the number of such prototypes is not predetermined as the training starts with just one prototype equal to an input vector randomly selected from the data-set **X**. Another randomly chosen data point **x** is compared with this first prototype $i = 1$ according to (A.1). If d_i fails to drop below the vigilance threshold ρ, the **x** becomes a second prototype $\mathbf{w}_g$.

Once there are three or more prototypes they begin to compete with each other such that the winner i^* with

$$\| \mathbf{x} - \mathbf{w}_{i^*} \| < \| \mathbf{x} - \mathbf{w}_i \|, \ \forall i, \tag{A.2}$$

and the co-winner i^{**} with

$$\| \mathbf{x} - \mathbf{w}_{i^{**}} \| < \| \mathbf{x} - \mathbf{w}_i \|, \ \forall i \neq i^*, \tag{A.3}$$

become eligible for a weight update. Before that the winner is subject to the vigilance test. If it fails, a new prototype g is introduced and takes the values of the current data point **x**. The adjacency matrix **S** indicating the connectivity among the prototypes is then updated in the following manner:

$$s_{gj} = \begin{cases} 1 & \text{if } j = i^* \\ 0 & \text{else} \end{cases} \tag{A.4}$$

$$t_{gj} = \begin{cases} 0 & \text{if } j = i^* \\ \infty & \text{else} \end{cases} \tag{A.5}$$

where t_{gj} is an age counter denoting the number of iterations covered since the creation or last refreshment of the connection s_{gj}.

If the winner i^* passes the vigilance test i^* and all its neighbours get updated by the following 'winner-takes-quota' learning rule:

$$\mathbf{w}_{i^*}(k) = s_{i,i} \ \lambda(k) \ \frac{\exp(-\eta(k) \ \|\mathbf{x}(k) - \mathbf{w}_{i^*}(k)\|^2)}{\displaystyle\sum_{j=1}^{L} s_{i,j} \ \exp(-\eta(k)\|\mathbf{x}(k) - \mathbf{w}_i(k)\|^2)} (\mathbf{x}(k) - \mathbf{w}_{i^*}(k)), \quad i = 1, \ldots, L \tag{A.6}$$

where $0 < \lambda(k) < 1$ is the learning rate that decays with the growing number of iterations $k = 0, 1, \ldots$; $\eta(k)$ is an annealing factor that increases during the training.

The last two steps in the DTRN procedure consider updating the connection lifetime record and the removal of superfluous prototypes. Age correction occurs via $t_{i,j} = t_{i,j} + 1$ and the removal of outdated connections, i.e. setting $s_{i,j} = 0$, happens for an age counter exceeding the lifetime, i.e. $t_{i,j} > t$. A prototype becomes redundant and is abolished if all its connections are zero.

The crucial parameter is the vigilance factor that controls the dynamic creation and demolition of prototypes. Si *et al.* suggest a schedule such as

$$\lambda = \lambda_0 \left(\frac{\lambda_1}{\lambda_0}\right)^{k/k_{max}} \qquad \text{with } \lambda_0 > \lambda_1 \tag{A.7}$$

and a maximum number of k_{max} iterations; this makes λ gradually decrease
from λ_0 to λ_1. The authors also provide ample evidence of the DTRN performance on synthetic data with known properties and thereby offer advice on
choosing meaningful parameter settings.

10 Narrative Design for Travel Recommender Systems

ULRIKE GRETZEL

1. Introduction

Travel is one of the top e-commerce categories and one of the most experiential and complex products sold online. Neither holistic sensory experience nor complexity lends themselves well to prevailing website design and its underlying computing structures. Consequently, tourism experiences are almost exclusively captured as pieces of pictorial or textual information that can be described in functional terms and, thus, easily translated into database structures. One would assume that the role of the interface is to reintegrate these information fragments into consistent wholes; however, online encounters of tourism information are currently restricted to interactions with interfaces that more or less directly mirror the ontology of the database systems to which they are connected. This dominance of the database perspective guiding travel recommender system design becomes apparent when looking at the search options and result displays these systems offer. Users are typically forced to express their preferences for certain aspects of travel destinations or other travel products and services as highly structured queries or choices among search options that more or less reflect the rows and columns in which the data are stored. Even when natural language query is supported, the structure of the output remains largely driven by database logic (Manovich, 2001). The resulting displays of bits and pieces of data in the form of item lists or collections of hyperlinks can only meet very specific, functional information needs and fail to reflect the complexity of the role tourism information plays in creating expectations and promoting travel experiences.

The goal of this chapter is to question the database approach in tourism interface design by reflecting on its limitations in terms of effectively conveying relevant information about holistic vacation experiences. As an alternative, an exploration of narratives as a means to organize and display tourism information in a way that can communicate the different aspects of travel experiences, including sensory and emotional components, is suggested. An integration of narrative principles is expected to lead to travel recommender systems that can better meet a multitude of informational needs, provide information that more closely matches human memory and communication patterns, support tourism decision-making throughout its various stages and increase user enjoyment of the recommendation process. In addition, narrative design is believed to enhance the persuasiveness of the recommendations provided by travel recommender systems.

2. Searching for Tourism Experiences

The enjoyment inherent in information search is a well-documented, self-oriented reward that can transform information search into a leisure experience in its own right (Bloch *et al.*, 1986). Mathwick and Rigdon (2004) report that flow and the experiential outcomes associated with it are relevant concepts in the study of online consumer behaviour, even when that behaviour is purposeful and goal-directed. Attitudes towards a firm's website and its brands appear enhanced when consumers participate in an engaging, enjoyable online experience. In addition, marketing and tourism scholars have argued that consumers often evaluate products more on experiential aspects than on 'objective' features such as price and availability (Vogt and Fesenmaier, 1998). Therefore, experiential information is not only entertaining and stimulating but also essential to the travel decision-making process as it allows consumers to understand and evaluate aspects of the travel product that cannot be easily described in functional terms or expressed as monetary values. Consequently, experiential information responds to the need for a holistic understanding of the specific travel experience to be evaluated. Despite the sequential nature of the travel decision-making process, whereby travellers move step by step through a series of hierarchically organized decision components, the information assimilated to serve as the basis for the various sub-decisions needs to eventually make sense as a whole (Fesenmaier and Jeng, 2000). Consumer decision-making usually involves trying to imagine the sequence of events that surrounds the purchase and consumption of a product or service and the consequences of its use (Adaval and Wyer, 1998). It is argued that information presented as unrelated items in a list or under separated categories makes it difficult for consumers to construct this cohesive picture of a travel experience and to evaluate how well such an experience would match their personal preferences. Further, expressing travel preferences and/or information needs in the form of structured queries using simple, functional terms is an entirely artificial approach driven by systems design rather than human nature. Traditional travel information search is dominated by narrative situations such as asking family and friends or consulting a travel agent. These human travel information providers typically supply contextual information and emphasize particular experiential aspects in a way that enables the information seeker to establish mental connections among the various trip elements. Whereas existing tourism information systems appear to be successful in providing functional information for specific components of travel decisions, they currently fail to address the need for holistic, experiential and conversational ways of communicating travel information. This is especially true for travel recommender systems that often require substantial simplification in order to facilitate matching procedures.

The appeal of the database logic for travel recommendation systems lies in its clarity and suitability for computational purposes. Manovich (2001) defines database as a conceptual way to represent the world as a list of items. Databases are highly structured collections of data that can be viewed, navigated and searched by their users. Interacting with a database is a linear experience that differs considerably from viewing films or playing computer games. There are no sequences and cause-and-effect trajectories of events incorporated in the way databases are organized. Database records are often displayed in arbitrary order or according to their relevance with regard to a certain search topic. Further, interfaces following database logic essentially communicate information in fragmentary pieces. Although possible, it requires additional cognitive effort to make mental connections between items that are displayed in a list. If no connections are established, the number of items that can be successfully remembered is rather limited. Further, whether or not these connections are made and how they are interpreted remains outside the control of the travel recommender system.

A lack of interpretation of the relationship between items is less problematic for unidimensional search concepts, e.g. a search for a hotel room. However, tourism experiences are typically multifaceted and it is often impossible to cognitively separate vacation aspects without a danger of losing coherence and, consequently, meaning. Searches for information or recommendations regarding entire vacation trips are problematic from a database perspective as they are open-ended, vague or imprecise, ill-defined, multidimensional and unconstrained. Interfaces that simply provide access to databases and feature queries and information displays modelled after database structures fail to acknowledge the complexity of travel experiences. The issue is creating an interface that can add relevance to the information it displays by supporting users in their efforts to express preferences and imagine or evaluate complex experiences. A growing stream of research in psychology and artificial intelligence suggests that narratives are a possible way for connecting seemingly unrelated items (Schank and Abelson, 1995). Narrative interfaces appear to be able to translate the underlying database into a different kind of user experience that is not only more entertaining but also more informative as it helps the user derive contextual information necessary for the interpretation of coherent experiences.

3. Narratives as Organizing Principles

Narratives can be described as event sequences that create a cause-and-effect trajectory of seemingly unordered items (Schank and Abelson, 1995;

Manovich, 2001). A narrative depicts at least two events and there must be 'some more or less loose, albeit non-logical, relation between the events' (Lamarque, 2004, p. 394). Moreover, there must be a temporal relation between the events, even if it is just that of simultaneity. Packer and Jordon (2001) define narratives as multithreaded networks that reflect the associative tendencies of the mind and collapse boundaries of space and time, drawing attention to previously undetected connections, creating links between disparate ideas and elements. Importantly, narratives provide structure, which itself has meaning (Shedroff, 2001). These structures or patterns inherent in narratives communicate some special kind of knowledge to our pattern-recognizing mental modules (Crawford, 2003a). In general, the imposition of structure, such as in the form of narratives, helps reduce the complexity of information, which is especially important in the case of travel recommender systems that need to convey complex travel experiences. Also, structure or information organization is often seen as a necessary condition for memory (Bower and Bryant, 1991), an argument that is frequently used to explain why stories can typically be more easily recalled than lists of items. Schank and Abelson (1995) discuss how stories, knowledge and memory are interrelated. They summarize the role of stories in individual and social understanding processes in three propositions:

1. Human knowledge is based on stories constructed around past experiences.
2. New experiences are interpreted in terms of old stories.
3. The content of story memories depends on whether and how they are told to others.

As Wyer *et al.* (2002) point out, given the central role of narrative-based representations of knowledge in comprehending experiences, narratives are likely to be an equally fundamental basis for judgements and behavioural decisions.

Stories are what we use to explain the underpinnings of reality (Meadows, 2003). Indeed, it has been argued that narrative is the primary form through which we understand and give meaning to our experiences. Umaschi and Cassell (1997) argue that narrative, including conversational stories of personal experience, serves at least three vital functions:

1. *A cognitive function.* Personal stories are fundamental constituents of human memory, and new experiences are interpreted in terms of old stories and generalized scripts (Schank and Abelson, 1995).
2. *A social function.* The tales that one knows and can tell define the social group or culture to which one belongs. Life stories are told and retold by adults according to certain conventions and in many different contexts.
3. *An emotional function.* Storytelling has been used in very different forms of psychotherapy.

In addition, stories are believed to be didactic (Schank and Berman, 2002) and, thus, serve an educational function. Narratives are significant means of conveying experiences as they facilitate our understanding of holistic relationships between things (Sengers, 2000). However, narratives not only allow for meaningful connections between pieces of information but they simultaneously afford the addition of emotional content and sensory details. The more details a description contains, the greater is its potential to trigger memories that make the information more personally relevant, and details also heighten the indexability of information, which makes a description easier to remember (Schank and Berman, 2002). Consequently, using narratives to communicate travel experiences offers the potential for particularly 'thick' descriptions of the experiential aspects of a trip, which are necessary to effectively evaluate the suitability of a specific travel option in light of one's personal preferences and needs.

Narratives serve an important communicative function in all aspects of our lives (Dautenhahn, 2002). Humans are constantly telling and retelling stories about themselves and others (Dautenhahn, 1999), including stories about vacation experiences. Travel stories help us understand and make meaning of our travel experiences and encourage us to relive and reflect upon trips, as well as integrate travel experiences with the rest of our experience and knowledge (Cassell and Smith, 1999). Narratives provide meaning, background and context, and create interest in what is next (Meadows, 2003). Thus, narratives can convey great quantities of information, especially of experiential nature, in a format that can quickly and easily be assimilated. Images, too, hold a considerable amount of information a viewer might grasp quickly, but images are susceptible to uncertainties and may require additional declarative statements (Gershon and Page, 2001). Recognizing the importance of narratives for communicating tourism information is not an issue of believing that narrative is the only organizing principle in human memory. Rather, it acknowledges the experiential nature and complexity of vacations and the importance of narratives as a means of communicating tourism experiences. Human beings have the ability to organize experience into narratives that help us make sense of the world (Mateas and Sengers, 1999). However, the focus of narratives is on meaning and relevance, not on precision. It has been found that getting information from a bulleted list taps the logical mode of the human mind; getting it from stories taps the human mind's creative and artistic mode (Gershon and Page, 2001). Similarly, stories are believed to induce an altered state of awareness that is less analytical, more receptive and better connected to unconscious imagination, and listening to stories can lower blood pressure and slow the heartbeat (Simmons, 2001). Thus, narratives provide guidance in terms of interpreting search results by making connections between items and assign meanings but also actively encourage imagination, which is necessary to make travel information personally relevant. Importantly, stories are compelling and even the most sceptic among narrative researchers acknowledge that stories are especially entertaining and influence our affective states (Brewer and Lichtenstein, 1982; Brewer, 1995).

4. Potential Benefits of Narrative Design

Most websites understand the Internet as being little more than a globally distributed brochure. The interactive, social and narrative capabilities of the Web remain unexplored (Meadows, 2003). Storytelling in virtual environments can meet the users' cognitive needs to interpret, understand and interact with the world in terms of stories. Such environments can be created so that they afford the narrativity underlying human perception, understanding and interaction with the world (Dautenhahn, 1999). However, computer-mediated environments should not simply display information but should create representations that engage humans in pleasurable ways (Laurel, 1986). Immersion is often seen as a necessary condition for compelling online experiences (Murray, 2001; Ryan, 2001; Mateas, 2004). Narratives have the ability to capture and hold our attention and to immerse us in another world much better than the most advanced technological systems (Shedroff, 2001). Further, people generally enjoy processing stories and seek out opportunities to do so (Graesser and Ottati, 1995). Enjoyment of the online information search experience has been found to have important consequences for the perception of a technology as well as website and brand attitudes formed online (Venkatesh, 2000; Blythe *et al.*, 2003; Mathwick and Rigdon, 2004). Consequently, narratives can greatly enhance the user experience while using a travel recommender system, thus having important implications for the acceptance of recommendations provided by the system as well as for the likelihood of using the system again in the future.

Narrative structure is fundamental to comprehension to the extent that its absence in certain forms of multimedia can seriously undermine comprehension and lead to unfocused and inconclusive learning behaviour (Laurillard, 1998). Narrative approaches to interface design can help solve the question of how to link content and navigation by structuring the information so that users can find what they are looking for without having to know how the system is organized (Don, 1990). Also, narrative design allows for the use of genres, which are 'conventional, familiar ways of setting expectations of the experience to come' (Oren, 1990, p. 471). Genres evoke memories of conventional stories, characters and handling of form and, thus, allow for immediate recognition rather than relearning of the basics when navigating a new system or learning about a new domain such as unfamiliar travel destinations (Oren, 1990). Computer-mediated environments intrigue us with interactivity; however, interaction requires decision-making, and because decision-making is not necessarily linear, we need to learn how to tell stories that facilitate choices (Meadows, 2003). We do not like to act randomly or without reason. In a sense, we must construct a story before taking an action to ensure coherence (Schank, 1990). The hope of narrative design is that narratives connected to the web-browsing experience will provide a user with an overall sense of cohesion and, thus, will support navigational choices (Mateas and Sengers, 1999). Accordingly, travel recommender systems can facilitate the navigation process by offering story cues or providing a storyline that guides the user through different navigational steps.

Stories simulate experience and, therefore, are especially important for 'selling' ideas or promoting intangible products such as vacations (Simmons, 2001). In fact, recent research suggests that consumers with relatively low familiarity with a service category prefer advertising appeals based on stories to appeals based on lists of service attributes (Mattila, 2000). Similarly, Adaval and Wyer (1998) found that consumers evaluated vacations at unfamiliar destinations more positively when they were described in a narrative format rather than a list of attributes. They argue that this advantage of narrative communication stems from the narrative's structural similarity to the information acquired through an actual travel experience, as well as from the narrative's ability to elicit positive affective reactions and hence induce holistic processing of the information. Such holistic information processing helps novices become aware of connections between the various pieces of information and can greatly enhance learning (Alba and Hutchinson, 1987). Since recommendations made by travel recommender systems will likely include vacations with which the user is at least partly unfamiliar, and sometimes even deliberately introduce novelty to satisfy variety-seeking needs, it is important for such systems to provide consumers with means to effectively process this information. Further, when unfavourable or inconsistent information is presented in the form of a list, it is typically weighted more heavily than favourable information (Wyer, 1974). It has been argued that undesirable or inconsistent features of a generally attractive vacation will have less impact if these features are described in a narrative than presented in an unordered list (Adaval and Wyer, 1998). Given the complexity of vacations and the small likelihood of exactly matching a specific trip with all the preferences of a user, systems that integrate narrative descriptions in their recommendations seem to have a clear advantage over those that do not. Research by Adaval and Wyer (1998) also suggests that pictures that accompany descriptions of vacations not only increase the impact of information conveyed in a narrative form but are also likely to decrease the impact of information that is presented in a disorganized list. Most travel recommender systems include pictures in their recommendations and, therefore, have to consider their impacts on the processing of the accompanying text.

In contrast to analytical processing, stories persuade via transportation, which can be defined as immersion or becoming 'lost' in a story (Green and Brock, 2002). This immersion typically involves mental simulation of the sequence of events; thus, narratives support mental imagery more successfully than other text genres (Brewer, 1988). Mental imagery can significantly influence attitudes and evaluations (Edson Escalas, 2004a) and is especially important in the context of experience goods such as vacations, for which trial experiences before the actual purchase are not readily available (Klein, 1998). Research by Keller and McGill (1994) suggests that consumers use an imagery heuristic in their decision-making process wherein they imagine the actual experience with a product alternative and then assess that alternative's desirability based on the affective response to imagining. Such mental simulation is especially persuasive when it is self-focused, and narrative forms of information are more likely than list forms to dispose individuals to imagine themselves experiencing the events described (Deighton *et al.*, 1989). Self-constructed mental simulation plays an important role in consumer decision-making because these consumption visions that involve self-enacting, detailed, product-related behaviours motivate future consumption behaviour (Philips *et al.*, 1995). Narrative processing has also been found to increase self-brand connections and it can be assumed that products or brands become more meaningful the more closely they are linked to the self, leading to more favourable attitudes and positive behavioural intentions (Edson Escalas, 2004b). Including narratives or narrative structures in travel recommender systems can, therefore, have a significant impact on users' evaluations of the trip alternatives recommended and their likelihood of actually purchasing a suggested vacation.

5. Implications for Travel Recommendation System Design

Given the inclusive nature of the narrative framework and its potential impact on information processing and decision-making, the significance of restructuring website visits, and particularly recommendation processes, into narrative experiences becomes apparent. If narratives are a closer match to human knowledge and communication structures in the travel domain, narrative approaches should be more effective in educating people about fuzzy or complex travel-related situations. Also, the ability of narratives to link items into logical and consistent wholes seems to be especially important for representing bundles of information in contrast to single-item concepts. This has significant implications for the recommendation of vacation packages that consist of a number of products and services. Further, the inherent entertainment value of narratives promises to engage website visitors at a much higher level than through interfaces that are direct representations of database structures. Finally, by providing a sequential path, plot or storyline, narrative approaches can potentially facilitate navigation through unknown knowledge territory. Thus, it appears that narratives provide a suitable means for linking pieces of information about the various functional and experiential aspects of a trip within the context of a travel recommender system.

The challenge of integrating a narrative approach into travel recommender systems is to translate non-linear patterns into interfaces that support narrative construction and goal-directed as well as experiential consumption of travel information. Since holistic experience is such an important part of travel, and narratives seem to be particularly suitable for supporting the communication of experiential aspects in a cohesive way, narrative design makes sense from both a human–computer interaction and a marketing perspective. The concept of the narrative should be perceived as an integral part of the tourism experience that begins with the information search process. This implies that it has to be understood as an underlying process for travel information search rather than an imposed design principle. Its integration into websites in general, and travel recommender systems in particular, goes beyond adding yet another story. The importance of narratives lies in applying the narrative concept to both information displays and navigational space in order to provide users with travel information that affords immediate comprehension, sense-making and ultimately high personal relevance. Alternative strategies have been proposed for integrating narrative design concepts into tourism information systems through the means of story matching and/or the use of narrative cues provided through an interactive display (Gretzel and Fesenmaier, 2002b). Narrative design has already been employed in other domains: online gaming and social agent development, for instance, have successfully integrated narrative principles into their designs (Mateas, 2004). It is proposed that travel recommender systems could greatly benefit from adopting narrative approaches developed in these areas. The ultimate goal of travel recommender systems is to provide recommendations that are relevant, enticing and easily comprehensible, and that can satisfy functional and hedonic information needs, as well as the need for coherence. Taking into account the ability of narratives to structure information and create experience, applying narrative principles appears to be an effective way to achieve this goal. Or, as Schank (1990, p. 243) puts it:

> If we can learn from a machine that is trying to respond to our needs and can do so in an entertaining way, then storytelling and learning may become what they were in the past – an interaction with an entity that knew something you wanted to know and was willing to tell it to you in the most interesting possible way.

Chapter Summary

Travel recommender system users are typically forced to express their preferences for travel products or services as highly structured queries or choices among search options that more or less reflect the rows and columns in which the data are stored. This chapter challenges the dominance of the database perspective underlying interface design by reflecting on their limitations in terms of effectively eliciting user preferences and conveying relevant information about holistic vacation experiences. Narratives are presented as a valuable alternative regarding the organization and display of tourism information. An integration of narrative principles is expected to lead to travel recommender systems that can better meet a multitude of informational needs, provide information that more closely matches human memory and communication patterns, support tourism decision-making throughout its various stages and increase user enjoyment of the recommendation process. Most importantly, it is argued that narrative design can enhance the persuasiveness of the recommendations provided by travel recommender systems.

11 Interface Metaphors on Travel-related Websites

ZHENG XIANG AND DANIEL R. FESENMAIER

1. Introduction

Travel-related websites offer numerous services including online booking, virtual tourist communities and advanced search functions on destinations, accommodations, activities and attractions. However, recent studies of online tourism have shown that travel planning on the Web can often be a frustrating experience (Radosevich, 1997; Stoltz, 1999). One important reason is that travel information search is highly dynamic and contingent on the information searchers' background knowledge, their individual characteristics, search tasks and stages of travel planning (Jeng, 1999). It is also argued that experiences form the foundation of travel, and the current approach most travel websites adopt fails to reflect the role tourism information plays and the capacity it possesses to affect travel-related choices (Gretzel and Fesenmaier, 2002b). It seems that the current paradigm in travel website site design does not take full advantage of the capacity of the 'hypermedium' (Hoffman and Novak, 1996), which accommodates rich, vivid and highly interactive representations of the website contents. Within the tourism context, such richness, vividness and high interactivity can be exemplified by the 'virtual tour', which presents, often in a metaphorical way, the information about a destination based upon the concept of telepresence and provides a means that allows the information user to experience or 'sample' a destination (Klein, 1998; Cho *et al.*, 2002).

Interface metaphors have been extensively documented in human–computer interaction (HCI) research and they can be regarded as important components in the computer interface that facilitate the interaction between the travel information searcher and the online information system (Pan, 2003). The merits of interface metaphors lie mainly in their capacity to improve computer interface learnability and usability (Neale and Carroll, 1997). In an online hypertext environment, the primary goal for using metaphors is to create a structured interface with easy navigation (Dix *et al.*, 1998). However, limited research has been conducted within the context of online information systems (Welles and Fuerst, 2000), and interface metaphors are interpreted only as navigation aids in a hypertext environment. Their connotations are far from clear, and within the tourism context their relationship with travellers' trip-planning experience remains undefined. Thus, it becomes imperative to understand and interpret interface metaphors in online travel-related websites because metaphors are ubiquitous on any computer system (Crawford, 2003a) and perhaps, more importantly, travel and tourism products are service-extensive and experiential products, and when prospective travellers cannot properly try the promised product in advance, metaphorical reassurances become the amplified necessity of the marketing effort (Levitt, 1981). Therefore, this article aims to: (i) conceptualize the notion of interface metaphor by reviewing the literature in HCI; (ii) examine interface metaphors within the context of travellers' online trip planning and provide a typological framework for better understanding interface metaphors; and (iii) explore some of the issues related to research on interface metaphors within the context of travel and tourism recommendation systems.

2. Interface Metaphors on Travel-related Websites

In order to establish the base for understanding interface metaphors within the online tourism context, this chapter first reviews the research on HCI. Then, it examines different types of interface metaphors on travel-related websites with respect to their functional roles, especially how they aid travellers to interact with the websites. Finally, it provides a typological view of interface metaphors for the interpretation.

2.1 What is an interface metaphor?

Lakoff and Johnson (1980) conceptualize metaphors as 'understanding and experiencing one kind of thing in terms of another' and claim that metaphors are not only pervasive in language, but they are a fundamental part of our conceptual system of thought and action. In contemporary HCI research, metaphors are conceived of as cross-domain mappings (Holyoak and Thagard, 1995); i.e. metaphors allow the transference or mapping of knowledge from a source domain (familiar area of knowledge) to a target domain (unfamiliar area of knowledge), enabling humans to use specific prior knowledge and experience for understanding and behaving in situations that are novel or unfamiliar. When a user is interacting with a computer system, the underlying operations of computer artefacts are imperceptible to the user and what is visible is conveyed through the user interface. Thus, metaphors play a critical role in HCI design and directly or indirectly shape the design of user interface (Neale and Carroll, 1997).

The use of metaphors for designing computer interface can be traced back to the notion of the 'ledger', which was used in the first electronic spreadsheet, VisiCalc. One of the currently most prevalent metaphors is the desktop metaphor, which was introduced by Xerox PARC and later popularized by the Apple Macintosh and Microsoft Windows operating system. Metaphors were first intended to facilitate learning to use a computer system. Studies have shown advantages for representing the designer's conceptual model with metaphors (Neale and Carroll, 1997). Carroll and Thomas (1982) posited that the activity of learning to use a computer system is structured by metaphoric comparisons. More recently, Masden (1994) found that metaphors affect the ease of using and learning computer software. They argued that system interface designs succeed or fail with respect to their learnability depending on the extent to which a metaphor helps computer users understand the purpose and function of software application (Boechler, 2001).

However, the notions of metaphor have been evolving due to the increased reliance on metaphors in general interface design (Neale and Carroll, 1997). Metaphors have become so ubiquitous that they exist on almost any software interface. Indeed, Crawford (2003a) argues that every icon ever used is a metaphor. Thus, much of the focus on metaphors has shifted from a primarily ease-of-learning focus to include a focus on ease of use. Understanding the roles of metaphors on a system is essential to the design of efficient computer interfaces. First, because user interfaces mimic actions and representations in an infinite variety of ways, and these concepts are artificial and arbitrary, metaphors of computer discourse are embedded deeply in the way computers have been thought about by designers. As a result, the process of design and the interfaces that result are both metaphorical. Second, the extent to which a metaphor is used in the designer's model and supported in the system image will directly structure the users' mental model that consists of their prior knowledge with source domain and their interaction process with the system (Collins, 1995). Thus, it can be argued that the appropriateness of an interface metaphor is highly related to the users' perception of the usefulness of the the interface.

2.2 Interface metaphors' functional roles on travel-related websites

Hutchins (1989) categorizes interface metaphors based on the functional roles they play on a system: (i) mode of interaction metaphors, which can organize understandings about the nature of the interaction with the computer; (ii) task domain metaphors, which provide an understanding of how tasks are structured; and (iii) activity metaphors, which refer to users' highest-level goals or to the institutional goals that are held for the users whether the users share them or not. Taking into account the characteristics of the hypertext and users' task domain, the functional roles of interface metaphors on a travel website can be understood based on how travellers interact with the website. Thus, interface metaphors can be categorized into three major types in terms of their roles for facilitating travellers' navigation, tasks and activities.

3. Interface Metaphor as Navigation Facilitator

A website visitor's dominant mode of interaction with a website is navigation. Navigation can be defined as an information searcher browses through certain web pages in order to find more relevant information. Internet websites exhibit hypertext character. The basic principle of hypertext is non-linearity, which means hypertext information is not necessarily represented in a typical hierarchical order. And hypertext reading has also been called associated reading, since the user determines the reading order dynamically in an associative way. Most hypertexts lack a perceivable structure, which is the main reason for the navigation problems to arise in these systems.

However, navigational problems are not inherently due to the hypertext concept but are caused by a user interface that fails to communicate the structure of the information to the user. Thus, it is necessary to provide tools or aids that make the information structure apparent and explicit to users and help answer the core navigation questions reliably and efficiently. Appropriate interface metaphors can fulfil this task. For instance, navigation elements such as 'home' and 'site map' can allow the user to quickly access the requested page and jump from page to page without 'getting lost'. Apparently, many websites use a 'restaurant menu' metaphor with the association for menu selection (Norman and Chin, 1988). A simple example is used to illustrate this in Fig. 11.1. It is obvious that without this metaphorical navigation aid, it would be difficult, sometimes even impossible, for travel information users to locate the page content they want to request. This type of metaphor is task-independent and determines how the user views the website structure (Hutchins, 1989). This is the reason why they not only exist on tourism websites but can also be found on virtually any websites. On travel-related websites, a number of metaphors have been used to facilitate navigation and decision-making and include photo or media gallery, slide show, information centre, and travel bag, travel case, etc. These metaphors are largely domain-oriented and can be understood as more contingent and arguably more relevant within the tourism context. An example is shown in Fig. 11.2, which uses the metaphor of a travel suitcase loaded with several travel necessity items, each standing for a different type of information category. The design is intuitive and provides such an obvious bricolage that even a first-time visitor to the website can instantly understand how to play with it.

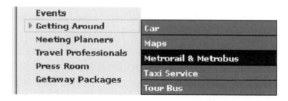

Fig. 11.1. A menu metaphor for accessing dynamically generated web pages.

Fig. 11.2. Navigational metaphors on a travel-related website
(http://www.vegasfreedom.com).

4. Interface Metaphor as Task Facilitator

Task-facilitating metaphors are task-dependent and provide an understanding of how tasks are structured and fulfilled. In hypertext systems, users' information task can be defined as searching for information by querying all documents to locate relevant ones (Conklin, 1987). For example, on an e-commerce website these tasks are more product related with the task domain being centred on product-related activities, such as carrying out a transaction or paying bills online.

An interface metaphor for product-related tasks can be exemplified with a 'shopping cart', which we have frequently seen on numerous commercial websites. It has often been used to allow online transactions, by which customers can 'add' and 'remove' items they select for purchase. The implementation of the 'shopping cart' might be different from website to website, but this term and its connotations, which are analogous to the shopping cart in a grocery store, can help first-time users intuitively imagine what the functional element allows them to do. On tourism websites, equivalent to 'shopping cart' is the metaphor of 'trip planner'. Instead of facilitating online transaction, it is more intended to help users keep a record of the attractions or events that they are interested in for trip planning and conveniently access for future reference (as illustrated by Fig. 11.3). This 'trip planner' works as a container wherein a travel information user can 'add' or 'delete' an itinerary, event, attraction or accommodation vendor. It also mimics the computer

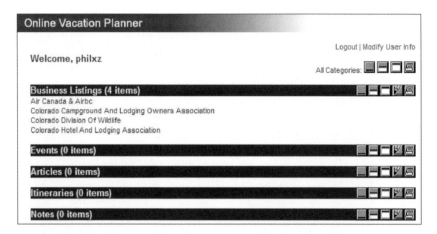

Fig. 11.3. A trip planner metaphor on a travel-related website.

file system on a graphical user interface (GUI) such as Microsoft Windows, which allows the file 'folders' to expand and collapse.

Another common task a traveller carries out on a website is querying the online database, which can often be implemented using metaphors like 'automated agents', 'online advisory' or 'online expert'. In HCI, studies (Catarci *et al.*, 1997) have established metaphorical design as being the basic paradigm for visual database interaction. They view database management systems as layered environments where multiple metaphors are used not only to understand the database content but also for extracting information. In line with these developments, travel-related websites, such as online recommendation systems (Delgado and Davidson, 2002; Ricci *et al.*, 2002a), are adopting interface metaphors to improve the 'ease-of-use' aspect of the websites. For example, Göker and Thompson (2000) proposed the 'Adaptive Place Advisor', a recommendation system designed to help users decide on a destination by establishing an interactive, conversational process facilitating the direct dialogue between the advisory system and the users.

5. Interface Metaphor as Activity Facilitator

As activity facilitator, interface metaphors can be used to help users achieve their highest-level goals and fulfil their expectations or intentions with respect to the outcome of the interaction (Hutchins, 1989). Users may perform different kinds of activities on a website such as playing an online game or communicating with other human beings, in addition to searching for information. In this respect, the users' goal of visiting the website plays a critical role in shaping their perception of how the website satisfies their needs. Actually, many websites provide various functions in order to facilitate users' heterogeneous online activities. Many examples can be easily identified on some web portals that provide various utilities using interface metaphors such as 'chat

Fig. 11.4.   Example of an online 'Chat Community' (http://www.habbohotel.com).

room', 'forum', 'bulletin board' and 'online games'. As illustrated by Fig. 11.4, the online chat function is implemented by using a graphical chat 'room', where people can walk around and look for partners they want to converse with. When interacting with these metaphorical interfaces, users are not only searching for information but also seeking experiences by communicating or competing with peer users (when playing a game). In tourism, the metaphor of 'virtual tourism community' exploits the concept of real-world community where groups of people who have like interests share travel information and experiences among the community members (Wang *et al.*, 2002).

It can be argued that these activity-based metaphors can sometimes play the same roles as the task-facilitating metaphors. Indeed, it would be difficult to completely distinguish them from each other. For example, people can participate in a virtual community with the goal of searching for information for planning a trip to a certain destination, and many people do. But these information tasks can be understood as subsequent goals of their top-level goals; i.e. they have to be a part of the community first and then they can carry out these tasks. More importantly, unlike the 'trip planner', which all travellers use only for the purpose of trip planning, people go to an online virtual community with different kinds of goals and needs (Wang *et al.*, 2002).

Table 11.1 provides a tentative typological framework for understanding interface metaphors within the context of online tourism. Note that the

Table 11.1. A typological view of interface metaphors on travel websites.

Metaphor functions	Characteristics	Examples
Navigation	Task-independent; helps travellers navigate the website with ease	Home
Facilitation		Site map Menu Media gallery Slide show Road sign Travel suitcase Information centre
Task facilitation	Task-dependent; helps travellers plan a trip	Trip planner Online Expert/advisory To-do list Shopping cart Calendar of events
Activity	Represents user's top-level goals, such as communicating with other people and playing games; not necessarily task-driven	Chat room
Facilitation		Forum Bulletin board Virtual community Virtual tour Press room Game(s) Storytelling

examples are not exhaustive. Although the interface metaphors are laid out in a typological way, it does not necessarily mean that there is a clear-cut distinction between them. In reality, they are often used and implemented in a combined style. As pointed out earlier, travellers who go to a virtual community may also have the goal of fulfilling their information task, and a 'chat room' designed like the example shown in Fig. 11.4 can facilitate website users' navigation as well. For example, by using those miniature human figures, it allows users to easily identify whom they want to have a dialogue with. Thus, this typological view is rather intended to help researchers establish a base for understanding and interpreting interface metaphors. For travel-related website developers it can be used to guide conceptualizing online information systems in order to improve website usability and match travellers' anticipations and expectations.

6. Implications for Travellers' Online Trip Planning

Interface metaphors are components of the website that represent an online travel information system. The website interface is the entry point through which users can exploit the system via navigating through the hypertext contents, querying the system database or carrying out other activities. That is, system functions and contents are visible and available to the user only through the website interface. The metaphors embedded in the interface work like mediators or facilitators between the user and the system, making the interaction effective. Thus, what travellers directly see and manipulate are the metaphorical components of the website, rather than the computer software programs that lie underneath them. This raises two issues: (i) the interface metaphors a website uses will influence the website usability; and (ii) the website usability will in turn affect travellers' level of satisfaction with respect to their experience on the website.

By definition, travel website usability refers to the extent to which the travellers can carry out their travel planning and information search task on the Internet effectively, successfully and with satisfaction (Pan, 2003). A recent study (Xiang, 2003) has shown that websites with the same contents and functions but designed using different interface metaphors are significantly different from each other in terms of users' perception of the websites' usability aspects, such as ease of use, learnability and users' overall experience. However, the study did not provide a generalizable conclusion that can be applied in the context of travellers' trip planning. Thus, it is necessary to investigate the relationship between interface metaphors and website usability, and how they are linked to travellers' online trip-planning experience.

Further, the hedonic values expressed through interface metaphors need to be explored since travel products are most of the time experiential products, and marketing and tourism scholars have argued that consumers often evaluate products more on experiential aspects than on 'objective' features such as price, availability, etc. (Vogt and Fesenmaier, 1998; Pine and Gilmore, 1999; Schmitt, 1999; Schlosser, 2003). Many researchers, for example, encourage designers to use metaphors to develop system interactivity (Nielsen, 1990; Crawford, 2003a). Imagine when a traveller interacts with an online expert recommendation system for trip planning, the search results can be dynamically generated according to the traveller's individual preferences. Thus, it establishes a real-time-like dialogue between the traveller and the information system and gives the traveller a sense of control and responsiveness. As suggested by Garrett (2003) another hedonic attribute of interface metaphors is its capability to increase website novelty, which makes it possible to enable trip planners to experience fun, excitement, playfulness and entertainment. Therefore, it can be argued that the ultimate goal for applying interface metaphors on travel-related websites is to enhance travellers' trip-planning experience, and, intuitively, the appropriateness of an interface metaphor on a specific website should be determined by the extent to which it satisfies the traveller.

7. Conclusions

Microsoft initiated the use of '.Net Passport' by which web users can visit a series of the corporate consumer websites, such as MSN, Expedia and Hotmail, and access customized web contents provided for individual visitors based on their profiles and personal preferences without logging in each time when they 'switch the channel'. This metaphorical representation of the technological innovation not only provides the website visitors with an assurance of a carefree experience and largely improves the ease of use of their websites but also gives the website architects an approach to tackle complex, cross-platform scenarios in the online environment. Indeed, the appropriate use of interface metaphors on travel websites not only can be used to enhance travellers' online trip-planning experience but also can benefit website designers and developers with its capacity to better conceptualize and represent software applications.

Research on interface metaphors should not be confined only to their functional roles, since interface metaphors can convey much richer and abundant meanings to trip planners, if implemented appropriately. Furthermore, the capacity of the current web technologies allows highly visual, multimedia and directly manipulative web interfaces to be designed using interface metaphors. These technologies will provide a rich environment for metaphor implementation because they can offer affordances that model much of what occurs in the real world (Neale and Carroll, 1997). In this sense, this provides a new horizon for research efforts on interface metaphors within the travel and tourism domain.

Chapter Summary

Interface metaphors are credited with the capability of facilitating interface usability and learnability from the human–computer interaction (HCI) perspective. On travel-related websites, they can help travellers plan their trips and make the trip-planning process more entertaining and engaging. This chapter conceptualizes interface metaphors on travel-related websites by examining the functional roles they play. Implications for research on interface metaphors and travellers' trip-planning experience are also discussed.

12 Playfulness on Website Interactions: Why Can Travel Recommendation Systems Not Be Fun?

Dae-Young Kim and Cristian Morosan

1. Introduction

In an online environment the concept of playfulness has emerged as an important factor that increases interactivity between the website and its visitors. Jeff Bezos of Amazon.com stated that one secret to his success was 'thinking of ways to make the online shopping experience more fun' (Star Tribune, 1999). The concept of playfulness has been of continuing interest, importance and controversy for many years. Initially, Dewey (1913) viewed playfulness as an individual's predisposition to be playful. Lieberman (1977) postulated the existence of a playfulness trait in young children, identifying five components of playfulness: (i) cognitive spontaneity; (ii) social spontaneity; (iii) physical spontaneity; (iv) manifest joy; and (v) sense of humour. Later, playfulness was viewed as a situational characteristic, describing the interaction between an individual and a situation (Lin *et al.*, 2004). In their study about computer usability, Webster and Martocchio (1992) argued that although the construct of playfulness is multifaceted, only cognitive spontaneity is critical in examining playfulness in human–computer interactions (HCIs).

The importance of playfulness in travel-related websites is evident in that it can lead to increased persuasiveness (Fogg, 2003). However, marketeers and designers have to understand what playfulness is, what its dimensions and impact are and what kind of playfulness applications can be incorporated into travel recommendation systems. The purpose of this chapter is to discuss the importance of the concept of playfulness from the *trait* and *state* viewpoints, and to examine several travel websites by discussing the increasing role of playfulness in the persuasive architecture of these recommendation systems. Specifically, the chapter defines the concept of playfulness, then examines the current status of the use of playful applications in travel-related

©CAB International 2006. *Destination Recommendation Systems: Behavioural Foundations and Applications* (eds D.R. Fesenmaier, K.W. Wöber and H. Werthner)

websites and, finally, discusses the implications of playfulness for the design of online travel recommendation systems.

2. The Concept of Playfulness

Although the importance of playfulness was recognized as early as 1910, its study in the context of marketing research can be traced back to the 1950s, when there was extensive discussion concerning the symbolic aspects of products in consumer behaviour studies (Gardner and Levy, 1955; Levy, 1959). Levy noted that '[p]eople buy products not only for what they can do, but also for what they mean' (p. 118). This line of thought was continued during the 1960s by incorporating the notion of congruence between a consumer's lifestyle and the symbolic meaning of products purchased (Levy, 1963). The 1970s were marked by a hiatus of research regarding product symbolism, possibly attributable to the excesses of the motivation research era, in spite of the potential benefits that could have been gained from exploring the aesthetic, intangible and subjective aspects of consumption (Hirschman, 1980; Holbrook, 1980). A number of characterizations of play have been proposed (Csikszentmihalyi, 1975; Day, 1981). Dewey (1913) defined the trait of playfulness as 'the capacity to draw satisfaction from the immediate intellectual development of a topic, irrespective of any ulterior motive' (p. 727). Barnett (1991) stated:

> Individuals with playful dispositions are said to be guided by internal motivation, an orientation toward process with self-imposed goals, a tendency to attribute their own meanings to objects or behaviors (that is, not to be dominated by a stimulus), a focus on pretense and nonliterality, a freedom from externally imposed rules, and active involvement.
>
> (Barnett, 1991, p. 52)

Berlyne (1969) pointed out the difficulties in identifying an adequate definition of play. He stated that 'there is, however, obvious disagreement on what ought to be regarded as the salient defining characteristics of play' (p. 814). Berlyne reviewed most of the available information in the field and concluded that the field is a 'discordant polyphony' (p. 840). Despite this, he proposed the following aspect of play:

1. It is repeatedly asserted that playful activities are carried on 'for their own sake' or for the sake of 'pleasure'. They are contrasted with 'serious' activities, which refer to readily identifiable bodily needs or external threats, or otherwise achieve specifiable practical ends.
2. Many researchers stress the 'unreality' or 'quasi-reality' of play. 'Reality' refers to the forms of interaction between the organism and its environment that occupy most of its waking hours.

Lepper *et al.* (1973) were among the first to examine play as a situational variable when they studied how children played with coloured pencils. In this study, half of the children were simply allowed to play with the pencils, while the other half were rewarded for doing so. The unrewarded children played with the pencils longer than those who had been rewarded. It was concluded that the intrinsic reward of the coloured pencils alone was a stronger incentive than the extrinsic reward offered for playing with them, and that offering the extrinsic reward weakened the attractiveness of the pencils. It was further posited that people with high playfulness would interact more playfully; in consequence, they would develop some of their skills through exploratory behaviours, resulting in enhanced task performance. Indeed, a series of studies clearly show that playfulness is positively associated with positive affect and satisfaction (Csikszentmihalyi, 1975; Levy, 1983; Sandelands *et al.*, 1983; McGrath and Kelly, 1986).

Webster and Martocchio (1992) viewed playfulness as a characteristic of an individual as well. They found that the individual attributes of cognitive playfulness were positively related to training outcomes of learning, mood and satisfaction. Cognitive playfulness generally related more strongly to learning, mood and satisfaction than computer anxiety or computer attitudes. The five dimensions of playfulness proposed by Lieberman (1977) have been adapted into HCI research; Table 12.1 shows how these dimensions were modified from their original context to fit the HCI. While the trait-based approach focuses on playfulness as the individual's characteristics, state-based research emphasizes playfulness as the individual's subjective experience of HCI.

The majority of the studies on playfulness are based on Csikszentmihalyi's (1975) Theory of Flow arguing that it provides the theoretical framework for examining the online information search experience. That is, when the challenges encountered in an environment are matched above a critical threshold to a person's ability, a person 'feels more active, alert, concentrated, happy, satisfied and creative, regardless of the task being performed' (Csikszentmihalyi and LeFevre, 1989, p. 816). If skill and challenge fail to combine in an optimal manner, however, the quality of the experience begins to deteriorate, and the associated value erodes. The four-channel flow model extends flow theory to identify four states of mind: (i) flow; (ii) boredom; (iii) apathy; and (iv) anxiety. Each state is associated with different levels of skill and challenge (Csikszentmihalyi and Csikszentmihalyi, 1988):

- Flow: challenge and skill are balanced and elevated above some critical threshold.
- Boredom: skill exceeds the level of challenge for a task.
- Apathy: skill and challenge fall below a critical threshold.
- Anxiety: challenge exceeds the skill level for a task.

Besides the two main approaches, one more possible approach is the interactionist approach (Woszczynski *et al.*, 2002). It takes the trait theorist viewpoint and combines it with situational factors to achieve a theory of behaviour that considers both viewpoints simultaneously. As a resolution to the trait vs state debate, many researchers now advocate this interactionist approach (Cantor and Mischel, 1979; Magnusson, 1981; Pervin, 1985; Caspi, 1987; Bowers, 1993). This approach suggests that traits provide long-term, stable and accurate predictions of behaviour, but the situation under which play occurs also should be considered.

Table 12.1. The dimensions of playfulness.

Playfulness dimension	Lieberman (1977)	Playfulness dimension in computer interaction	Ours
Physical spontaneity	How often do people engage in spontaneous physical movement and activity during play? How is their motor coordination during physical activity?	Web spontaneity	How often do web visitors visit web pages that they otherwise would not have visited?
Social spontaneity	While playing, how often do people show flexibility in their interaction with the surrounding group structure? With what degree of ease do people move?	Involvement	How deeply web users get involved in web activities?
Cognitive spontaneity	How often do people show spontaneity during expressive and dramatic play? What degree of imagination do people show in their expressive dramatic play?	Cognitive spontaneity	How often do web users engage in spontaneous playful web interface and syntax of the Web during web-surfing activity?
Manifest joy	How often do people show joy in, or during, their play activities? With what freedom of expression do they show joy?	Manifest joy	How often do people show joy in or during their web activities?
Sense of humour	How often do people show a sense of humour during play? With what degree of consistency is humour shown?	Sense of humour	How often do people show a sense of humour during web activities?

3. Application in Travel Recommendation Systems

Due to the multitude of websites containing travel information and allowing travellers to make their travel arrangements online, presenting information in an efficient and user-friendly manner might not be enough to be successful. This is why marketeers and website designers have to rely upon applications capable of stimulating web visitors' interest beyond the basic, functional purposes of the websites. They have to build websites that are fun, entertaining and capable of retaining visitors by using playful applications.

Travel is a fruitful domain for the application of playfulness. Due to its playful consumption, travel is associated with a broad class of intrinsically motivated consumer behaviours that includes leisure activities (Unger and Kernan, 1983), games (Huizinga, 1938), sports (Mihalich, 1982) and aesthetic appreciation (Osborne, 1979). Playful consumption involves using products to fulfil fantasies and satisfy emotions (Assael, 1998). Therefore, it is more likely to be based on pleasurable experiences and emotions that result from using the brand rather than on the brand's utilitarian performance and economic value. As a result, the traveller is likely to form an overall judgement of satisfaction based on the overall consumption experience.

The travel web community consists of a large number of websites in fierce competition with each other. The common feature of all these websites is that they present travel-related information or offer online transaction capabilities. Most of these websites have excellent functionality; however, in order to be able to attract travellers and retain them, the web visitors' experiences have to become memorable. Presenting information in a functional way might not be enough to attract and retain the web visitors; travel websites today have to incorporate attributes that are interactive and fun. One example of a website that incorporates a large variety of playful applications is that of Walt Disney (Fig. 12.1). This website contains a series of animations that allow visitors to taste the playful nature of the company by playing online games and downloading ringtones and screensavers. This is a good example of a company that is delivering messages about its core value on the website, not only by incorporating these into the functionality but also on the playfulness of the website (The Walt Disney Company, 2005).

Another common web application with playful connotations is the interactive map. This type of map that enables visitors to click on a portion of the map to zoom in and look for attractions is present on almost all state-sponsored tourism websites. Although not new, this type of feature has demonstrated its effectiveness by providing website visitors with an interactive browsing experience that is entertaining and fun. Figure 12.2 presents an excellent example of an interactive map from Kansas Travel and Tourism (2005).

A widely used category of travel recommendation systems is represented by travel aid websites (i.e. maps and driving directions). Due to their interactive nature, travel aids can easily combine functionality with playfulness. A noteworthy example of successful integration of playfulness into a travel aid is the map or driving directions section of Google search engine (Google, 2005). Along with the traditional, interactive online maps, one of the recently added features is the satellite view (or a hybrid between satellite and traditional view), which adds fun to the otherwise unexciting task of searching for driving directions or finding a destination. Although

Fig. 12.1. Online games pop-up menus on a travel-related website.

two well-respected map websites (Yahoo.com and Mapquest.com) use functionality in a brilliant way, Google's map section is more entertaining and fun (Fig. 12.3).

Another illustration of the integration of playful applications into a state-sponsored website can be found at Texas Travel (2005). The synergy between the organizational goals and the website attributes is reflected here through inclusion of interactive web cams showing activities specific to the state. Figure 12.4 shows an excellent way to capitalize on a cattle show in Texas. A similar example is a personalization of a 'hula postcard' on the Hawaii state tourism website (Hawaii Visitors and Convention Bureau, 2005). The state-sponsored tourism websites have a general leisurely character. Therefore, it is easy to include interactive elements. An example of such integration is the California tourism website (Fig. 12.5), where an entire section is dedicated to online interactive activities such as fun facts, trivia and online games (California Tourism, 2005).

Similar to the interactive maps and driving directions, another way of using interactive elements on a travel recommendation website is by making the transition from boring to fun tasks. As most tasks associated with information search are goal-directed and, by their nature, not very exciting, the successful integration of playful applications could actually help web visitors

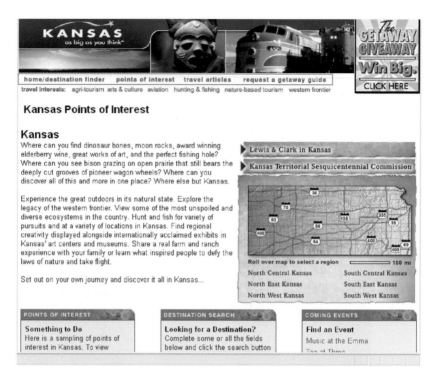

Fig. 12.2. Interactive maps from a state-sponsored tourism website.

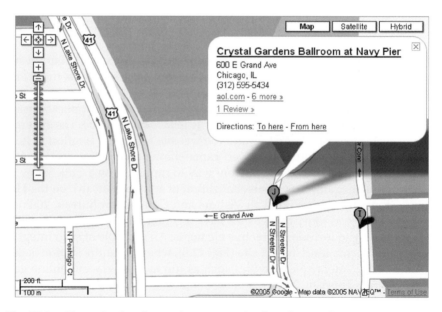

Fig. 12.3. Example of an interactive map on the Google search engine.

Fig. 12.4. Example of playful applications of Texas official tourism website – Texas cams.

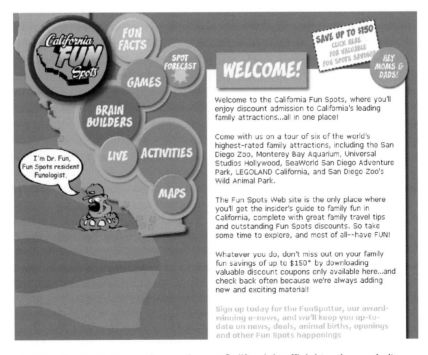

Fig. 12.5. Creating website interaction on California's official tourism website.

Fig. 12.6. Interactive elements make it fun to navigate through a series of locations – the Six Flags Theme Parks.

spend more time and have more fun on the website, while performing these tasks. For example, the Six Flags Theme Parks allows their website visitors to find a theme park location in a very entertaining manner, by using a fun way to navigate through the US map (Fig. 12.6) (Six Flags Theme Parks Inc., 2005).

These are just a few examples of successful integration of playfulness applications into travel recommendation systems. Successful integration into recommendation system design requires that marketeers and website designers know: (i) what types of applications suit their organizations; (ii) which audience they target these applications at; and (iii) what level of interactivity they want to achieve on their websites. On these websites, playful applications impact web visitors by various physical factors in the visual and auditory fields including movement, size, intensity and sound. It is much easier to notice things that move, unique objects, more intense or more attractive stimuli, and bright or loud things. However, marketeers and website designers should use these elements with caution. If everything moves and sounds loudly on a website, nothing on the page will stand out and cause motivation. Therefore, using these playful applications should be reserved for presenting the most critical parts of the general message delivered through the website.

4. Integrating Fun into Travel Recommendation Systems

In this chapter we looked at why playfulness is important for the design of travel recommendation systems. It is argued that a technology-oriented perspective that attempts to treat a website as simply information rather than an immersive, hedonic environment is likely to be misguided, especially for products with strong hedonic attributes such as travel. Thus, travel recommendation systems must be considered within the context of playfulness and the design characteristics leading to it. While focusing on the functionality of the online environment has proved beneficial, this chapter argues that the playfulness of travel recommendation systems can improve visitors' experiences online by allowing them to fully immerse into the online experience. As a result, the content of the travel recommendation system becomes more credible, with a direct impact on the persuasiveness of its messages.

Playfulness was proved an important predictor of attitudes towards online information search process and systems adoption (Lin *et al.*, 2005). This takes into consideration that consumers' attitudes, expectations and preferences for interactive web environments may differ from those held in a physical retail environment for identical products. Consumers may, in general, expect to find more playfulness in interactive environments than they do when searching information in physical environments.

Many aspects of the civilized lifestyle are dominated by the continuous preoccupation of making everything efficient. However, according to Sengers (2003), it makes little sense to try to optimize all of the processes and tasks, because some of them, although inefficient, afford people considerable pleasure. Similarly, it is believed that most information systems were designed having only functionality in mind, with no thought about playfulness. Comprising a wide range of products and services traded online, travel is one of those domains that cannot rely on functionality alone. This is due to the intangible nature of travel products. For this reason, playfulness could help diminish the intangibility of most travel-related products. Despite the fact that most information technology applications in travel relate to functionality (i.e. how to optimize the task of making a hotel or airline reservation at the lowest possible rate on the Web), there are multiple ways in which travel can incorporate interactive and playful applications in order to make the overall users' experience more enjoyable.

In addition to the flexibility and convenience of the Internet, novel, intrinsically enjoyable, virtual elements should be featured in the design of online travel recommendation systems. Creating a playful and enjoyable environment may require the use of powerful design tools, and the inclusion of images, videos, colours, humour, sounds, music, games and animation. Even in goal-driven e-commerce environments, such as discount travel agents, playfulness elements such as interactive design, games and 3D product videos are likely to improve information search and transactions, while differentiating the websites from their competitors.

The examples presented in this chapter illustrate how a variety of applications can be used successfully to increase interactivity of the travel recommendation systems by creating a playful environment. Norman (2004) suggested that information should not be simply presented online – information should be presented in a playful manner, to make visitors enjoy or even increase visitation. As demonstrated in the above examples, today's travel organizations became more concerned with presenting their content not just in a functional but also in a playful way. As a result, they used their imagination to add a variety of playful applications to their websites. However, a question remains: Do these organizations really understand the advantages of combining functionality with playfulness? Overbeeke *et al.* (2003) found that often most computer systems are designed based on functionality, and then playfulness is just attached to the new system. They asserted that to really use all the benefits of playfulness, it should be integrated at every level in the design of all information technology applications. But, in today's travel, can we really talk about seamless integration between functionality and playfulness at every stage of the website design level?

From a strategic viewpoint, seamless integration is needed between functionality and playfulness, making sure that the core elements of the organization are communicated consistently through both types of applications. Such integration would not only give competitive advantages to travel organizations by making them unique but would also induce a new way of thinking within the organizations, based on an optimal balance between functionality and playfulness, with beneficial long-term effects.

Another key aspect in the integration of playfulness in travel recommendation systems is continuous adaptation. People tend to pay less attention to things that are familiar and, therefore, from both marketing and website design perspectives, modifying the structure of online content could have a substantial impact on the way this content is perceived. To increase their responses or usage to websites over time, marketeers and designers must be concerned with the possibility of continuous change.

The theoretical foundations and the applications discussed in this chapter illustrate sufficiently that playfulness is a concept with high applicability in travel. Not only can it serve the purpose of transforming boring web experiences into memorable ones and making the organization more persuasive but it can also help convey the strategic messages from the organizations to the travellers more easily and effectively. Thus, we believe that playfulness is a concept too important to be ignored. We emphasize that the future belongs to those organizations that can successfully integrate their functionality with their playfulness applications.

Chapter Summary

With a considerable impact on the number and nature of business applications, the Internet has become the foundation for the world's new information infrastructure. To be able to attract consumers, websites have to incorporate not only functional but also playful attributes. While the importance of functionality has been discussed extensively, a newer paradigm, focusing on the playfulness of a website, has gained substantial interest. Playfulness is viewed not only as a personal trait but also as a situational variable: trait influences are captured through personality factors, whereas state influences are captured by flow theory. This chapter has discussed the importance of playfulness and illustrates how it can be successfully integrated in travel rec-ommendation systems. Moreover, the chapter asserts that, by interactivity, playfulness allows website visitors to fully immerse in their web visitation experience, with a direct impact on the credibility of the messages delivered by the travel recommendation systems. Finally, the chapter emphasizes that playfulness applications must be incorporated in all travel recommendation systems, at every level of their design, and be continuously adapted.

III Case Studies in Destination Recommendation System Development

13 Domain-specific Search Engines

KARL W. WÖBER

1. Accessibility of Tourism-related Information on the Internet

Today, the Web comprises billions of documents, authored by millions of diverse people. The volume of web data increases daily and so does its usage. What at first glance sounds superb becomes more and more a burden for users as well as for many tourism managers. Today, an increasing number of people planning a trip use the Web for obtaining information about their prospective destination, and in a study realized by Jung *et al.* (2002) the Web is already regarded as the second most important source of information. The Web grows freely, is not subject to discipline and contains information whose quality can be excellent, dubious, unacceptable or simply unknown. The richness of Web content has made it progressively more difficult for users to leverage the value of information.

Given the quantity of text that Internet users must deal with, techniques for browsing full-text systems are important. Search engines are the most popular access points for users on the Internet. According to Lawrence and Giles (1999), 85% of web users employ search engines to find information. The market for Internet search engines is currently dominated by several big companies, which, with immense effort (e.g. Google used 16,000 Linux servers in 2002), try to index all pages available on the Web (Calishain and Dornfest, 2003).

The main search engines like Google (www.google.com), AlltheWeb (www.alltheweb.com), Hotbot (www.hotbot.com), AltaVista (www.altavista. com), MSN Search (search.msn.com), Teoma (teoma.com), WiseNut (wisenut. com) and Gigablast (gigablast.com) possess full-text searching capabilities. Because a single search engine can cover only a small portion of the Web (Lawrence and Giles, 1999), some information request services use several search engines for their automated searches. A system that forwards user queries to several search engines, aggregates the returned results and presents the combined (usually re-ranked) results to the user is referred to as a metasearch engine. For example, Yahoo! (www.yahoo.com) used Inktomi as well as Google's search engine and recently also acquired Overture (www.overture.com). In Yahoo!, web pages are manually grouped into categories to create a hierarchical directory of a subset of the Internet in order to retrieve pages more easily. NorthernLight (www.northernlight.com), a commercial search engine, categorizes retrieved web pages into predefined search categories and provides these customized results to their paying clients. Other metasearch engines include MetaCrawler (www.metacrawler.com), DogPile (www.dogpile.com) and 37.com (www.37.com). Interestingly, Ask Jeeves (www.ask.com) provides its own human-compiled directory of responses to questions, as well as metasearch results from several popular search engines.

Travellers use search engines to locate a vacation destination, find sites where they can arrange their transportation and find web offers that allow them to plan their leisure activities before departure or upon arrival. The global information request services let us find pages that contain (or do not contain) travel-related keywords and phrases. Tenopir (1985) noted that full-text searching allows users to make immediate judgements about relevance. However, for such a complex knowledge domain like tourism, this leaves much to be desired. For most broad queries (e.g. 'hotel' or 'restaurant') there are millions of qualifying pages. There is little support to disambiguate short queries like 'hotel' unless embedded in a longer, more specific query. Furthermore, the medium has no inherent requirements of editorship and approval from authority. Hence, there is no authoritative information about the reliability and prestige of a web document or a site. Internet users who are looking for accurate and reliable information when they are planning or preparing their vacation or business trip sometimes find it very difficult to trust the information provided by the great number of different content providers available for one specific destination. Moreover, the current state of search engines is updated irregularly, is biased towards listing more popular information and has most of the pages ripped out. Also, the immense size of the Web and the increasing proportion of invisible web pages, caused by either file formats unreadable for standard robot technology or backend databases, is stopping the major search engines from providing anywhere near complete search. But the number of pages available on the Internet is growing faster than can be indexed and, therefore, finding relevant information becomes increasingly difficult (Chakrabarti, 2003).

Due to the vital role of tourism in many countries and regions in Europe, a number of programs concerning tourism promotion have been installed. Government and private tourism organizations have been established in order to strengthen a tourism destination. The basic content and most of the information about destinations are, today, produced by the local or regional tourism authorities and, in most countries in the world, co-coordinated by a National Tourism Organization. These organizations, commonly referred to as destination marketing organizations (DMOs), are the main suppliers of up-to-date information for people who travel to a certain destination. In Europe, tourism is among the most advanced economic sectors for the use of Internet for e-commerce and for the percentage of actors with a website (EC, 2003). The Internet provides unprecedented opportunities for DMOs, as there are only few other economic activities where the generation, gathering, processing, application and communication of information is so important for day-to-day operations (WTO, 2001). In fact, the Web has revolutionized the conception of communication and interaction for many DMOs (Buhalis, 2003). It offers new ways of business-to-business and business-to-consumer transactions, new mechanisms for person-to-person communication and new means of discovering and obtaining information, services and products electronically.

The complexity and inscrutability of the net makes it more and more difficult for DMOs to make their offer visible and accessible for potential tourists or actual visitors who want to prepare themselves before or during their stay. As a consequence, research on the effectiveness of tourism websites has gained significant popularity (Tierney, 2000; Buhalis and Spada, 2000; Bauernfeind et al., 2002). The vast majority of authors agree that accessibility and visibility has become a basic requirement for DMOs who want to market their destination on the Web effectively.

However, considering the characteristics of the Web, this is not a trivial task as can be seen from a study the author conducted in order to evaluate the ranking of 299 European cities' tourism organizations' (CTOs) websites on the three most popular search engines in 2002. Evaluation of web rankings, which was carried out by a group of 25 students participating in a seminar on Tourism Information Systems supervised by the author, considered two alternative search strategies ('tasks') to gather accommodation and other types of travel-related information before departure or upon arrival in a city. Specifically, in the first task, students were asked to look up the name of each of the cities on AltaVista, Google and Yahoo! using the English and native spelling (e.g. 'Prague' and 'Praha') and to annotate the ranking of the first page referencing to the official DMO's website. In the second slightly altered task, students were asked to analyse the ranking when the city's name was entered together with the keyword 'hotel' connected by the Boolean operator AND.

The findings of this research are summarized in Table 13.1. By far, the best results are achieved when someone enters the city name in its native language only. In Google this strategy will work for 84% of the cities where the official website will appear among the top 20 links recommended by the search engine. Yahoo! delivered similar results as Google, whereas AltaVista made it more difficult to find an official DMO's website. The average ranking of a website listed among the top 20 recommendations varies between 3 and 4. When a city is searched by its English name, official tourism offices' websites are less likely to be found; the chances of appearing among the first 20 recommendations drop by approximately 5% throughout all three search engines.

The likelihood of a DMO website being recommended by one of the main search engines dramatically decreases when someone particularizes

Table 13.1. How difficult is it to find information of official city tourist offices' websites in Europe by using global search engines?

| | Keywords used: city name | | | | | |
| | In English | | | In native language | | |
	AltaVista	Google	Yahoo!	AltaVista	Google	Yahoo!
Top 20 appearances	156	201	187	167	213	196
Percentage	**61.7**	**79.4**	**73.9**	**66.0**	**84.2**	**77.5**
Average top 20 rank	4.7	3.9	3.7	4.5	4.0	3.8
Standard deviation	4.4	4.1	3.9	4.3	4.2	4.1

| | Keywords used: city name + 'hotel' | | | | | |
| | In English | | | In native language | | |
	AltaVista	Google	Yahoo!	AltaVista	Google	Yahoo!
Top 20 appearances	26	25	44	27	21	46
Percentage	**10.3**	**9.9**	**17.4**	**10.7**	**8.3**	**18.2**
Average top 20 rank	9.1	6.4	8.6	10.1	8.3	9.7
Standard deviation	5.8	4.6	6.5	5.8	5.7	6.5

search by adding an additional search term. Search engines' responses for the names of 299 European cities and the keyword 'hotel' frequently led to a great number of websites, among which were many offerings of individual hotels, but comprehensive hotel lists were commonly offered by CTOs' websites. Official tourist offices' websites were largely not found in this examination; only 18% of all evaluated DMO websites were included among the first 20 recommendations on Yahoo!. This ratio drops to only 11% and 10% when the same search terms are launched on AltaVista and Google.

This survey clearly shows that it is very difficult for DMOs to be found by visitors and potential city-break tourists. The problem becomes even worse for large cities like London, Paris or Rome, where information provided by the local DMO competes with a much greater number of similar contents provided by other companies. The DMO's Internet accessibility also varies by country of origin (see Table 13.2). DMOs in French and Italian cities were significantly less frequently listed among the first 20 pages recommended by the main search engines than in cities located in other European countries.

2. Domain-specific Search Engines

A necessary response to these search problems is the creation of domain-specific web portals and specialized search engines. Even though generic search engines are currently the most important way for users to find information on the Web, there are compelling reasons for the continuing development of specialized search engines. These reasons include technical and economical advantages, as well as improvements to search ability (Steele, 2001). The

Table 13.2. Accessibility of official city tourist offices' websites by different European countries.

Country	Number of cities	Percentage found among top 20	Average top 20 rank	Standard deviation
Germany	70	**51**	6.1	4.8
Spain	14	**49**	10.4	4.7
Great Britain	25	**46**	5.4	4.6
Other cities	75	**44**	6.4	5.1
Netherlands	20	**44**	8.1	4.1
Italy	24	**41**	5.8	4.5
France	25	**37**	6.2	5.4

technical problem is that it is becoming increasingly difficult, if not impossible, for the general search engines to index the entire contents of the Web. This is also an economic hurdle as it is not cost-effective given the revenue a search engine can receive to build such an index. Also, the quality of search provided by specialized search engines can add more to the searching experiences by: (i) allowing searching of pages that are currently not searchable from the major search engines at all; (ii) providing a more up-to-date search; and (iii) adding more functionality and search power in the searching of all searchable pages (see also Steele, 2001).

Domain-specific search engines are also becoming increasingly popular because they offer increased accuracy and extra features not possible with the general, web-wide search engines (McCallum *et al.*, 1999). They allow users to search for information that they currently cannot easily search for in a number of ways. Broadly speaking, this may involve more thorough searching of the static Web or parts of the Invisible Web (something not currently done by the major search engines). Each specialized search engine can allow searching of just a subset of these pages currently not searchable from the major search engines. For instance, many DMOs maintain their calendar of events so that it can be accessed by the user solely by filling out a form indicating the anticipated travel period and interest in various topics (e.g. opera, musical, museum, folk or sport events). Information that is maintained in this form can hardly be accessed by the common web spiders and, hence, are not available on the global search engines. Moreover, the major search engines often do not thoroughly search through websites. They may index all pages that are a few links down from the site's home page but may not enable access to deeper content. Finally, the major search engines generally can not maintain up-to-date indexes, which is a result of the vast number of pages that must be crawled. A specialized search engine, as it has a smaller number of pages to monitor, can more frequently crawl these, which leads to more up-to-date search results for users.

Extra functionality refers to the presentation of more sophisticated interfaces to users that are configured for the particular domain of search. Since all users visiting a domain-specific search engine belong to a group of people with similar interests and desires, domain-specific search engines can more effectively employ user profile information to make meaningful recommendations to users who have difficulties specifying their interests and needs. Also the fact that pages of only a targeted category or subject matter appear in the results list can improve the users' search experience.

There is an increasing number of tourism-related portals that apply domain-specific search engine technologies (e.g. www.travel-finder.com, www.campsearch.com, www.visiteuropeancities.com). Following Steele (2001), specialized search engines can be classified according to the way they build their index: (i) crawling a predefined set of qualified websites; (ii) collecting domain-specific pages preferentially using machine-learning techniques; and (iii) crawling at query time using semantic web technology.

2.1 Crawling a predefined set of qualified websites

Limiting the scope of web crawlers to websites with similar information is the easiest way to build a domain-specific search engine. Moreover, architects of this type of search engine have the opportunity to thoroughly investigate each of the websites included in the list of potentially interesting sites, and to develop tailor-made tools that extend the search coverage of general search engines. Today, almost every DMO has established searchable databases with important travel information, similar upcoming events or hotel information. Metasearching these specialized databases is a way to allow the searching of content that is not crawled by the general search engines (Wu *et al.*, 2001) and that is very valuable information for a traveller who wants to look up a particular event or activity in any of the destinations covered by the portal. A downside to building a metasearch engine is that the interfaces to the various sites to be searched can change frequently. This means that the developers of the metasearcher need to continually update their software to reflect these changes.

LawCrawler (www.lawcrawler.com) is a domain-specific search engine that searches for legal information on the Web. Moreover, www.moreover. com searches for the latest news from crawling a set of over 1800 respected news sites up to four times per hour. There are a number of specialized search engines using a predefined set of qualified websites. A specific example for tourism is www.visiteuropeancities.info, the web portal of European City Tourism, which will be outlined and discussed below.

2.2 Collecting domain-specific pages preferentially using machine-learning techniques

When qualified websites cannot be identified, constraining the contents of the search index to a particular topic or category by using machine-learning filtering techniques may become the only alternative in order to build a specialized search engine. In this approach the search engine's index is generated automatically using a filtering technique (Chau and Chen, 2003a,b) which may be enhanced by an adaptive reinforcement procedure (Kaelbling *et al.*, 1996; Rennie and McCallum, 1999; McCallum *et al.*, 1999; Chau *et al.*, 2003). In these techniques a robot is given a few starting nodes on the Web where its goal is to seek out and collect other nodes that satisfy specific requirements that are defined by a human or machine classifier. Chakrabarti has outlined the general framework of a focused crawler using a machine-learning approach (Chakrabarti *et al.*, 1999; Chakrabarti, 2003, p. 270). First, he suggests that a suitable sample of pages from the Web need to be marked by human effort as positive and negative samples for the domain under consideration. A supervised classifier is trained to distinguish the positive and negative samples, which are then evaluated using new web pages. If the classifier judges that the page is positive, outlinks from this page will be added to the work pool as with standard crawlers; otherwise they will not be considered for further crawling.

Although there are a growing number of applications in the automatic information extraction and domain-specific processing arena, none of these have relevance for tourism. ResearchIndex (formerly CiteSeer, see researchindex.org) is a specialized search engine for automatically finding computer science papers (Lawrence *et al.*, 1999). It is a free public service and is currently indexing more than 300,000 articles containing over 3 million citations (Lawrence, 2000). ResearchIndex automates the creation of citation indices for scientific literature, provides easy access to the context of citations in papers and has specialized functionality for extracting information commonly found in research articles.

Other specialized search engines automatically parsing the Web include Deadliner (Kruger *et al.*, 2000) for finding conference deadlines, Hpsearch (http://paulin.uni-trier.de/hp/) for finding personal home pages of computer scientists (Hoff and Mundhenk, 2001) and FlipDog (www.flipdog.com), which looks at job postings on websites. In the case of Deadliner the document retrieval phase starts by crawling sites that are known to contain conference deadline postings; then, the system makes use of a focused crawler to find other relevant pages. In addition, major search engines are metasearched to find even more pages. Finally, support Vector Machines are trained and later used to rigorously filter out irrelevant documents.

2.3 Crawling at query time using semantic web technology

Extra crawling at query time is difficult for a generic search engine since there are too many possible sites and pages to attempt to crawl at query time. It may, however, be possible when the search engine is dealing with a specific topic and has a domain-specific knowledge about where to look. Developments that promise real-time querying of the web space are current research activities in the field of XML and semantic web services. Both are trying to create a web of machine-readable data. The semantic web is an extension of the current web in which information is given well-defined meaning, better enabling computers and people to work in cooperation (Hendler *et al.*, 2002). This new format of the World Wide Web is envisioned to be as capable as the current World Wide Web (WWW), but consists of machine-readable data, which has the potential for having a major impact on searching the Web.

There are a number of international research groups jointly working on building semantic web services. Activity-based searching (ABS), for instance, is a distributed project involving researchers from the Knowledge Systems Laboratory at Stanford, Knowledge Management Group at IBM Almaden and W3C's Semantic Web Advanced Development Initiatives (http://tap. stanford.edu/). ABS, for instance, applies TAP to the problem of searching for information on the Internet. TAP-based results complement traditional search results by determining the kinds of activities that are typically associated with a concept a search term belongs to. In the case that the search term has multiple denotations (e.g. 'jaguar' could denote the animal or the car), the system selects one and offers the user the ability to choose the other denotation. Given the search query, ABS retrieves real-time data relevant to that query augmented by the knowledge base.

The creation of a tourism-related ontology as well as ontology-based applications are a precondition for effectively using this technology in a tourism-specific search engine (Maedche and Staab, 2002; Maedche *et al.*, 2003). Although the experimental knowledge base in Stanford already includes knowledge about places and tourist attractions, the ontology is still too simple and incomplete to be adopted by the industry. Other systems such as Cyc (http://www.cyc.com/) have a deep knowledge about basic, common-sense phenomena, but do not have knowledge about particulars. Although Resource Description Framework (RDF) and extensible markup language (XML) are becoming widely recognized as the standard vehicle for describing metadata (Berners-Lee *et al.*, 2001), an enormous amount of semantic data is encoded in hypertext markup language (HTML) documents. However, systems that offer automated techniques, which support the creation of an ontology, for instance, by means of small samples of relevant websites, are currently being developed (Davulcu *et al.*, 2003).

Other approaches that integrate some aspects of real-time querying for domain-specific search engines are post-retrieval analysis of metasearch engine results (Chen *et al.*, 1998, 2001; Glover *et al.*, 1999) and domain-specific web search with keyword spices (Oyama *et al.*, 2003). When a metasearch engine returns a ranked list of links to a set of web pages relevant to a user query, the user has to go through these web pages manually to gain a comprehensive understanding of them and judge their relevance to the original query. This browsing process can be very time-consuming and requires substantial mental effort. Chen *et al.* (1998, 2001) have demonstrated that web content-mining techniques involving self-organizing map (SOM) algorithms can be applied to perform post-retrieval analysis of a retrieved document set that generally improves the searching experience. A major drawback of post-retrieval analysis is the computation time and resources needed. While a simple ranked list of search results usually can be returned to the user within a few seconds, post-retrieval analysis may take much longer, from several seconds up to a few minutes. Also, more computation, time and memory are often required. These limitations may be severe, especially for web-based search engines, which have to handle thousands to millions of search queries per day.

3. Travel Web Portals

Travel portals aim to provide information request services, travel-related physical products and exchange services for travellers. Offering just one of these services or all services for only one destination has not been economically viable; however, the bundle of offerings by portals is likely to provide the basis for economic success (Singh, 2004). Portals aggregate the informational functions of the different types of online firms. However, different stages of development as well as different business models exist (Singh, 2004). Depending on the business model they offer a broad array of resources and services such as search engines, e-mail lists, forums and booking services for suppliers who usually are located elsewhere. The objectives of web portals can vary and range from information exchange and community-building services for the clients, providing recommendation functions that support potential travellers in their travel decision-making process, to systems that provide full e-commerce capabilities when individual products or packages are sold directly by the site. Prominent examples for the latter type of commercially oriented travel portals are Travelocity (metamorphosing from being just an exchange website) and Microsoft's Expedia.

For a DMO, whose primary objective is marketing its destination by providing interesting and accurate travel information (and not selling particular travel arrangements), commercially oriented travel portals are not appropriate. Furthermore, in many destinations the legal form of the DMO and its affiliation to the local government prevents the management to enter into a business relationship with privately organized companies offering travel-related portal services. As a consequence, DMOs have started building their own portal services by first vertically, and later horizontally, expanding their content. The vertical integration started by including information on local tourism suppliers (accommodation, transportation, museums, etc.), who – to a varying extent – use the DMO platform to present themselves and the services they provide. An increasing number of DMOs apply sophisticated content management tools in order to administrate their web appearance and to integrate other local content providers in their platform.

Horizontal integration is a relatively new area that has also been recently recognized by the European Commission and funded in the context of the Interchange of Data between Administration (IDA) program. The European Tourism Destination Portal is the implementation of this initiative foreseen in the eEurope 2005 action plan under the heading 'Modern online public services'. The aim of this project is to develop a European portal to promote European destinations and contribute to maintain, as much as possible, the current international tourism market share of Europe. For this to happen, the portal must address needs of both tourists originating from outside and within the region. The main objective of such a horizontal portal is to serve potential or actual visitors (undecided or decided customers) who want to access one or more of the official tourism websites in order to satisfy their information needs.

Access to existing content and the interoperability of tourism information platforms is difficult. The technical realization of such a platform, which serves on top of several other vertical platforms, can be accomplished either by means of manual content aggregation supported by traditional content management tools or by self-organizing, automatic content gathering and access procedures as provided by domain-specific search engines. The former approach holds the danger that the operator of the portal will more and more centralize information of its clients and therefore will increasingly compete with the currently existing content providers. This will create resistance not only for reasons of individual identity loss of each participating destination but also as DMOs will fear to lose their core competence as information providers. The second approach, deploying domain-specific search engine technology, foresees that all participating DMOs remain independent organizations.

4. Case Study: The European City Tourism Web Portal

The European City Tourism web portal is an initiative of European Cities Tourism (ECT), an association of currently more than 80 CTOs (see www.europeancitiestourism.com) representing 31 European countries (Wöber, 2003). It demonstrates the applicability of the concept of domain-specific search engines not only for tourism web portals but also for being a powerful market research tool, which delivers highly relevant comparative information for tourism managers.

The ECT web portal belongs to the group of domain-specific search engines whose database is generated by robots crawling a predefined set of qualified websites. The web server and database system, which has been developed by a team of researchers at the Institute for Tourism and Leisure Studies at the Vienna University of Economics and Business Administration, consists of the following components:

1. Domain database.
2. Graphical user interface for the managers operating and using the system.
3. Graphical user interface for the users of the portal.
4. Query processor.
5. Source database.
6. Scoring module.
7. User log file.
8. Management information system module.
9. Web crawler.
10. Text processor/web content miner.
11. Recommender module.

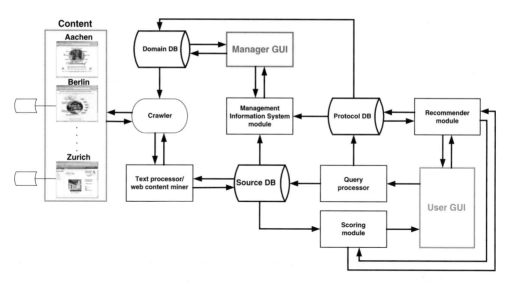

Fig. 13.1. The architecture of the ECT web portal.

The architecture of the ECT web portal is outlined in Fig. 13.1. The **domain database** defines the boundaries of the domain and therefore the system's capabilities. The principal component of the domain database is the list of uniform resource locator (URL) addresses of tourism-related websites for each city served by the ECT web portal, supplemented by general information for each city required for some other information services offered by the web portal. Currently, 300 European cities are served by the ECT web portal. The respective URL addresses are maintained by each individual DMO and the ECT secretariat by means of the user-friendly graphical user interface (GUI) for tourism managers (**manager GUI**).

Normally, the official tourist board's website will be the only data source represented for each individual city in the data repository. However, since some tourism organizations have outsourced all or parts of their services (e.g. booking services) to various content providers, the web portal also offers the opportunity to define several websites that jointly represent the web content recommended by the official tourism authority.

Additional data stored in the domain database refers to structured information, which is relatively static in nature and is available for all cities. Examples are a short description or slogan of the city, longitude and latitude information to identify the city on a dynamically generated map, name of the country the city belongs to, population, currency, passport and visa requirement, official language(s), a standard picture, etc. Although this information is centrally stored by the web portal's server, it is also maintained by a city board's website operator.

The next component is the **user interface**, which is responsible for accepting user input and presenting the output (see Fig. 13.2). The user interface allows users to query the database and customize their searches. The appearance of the ECT web portal's home page is very simple. The

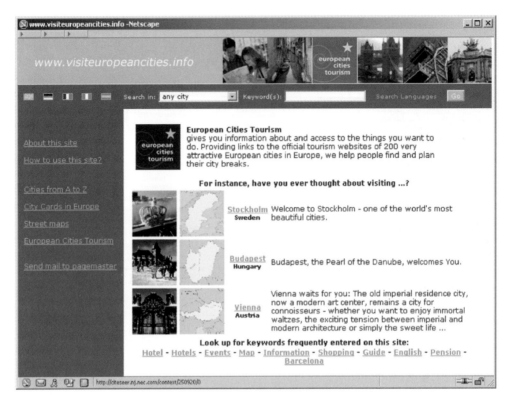

Fig. 13.2.   The ECT web portal's user interface.

basic query feature requires the user either to enter a keyword (or phrase) or to select a city from a list, or both. Users can search documents using keywords together with appropriate Boolean operators thanks to the **query processor**, which generates a reasonable database query from the user input. If the keyword or phrase specified by the user is available in the **source database**, the system will retrieve and present all available web pages ranked by its relevance (see Fig. 13.3). Responsible for the ranking is the **scoring module**, which processes each result before sending the result to the user interface for display. Each search result features a page link, the name of the city the page is associated with, a rating that indicates the relative number of times the term was found on the page (compared to the number of other terms that appear on the page), as well as an abstract.

The majority of DMO web pages have URLs from where the user cannot guess which information a specific page provides. Therefore, the abstracts that are retrieved from the text of the respective page and presented on the screen are the only source users can base their decisions on as to which of the suggested links they will select for closer inspection. The procedure that generates the abstract also selects the text fragment of up to 300 characters which contains the maximum occurrence of the searched keyword(s).

Fig. 13.3. Results when searching for 'Hotel' (2946 links found).

In addition to the keyword retrieval system, three cities are randomly featured on the home page using icons and little descriptions to help users think of destination alternatives (see Fig. 13.2). Each icon is linked to a city-specific page that features mapping tools, a link to the city home page, a top ten list of city-specific keywords and a list of neighbouring cities (see Fig. 13.4).

The portal monitors all user activities in a **user log file** including the text and/or city the user has selected or entered into the system, and the web pages the user has actually selected for viewing. In case the user has specified a keyword that is unknown by the system, the word will also be stored in the user log file. Analysis of the user log file helps to identify outdated web pages that need to be refreshed by the crawler. Moreover, the user log file is regularly analysed by the **management information system (MIS) module**. The MIS module generates a list of highly interesting key indicators that supports managers in evaluating and benchmarking the performance of their website.

Traditional website evaluation studies rely either on qualitative methods by collecting and analysing user or expert opinions (Benbunan-Fich, 2001; Jeong and Lambert, 2001) or on applying quantitative measures from automated website-analysing tools (Ivory *et. al.*, 2000; Scharl, 2000; Olsina and Rossi, 2001; Wöber *et al.*, 2002; Ivory, 2003). A combination of quantitative

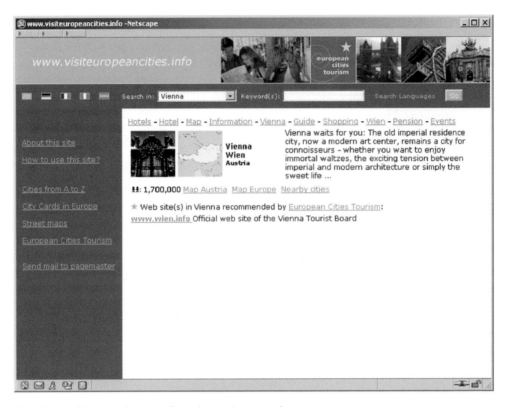

Fig. 13.4. City-specific page featuring various services.

and qualitative assessment for the evaluation of European city tourism and national tourism organizations' websites was introduced by Bauernfeind *et al.* (2002). In this study the authors complemented web content-mining data generated by a web crawler with success indicators such as number of visits or inquiries retrieved by a survey among the managers of the corresponding tourism organizations.

Automated website-analysing tools can be used to obtain information about navigation, interactivity, layout and textual features. The strengths of this computer-supported type of evaluation lie in the inclusion of more objective measures and, by means of larger samples, in the chance to draw more general conclusions compared with solely qualitative studies. Weaknesses remain concerning the comparability and significance of the success measures and the fact that the actual user needs are not considered in the evaluation process (Jansen *et al.*, 2000). For example, a large number of page views recorded by a tourism website may be a sign of a management's success in effectively marketing an organization's website more than an indicator for a demand-oriented and informative content that is available through a well-designed, easy-to-use system. The ECT web portal, following a collaborative information provision concept, provides a solution to this major drawback in tourism website evaluation research.

For monitoring the success and development of a CTO's website, the ECT web portal regularly generates comprehensive reports based on the constantly updated access statistics. These comparative studies are communicated either through the manager interface or by automatically sending an e-mail to all managers involved (i.e. members of ECT).

The studies provide highly relevant information for tourism management and include figures describing:

- content provided by a certain destination's website compared to content provided by other destinations in the database (i.e. uniqueness of offer);
- content requested by the users vs content actually provided by the DMO's website (i.e. usefulness of information); and
- language versions requested by the users vs languages actually offered by a particular DMO website.

An indexer compares keywords extracted from each individual web page with information commonly requested by users. Congruencies are analysed and indices are stored into the database. Information that is extracted from the user log file can be classified into three categories:

1.   Information that describes system usage as an indicator for the success in marketing the tourism web portal as an effective tool for undecided and decided city-break travellers. Typical key indicators in this category are the total number of visitations and queries made to the system and the distribution of languages selected by the visitors.

2.   Information that describes the users' interests is available from the text they enter in the fields 'keyword' and 'city' (see Table 13.3). Information collected here is comparable to the unaided response frequently applied in travel surveys where customers are asked where they want to spend their vacation and/or what they are actually interested in during their stay. Valuable information can be generated that includes the most frequently asked keywords and cities and the distribution of query styles applied by users (i.e. number of times users have specified only a keyword, a city name or both). This data can be further used to estimate the users' stage in the decision-making process.

3.   Relative measures for each participating city based on comparative information and analysis. The analysis of 'city bundles', i.e. groups of cities that are commonly requested by a single web user, is a precondition for effective city tourism management collaborations and, therefore, highly interesting information from a managerial point of view. Another example of comparative information, which can be derived from the user log file, is the relative user interest for a particular city expressed by the number of times a city's website was clicked by the user divided by the number of links the web portal returned (offered) to the user.

Another important component is the domain-specific **web crawler**, which is directly connected to the **text-processing and web content-mining module**. The web crawler collects web pages from all the database-specified websites in the domain (i.e. servers). One characteristic of tourism web pages,

Table 13.3. Most frequently searched keywords and cities on www.visiteuropeancities.info (June–December 2003).

Top ten keywords and phrases			
The user has selected from suggestions	Percentage	Entered by the user in form	Percentage
Hotels	21.5	Hotel	17.3
Map	17.4	Events	15.9
Hotel	16.3	Hotels	15.8
Information	10.4	Map	14.7
Guide	7.1	Information	9.7
Events	7.1	Shopping	7.2
English	4.4	Guide	6.9
Pension	4.1	English	3.5
Shopping	3.5	Pension	2.0
Points of interest	2.2	Guides	1.9
Most requested cities	Percentage	Most frequently visited web pages	Percentage
Vienna	24.5	Dublin	12.5
Stockholm	7.5	Vienna	11.6
Barcelona	7.3	London	7.2
Brussels	5.1	Reykjavik	6.3
Gothenborg	4.9	Gothenborg	5.5
Amsterdam	4.5	Barcelona	5.3
Paris	4.4	Paris	4.5
Seville	4.3	Glasgow	4.5
Prague	4.2	Prague	4.5
Budapest	4.0	Copenhagen	4.5
Warsaw	3.7	Liverpool	4.1
Aachen	3.7	Brussels	3.6
Berlin	3.2	Berlin	3.3
Luxembourg	2.6	Birmingham	2.5
Dublin	2.5	Bergen	1.7
London	2.3	Cardiff	1.7
Zagreb	1.6	Luxembourg	1.6
Heidelberg	1.4	Zagreb	1.4
Rome	1.2	Stockholm	1.3
Birmingham	1.1	Aachen	1.3

Note: Cities providing a back-link to the ECT web portal and members of ECT are better ranked by the ECT web portal.

particularly in Europe, is that the information is commonly displayed in various languages. DMOs that experience many international visitors from different countries frequently offer their website in more than five languages (www.wien.info, the website of the Vienna tourist board, for example, is offered in nine languages).

What sounds superb at first glance becomes a problem when a user who is not capable of multiple languages inspects results from a query with keywords that exist in different languages. For example, the word 'information' exists in (at least) three languages: English, German and French. A search for 'information' would, therefore, result in all pages from 300 CTOs, regardless of whether the content can actually be understood by the user. In order to avoid the problem of users being offered pages that lead to websites they cannot read, search engines must offer tools where users can specify their language capabilities, and eliminate pages from search results according to this preference. However, this requires search engines to categorize web documents by their language, which is a typical text-processing task.

Similar to other search engines providing multilingual search services, the ECT text-processing module uses an N-gram-based approach for language classification (Cavnar and Trenkle, 1994). The system is based on calculating and comparing profiles of N-gram frequencies. First, the system computes profiles on training set data that represent samples for 13 different languages (English, German, Spanish, French, Italian, Dutch, Swedish, Finnish, Czech, Danish, Hungarian, Portuguese and Norwegian). Then the system computes a profile for a particular document that is to be classified. Finally, the system computes a distance measure between the document's profile and each of the category profiles. It then selects the category whose profile has the smallest distance to the document's profile. The profiles involved are quite small, typically 10 kilobytes for a category training set. For individual pages the minimum number of characters required to correctly identify the language is less then 300. This procedure is small, fast and robust. It works extremely well for language classification, achieving a 99% correct classification rate on city tourism websites available on www.visiteuropeancities.info.

The final component is the **recommender module**. The recommender module leverages content and community information to target the optimal website to consumers. Gretzel and Wöber (2004) have proposed a unified framework for merging collaborative and content-based recommendations. As a complement to the MIS module that supports tourism managers for improving their web appearance, the recommender module represents a learning opportunity for users.

Previous studies on the travel destination decision process have shown that a travel recommender system ideally deals with various consumer decision styles (Grabler and Zins, 2002; Zins, 2003). The process of creating and offering tailor-made products for people who are swamped with information on the Internet becomes increasingly important. In tourism, a growing number of consumers have a highly undefined mental mode when they plan a trip. These recommendation-oriented users, as labelled by Grabler and Zins (2002), have a tendency to last minute travels as well as completely individual travel arrangements and, in comparison to others, they do not feel bound to certain destinations or accommodation types. However, they show a high affinity to recommendations because they wish to be inspired by the system.

The recommender module built into the ECT web portal offers several ways in which users are provided with an initial information seed. For users looking for general inspiration, the site provides a list of European cities from A to Z with links to the respective city tourism office websites. Additionally, the system presents users with a drop-down list of cities that represent the sub-domains to which a search could be restricted. Most importantly, the results page features a list of ten keywords suggested by the system as possible terms to be used by the user. These keywords are the most frequently searched keywords by other users who have previously visited the system. Only terms that are entered in the form are considered for the permanently updated list of most frequently searched keywords. To avoid a premature saturation of items, selections from the top ten suggestions do not count in the updating procedure. Keywords are also suggested when someone has decided on a specific destination. In this case, the system considers only keywords that have been selected by other users when they were searching for information on this particular city.

The recommender module requires continuous analysis of the user log file. In order to react to changes in the visitors' interests during the year (e.g. winter and summer sport activities) and to adapt to the general evolution of peoples' travel motives and information needs, only the last 2 months of entries are considered in the analysis of keywords. By this means the web portal learns from actual system usage and adapts itself automatically to changes in customers' preferences. As the frequency distribution of keywords is relatively stable over a short period of time, the procedures do not have to be launched at run time. Currently, the recommender module updates its knowledge base every 2 h.

As discussed by Grabler and Zins in Chapter 7, empirically testing the significance of various mental modes of users planning a trip is not a trivial task. The analysis of the log files generated by the ECT web portal has shown that the inspirational features of the system are heavily used, suggesting that many users are looking for a clue where they could start their search. Between June and December 2003, www.visiteuropeancities.info experienced 39,894 visitors (distinct Internet Protocol (IP) addresses) who have requested 256,179 pages (URL addresses) from the portal. About 64,350 (25%) of all requested pages refer to the portal's home page as illustrated in Fig. 13.5. The analysis of the user dialogue provides two principal phases of the recommendation process: (i) the **information-searching phase**; and (ii) the **activity selection phase** where the user decides for internal or external information sources. Non-task-specific activities, like users searching for online help or reading the imprint, are ignored since it accounts for only 4.2% of all activities.

Activities in the information-searching phase are grouped according to the user's information search behaviour into *retrieving* or *browsing* activities. According to Stephenson (1988), a user is retrieving when he or she knows what information is wanted. A user who wants to retrieve information needs to be aware of the system's content and functionality and how to set up a database query. During the first 7 months when the system was in operation, typical retrieving functions (e.g. looking up for a particular keyword or

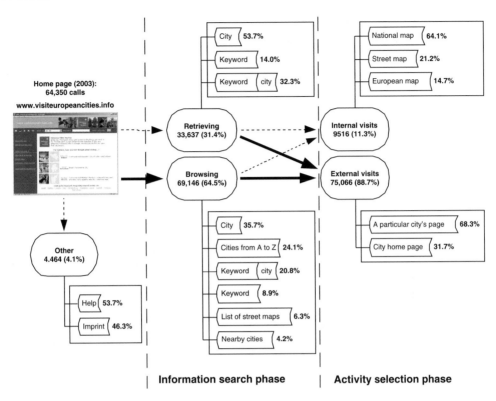

Fig. 13.5.   User activities on the ECT B2C web portal.

phrase or a city, or both) accounted for 31.4% of all system activities in the information-searching phase.

When users are unsure of what information they are exactly looking for, or where to look to find the necessary information support, they tend to browse around the website. During the first 7 months of operation, browsing activities clearly dominated the information-searching phase on the ECT web portal. Almost 65% of all user activities on the ECT web portal's entry phase were observed for this type of information search behaviour. This result is a clear indication of the significance of the system's inspirational features and stresses the importance of research activities in this field.

The 'activity selection phase' starts when users receive a list of recommended web pages (sorted list of links), where they need to decide between none, one or more of the offered services. Services are divided into external and internal services. External services refer to users who are leaving the portal to visit one of the recommended web pages; 88.7% of all user activities in this phase, or 29.3% of all activities on the portal, are user requests for visiting DMO web pages. A high number of external links are welcomed by the operators of the system, since the main purpose of the web portal is to recommend other websites' pages. Graphics generated for locating a city on various maps is the only internal information service currently supported by the system. A total of 11.3% of all activities in the final phase of the recommendation process refer to this service.

The results of the analysis of the user log files stress the importance of the recommendation services provided by the ECT web portal. Further improvements of the recommender module are currently under way. For example, Gretzel and Wöber (2004) have suggested an extension to the basic procedure that supports users in refining and expanding a query when someone has entered a specific search term.

5. Summary and Future Research

The regional and/or national websites are, and will remain, the source of tourism information, and will continue to be responsible for their image and the quality of the information made available. Networks of tourism organizations where all members are able to exchange information on the success of their systems not only help to learn and improve present tourism websites but also contribute to the standardization and harmonization of design and data models. Interorganizational relations among tourism organizations have therefore become an interest of tourism practitioners and academics (Selin and Beason, 1990). The effectiveness of these relations depends on the ability of each participating organization to generate any additional value for its customers. One of the main drawbacks for a customer who browses various tourism websites is the lack of standardization that exists. This heterogeneity refers not only to the content, which is actually provided by the different organizations, but also to the style of presentation and the way users are navigated through a system. Furthermore, the information overload on the Internet hampers users who are interested in the most accurate and relevant travel information to identify official tourist offices' websites among the many sources usually presented by traditional search engines. To address this information and cognitive overload problem, research must develop new techniques and tools to analyse, categorize and visualize specialized collections of web pages. Hence, a variety of tools are needed to assist searching, gathering, monitoring and analysing information on the Internet.

This chapter has discussed state-of-the-art search engine technology and its use for travel planning on the WWW. The current major search engines fail to provide ideal search in a number of ways. They cover a relatively small proportion of the static web pages, their indexes can be significantly out of date, they do not search the vast number of pages in the Invisible Web and they fail to provide sophisticated search when the user has a specialized category or topic of search in mind. Moreover, they fail to provide any meaningful suggestions if the user wants to be inspired.

Based on requirements of people who want to plan a trip on the Web, it seems possible to improve the traditional approaches by means of domain-specific search engines. Specialized search engines can search more of the Web and in a more up-to-date fashion within their domain. They can provide more search functionality, superior search in their domain vs the major search engines in terms of standard retrieval metrics, and provide better structured search results.

A big disadvantage with specialized search engines is that people simply want to use one all-purpose search engine. Finding the best specialized search engine becomes a difficult task when the number of search engines on the Internet increases. Furthermore, it could be argued that if search engines index many pages that are of interest to very few people this might not be economically viable and the search engines would need to cut back on indexing these low-interest pages.

The applicability of specialized search engines is demonstrated by www.visiteuropeancities.info, the web portal of ECT. The system consists of a focused web crawler, which seeks, acquires, indexes and maintains pages of European CTOs. Information from the web crawler accompanied by data generated from the server's access logs is analysed in order to provide decision style-dependent recommendation services as well as indicators for improving the websites of all participating tourism organizations. The ECT web portal consists of a number of innovative features like automatic removal and alert functions for websites with broken links, and functions that allow the calculation of distances in order to identify nearby cities. Furthermore, the system consists of sophisticated features that support the concept of decentralized maintenance for all participating DMOs.

The services offered by the European portal are designed to complement the services offered by national or regional tourism sites, so as to avoid any form of competition between them. The portal provides a more integrated chain of European services leading the potential tourist to the most relevant CTOs' websites, making the tourist's research easier through a user-friendly dialogue. In addition, the ECT web portal contributes to increase the number of visitors on a single city tourism website by improving its visibility worldwide. For the tourists, the portal contributes to making European cities more attractive and desirable. The multilingual dialogue, standardized presentation of information and guidance for retrieving the most accurate information by means of a user-friendly interface help potential travellers in their decision-making process. In addition to fulfilling customers' actual needs, the tourism portal provides a platform for tourism organizations to bundle their destinations' websites and, therefore, allows joint marketing activities. The concept also opens valuable opportunities to gain insights into the consumers' decision-making process by tracking the users' information needs. Further benefits refer to the low operational costs of the presented technology. The cost effectiveness of the ECT web portal puts pressure on all tourism actors to use common standards and, therefore, facilitates the integration of tourism information sites in Europe.

Chapter Summary

This chapter has discussed the advantages and limitations of domain-specific search engine technology for the development of tourism web portals. The case example outlined here focused on www.visiteuropeancities.info – the B2C site offered by European Cities Tourism (ECT), a pan-European association currently consisting of 90 European city tourism boards representing more than 30 European countries. Along with a comprehensive introduction to the application of web content-mining and web usage-mining techniques in domain-specific search engines, this chapter has also provided detailed information on the technical outline of the system and on the first users' responses after a 7-month trial period.

14 DieToRecs: A Case-based Travel Advisory System

FRANCESCO RICCI, DANIEL R. FESENMAIER, NADER MIRZADEH, HILDEGARD RUMETSHOFER, ERWIN SCHAUMLECHNER, ADRIANO VENTURINI, KARL W. WÖBER AND ANDREAS H. ZINS

1. Introduction

There is a growing number of websites that support a traveller in the selection of travel destinations or travel products (e.g. flight or hotel). Typically, the user is required to input product constraints or preferences, which are matched by the system in an electronic catalogue. Major e-commerce websites dedicated to tourism such as Expedia, Travelocity and TISCover have started to cope with travel planning by incorporating recommender systems, i.e. applications that provide advice to users about products (Schafer *et al.*, 2001). Recommender systems for travel planning try to mimic the interactivity observed in traditional counselling sessions with travel agents (Delgado and Davidson, 2002). The current generation of travel recommender systems focuses on destination selection and does not support the user through a personalized interaction in bundling a tailor-made trip comprising one or more locations to visit, an accommodation and additional attractions (museum, theatre, etc.).

The DieToRecs[10] system extends current recommender systems by incorporating a human choice model extracted from both the literature and the empirical analysis of the traveller's behaviour. DieToRecs supports the selection of travel products (e.g. a hotel or a visit to a museum or a climbing school) and building a 'travel bag', i.e. a coherent (from the user point of view) bundling of products. DieToRecs also supports multiple decision styles by letting the user 'enter' the system through three main 'doors': iterative single-item selection, complete travel selection and inspiration-driven selection. The first

[10] This work has been partially funded by the European Union's Fifth RTD Framework Programme (under contract DIETORECS IST–2000–29474).

door enables the most experienced user to efficiently navigate the potentially overwhelming information provided by the two integrated databases (TISCover and APT Trentino). The user is allowed to select whatever products he or she likes and in the preferred order using the selections done up to a certain point (and in the past) to personalize the next stage. The second 'door' enables the user to select a personalized trip that bundles together items available in the catalogue. The personalized plan is constructed by 'reusing' the structure and main content of trips either built by other users or available from some providers. The third door allows an inspiration-seeking user to choose a complete trip by exploiting a simpler user interface (icon-based) as well as an interaction, which is kept at the minimum length as possible. It must be stressed that all these decision styles are supported in a uniform and seamless way by means of a graphical user interface. Hence, switching from one style to another is always possible and easy to do.

Sections 2 and 3 describe our conceptual approach to travel planning and illustrate how the notion of decision styles emerged from the research. Then, we describe the fundamental element of the designed application and its technological implementation. We end the chapter by summarizing the results of this project and discussing some still open issues to recommendation system development.

2. Travel Decision Styles

Ideally, the system must enable a (new) user entering the travel destination recommendation system to be classified quickly in order to provide him or her the optimal navigational path and mode of presentation (type and sequence of questions, graphical widgets selection, length of interaction, etc.). The user should be able to influence the dialogue management component by explicitly volunteering information that is useful to determine his or her decision style. This can be achieved by self-selection of the decision style, for instance, by presenting iconic descriptions of the styles. Although Grabler and Zins (Chapter 12, this volume) recommend that information on a user's decision style should be acquired at a very early stage in the session, the system should provide the possibility of switching between different interface styles. Again, this can be achieved by self-selection of the user or derived from a pattern of user interaction with the computer. Information presented at a later stage of the user session should be structured differently according to the requirements of the respective decision styles. However, the following three stages are used to decompose the dialogue:

1.   Filtering: The user must be able to enter the primary variables or constraints that describe his or her decision style; however, not all information categories are required at the beginning of the dialogue.
2.   Specification: Additional information related to the responses provided in the first stage are presented to the user. An important aspect of this stage is that the user believes that only personally 'important' features are asked.
3.   Selection or sorting: The user must be able to make his final decision

based on a small number of alternatives presented. This list may be sorted by one (or more) of the key factors associated with the identified decision style and/or specified during the decision process by the user.

As the number of possible offers should be counted and provided to the user at any time, it is possible that a specific user session does not require all three stages as the number of matched offers may be limited. Additional information, which appears to be important in describing the characteristics of the decision process and therefore needs to be monitored and stored during a session, includes: usage type, sequence of sub-decisions, flexibility or rigidity of trip characteristics, degree of pre-specification, number of alternatives, decision style and experiential proneness.

3. The Proposed Approach

The theoretical considerations provided above set the requirements for a travel-planning recommender system that must support, by means of an adaptive behaviour, rather different decision styles and must personalize the suggestions on the base of both personal and travel characteristics. In this section we shall describe the basic design choices of the DieToRecs recommender system and illustrate a typical man–machine interaction. The DieToRecs system is based on the following elements:

- **Bundling a mix-and-match travel.** DieToRecs basically supports the user in building a personalized travel plan that can either comprise a pre-packaged offer or can be obtained by iteratively selecting tourist products (travel items) such as locations to visit, accommodations and activities. Item selection dialogue is driven by the personal and travel characteristics that are structurally decomposed into what are referred to as 'general travel wishes' and 'detailed travel wishes'. General travel wishes provide basic information about the nature of the travel the user is going to plan, like its duration, the travel party and the budget. Detailed travel wishes are preferences and constraints that the user expresses on features of the specific products (destinations, accommodations and activities) to be included in the 'travel bag'.
- **Allow the user to enter through three functional doors.** Users can build (configure) their travel plan by means of three top system functions, which act as different doors to enter the system. These doors enable users to provide in whatever order and amount they like general and detailed travel wishes. The first door allows the users to select whatever products they like and in the preferred order (Single-item Recommendation). The second door enables the users to select a personalized trip that bundles together items available in the catalogues (Complete Travel). The third door enables inspiration-seeking users to choose a complete trip exploiting (selecting and modifying) examples of travels shown by means of a user interface, which is strongly based on images and which minimizes the interaction length (Seeking for Inspiration). At any

moment users can switch from one system function to the other preserving the choices already done, allowing the users to build their travel by combining the three approaches; for example, the user can bundle his personalized travel first by selecting a complete trip using the second or third door and then by completing it with additional products from the catalogues using the first door.

- **Decision styles and functional doors.** Decision styles are initially mapped (probabilistically) to these functional doors. This means that DieToRecs is bootstrapped with a default assignment of decision styles to doors (e.g. the 'highly predefined user' to the first door), but user activity logs, stored as cases, will provide data for training the DieToRecs classifier to: (i) identify the decision style; and (ii) suggesting the user switch to another door.

- **Wizard-like GUI approach.** The system drives the users through the logical steps needed to define the travel. At any step of the decisional process, the system displays the next alternative steps that can be followed to complete the task. The sequence of steps depends on the functional door chosen. We will now describe this approach by means of a sample user session.

- **Register the user interaction session as a case.** The adaptive behaviour of DieToRecs is based on a structured representation of the interaction session that is stored as a case in a case-based reasoning system (Ricci *et al.*, 2002a). A case includes general travel and detailed travel wishes acquired during the interaction, items in the 'travel bag', feedback provided by the user on the items selected and an ordered list of the system functions called during the interaction (activity log).

- **Personalize the questions posed to the user using cases and catalogue analysis.** DieToRecs exploits Intelligent Query Management techniques to help the user identify his query. After having acquired some travel wishes from the user, DieToRecs poses in-context questions, trying either to further specify the travel wishes, whose effect is to tighten the search, or to relax conditions that cannot be satisfied. The identification of those travel wishes that could be asked or should be relaxed relies on: (i) the analysis of the users behaviours stored in the cases (statistics over user explicit preferences); (ii) constraint relaxation techniques; and (iii) information theory indicators, such as entropy, computed on the catalogues of products (Ricci *et al.*, 2002b).

- **Personalize the recommendations using collaboration filtering through case similarity.** The items (and the complete trips) suggested by DieToRecs are ranked according to a collaboration-via-content-based approach (Pazzani, 1999). In fact, items filtered according to the user travel item preferences are then sorted such that those contained in (or more similar to) similar recommendation sessions (cases) are scored best. In this respect DieToRecs is a hybrid recommender system that overcomes classical problems of pure collaborative-based approaches such as huge amounts of registered user logs data needed to deliver recommendations.

Details about the case structure, the recommendation methodology and the Intelligent Query Management technique can be found in Chapter 6 of this book. The rest of this section describes how tourists can bundle their trip by using DieToRecs. When starting to use the system, the users must first decide how to search through the travel and product catalogues managed by the system. If the users want to build their trip by selecting each travel item (destinations, accommodations, activities) matching specific detailed travel wishes, they should choose the 'Single-item Recommendation' function. If the users want to select a complete trip already including a set of products by specifying general travel wishes, they should choose the 'Complete Travel' function. If they want to find their travel by browsing complete trips suggested by the system, they should choose the 'Seeking for Inspiration' function. Sections 3.1 and 3.2 will describe sample sessions for the 'Single-item Recommendation' and the 'Seeking for Inspiration' functions. The interaction supported by the Complete Travel is not explicitly described since it is quite similar to the 'Single-item Recommendation'.

3.1 Single-item Recommendation

When tourists have highly detailed wishes about the trip (destinations, accommodations, activities), they normally use the Single-item Recommendation function (first door). The wizard-like interface drives them through the sequence of steps normally needed to self-bundle a complete travel. The typical sequence of steps is:

- **General Travel Preference Specification.** In this first step (Fig. 14.1), the system asks the user the most important features characterizing his or her travel (destination, travel party, budget, duration). The (optionally) provided data will be exploited by the system to provide personalized recommendations. On the right frame (Fig. 14.1), the system suggests the possible next alternative steps: further specifying travel preferences (advanced travel preferences), searching for a destination, an accommodation or activities. Let us assume that the user first decides to search for the main destination.
- **Destination Preferences.** The user is prompted for specific preferences about the sought destination. Two kinds of searches are provided: the geographical search, in case the user wants to select a village in a certain tourist area or region; or the search by activity, if the user wants to find destinations that allow practising his or her preferred activities (Fig. 14.2). After having specified the interests, the user can ask for the recommended destinations by following the 'Search for Destination' link. Two cases may occur. If the preferences specified by the user allow to select a reasonable number of results (neither zero nor too many), the destinations matching the criteria are ranked and shown to the user (Destination Recommendation step). Otherwise, the system initiates an interaction with the user to better clarify his or her needs (Relaxation and Tightening step).

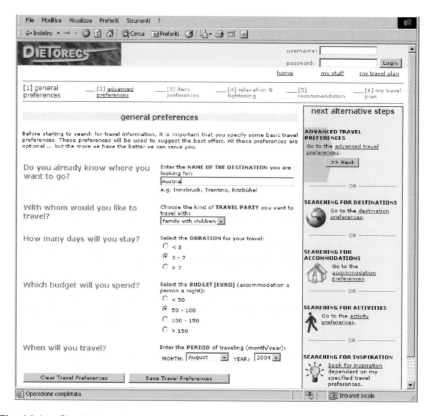

Fig. 14.1. Single-item Recommendation: General Travel Preference.

Fig. 14.2. Single-item Recommendation: Search by Activity.

- **Relaxation and Tightening.** This step is initiated by the system when it is not able to select a reasonable number of products. In this case, the system suggests to the user how he or she can change the preferences to improve the result set. Two situations may take place. If too many destinations are selected, the system suggests additional preferences that could be set to reduce the result set (tightening). If no destination matches the preferences specified by the user, the system suggests which preferences should be changed (relaxed) to get results. After the user revises the preferences, the system either recommends some destinations or, if it is not able to select a reasonable number of products, provides further relaxation or tightening suggestions.

- **Destination Recommendation.** When the specified destination preferences enable the system to select a reasonable number of destinations, they are ranked and shown to the user (Fig. 14.3). Specifically, the system ranks the selected destinations exploiting all the information acquired from the user during the interaction and the past travels built by other users in similar situations. The user can obtain an explanation about why the recommended destination fits his preferences ('Explain Why' link), browse the next recommended destinations and when he or she finds the one suited to his or her needs, adds it to the 'travel bag'.

Fig. 14.3. Single-item Recommendation: Destination Recommendation.

With a similar interaction, the user can then select and add to his or her personal 'travel bag' additional destinations to visit, the accommodation to stay and the activities to practise.

3.2 Seeking for Inspiration

If the tourist is more recommendation-driven, the selection process will be supported from the system in the form of pictorial representations of former trips (third door). In this case, the user does not have to specify general travel or travel item preferences to obtain recommendations, but rather immediately receives six complete trips, represented by images about the destination and the accommodation and the two most important and characterizing features (Fig. 14.4). The user can then access detailed information about each trip. After examining the recommendations, or, simply, inspired by the shown images, the user can get six new different recommendations simply by expressing interest about one of them; the system, exploiting the fact that the user is interested in that particular alternative, proposes six other alternatives more focused on the user wishes. In this way, the user can browse the catalogue space without explicitly specifying constraints and wishes. When the user finds the proposal that suits the needs, he or she can add the suggested products to the personal travel bag.

Fig. 14.4. Seeking for Inspiration.

4. System Logical Architecture Implementation – System Architecture

The system exploits a case base of travel bags that is built by the community of DieToRecs users as well as catalogues provided by TISCover AG and APT Trentino (DMO). The case structure is hierarchical (Ricci *et al.*, 2002b) and implemented as an XML view over a relational database. DieToRecs integrates case-based reasoning with interactive query management. When asked to retrieve a travel product, DieToRecs tries to cope strictly with user needs and, if this is not possible, it suggests query changes that will produce acceptable results. Similarity-based retrieval is exploited: (i) when a complete travel is searched (second and third door); and (ii) when the single products (as the result set of the user's query) must be ranked (first door).

The system is structured into two main components: (i) the GUI component, which manages the interaction with the user, gets the inputs, handles customization and shows the results; and (ii) the recommendation component, which is responsible for the work behind the interface – the database access, user case management and the recommendation process itself. Sections 4.1 and 4.2 describe these two components in more detail.

4.1 DieToRecs GUI structure

The DieToRecs system was developed as component-based architecture and consists of several components that interact with each other. The units encapsulate functionalities essential for managing the DieToRecs system and are described below. Figure 14.5 shows the cooperation among these engines.

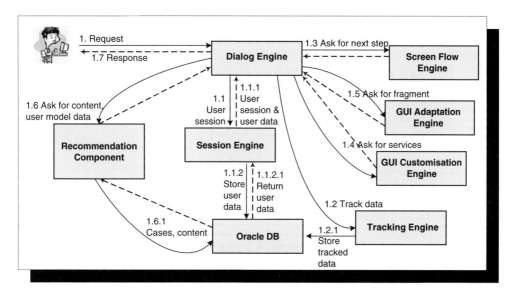

Fig. 14.5. Cooperation among engines in the DieToRecs system.

The Dialog Engine serves as a central management component to support the interaction between user and system, to read the input, to validate it, to manage the workflow and to return the response back to the user. This demonstrates that the Dialog Engine is responsible not only for the representation but also for the control of the user navigation. The engine consists of four main components to handle the user input validation and session handling, the workflow steering, the recommendation process and the integration of data from the recommendation component into the visualization fragments.

In close cooperation with the Dialog Engine two other engines work in the background to administrate information on session level and, if activated, on permanent level. The Session Engine is responsible for authenticating and authorizing users according to their identification and permission rights as well as guaranteeing that a user's session will not be lost during interaction. It overcomes stateless hypertext transfer protocol (HTTP) connections by keeping sessions alive. The Tracking Engine manages tracking of interesting data such as user input or user behaviour. Tracked data is logged in the local database and provides methods to retrieve once tracked and logged data to support the recommendation process.

The Screen Flow Engine informs state-dependent engines about workflow sequences. It is responsible for delivering information about what is the next step that should be delivered to the user. The request comes from the Dialog Engine. To be able to respond the Screen Flow Engine needs to know the current status from this request. Consequently, depending on this current status and certain other conditions, the next step will be explored and delivered back to the Dialog Engine.

The GUI Adaptation Engine handles all relevant actions for supporting the Dialog Engine with essential layout information for the next required step that has to be visualized and delivered to the user. It assembles a web page through the adaptation of single fragments described in HTML, XML or JavaServer Pages (JSP). Following the engine model it only performs work in case the Dialog Engine requests some information; so, it is not active by itself. The key part of the GUI Adaptation Engine asks its subworkers for information, combines this information, prepares the necessary fragments and sends them to the requester, all based on the state information received with the request.

The GUI Customization Engine provides interaction services independent from content that have to be customized for an individual user. More generally, it supports an individualized interaction between a specific user and the system. An example of such services is a personalized welcome message for registered users after logging into the system. The GUI Customization Engine supports the Dialog Engine in the same manner as the GUI Adaptation Engine. It reacts in case the Dialog Engine requests some information. To minimize system traffic the engine has to know the next step of the GUI sequence from the Dialog Engine to retrieve only those services that are relevant for the specific user and also relevant for the concerned step.

4.2 Recommendation component structure

The main goal of the recommendation component is to enable the application to provide personalized recommendations about products stored in the product catalogues. This component has been designed to be easily integrated in existing tourist websites to enable recommendation functions. Figure 14.6 shows the overall structure of the recommendation component.

It is structured in the following main components:

- **The CaseManager.** Is the component devoted to the management of the current user's case? It collects all the session data acquired from the user during the interaction, like the expressed travel wishes and the products added to the user's travel bag, and makes them available to the Recommendation Engine component.
- **The Recommendation Engine.** Exploiting the current case and the case base implements the recommendation algorithms to find the products to be recommended to the user. In particular, it provides the Single-item Recommendation, the Complete Travel and the Seeking for Inspiration functions. It uses the XML Mediator and the Metric components.
- **XML Mediator.** It allows storing and retrieving data (XML documents) from existing data repositories. XML Mediator returns the XML documents matching queries that are expressed by means of a query language we have defined. In this integration architecture, the existing repositories contain data modelled according to their local data models. One role of

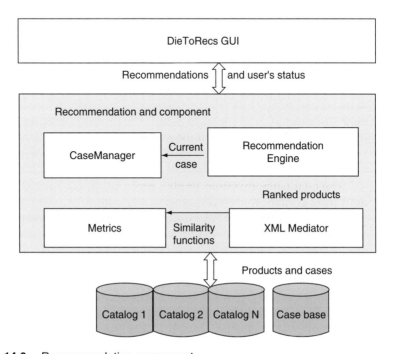

Fig. 14.6. Recommendation component.

the XML Mediator is to expose a unified integrated data model, which is mapped into the underlying local data models (Global as View approach) (Manolescu *et al.*, 2001). The XML Mediator has to translate the query expressed on the integrated data model and produce the XML documents having the structure defined by the integrated data model by collecting the pieces of information from the local data models of the integrated repositories. Furthermore, XML Mediator implements the Intelligent Query Management technology, identifying the query refinement suggestions to be proposed to the user.

- **The Metrics.** This component provides the tools for measuring similarity among XML documents and for sorting these documents, which can be products or recommendation sessions (cases). The recommendation algorithms implemented in the Recommendation Engine exploit similarities among products and recommendation sessions to identify the products to be recommended. The reader is referred to Chapter 8 for more details on this.

XML is widely used by all the components. All the data passed to, and provided by, the component to the application are XML documents, making certain that the functions are available to different web architectures. In addition, XML enables the document structures to be dynamic and allows the framework to work with different data models and case structures.

5. Conclusions

The DieToRecs system represents a new generation of travel recommender systems that can cope with individual differences in travel wishes and decision styles. We have empirically validated the system by A/B comparisons with more traditional approaches. The validation was conducted in Austria and has shown that the recommendation functions included in this system help users in travel planning by increasing ease of use and overall satisfaction. Perhaps, most importantly, users tend to accept the products that are recommended. A second evaluation has been done in Europe (Italy and Austria) and in the USA and has produced a large number of cases that will be used as training cases for the adaptive behaviour of DieToRecs. However, both research and software engineering issues are still open. From the research side, the most important aspects are how to dynamically adapt the recommendation algorithms to the current user, how to dynamically bundle travel proposals based on other users' past cases and how to manage cases that contain incomplete information (i.e. unspecified travel preferences). From the software engineering point of view, integrating recommendation technologies in commercial tourism sites poses specific challenges: the algorithms should be optimized to be able to handle the workload in terms of concurrent users and number of recommendations per seconds that such systems require; the number of cases produced by the system becomes quickly very large and, thus, algorithms for case base management should be identified; tourism products change often and, thus, recommendation algorithms should cope with a case base, which may contain products changed or not existing any more, by adapting the recommendations to the new context.

Chapter Summary

This chapter has presented DieToRecs, a novel case-based travel advisory system. DieToRecs has been designed by incorporating a human decision model that stresses individual differences in decision styles. DieToRecs supports multiple decision styles and provides personalized recommendations exploiting a case base of recommendation sessions, which are stored by the system. Users can access the system through three main functional doors that fit to complementary groups of decision styles. Whichever the door used to enter the system, users can eventually switch the type of support required. The application relies on a component-based architecture, featuring a set of computational engines. One of these engines encapsulates the core functionality of the system – the methodologies used to rank products and manage queries. Other engines are dedicated to the personalization of the GUI and to track user activity. The system has been empirically validated and represents a value-added service for future destination management systems.

15 Evaluating Travel Recommender Systems: A Case Study of DieToRecs

ANDREAS H. ZINS AND ULRIKE BAUERNFEIND

1. Introduction

When creating a recommender system, the ultimate objective is to suggest items valuable to the users. Due to the inherent complexities of the product and the decision-making process, the creation of a travel recommender system is a time-consuming and cost-intensive process. However, before improvements on the prototypes can be made, intermediary steps of evaluation should be taken to discover shortcomings. According to Lindgaard (1994) usability is defined as the ease of learning and using computer systems (for novices as well as for experienced users). In ISO 9241 usability is 'the extent to which a product can be used by specified users to achieve specified goals with effectiveness, efficiency and satisfaction in a specified context of use'. Different approaches for usability evaluation methods exist. One possibility is to distinguish between formative and summative evaluation. The first is the assessment of a system still in the prototype design stage, whereas the latter focuses on a final, already fully operational system with the goal to measure efficacy or to compare two systems (Hartson *et al.*, 2001). Hilbert and Redmiles (2000) classify evaluation methods if they are predictive, observational or participative. The first one includes cognitive walkthroughs or expert reviews. Observational evaluation is based on the observation of users while testing a prototype or an already functioning system. Participative evaluation is the collection of users' subjective reports by questionnaires or interviews.

An adapted version of Oppermann and Reiterer's four-step classification scheme (1997) for usability evaluation will serve as a basis to distinguish between the broad categories of evaluation:

1. Subjective evaluation methods
   Questionnaires
   Interviews
2. Objective evaluation methods
   Observations
   Video recording
   Interaction-based (e.g. logging)
3. Expert evaluation methods
   Checklists and guidelines
   (Cognitive) walkthroughs
   Specialists' reports and heuristic evaluation
4. Experimental evaluation methods

Only selected methods listed in each category above will be discussed in greater detail. Starting with subjective evaluation methods, questionnaires are popular and widespread to collect user opinions. Therefore, several of so-called 'standard questionnaires' had been developed to act as a reliable tool measuring the users' point of view and covering all relevant areas of system evaluation. Approaches range from very simple and quick questionnaires, e.g. System Usability Scale (SUS; Brooke, 1986), Nielsen's Heuristic Evaluation and Nielsen's Attributes of Usability (Nielsen, 1993) to more comprehensive ones. The Software Usability Measurement Inventory (SUMI; Human Factors Research Group, 1993/2000) contains around 50 questions, the Questionnaire for User Interaction Satisfaction (QUIS; Chin *et al.*, 1988) covers five areas to be rated: overall reactions to the system, screen, terminology and system information, learning and system capabilities. IBM developed some usability satisfaction questionnaires (Lewis, 1995): the After-Scenario Questionnaire (ASQ), the Post-Study System Usability Questionnaire (PSSUQ) and the Computer System Usability Questionnaire (CSUQ). An extensive questionnaire was created by Lin *et al.* (1997): the Purdue Usability Testing Questionnaire (PUTQ) consisting of 100 questions. Table 15.1 gives an overview of the topics covered by PUTQ and a few example questions for each area.

Another form of subjective assessment, open-format interviews, are often time-consuming and staff-intensive although they can be productive by giving new insights (which would not be covered by a predefined questionnaire) because the interviewer can address specific issues of concern (Shneiderman, 1992). Interviews are particularly useful when the study is an exploratory one (Oppermann and Reiterer, 1997).

Objective evaluation methods include observations that can be conducted either in the field or in the laboratory. Since observations are complex tasks, they are often complemented by videotaping or the logging of data (Lindgaard, 1994). Videotaping is a useful method because every reaction of the users such as eye movements can be tracked and analysed. The use of an automated data-tracking method by collecting and analysing usage data seems to be the most comprehensive approach of objective evaluation methods. All possible interactions can be tracked: number of errors, trials,

Table 15.1. An overview of the Purdue Usability Testing Questionnaire (PUTQ)
(Lin *et al.*, 1997).

Compatibility
   Is the wording familiar?
   Is the control matched to user skill?

Consistency
   Is the feedback consistent?
   Is the wording consistent with user guidance?

Flexibility
   Does it provide flexible user guidance?
   Are users allowed to customize windows?

Learnability
   Is the ordering of menu options logical?
   Is the data grouping reasonable for easy learning?

Minimal action
   Does it provide default values?
   Does it require minimal steps in sequential menu selection?

Minimal memory load
   Are selected data highlighted?
   Are prior answers recapitulated?

Perceptual limitation
   Does it provide easily distinguishable colours?
   Are groups of information demarcated?

User guidance
   Is HELP provided?
   System feedback: how helpful is the error message?

task time, etc. At two different levels logging user–system interaction is feasible: (i) logging the screen flow capturing the whole PC screen or a particular window together with actions; and (ii) logging predefined activities, events and results logically by the means of a logging component, which runs 'backstage' and stores events and processes. Expert evaluation methods range from simple guidelines or checklist reviews to more extensive approaches. The cognitive walkthrough is a technique for evaluating the design of a user interface with special attention to how well the interface supports 'exploratory learning', i.e. first-time use without formal training (Rieman *et al.*, 1995). Another technique, the heuristic evaluation, is defined by Lindgaard (1994) as a detailed, informal, subjective usability analysis conducted by experts simulating the perspective of a typical end user. The evaluators do not follow a specific set of methods, rules or procedures; instead, they rely on a set of vague guidelines. By performing a heuristic evaluation the experts identify violations of certain heuristics, i.e. some predefined principles (Ivory and Hearst, 2001). In addition to the cognitive walkthrough, the heuristic evaluation is an in-depth analysis collecting all occurred problems, from the highly serious to the most trivial. However, the judgements of experts underlie some subjectivity and are influenced by their experience, background and talent in anticipating what users find easy or difficult when using a system (Oppermann and Reiterer, 1997).

The literature distinguishes qualitative measures (e.g. Benbunan-Fich, 2001) or quantitative methods (e.g. Ivory *et al.*, 2000; Olsina and Rossi, 2001; Wöber *et al.*, 2002). Although qualitative investigations allow an in-depth analysis and the discovery of specific problems occurring, they tend to be more subjective and less comparable. Quantitative website evaluation can be performed in the way of judging site structure, technical parameters and content or server characteristics. Predetermined categories and attributes are used to assess the website. Log file analysis is a typical example of a method relying solely on a quantitative data collection by using traffic-based characteristics to establish usage patterns. By using these quantitative methods the evaluation process is likely to be structured, accurate and comprehensible (Olsina and Rossi, 2001).

Substantial effort has been made in developing quantitative approaches for website measurement. These contributions range from developing benchmarking metrics and specifications (e.g. Johnson and Misic, 1999; Jutla *et al.*, 1999; Ivory *et al.*, 2001) to highly sophisticated web-mining tools. A large research area consisting of automated quantitative website analysis was developed by means of web-mining methods. Originally, web-mining methods stem from the large research field of data mining. Data mining is defined as the extraction and the discovery of previously unknown but useful and interesting information and interrelations in large databases to infer new knowledge (Nestorov and Tsur, 1999; Spiliopoulou, 2000). Web mining enables the systematic discovery, extraction and analysis of World Wide Web (WWW) information sources (Cooley *et al.*, 1997; Kosala and Blockeel, 2000). Web mining can be basically divided into three areas: web content, web structure and web usage mining (Zaiane, 1998; Srivastava *et al.*, 2000). Web content mining is defined as the discovery and analysis of content and data of the Web. Web structure mining is concerned with the structure of hyperlinks, whereas web usage mining analyses the user behaviour (Kosala and Blockeel, 2000).

A qualitative method that can be found in the category of testing is the think-aloud method or protocol analysis (e.g. Waes, 2000; Benbunan-Fich, 2001). Test persons are asked to say what they are thinking about the website they are surfing or when problems are occuring. Although protocol analysis is a feasible and efficient approach (Benbunan-Fich, 2001), there are also some drawbacks such as that the situation can be quite unnatural for the test persons. A variation of the think-aloud verbal protocol analysis is the cooperative evaluation technique. Users and designers assess a system together; users are encouraged to ask questions during the interaction with the system. Similarly, evaluators can ask the user questions if problems or misunderstandings are occurring, or at any other time during the evaluation (Marsh and Wright, 1999; Yong and Kong, 1999). The obvious advantage is that the process is more natural than the 'pure' think-aloud method. Additionally, more insights can be gained because the evaluator can immediately ask about problems when he or she recognizes any dissatisfaction of the users. Another popular qualitative method of website evaluation is the cognitive walkthrough (e.g. discussed in Blackmon *et al.*, 2002 or applied in Jacobsen and John, 2000).

Another criterion addresses the question as to whether the assessment was conducted by automated tools or by a manual method (e.g. expert review). While manual methods for system assessment can be valuable giving deeper insight, this type of evaluation is time-consuming and complex (particularly when a large number of websites are to be evaluated). Besides, a certain degree of subjectivity cannot be completely avoided. An automated data-gathering process is an invaluable opportunity for assessing dynamic media such as the WWW (Scharl, 2000). Olsina (2003) divided evaluation methods into the following categories: testing, inspection, inquiry, analytical modelling and simulation. A similar categorization can be found in Ivory (2003). The respective methods for each category (derived from Nielsen, 1993; Ivory, 2003; Olsina, 2003) are shown in Table 15.2.

Table 15.2. Evaluation methods by categories (Nielsen, 1993; Ivory, 2003; Olsina, 2003).

- Testing
    - *Thinking-aloud Protocol* (users talk aloud while testing a website)
    - *Testing of system performance* (e.g. speed)
    - *Web log-file analysis* (data recording of a user interaction)
    - *Remote testing* (users and evaluators are separated)
    - *Contents testing* (relevancy, consistency, timeliness of the content)

- Inspection
  (performed by one or more experts)
    - *Guideline review*
    - *Heuristic evaluation* (review of usability principles, i.e. heuristics) *and estimation* (an evaluator's prediction of usability)
    - *Cognitive walkthrough* (simulation of users' problem-solving task)
    - *Feature, consistency, standards and formal usability inspection* (e.g. review of ISO standards)

- Inquiry
    - *Field observation* (users interact with a site in their environment)
    - *Survey* (users are asked some specific questions)
    - *Questionnaires* (such as PSSUQ and SUMI, discussed in Chapter 3)
    - *User feedback* (users submit comments and suggestions)
    - *Focus groups* (user discussion)

- Analytical modelling
  (model of the interface or user allowing the evaluator to expect usability, not yet developed for website evaluation)

- Simulation methods
  (simulation of a user–site interaction)

2. Evaluation of Recommender Systems: A Case Study of DieToRecs

Recommender systems require a particularly careful and thorough assessment since there are functions involved that the systems heavily depend upon the recommendation functions. A possible evaluation framework will be presented first followed by the description of the assessment procedure of a couple of recommender systems. Konstan and Riedl (1999) argued that recommender systems' research can be basically divided into two areas: off-line and online research. Whereas off-line research or off-line retrospective analysis is concerned with the evaluation of existing, already collected data, online research (conducted by exploratory online experiments) covers the evaluation of the performance of a running, live system. DieToRecs serves as an example to show how various evaluation methods can be used to improve the system development (Zins *et al.*, 2004a,b).

2.1 Formative evaluation

Before describing the evaluation measures applied, a short description of DieToRecs and its features will be given. First, DieToRecs is a destination advisory system based on case-based reasoning (CBR). As discussed elsewhere in this book, CBR is a methodology that solves a problem by retrieving and using a similar, already solved case. Second, a collaborative filtering system, based on similarity of sessions rather than the classical correlation of votes, is employed enabling the reuse of travel plans built by similar users. Finally, the system is a conversational tool, meaning that the users should feel like interacting with a human being. Queries and suggestions follow successively, thus providing a vivid question and answer process. Interactive query management is employed to handle queries more efficiently. The system helps the users to redefine queries: they are relaxed or tightened in order to display a desired number of ranked results.

The stages of evaluation are presented in Fig. 15.1. Each section (i.e. evaluation step) addresses three areas of interest: the starting situation and objective; a short description of the applied method and the procedure; a brief summary of the results and the lessons learned for the general use of evaluative techniques.

2.2 Concept test with a horizontal prototype

From literature review and an additional observational study the user model for the destination recommender system was elaborated. One of the basic premises was that the system has to serve users with different decision styles (Grabler and Zins, 2002). Therefore, a concept test (Dalgleish, 2000) had been conducted in an early stage of the prototype development (Pearrow, 2000). The purpose was to investigate the potential benefits of two

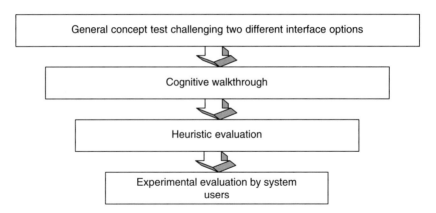

Fig. 15.1.   Stages of evaluation.

effects of the human–computer interaction: (i) giving the users the choice
to select among two alternative navigational options: A (more sequential)
and B (more pictorial-holistic); and (ii) classifying the users in advance
into one of two broad categories of cognitive styles – A' (analytical) and
B' (holistic) – to direct them to the potentially more suitable navigational
option.

For the empirical test a horizontal prototype (Nielsen, 1993; Rudd and
Isensee, 1994) or so-called demonstrator (i.e. a not yet fully operable system of related web pages to collect or identify the users' travel preferences
and wishes) was developed and presented to 176 test persons (Internet users
only). As the graphical user interface was already in an advanced stage of
the system development and responded to a limited set of keyboard and
PC-mouse inputs, it can be recognized as a high-fidelity prototype (Walker
et al., 2002).

Results had been encouraging and in favour of offering two alternative
system accesses: a classical interface with check boxes and structured input
fields and another more holistic approach using sketches of already existing
travel bundles for revealing someone's travel preferences and constraints.
The analysis indicated that users should be classified in advance to one of the
corresponding cognitive styles. This is based on the observation that asking
the users first to think about their learning styles and let them choose afterwards between two interface options leads to a substantial rate of a mislead-
ing self-selection. The likely consequences are reduced user satisfaction and,
in the worst case, a lost customer.

Still unresolved problems and areas at this stage were: (i) finding and
applying well-performing and not tiring a priori classification instruments
to detect the users' appropriate cognitive style; (ii) testing multiple interface
alternatives to better address the inhomogeneous audience; and (iii) comparing the performance and user evaluation of competing fully functional
recommender systems with alternative presentation and interaction designs
as proposed by Rumetshofer *et al.* (2003).

2.3 Cognitive walkthrough and first heuristic inspection

The primary goal of this stage of the study was to detect substantial weaknesses of the user interface design using two different techniques: cognitive walkthrough and heuristic evaluation. According to Ivory and Hearst (2001) the cognitive walkthrough method is used to simulate the users' problem-solving process. Proposed by Nielsen (1993), the latter is a technique to identify violations of heuristics (Ivory and Hearst, 2001). The usability guidelines applied for this evaluation follow from Nielsen (1999), which had been adapted to define the following principles: (P1) know your user; (P2) reduce the cognitive work; (P3) design for errors; and (P4) keep the consistency with your internal systems and with respect to common practices.

Important improvements had been achieved following the focal, critical comments on consistent labelling, navigational and menu aspects as well as design considerations. Changes resulting from the inspection were a re-arrangement of the menus (new design, change of grouping, visualization through icons, renaming for the purpose of being consistent). The start page of the main area was unified with the menus and the registration process was simplified and better explained to the user. Resolution problems concerning the display of the interface were solved. Furthermore, a clearer presentation of the recommendation results was implemented and some inconsistencies in the use of terminology were eliminated.

Although the re-engineering process of the cognitive walkthrough is tedious to perform, and inconsistencies and general and recurring problems could be missed, the method is appropriate in an early prototypical stage. In particular, it is possible to detect substantial weaknesses before a prototype is built. A general problem occurring with cognitive walkthrough and heuristic evaluation is the difficult position of the evaluator. He has to act as a user with the opinion of an expert, which leads to ambiguous roles.

2.4 Heuristic and standardized evaluation by experts

A major evaluation goal of heuristic evaluation was to eliminate the major interface and interaction shortcomings prior to the experimental test. This step seemed to be necessary given the stage of system development. Due to the subjective judgements and the missing structure of the heuristic evaluation, a standardized instrument was used to enable comparisons between the judges and to assess the actual development stage.

The comparable evaluation was carried out using the Purdue Usability Testing Questionnaire (PUTQ). Its essential advantage is the possibility to compute an index based on the ratings and to put it in relation to the possible perfect (maximum) score (Lin *et al.*, 1997). The heuristic evaluation was carried out using five experienced interface judges. These evaluators had to:

- provide comparative judgements, rating the system on a variety of dimensions by the PUTQ;

- perform a detailed analysis of the general system functionality, of the interface and of the user–system interaction aspects.

The heuristic evaluation results were grouped into the following categories: start page, navigation, layout and design, travel-planning process, recommendation process and results, and sorted by their importance. The most critical issues were solved before the experimental user evaluation took place. A lot of changes were made. However, a few examples of detailed problems will serve for better illustration:

- expiration of intermediary result pages;
- loading speed;
- content descriptors not adequate for real use; and
- consistency of used terms.

Overall, the experts gave the system a good-quality total grade (PUTQ index: 65.0 – the higher the score, the better the usability result; scale of 100), especially with respect to perceptual limitations, compatibility and learnability. Deficiencies were identified in user guidance and flexibility, which mainly resulted from functions not available due to the prototypical status. The results of heuristic evaluation revealed that additional work should be invested to avoid typical prototype troubles such as further extension of the database, help functions and error messages. The recommendation process was one of the major issues for further development.

The heuristic evaluation was an important second step in the re-engineering process of the first prototype. PUTQ, as a standardized questionnaire, turned out to be a valuable tool allowing comparisons. On the other hand, the questionnaire is tailored to general computer interfaces and, therefore, some application problems on web-based systems arose. Furthermore, some web-specific problem areas remain unconsidered. Hence, it is suggested that PUTQ should be modified to better reflect the nature of the system under evaluation.

2.5 Experimental evaluation by potential users

The final step of evaluation process was conceived to assess the implementation of the recommendation functions, which were supposed to be general enough to be integrated into a variety of destination-related websites. The system prototype is a tool that allowed testing of these general functions in a more controlled, yet flexible, way, i.e. without having to cope with the engineering problems regarding the real integration of the recommendation components into an existing application. The approach consisted of building a limited set of variants of the DieToRecs prototype to test hypotheses regarding performance of the system. The main hypotheses concerned the users' search and choice behaviour, and their satisfaction.

Three variants were to be tested:

- **DTR-A:** interactive query management only, i.e. supporting the user in case of query failures (too many or no results) but not using a case base of previously built travel plans and therefore not providing any recommendation support via sorting (Ricci *et al.*, 2002b);

- **DTR-B:** single-item recommendation with interactive query management and ranking based on a case base of 25 cases extracted from the database of the Austrian National Guest Survey 1997/98; and
- **DTR-C:** this variant allows a user to navigate among complete travel recommendations starting from the link 'Seeking for Inspiration'. Six travel examples are shown for each page. Then the user is requested to provide a feedback on the presented alternatives in a simple form ('I like this' vs 'I do not like this'). Finally, the system updates the proposed alternatives by means of the feedback provided by the user, and the similarity-based retrieval in the case base is performed again.

The main hypotheses refer to the the users' search and choice behaviour, and their satisfaction:

H1: *The recommendation-enhanced system is able to deliver useful recommendations.*

H2: *The recommendation-enhanced system is able to facilitate the construction of good travel plans.*

H3: *The recommendation-enhanced system allows a more efficient search.*

H4: *The recommendation-enhanced system heightens the user satisfaction.*

Participants from a student population randomly assigned to the experimental groups were asked to use both a DieToRecs variant and a so-called 'baseline system'. In this study the baseline system was the TISCover.com online travel agency website. The DieToRecs recommender system and its variants were fed by a substantial subset of the travel items represented in the TISCover system. An additional small number of participants were assigned to a full functionality design (corresponding to a variant recommending complete travel arrangements called DTR-C), to obtain some exploratory indications on the users' interaction with a system resembling the final development of the DieToRecs project. The users were asked to perform a series of tasks within the general context of 'planning a travel in Tyrol, Austria'. A series of objective and subjective measures were recorded, both automatically during the interaction (by means of the logging component; DTR-variants only) and by asking the user to fill a questionnaire after each test session. To insure a sense of external validity it was necessary to design tasks that are representative of the typical usage of the system in the real world. Thus, the participants were requested to choose a different geographical area for the execution of the two test tasks, thus trying to avoid content-specific learning.

Besides sociodemographic and Internet usage characteristics, the questionnaire focused on the process and outcome evaluation of the trip-planning task. After having screened a list of potential standardized measurement instruments devised to capture aspects of usability criteria the Post-Study Satisfaction User Questionnaire (PSSUQ with 19 statements; Lewis, 1995) was chosen, slightly adapted to a non-technical wording and extended by typical aspects relevant for recommendation systems (resulting in

23 statements as shown in Table 15.3). Although the psychometric properties have been documented by Lewis (1995), the dimensional structure (system usefulness, information quality and interface quality) and content (e.g. satisfaction aspects mixed with functional qualities) of this instrument should be treated with caution.

3. Results

The following analysis considers hypotheses 1–4 step by step. It is based on a sample of 47 test persons with a share of 63% females. One quarter belongs to an age group older than 25, and the majority is under 25 years. General Internet usage was rather high with a share of 62% using the Web for 4–6 years. No participant showed an experience less than 1 year. The students' population was well captured by a 72% share of test persons using the Internet daily. Another 20% indicated the use of the Internet several times a week. Almost everybody (96%) used the Internet for information retrieval. About 75% bought some product or service at least once a year over the Internet. With regard to the travel domain the usage rates are comparable: 98% used this source for some information; almost 80% purchased some travel-specific product on the Internet at least once a year. One-third of the test persons were unfamiliar with Tyrol.

The usefulness of the different recommendation functions implemented in the three DieToRecs variants was tested. The log data provided the average position of each item in the presented result list of queries. Those items selected and put into the travel plan are taken here to compare the relative position (DTR-C does not provide single-item result lists as it recommends in the initial step complete travel plans only). The differences between DTR-A and DTR-B were substantial for all item categories. This can be interpreted as a sign of consistency though the sample size does not suffice to deliver statistically significant results ($\Rightarrow$ H1 accepted without statistical proof).

Next, a model for explaining user satisfaction with a typical structure as outlined in Fig. 15.2 was the starting point for the investigation of evaluative dimensions. The original three-dimensional configuration (PSSUQ; Lewis, 1995) could not be identified with the empirical data of this study. Instead, the following three dimensions turned out to represent a very consistent way of how the respondents evaluated the baseline and experimental recommender systems: ease of use combined with design aspects and learnability; outcome combined with functionality and effectiveness; and reliability strongly related with error handling (Fig. 15.2; Cronbachs Alpha coefficients below, for loading indicators cf. Table 15.3).

When testing the criterion validity by applying linear regression analyses – separately for the two systems evaluated by each respondent – on the dependent satisfaction dimension, very similar structural effects were detected (cf. Fig. 15.2). Both models explained a high proportion of the satisfaction variance (DTR-R^2: 0.94; TIS-R^2: 0.87). The standardized regression coefficients do not differ substantially. Finally, the reliability dimension does

Table 15.3. Usability and User Satisfaction Questionnaire (adapted from PSSUQ).

Items	PSSUQ	Ease of use	Effectiveness	Reliability	Satisfaction
Design/layout					
I liked using the interface of the system	o	x			
The organization of information presented by the system was clear	c	x			
The interface of this system was pleasant to use	c	x			
Functionality					
This system has all the functions and capabilities that I expect it to have	o		x		
The information retrieved by the system was effective in helping me to complete the tasks	c		x		
The products listed by the system as a reply to my request were suitable for my travel	n		x		
I found the 'recommend (the whole) travel' function useful	n				
Ease of use					
It was simple to use this system	o	x			
It was easy to find the information I needed	o	x			
The information (such as online help, on-screen messages and other documentation) provided with this system was clear	o			x	
Overall, this system was easy to use	c	x			
Learnability					
It was easy to learn to use the system	o	x			
There was too much information to read before I could use the system	n				
The information provided by the system was easy to understand	c	x			
Satisfaction					
I felt comfortable using this system	o				x
I enjoyed constructing my travel plans through this system	n				x
Overall, I am satisfied with this system	o				x
Outcome/future use					
I was able to complete the task quickly using this system	c		x		
I could not complete the task in the preset time frame	n		x		
I believe I could become productive quickly using this system	o	x			
The system was able to convince me that the recommendations are of value	n		x		
From my current experience with using the system, I think I would use it regularly	n		x		
Errors/system reliability					
Whenever I made a mistake using the system, I could recover easily and quickly	o			x	
The system gave error messages that clearly told me how to fix problems	o			x	

Note: 'o' = unchanged items; 'c' = changed wording; 'n' = new items added; 'x' = highly loading variables (one variable without 'x' was an outlier and did not load on any of the factors).

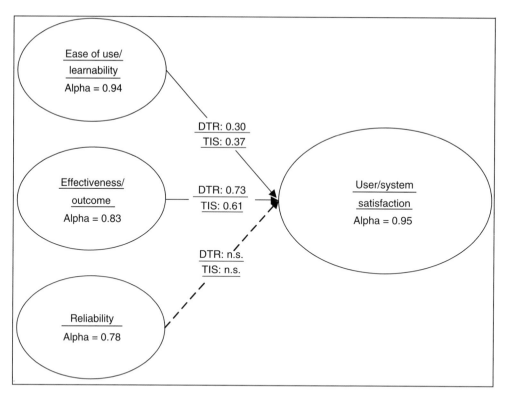

Fig. 15.2.   Explanatory model for user–system satisfaction.

not contribute directly to the process and outcome evaluation in terms of user satisfaction ratings. From the point of view of content validity this configuration seems to converge towards the widely acknowledged Technology Acceptance Model (Davis, 1989; Lederer *et al.*, 2000), which proposes two factors for explaining system usage: perceived usefulness and perceived ease of use.

Overall, the evaluation indicates a solid superiority for the baseline TISCover system. This result was expected and explained within hypotheses 2 and 4 (see above) and is, apparently, due to the mature developmental stage and the huge and detailed data available. Another indicator of this performance difference can be derived from the subjective declaration whether the planning task could have been accomplished successfully or not: DieToRecs achieved a 30% ratio; TISCover 64%.

In terms of differences of the item ratings between the DieToRecs variants Table 15.4 exhibits a clear and confirming picture. The more intelligent recommendation functions were in operation, the better the satisfaction ratings were. Overall, relatively more respondents succeeded in finishing their plans during the given time frame successfully. For the destination recommendations the DTR-C variant holds a significantly better position compared to that of the modest DTR-A variant. The differences of the accommodation

Table 15.4. Satisfaction ratings for travel plan elements by DieToRecs variants.

		System variants			
Travel plan element	Average	DTR-A	DTR-B	DTR-C	*p*-value
Finished plans	30%	10%	30%	100%	0.001
Ratings					
Destination	4.0	2.8	4.5	5.3	0.10
significant A–C		0.10			
Accommodation	4.1	4.1	3.6	5.9	0.15
significant B–C			0.01		
significant A–C		0.05			
Activities	4.2	3.2	4.9	7.0	0.05
significant A–B		0.1			
significant B–C			0.01		
significant A–C		0.001			

Note: '1' = very dissatisfied; '7' = very satisfied.

ratings are even more distinct: the DTR-C variant works better than DTR-A and DTR-B.

As outlined in hypothesis 3 the objective measures of the system evaluation were derived from the user logging component and are exhibited in Table 15.5. Considering the different success rates in terms of finished travel plans (see Table 15.4) the irrelevant differences in the number of queries and page visits turn into some more encouraging findings ($\Rightarrow$ H3 confirmed). Session time has to be taken with caution because the experimental process strictly limits the granted time for the travel plan assembly. Nevertheless, the improved recommendation functions help to reduce the necessary planning time. From the number of query refinement options applied we can learn

Table 15.5. Objective efficiency measures by DieToRecs variants.

	System variants			
	DTR-A	DTR-B	DTR-C	*p*-value
Total number of queries	12.9	13.3	9.5	n.s.
Accommodation queries	5.5	6.5	4.0	n.s.
Destination queries	4.3	2.1	2.3	n.s.
Interest queries	3.1	4.6	1.8	n.s.
Number of pages visited	20.2	18.8	8.8	n.s.
Number of query relaxations applied	5.8	4.6	4.0	n.s.
Number of query tightening applied	0.6	0.2	0	n.s.
Session time in minutes	25	20	23	>0.1

Note: n.s. = not significant.

that in most of the cases the result lists are too short (and maybe more often empty) than too long. No apparent differences can be detected.

In order to test hypothesis 4, the variation of the evaluation scores (see Table 15.6) was decomposed with respect to the within-subject (i.e. sequence order) and the between-subject (i.e. variant comparison) effects. In general, a significant order or sequence effect could be detected which affected each dimension except reliability. As initially assumed, a learning effect appeared which favoured the ratings for the second trip-planning task. On average, this learning effect was much more pronounced in the situation in which the baseline system was used and evaluated in second place. The effect size was rather similar for the system satisfaction scale, whereas for the ease-of-use scale it was more than double and for the outcome scale even more than eight times as large.

Considering the sequence effect simultaneously with the between-subject effect of comparing different system variants (only DTR-A and DTR-B due to the small sample size) a considerable scale difference remains for each scale (ease of use: 0.43 [$p = 0.39$]; outcome: 0.32 [$p = 0.47$]; reliability: 0.60 [$p = 0.26$]; satisfaction: 0.70 [$p = 0.2$]). Additionally, the comparisons between respondent ratings without order effect to those respondents using only the DTR-C variant indicate that each dimension scores higher for the DieToRecs system, except ease of use (see Table 15.6). Hence, in principle, hypothesis 4 cannot be corroborated entirely, though when taking the small sample size into account the results show the expected direction.

4. Discussion

The travel recommender system prototype DieToRecs and a reference system (TISCover) were tested and evaluated by users with the basic goal to discover weaknesses in the new DieToRecs recommendation system. Although the assessment of TISCover was significantly better than for DieToRecs, the higher satisfaction ratings for the DieToRecs variant with more recommendation functions confirm the appropriate direction of system design development. A certain familiarization effect for the TISCover system cannot be

Table 15.6. Average ratings and differences on the evaluation dimensions by system variants.

	TISCover Ø	DieToRecs Ø	DTR-A – TISCover	DTR-B – TISCover	DTR-C – TISCover
User satisfaction	3.2	4.6	2.33	1.05*	−0.50*
Ease of use	2.8	3.6	1.34	0.45*	0.31*
Effectiveness/outcome	3.4	4.6	1.71	1.01	−0.50*
Reliability	3.5	3.7	0.60*	0.05*	−0.22*

Note: '1' = strongly agree; '7' = strongly disagree; * = not significant.

completely denied in that the user sample employed for this assessment was very likely to know the system and might have used it before. Also, TISCover as a fully functioning travel recommendation system provides a greater variety of travel items than the DieToRecs subset. Nevertheless, it can be assumed that these differences of scope are minor compared to a system comparison, which would be based on completely different databases. Hence, the evaluation relies much more on process differences than on those of content.

As far as the survey instrument and the explanatory model for user–system satisfaction are concerned, the three-dimensions (i.e. system usefulness, information quality and interface quality) explaining user–system satisfaction proposed by Lewis (1995) were not confirmed. Instead, a three-factor solution for explaining overall system satisfaction could be ascertained. These factors were labelled ease of use or learnability, effectiveness or outcome and reliability. Finally, the approach used in this study to generate empirical data is a promising one since the combination of objective and subjective measures enables the assessment from a twofold point of view: the satisfaction ratings delivered by the user and the interaction data showing the users' search and selection behaviour.

From the experiences of this experimental evaluation, several aspects and suggestions should be mentioned:

1. Building recommender systems for such a complex product like tourism destinations and the main services a traveller regularly consumes in this place challenges the existing evaluation procedures. The simulation of a real travel-planning task within a test situation immediately touches some restrictions such as the available information space, the time span for planning a trip, the seriousness of travel preferences and budget constraints. Hence, the technical feasibility of the implemented routines can be seen as a necessary but not sufficient condition from the usability point of view.
2. The performance tests have to be embedded in an environment that reflects realistic and, therefore, complete applications. This requirement raises preparatory costs and comprises functionality, interface design, quality and scope of the database of travel items as well as those of CBR cases.
3. There are no adequate user satisfaction instruments available that cover the world of recommender systems. Some additional time and resources have to be reserved for adapting, testing and improving.
4. The proposed remedies in short are as follows: (i) increase sample size; (ii) adopt better measures; (iii) complement laboratory experiments with web experiments; and (iv) use simulations.

In general, evaluating recommender systems means being at least one step ahead in terms of sophistication of the available evaluation instruments. The space of information and communication results is not strictly limited and determined. It depends closely on the users' contingencies as well as on the design of the whole interaction process. As a consequence, different results (complete or ad hoc assembled travel bundles) may lead to similar satisfaction levels while identical suggestions from the recommender system may cause different evaluations due to different paths on which the system guided the users to meet their needs and preferences.

Chapter Summary

The evaluation of a recommender system is a crucial step in eliminating possible shortcomings and weaknesses. This chapter has used DieToRecs as a case study to illustrate how different evaluation methods can be used to improve system design.

Acknowledgement

This work has been partially funded by the European Union's Fifth RTD Framework Programme (under contract DIETORECS IST-2000-29474). The authors would like to thank all other colleagues of the DieToRecs (http:// dietorecs.itc.it/) team for their valuable contribution to this chapter.

16 TourBO: A Prototype of a Regional Tourism Advising System in Germany

THOMAS FRANKE

1. Introduction

Besides natural resources, tourism destinations are typically characterized by a relatively large number of autonomous service providers. However, customers' decision regarding where to travel or not is based on their total impression of the site rather than on the single 'places and things' available. Therefore, it is vital for the individual 'experience providers' to cooperate in the presentation of an overall image or brand of the destination (Williams and Palmer, 1999; King, 2002, p. 107). The Internet provides a well-suited tool for reaching this end, either by creating decentralized 'virtual tourism destinations' (Palmer and McCole, 2000, p. 199) (where cooperation is achieved by forming a 'web-ring' that hyperlinks the different actors of the destination) or via central document management system (DMS). In any case the desired tourism information or product has to be easily retrievable (Pröll and Retschitzegger, 2000, p. 182). This is why the development of mass customization capabilities, which tailor products to the customers' individual needs, is an important issue (King, 2002, p. 108).

However, intelligent information systems that aim in this direction are still scarce. Although the travel industry is one of those fields in the economy that are heavily affected by the growing disintermediation through the Internet (Clemons and Il-Horn, 1999, pp. 13–15; Gilbert and Bacheldor, 2000), this trend is mainly constricted to simple travel products like hotel rooms or flight tickets. As the complexity of products increases, online assistance gets sparse, although it is actually needed more (Björk and Guss, 1999). Consequently, many tourists still book their journeys at a travel agent after having gathered information online.

The demand for personalized travel systems described above is actually backed up by the development of the necessary technologies to produce

them, e.g. user modelling, soft computing algorithms and efficient computers. Nevertheless, practical implementations still seem to be limited because
of complicated privacy regulations, high expenditures and particularly the
dilemma of how to profile a user without long questionnaires. Only recently
individualized products seem to be emerging on the online travel market,
e.g. dynamic packaging that combines flight tickets, hotel rooms from different categories and even excursions to a complete travel package (Kiani-Kress,
2003). In order to support this trend, we developed a couple of computer-
assisted consulting, decision support and offering systems in cooperation
with German firms and public administration (Franke and Mertens, 2001).
A guideline in all of our work is to pragmatically individualize the dialogue
between man and machine by user modelling. One of these systems, which
is called TourBO (Touristic Browser and Organizer), contributes to this task
by providing individualized travel information based on the users' (interest)
profile. It comprises predefined travel suggestions for common situations
(like annual company outings), a customizable timetable for the stay, which
is filled in with the system's assistance, or a recommendation module for
appropriate leisure partners, e.g. for playing tennis.

 This chapter first discusses the structure and contents of TourBO's user
profile. Subsequently, it walks the reader through the advising process from
profile generation to the explanation of recommendations made by several
program modules. Among these modules are a fuzzy stereotyping engine for
easy profile assessment, several approaches to support travel group counselling and an explanation component that partly depends on customers'
personality traits. All of them are not 'typical' modules of a consulting system but try to address more peripheral, yet specific, problems that are often
overlooked.

2. User Profile

TourBO needs individual data for most of the services it makes available.
First, the system gathers some hard facts about the user, specifically age and
gender. The main part of the user model consists of an interest profile that
stores the customer's leisure preferences. To derive this, we structured the
domain of leisure activities in six categories: 'sightseeing', 'music', 'sports',
'cultural activities', 'nightlife' and 'shopping'. These in turn are subdivided
into 31 more detailed rubrics (e.g. 'theatre', 'opera', 'art and exhibitions' and
'children's theatre' in the case of 'cultural activities'). In each of these subdi-
visions the user may specify his interests in six degrees from 'no interest at
all' to 'very high interest'. Finally, the user can tell the system whether he or
she prefers rather unhurried, balanced or active leisure programmes (degree
of activity), with regard to the number of recommended activities per period
of time and the estimated duration of these. This means that for a customer
who prefers an unhurried schedule the system calculates a longer duration
for visiting a museum and, therefore, would recommend fewer activities on
that day.

More formally, the profile of interests could be represented as a vector of 31 interest ratings ranging from 0 to 5 (according to the interest degree):

$$\vec{p} = (r_0, r_1, \ldots, r_{30}), \quad r_i \in [r_{min}; r_{max}] = [0; 5]$$

with $\vec{p}$ = profile vector; r_i = interest value of the profile in rubric i; r_{min} = lowest possible interest value; r_{max} = highest possible interest value.

A given sight or activity could be analogically represented with a vector of 31 values, which indicate to what extent the attraction covers the respective rubric and its ability to provide corresponding content:

$$\vec{s} = \begin{pmatrix} a_0 \\ a_1 \\ \vdots \\ a_{30} \end{pmatrix}, \quad a_i \in [a_{min}; a_{max}] = \{0; 1\}, \quad \sum a_i = 1$$

with $\vec{s}$ = sight vector and a_i = ability of the sight to provide content related to rubric i.

In this case, the scalar product of the two vectors ($\vec{p} \cdot \vec{s}$) could be interpreted as the attractiveness of the sight in analogy to Hu and Brent Ritchie (1993), who define a destination's attractiveness via 'the relative importance of individual benefits and the perceived ability of the destination to deliver' them. The user's perception of this ability has, however, been exchanged by the system's estimation, as it is the computer which is making the recommendation. Figure 16.1 shows the classification of the profile on hand within the framework for user models that Mertens and Höhl (1999) proposed; the appropriate attribute values are shaded in a darker grey than the others. In detail, this means that the used profile aims at *selecting* those pieces of information from a large amount of data which are most relevant for an addressee rather than rehashing and presenting data on the screen according to his or her preferences. The addressee may be a single *customer* of the system or a whole *group* (e.g. a tourist party), and in most cases the addressee of the gathered information is also the *operator* of the system.

Customers may each specify their own *individual profile* as opposed to being assigned to a stereotypical group. However, an elaborate *stereotypical approach* is considered and developed (see Section 3) too. The profile stores only *hard facts* that the users have explicitly keyed in before entering the system (*ex ante*), and does not make any implicit assumptions about other 'softer' factors. The customers may give feedback about recommendations they were given and thereby adapt their profile (*explicit, ex post extraction*). As the entered data are stored in a database between two sessions, it is a *long-term profile*, which can be viewed by the customer at any given time (*transparent*). The *dynamic* user model may be changed *manually* during advising sessions as well as in between them but never does so automatically (Schuhbauer, 1999).

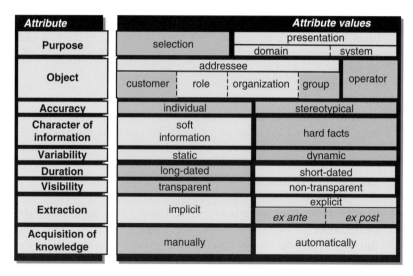

Attribute	Attribute values				
Purpose	selection	presentation			
		domain		system	
Object	addressee				operator
	customer	role	organization	group	
Accuracy	individual		stereotypical		
Character of information	soft information		hard facts		
Variability	static		dynamic		
Duration	long-dated		short-dated		
Visibility	transparent		non-transparent		
Extraction	implicit		explicit		
			ex ante	ex post	
Acquisition of knowledge	manually		automatically		

Fig. 16.1.   Classification of TourBO's user model.

3. Fuzzy stereotyping

If the system gathers the interest values of the 31 subcategories with the help of a questionnaire directly from the customers, the latter have to enter lots of data into the computer and make many decisions. Stereotypical profiles, which are assigned to users after they have entered very few key data (so-called triggers) could help to find a remedy for this problem. The drawback of this approach is that only a relatively small number of predefined data-sets can be stored in the system, leading to a rather limited variety of possible starting profiles for new users. Consequently, the assignment process is often ambiguous, because an individual might belong to two or more stereotypes according to his 'triggers'. The following sections show how the introduction of fuzzy logic methods into the stereotyping process may help negating these negative side effects.

3.1 Identification of possible stereotypes

Most of the tourist role systems that have been identified in the literature are closely connected to the stereotype approach. Therefore, it seems to be help-ful to base the TourBO-stereotypes on these works. One of the first role sys-tems that categorized tourists into groups or roles based on their preferences has been suggested by Cohen (1972). He placed the different roles along a familiarity–novelty continuum, ranging from the organized mass tourist to the so-called 'drifter'. The development of the International Tourist Role Scale (ITR) has taken into account that Cohen's unidimensional familiarity–novelty model cannot adequately represent the different facets described by these two terms (Mo *et al.*, 1994, p. 25; Jiang *et al.*, 2000, p. 966). Therefore, the

ITR differentiates between three dimensions: destination-oriented dimension (new vs familiar); travel-services dimension (organized vs individual); and social contact dimension (many vs few contacts to local people). Four basic stereotypes with different emphases in the various dimensions are identified. The Tourist Role Preference Questionnaire (TRPQ) is structurally similar to the ITR, as it also identifies three dimensions (Gibson and Yiannakis, 1992). The only difference is that instead of the social contact dimension the TRPQ measures if a tourist prefers a stimulating or quiet environment. However, a much greater number of individual roles (i.e. 15) are defined.

Besides the general classifications described above, several role systems for specific areas of the tourism sector have been suggested, e.g. for sports (Hinch and Higham, 2001). McKercher finds five different kinds of cultural tourists based on the importance of the cultural aspect in the decision for a destination and on the deepness of the experiences actually made during the stay. It can be shown that the longer the distance to the destination, the stronger the influence of culture on the decision to travel and the deeper the experiences made (i.e. not only the main attractions but also less spectacular objects are visited) (McKercher and du Cros, 2003, p. 53). Table 16.1 gives an overview of the dimensions on which the stereotypes in TourBO are based.

These studies led to the development of five stereotypes for the proto-type:

1. *Cultural tourists* are mainly interested in art and culture. They like making new experiences at another destination on every trip and they want to visit cultural and historic sites. Besides museums, exhibitions, churches and monuments this includes theatre plays and concerts (Opaschowski, 2002, p. 255). Cultural tourists prefer relatively short trips during the summer months and mainly visit big European cities (Diem, 1996; Dreyer, 2000).

2. For *leisure travellers* it is much more important to relax during the holidays than to make new experiences. As the main goal is to recover from the stress in everyday life, they prefer comprehensive travel services. Often leisure travellers participate in so-called wellness programmes with a strong focus on health issues (Lohmann, 1997). Nevertheless, a partial interest in historic and cultural sites remains. The length of stay is usually slightly longer than the one of the cultural tourists (Diem, 1996).

3. The group of *young single travellers* comprises globetrotters, who travel from city to city in a self-organized way and always stay only for a few days,

Table 16.1. Preference ranges of different role systems.

Many new experiences	No new experiences
Novelty of destination	Familiarity of destination
Organized travel service	Self-organized travel
Many social contacts	Few social contacts
Stimulating environment	Quiet environment
Active participation in sports events	Passive participation in sports events
Cultural aspect important	Cultural aspect unimportant

as well as tourists who travel without their partner but with friends (also mostly on a relatively low-service level). Single travellers want to visit the most important sights of their destinations. As another focal point is getting to know new people, nightlife and sport activities are very important (Opaschowski, 2002, pp. 71, 100).

4. *Adventurers* are mainly interested in activities that allow them to make mental and physical experiences, which take them to their limits. This includes activities that give them a special 'psychological kick' (Kutsch, 2001, p. 12) and let them stay away from the average tourists with extraordinary achievements under extreme conditions (Voigt, 1997) (e.g. rafting, bungee jumping, canyoning).

5. Typical *family tourists* include partners and children. The well-being of all family members is the focal point and all their special interests are taken into account. Especially when there are smaller children and the service at a certain destination is really good, the desire to make new experiences and visit new locations becomes less important and the same destination is visited more than once. Leisure activities are often the focus of participating children (Vester, 1988; Turley, 2001, p. 1) and are selected with the intention of helping their education (Shaw and Dawson, 2001, p. 225).

For each stereotype the system stores 31 standard values in a predefined interest profile $\bar{p}_i$ with $i \in \{C, L, S, A, F\}$, which represents the preferences of cultural, leisure, single travellers, etc.

3.2 Identification and acquisition of triggers

The main goal of the fuzzy sterotyping engine is to generate a satisfying profile with minimal data input from the user. Before the questions to acquire these triggers can be formulated, the determining factors of tourist behaviour have to be examined. Besides biological and socio-economic factors this includes psychological and biographical components (see Fig. 16.2). Based on these data, a probability for the classification of a person as a certain tourist type can be determined (Vester, 1988).

For the TourBO prototype, seven pieces of information have been identified that seem sufficient for the classification without intruding too far into the user's privacy. The *age* of the user is entered as a concrete figure, e.g. '28', because it allows conclusions concerning the leisure and tourist behaviour (Gibson and Yiannakis, 2002, pp. 360–363). Another important information is the user's *familiarity with the destination* as the points of interest vary with the number of previous visits. The customer enters this figure into the system with a slider on a scale ranging from *never* to *often*, which is internally represented as a value between 0 and 100. Another factor that highly influences the tourist's interests is his or her *level of education*. As this is a relatively delicate question, which might not be answered in a completely truthful way by all the users, the system provides a relatively high number of different education levels. In this way, a (purposeful) deviation from the actual level by a

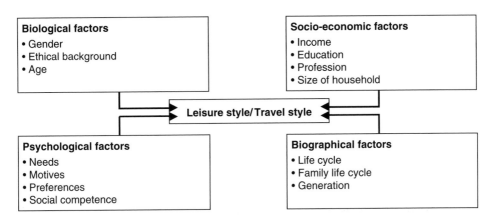

Fig. 16.2. Determining factors of tourist behaviour (from Depner, 2002, p. 17).

few nuances influences the result of the classification to a smaller degree. The *interest in nightlife activities* includes bars, discos and parties. In combination with the user's age this can be especially helpful for the classification process. The same is true for the *interest in outdoor activities,* which can be seen as one of four main factors for classifying tourists according to Madrigal and Kahle (1994, p. 26). Both input variables as well as familiarity are represented on a scale between 0 and 100. Another important factor for describing a travel programme is the *travel company.* It ranges from single trips to families with children. If the user tells the system that he or she is travelling with children, the seventh question concerning the *childrens' age* is activated.

3.3 Fuzzification

Fuzzy theory is an extension of the classical Boolean logic where a statement is either completely true (1) or false (0). In contrast to this, the fuzzy concept allows membership values between 0 and 1 for a statement. In order to represent the trigger data in a fuzzy-compatible way, the system uses so-called linguistic variables (LV). There is one LV for each trigger and an additional eighth one for the suitability of the different stereotypes. Table 16.2 shows their possible expressions.

The connection between a numeric input variable and the linguistic expression is established via the so-called membership function μ. For each numeric value g from a basic set $G = [g_{min}, g_{max}]$ the function calculates a membership value $\mu(g,l_i)$ to a certain linguistic expression l_i of the LV, with $0 \leq \mu(g,l_i) \leq 1$ (Börcsök, 2000). The combinations of function and linguistic expression are called fuzzy sets. The most common forms are triangular, trapezoid and bell-shaped curve (see Fig. 16.3).

For example, in the case of a 28-year-old user, the approach to fuzzification led to a categorization as 80% young and 20% middle-aged (see Fig. 16.3). The other forms produce different results; in the case of the bell-shaped curves

Table 16.2. Possible values of the linguistic variables.

Linguistic variable	Possible expression
Age	Very young, young, middle-aged, old, very old
Visits	None, few, many
Education	Very low, low, medium, high, very high
Nightlife	Very low, low, medium, high
Outdoor	Very low, low, medium, high, very high
Company	Single, partner
Childrens' age	Young, medium, old
Suitability	Very low, low, medium, high, very high

there are even three fuzzy sets that are overlapping at this point. All trigger variables are translated in this way and in the end each of them is assigned to one or more fuzzy sets with a certain membership value and forms the input for the rules of the inference engine.

3.4 Inference engine and rule base

The purpose of the rule base is to identify combinations of input variables that indicate a high or low suitability of a certain stereotype for the user in question. For example, the stereotype 'cultural tourist' is especially well-suited

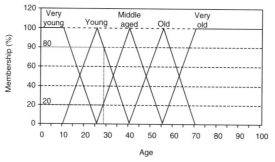

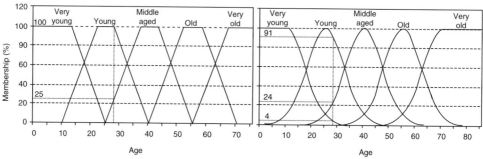

Fig. 16.3. Different forms of membership functions.

for travellers with a high degree of education (Dreyer, 2000) between 30 and 50 years of age. As they often visit new locations, a low familiarity value indicates high suitability as well as a relatively high appreciation of outdoor activities (for sightseeing tours, etc.) as well as this kind of tourist travels alone or in groups without children (Diem, 1996, p. 31).

In order to be processed by the inference engine, verbal descriptions like the one above have to be formalized and transferred into rules. In TourBO this is achieved with the help of a rule editor. One rule consists of one or more conditions connected with the AND-operator and one conclusion. Table 16.3 shows part of the rule set for the stereotype family tourist with the membership values printed above the conditions.

The rule base is evaluated in two steps. First, the computer calculates a value for the conclusion of each rule by aggregating the membership values of the conditions. Second, the rules with the same conclusion but different membership values (see rules 1 and 2 in the example) are accumulated in order to get only one value for each suitability-fuzzy set. There are pairs of operators for aggregation and accumulation that are called t- and s-norms. TourBO uses three of these pairs (see Table 16.4).

Although the first pair is the easiest to calculate, it is also the one that disregards most of the information available in the rules. For example, a high membership value in one condition can never compensate for a low one. On the other hand, when using the algebraic product, each new condition added to a rule automatically decreases the result of the rule regardless of how well the condition is met. This is due to the multiplication with a number ≤ 1. When the single rules have different numbers of conditions, the outcome of the rule set can be influenced by the algebraic operators.

The evaluation of the rules in Table 16.3 with the operators described above leads to the results in Table 16.5. It can be seen that the accumulated membership value of rules 1 and 2 is higher when t_2/s_2 or t_3/s_3 are used instead of t_1/s_1, although their single values after the aggregation were still significantly lower. This also leads to a different overall estimation: leaving

Table 16.3. Rule base for family tourists.

No.	Condition		Conclusion
1	IF 0.8; 1.0; 0.85 Age = 'young' AND Partner = 'yes' AND Children = 'young'	THEN	??? Suitability = 'very high'
2	IF 0.85; 0.75; 0.95 Children = 'young' AND Visits = 'many' AND Outdoor = 'medium'	THEN	??? Suitability = 'very high'
3	IF 1.0; 0.1; 0.15 Partner = 'yes' AND Children = 'medium' AND Nightlife = 'medium'	THEN	??? Suitability = 'high'
4	IF 0.8; 0.85 Nightlife = 'high' AND Children = 'young'	THEN	??? Suitability = 'low'

Table 16.4. *t*- and *s*-norms.

Aggregation of conditions (*t*-norm)	Accumulation of identical conclusions (*s*-norm)
Minimum operator t_1:	Maximum operator s_1:
$t_1\left(\mu_A,\mu_B\right) = \min\left(\mu_A;\mu_B\right)$	$s_1\left(\mu_A,\mu_B\right) = \max\left(\mu_A;\mu_B\right)$
Hamacher product t_2:	Hamacher sum s_2:
$t_2\left(\mu_A,\mu_B\right) = \dfrac{\mu_A \cdot \mu_B}{\mu_A + \mu_B - \left(\mu_A \cdot \mu_B\right)}$	$s_2\left(\mu_A,\mu_B\right) = \dfrac{\mu_A + \mu_B - 2 \cdot \mu_A \cdot \mu_B}{1 - \left(\mu_A \cdot \mu_B\right)}$
Algebraic product t_3:	Algebraic sum s_3:
$t_3\left(\mu_A,\mu_B\right) = \mu_A \cdot \mu_B$	$s_3\left(\mu_A,\mu_B\right) = \mu_A + \mu_B - \left(\mu_A \cdot \mu_B\right)$
With $t_1 \geq t_2 \geq t_3$ for identical μ_A, μ_B	With $s_1 \leq s_2 \leq s_3$ for identical μ_A, μ_B

out rule 3, the min/max operators judge the suitability of stereotype 'family tourist' as 'very high' (0.8) and 'low' (0.8) to the same degree. As opposed to that, with the combination of algebraic product or sum, the very high suitability (0.874) is rated 30% higher than the low one (0.68).

3.5 Defuzzification and assignment of stereotypes

After the inference engine has evaluated the complete rule base, it returns expressions of the following kind for each of the predefined profiles: 'The stereotype *n* is well suited for the user with *x*% and very suitable with *y*%, but also has a low suitability with *z*%.' Formally, these are fuzzy sets of the LV 'suitability'. In the next step, these expressions have to be transformed into a numeric value *S* in order to be able to compare the different stereotypes. To do this, the system translates the results of the rule sets with the help of the membership function into a 'suitability ridge' (see Fig. 16.4, grey area), which again is a fuzzy set.

TourBO implements two methods to calculate a numeric value from this geometric form. The easier one is the maximum method, which simply checks which point(s) of the ridge the membership value $\mu(s)$ is (are) the highest. The corresponding value on the *x*-axis is the stereotype's suitability. In case there is more than one maximum point their average is calculated (Börcsök, 2000). In our example the result is $S_{max} = (100 + 83)/2 = 91.5$. One can see that this calculation completely ignores the areas under the fuzzy sets 'low' and 'high', i.e. it overestimates the fuzzy set(s) with the highest membership value. In contrast to this, the centre of gravity (COG) method takes

Table 16.5. Evaluation of the rule base.

		Rule 1			Rule 2			Rule 3			Rule 4	
Conditions		0.8	1.0	0.85	0.85	0.75	0.95	1.0	0.1	0.15	0.8	0.8	0.85
Aggregation	t_1	0.8			0.75			0.1			0.8		
	t_2	0.701			0.640			0.064			0.701		
	t_3	0.68			0.606			0.015			0.68		
Conclusion					Suitability = 'very high'			Suitability = 'high'			Suitability = 'low'		

Accumulation	
s_1	0.8
s_2	0.805
s_3	0.874
Suitability = 'very high'	

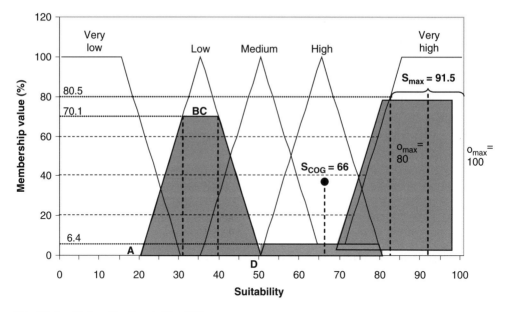

Fig. 16.4. Defuzzification in TourBO.

into account the complete suitability ridge. After calculating the COG of the grey area the corresponding x-value represents the suitability. It is, of course, much lower than the one calculated with the maximum method because it does not neglect the more pessimistic rules.

After having assigned a suitability value to each stereotype the system could simply select the best one for the user in question. However, this would not solve the problem of having a limited variety of starting profiles. Therefore, TourBO creates a mixed profile from those stereotypes that have a similar suitability. As this mix only includes the n best stereotypes, the latter are sorted in a first step (see Fig. 16.5).

How many candidates finally belong to the top group is determined with the help of the relative distance of their suitability values. If this distance exceeds a predefined threshold d_{max} (e.g. 10%), the stereotype i is not calculated into the mixed profile.

$$\frac{S_i}{S_{i-1}} < 1 - \frac{d_{max}}{100} \quad \rightarrow \text{stereotype } i \notin MP$$

with S_i = suitability value of ith stereotype; d_{max} = threshold value for the relative distance of two adjacent profiles; and MP = set of all stereotypes that are calculated into the mixed profile.

In the example the final profile includes only the cultural and the family tourist (with a threshold value of $d_{max} = 10$), as $S_2/S_1 = 66/70 \geq 0.9$, but $S_3/S_2 = 51/66 < 0.9$.

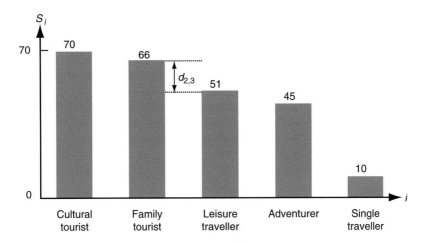

Fig. 16.5. Ranking of stereotypes.

For the actual fusion of the selected stereotypes $\vec{p}_i \in MP$ into the mixed profile $\vec{p}_M$, TourBO provides two alternatives:

$$\vec{p}_M = \begin{pmatrix} r_0^M & r_1^M & \cdots & r_{30}^M \end{pmatrix}; \; MP = \{\vec{p}_1, \ldots, \vec{p}_n\} \subseteq \{\vec{p}_C, \vec{p}_L, \vec{p}_S, \vec{p}_A, \vec{p}_F\}$$

Alternative 1:   *Alternative 2:*

$$r_i^M = \max_k \left(r_i^k \right), \; \forall k \,|\, \vec{p}_k \in MP \qquad r_i^M = \frac{\sum_k r_i^k \cdot S_k}{\sum_k S_k}$$

with r_i^M = ith interest value of the mixed profile and r_i^k = ith interest value of the kth stereotype in MP.

The first alternative assigns the maximum interest of all candidate profiles to the user. In doing so, all the profiles are simply treated in the same way, including the last one, which has barely been qualified. The second method takes into account the varying suitability of the candidates and calculates a weighted sum of their single interest values.

4. Integration of Group Support Tools

It is interesting that most publications on user profiling and computer-generated recommendations deal with the modelling of single individuals' interests, but usually fail to (or rather do not attempt or want to) extend the proposed solutions to the profiling of groups (e.g. Madrigal, 1995; Zins, 1998; Cotte and Ratneshwar, 2001). Therefore, the following describes some ideas as to the integration of group support tools into an advising system like TourBO.

One opportunity to add group functionality to an advising system is to make special offers for them. This could be commercial products as well as private activities that require a minimum number of participants in order to take place, e.g. special guided tours in museums or the participation at an amateur football tournament. With the help of a web interface interested users can book a place in such a group event until the maximum number of participants is reached. After that, they may communicate with the other group members over an internal messaging system or dynamically generated mailing lists. Perhaps a central coordination authority (like the advising system) might help the users to save money via discount offerings, similar to the bulk-buying or power-buying concepts of electronic marketplaces like atrada.de (Slawinski, 2001). However, opportunities for group support can be found not only in the execution stage of the service process but also in the previous phases.

4.1 Assisting a 'moderator' in profiling a group of persons

When a group is travelling together, often one 'moderator' or group leader is responsible for planning the journey for the whole company. Thus, a first step towards group support could be assisting this person in profiling the people he or she is responsible for, e.g. by reminding the leader of facts he or she is likely to forget, because he or she is not immediately concerned with them (like the needs of smaller children or wheelchair-bound people in the group). One means to reach this end are intelligent checklists and knowledge-based systems that generate adaptable questionnaires based on rules and depending on previous responses (see Fig. 16.6).

This means that answers to earlier questions may determine or at least influence replies to inquiries in later stages of the list. Consequently, these questions may be skipped or their range of possible answers may be narrowed, rendering the profiling process as lean as possible.

4.2 Assembling potentially cohesive groups

Another idea in this context is to assemble potentially cohesive groups from a pool of individuals. This becomes relevant in those cases where single travellers book a journey, which then takes place in several groups (bike tours, safaris, bus journeys, etc.). For example, if a number of single travellers book bus journeys or other team-oriented travels, one should assign the people to the different buses respectively as teams, in such a way that they fit together as well as possible according to their user models in order to prevent or minimize possible conflicts.

As finding the best-suited leisure partner for an individual is rather similar to the accumulation of a group of people, but on a lower level of

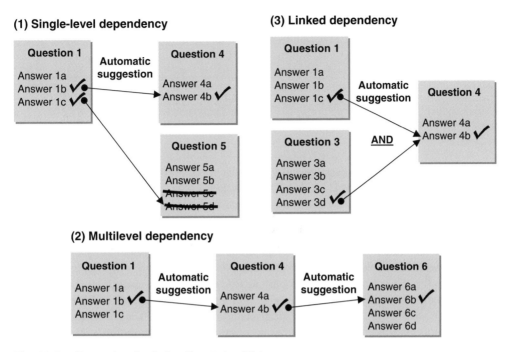

Fig. 16.6.   Dependencies in intelligent checklists.

complexity, we tried to do this first. If, for example, somebody wants to play tennis during the trip, there is always the problem of finding a suitable partner. The same is true if the person wants to go clubbing, to the theatre or other cultural activities, but does not know at all where to go and with whom. In this situation, our partner recommendation module can determine the best-suited partners using a three-level process. The first step verifies the KO criteria given by the customer (e.g. desired age, gender) and singles out all candidates that do not meet these. Subsequently, we try to find out those profiles that closely resemble the seeker's, taking into account both the absolute distance between the profiles and their correlation. The former (see Fig. 16.7, arrows indicate the distance) is calculated using an adapted version of the square Euclidean distance (Backhaus *et al.*, 2000, pp. 340–341):

$$d_{A,B} = \frac{\sum_{i=1}^{N} w_i \cdot (r_{Ai} - r_{Bi})^2}{(r_{max} - r_{min})^2 \cdot \sum_{i=1}^{N} w_i}$$

with $d_{A,B}$ = distance of profiles A and B; $d_{A,B} \in [0;1]$; r_{Ai}/r_{Bi} = interest value of profile A/B in rubric i; w_i = weight of ith rubric; $w_i \in \{1, 2, 3\}$; N = number of rubrics in a profile.

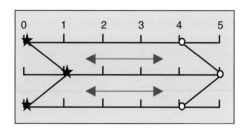

Fig. 16.7. Absolute distance of two profiles.

As it is a square distance, one large divergence has a higher influence than several minor ones with the same absolute value. The following adaptations of the conventional Euclidean distance make it better suited to our requirements: First, the rubrics of the profile get different weights according to their relevance in the concrete situation. Those activities the user seeks a partner for are weighted three times, rubrics in the same superior category are given a weight of two and the rest gets one.

As the sum of weights can differ between two searches, the result is finally normalized to a range of values between 0 and 1. All candidates whose profiles exceed a marginal distance value (e.g. 0.3) are sorted out. Subsequently, the correlation of the remaining profiles is checked, whereby profiles that are exactly parallel to each other are considered to be most similar regardless of their absolute distance, because we assume that the correlation of profiles becomes more important than their absolute distance, once the latter ranges within an acceptable limit. The q-correlation coefficient, which compares the divergences of the single values in a profile from its average value, is able to determine this kind of similarity (Backhaus *et al.*, 2000, p. 343).

$$S_{A,B} = \frac{\sum_{i=1}^{N} (r_{Ai} - \overline{r_A}) \cdot (r_{Bi} - \overline{r_B})}{\sqrt{\sum_{i=1}^{N} (r_{Ai} - \overline{r_A})^2 \cdot \sum_{i=1}^{N} (r_{Bi} - \overline{r_B})^2}}$$

with $S_{A,B}$ = similarity of profiles A and B; $S_{A,B} \in [-1;1]$; $\overline{r_A}$ = average of all interest values in profile A; $\overline{r_B}$ = average of all interest values in profile B.

Figure 16.8 shows two examples of profiles with the same absolute distance; however, in (A) they run exactly parallel resulting in a q-correlation coefficient of 1, whereas in (B) they are inverted entailing a value of −1. According to their performance in this final matching step, the system sorts the partners and recommends the best three matches to the inquiring customer.

Assembling whole groups of individuals, rather than matching only two persons, adds a lot of complexity to the problem. Therefore, we decided to take into account only the distances between the profiles and to neglect their correlation. To do so, we made use of clustering algorithms that categorize individuals in such a way that there is uniformity within the categories and

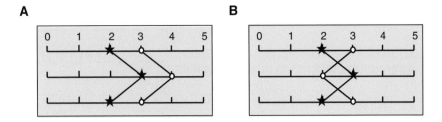

Fig. 16.8. Examples for similarities of profiles.

heterogeneity between them. The best-suited procedure for our purposes is a fusion algorithm, which starts with clusters of single individuals and successively merges the two collections with the smallest distance in the distance matrix. In our example, this would be the clusters 1 and 3, having a distance of 1 (see Fig. 16.9A). Therefore, the elements of group 3 are put into group 1 and the former is deleted.

After the merging, the new distances in the reduced matrix are calculated (see Fig. 16.9B) using the Ward method:

$$D(R,P+Q)=\frac{NR+NP}{NR+NP+NQ}\cdot D(R,P)+\frac{NR+NQ}{NR+NP+NQ}\cdot D(R,Q)-\frac{NR}{NR+NP+NQ}\cdot D(P,Q)$$

with $D(x,y)$ = distance of groups x and y and Nx = number of objects in group x.

The distance between an unchanged cluster and the newly merged one consists of a weighted sum (according to the number of objects involved) of its former distances to the individual pre-merger clusters. The resulting value is reduced by a fraction of the now intracluster distance between the

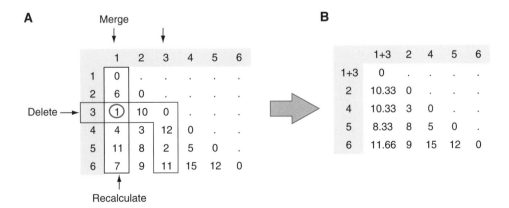

Fig. 16.9. Fusion algorithm.

merged groups. This method tends to produce even-sized clusters, thus suiting our needs (Backhaus et al., 2000, pp. 354, 365).

4.3 Aggregating individual interest profiles

Having identified travel groups, the next step in the advising process is to aggregate the individual profiles to a single 'group profile'. Our first consideration was to employ scoring models by weighting the specific values. However, we found it more practicable to generate a so-called 'matrix of contentment', whose structure is depicted in Fig. 16.10. As can be seen, the first column (❶) includes a generated travel programme, i.e. the sequence of activities and breaks. The following columns show the ratings of the group members (❷). For example, member 1 gives 1 point to activity A, whereas member 2 awards 7 points to it. Breaks and idle times resulting from transfers between locations are negatively rated, more so with increasing duration, less if a user desires an unhurried tour. The sums of the column values indicate a member's individual approval of the programme in question (❸). If this value is very low, the system could either dynamically increase the weight of this member's rating in order to lessen his or her disadvantage or recommend that he or she should change into another group that fits his or her interests better. On the other hand, the sums of the lines show the group's collective opinion of an activity (❹): the higher this value, the bigger the contribution of the activity to a high overall programme rating. Furthermore, the matrix provides another indicator for the quality of an element: in the rightmost column the standard deviation of the members' opinions is calculated (❺). For example, activities A and C have the same overall rating, whereas the standard deviation of A is way beyond that of C. This means there is a higher degree of consensus on activity C in the group; hence it should be preferred

❶	Grade 1	❷ Grade 2		Grade N	❹ Σ	❺ σ
Activity A	1	7		2	10	2.6
Break	−3	−2		−1	−6	0.8
Activity B	6	9		10	25	1.7
Break	−6	−3		−2	−11	1.7
Activity C	4	3		3	10	0.5
⋮	⋮	⋮	......	⋮		
Activity N	10	2		5	17	3.3
Σ	12 ❸	16		17	45 ❻	2.2

Fig. 16.10.   Matrix of contentment.

by the system. Finally, the overall sum of the matrix (❻) provides additional information about the programme's quality. By combining these values of the matrix, a target function for generating sightseeing tours for groups with an evolutionary algorithm (Franke and Mertens, 2003).

4.4 Support decision-making processes

It is difficult for the system to decide which of the generated programme alternatives is 'best' for the group. Therefore, it presents the two or three with the highest ratings. Now, it is up to the group to decide which alternative to take while the computer can support this decision-making in analogy to conventional group decision support systems. To do so, we use a modified version of the well-known Delphi method containing the following steps:

1. Creation of a ranking order by the participants.
2. Calculation of key figures (average, variance) by the system.
3. Communication of results to the participants.
4. Reconsideration of results and possible correction.
5. Recurring evaluation and correction turn.
6. Finish when variance is sufficiently small.

The necessary communication takes place over mailing lists or (as mentioned above) with the help of an internal messaging system.

5. Explanation Component

The following sections describe an approach for an explanation component in TourBO. These modules are normally parts of expert systems that tell the user which rules in the knowledge base lead to the presented result.

5.1 Direct explanations

Direct explanations try to make the problem-solving process of the system transparent for the user by telling the user how a certain decision was made. When a leisure programme is generated, there are three different possibilities of choosing a certain activity for the programme (see Fig. 16.11). It may be found in the content-based search, if the interest profile of the customer shows at least a *high* interest in the corresponding category. The second channel works as recommender system and determines those people as the user's reference group, who have rated activities in the past in a very similar way as the customer has. Suggestions that have not yet been made to the user in question and that have been rated with an average of 7 points or higher on a scale from 1 to 10 by the reference group are then picked for the leisure programme, provided that there is at least a *very low* interest in the category. In both cases TourBO checks if there are additional activities available in the immediate vicinity of

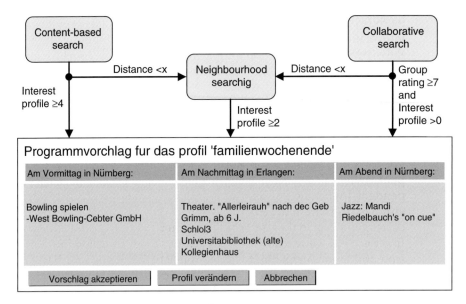

Fig. 16.11.   Program generation modes.

the one just added to the programme. If this is the case and the customer has at least low interest in this category, the system suggests these too. The structure of the direct part of the explanation component follows directly from the three selection channels. There are text blocks for all possible combinations that are combined according to Table 16.6. The text parts in bold print represent

Table 16.6.   Text blocks for direct explanations.

	Interest value	
Search mode	≥4	<4
Content-based	Your profile shows {*high/very high*} interest in {*%category*}.	–
Collaborative	The other {*%count*} users with a taste similar to yours have given {*%activity*} an average rating of {*%x*} out of 10 points. Furthermore your profile shows {*high/very high*} interest in {*%category*}.	Although your profile shows only {*very low/low/average*} interest in {*%category*}, the other {*%count*} users with a taste similar to yours have given {*%activity*} an average rating of {*%x*} out of 10 points.
Neighbourhood	{*%activity*} lies in the vicinity of {*%reference activity*}. Furthermore your profile shows {*high/very high*} interest in {*%category*}.	Although your profile shows only {*low/average*} interest in {*%category*}, {*%activity*} lies in the vicinity of {*%reference activity*}. Perhaps you want to have a look?

dynamically generated sections; the percentage sign means that the following part is a variable that is filled at runtime. TourBO combines the generated texts with the indirect explanations and displays them on demand.

5.2 Indirect explanations

Indirect explanations include those parts of an illustration that exceed the mere tracing of the selection algorithm. Often, it is appropriate to describe the object of the explanation from a different point of view. TourBO uses personality traits of the user for this purpose, i.e. characteristics that are independent from time or situational influences (Pervin, 2000, p. 225). Thus, it emphasizes those aspects of the activity to be explained in its description that correspond best to the user's character. In a very early model Eysenck identified two basic dimensions of personality, which he called intro- or extraversion and emotional stability or neuroticism (Amelang and Bartussek, 2001, pp. 327–331). Since the 1960s these two criteria have more and more been judged as not sufficient and several different studies identified more or less the same five factors under slightly different names (Amelang and Bartussek, 2001, pp. 364–385; Borkenau and Ostendorf, 2001):

- *Neuroticism.* This scale describes a person's emotional stability without making any statements about psychological disturbances. The focus lies rather on the way people experience and react to (especially negative) emotions. A high neuroticism value often results in people being more easily concerned and reacting as shocked, ashamed or afraid, while in the opposite case, the person hardly ever worries about anything at all.
- *Extraversion.* Socializing is one main characteristic of people with a strong extraversion factor. They are open to new acquaintances, are talkative and comfortable in groups or at social events. Being optimistic and active are also traits of extraverted people. The more introverted counterpart, however, does not like to be among other people, but rather wants to spend time alone by himself or herself in a quiet environment.
- *Openness.* This dimension measures the desire to learn from new experiences and impressions. People with a high value are often creative and perceive their feelings (positive and negative) very strongly. They often act in an impulsive way and are ready to try new approaches to solve problems. On the other hand, less open people tend to behave in a more conventional way and to have a more conservative attitude. They prefer familiar things and do not react very emotionally.
- *Agreeableness.* This factor mainly describes interpersonal behaviour. One extreme are very altruistic people with a great desire for harmony. On the other side, one finds egocentric persons who always compete with others and do not trust anyone.
- *Conscientiousness.* This refers to the process of planning, organizing and solving tasks. Naturally a high value is connected to being determined, ambitious, disciplined and almost overly thorough. Persons with a low

value describe themselves as rather careless, indifferent and unstable. They pursue their goals with less effort.

The best known and most widely spread tool to record these dimensions is the NEO-FFI by Costa and McCrae (1992; see also Amelang and Bartussek, 2001, p. 377), which is a standardized questionnaire with 12 items per factor. The person answering the questionnaire rates these items on a 5-point scale represented as 0 to 4 points. The value of each factor is calculated as the average of the 12 corresponding questions.

TourBO's explanation component takes into account the first three dimensions, because it is argued that agreeableness has a solely interpersonal focus (giving hardly any information concerning personal recommendations). Conscientiousness, on the other hand, plays a much greater role in the professional environment than in the field of tourism and leisure. Furthermore, this approach reduces the time to complete the questionnaire from about 10 to 6 min. Table 16.7 provides an overview of the factors together with the average values and their standard deviations, which have been gathered in several studies with more than 2000 participants in Germany (Borkenau and Ostendorf, 1993, pp. 12–13). The numbers are given separately for men and women, as well as overall.

In order to enable the system to display not only the tracing of the plan generation (see above) but also the parts of the indirect explanations, the user, first, has to complete the shortened NEO-FFI on the computer. Then, the system calculates the distance x_i from the user's factor scores to the corresponding average and categorizes him or her in analogy to Table 16.8 into one of five groups.

If the customer's gender is known, the system uses the corresponding averages, otherwise, the general figures. A woman with a neuroticism value of 2.33 would, therefore, still be classified as neutral, because she is less than half of the standard deviation (0.345) away from the women's average (1.99),

Table 16.7. Overview of 5-factor model.

				Score factor	
				Rather low	Rather high
	Neuroticism				
	m	w	ges.	Calm, relaxed, balanced,	Worried, nervous, unsure,
Ø	1.66	1.99	1.84	fearless, self-confident	hypochondriac, afraid, self-
σ	0.67	0.69	0.70		conscious, touchy
	Extraversion			Reserved, matter-of-fact,	Sociable, active, talkative,
	m	w	ges.	controlled, quiet, inde-	energetic, optimistic, fun-
Ø	2.34	2.39	2.36	pendent, shy, withdrawn	loving, cheerful
σ	0.56	0.58	0.57		
	Openness			Traditional, down-to-earth,	Curious, creative, original,
	m	w	ges.	narrow minded, conserva-	imaginative, intellectual
Ø	2.65	2.75	2.71	tive, uncreative, habitual-	
σ	0.53	0.51	0.52	ised	

Table 16.8. Classification intervals.

Very low	Low	Neutral	High	Very high
$x_i < -1.5\sigma$	$-1.5\sigma \leq x_i < -0.5\sigma$	$-0.5\sigma \leq x_i \leq 0.5\sigma$	$0.5\sigma < x_i \leq 1.5\sigma$	$x_i > 1.5\sigma$

whereas a man with the value 2 (>1.66 + 0.335) would already be sorted into the *high* interval. If the gender was unknown, the first example would lead to a *high*, and the second one to a *neutral*, classification. To generate the explanations, the prototype stores a text block for each profile category of leisure activities in each interval of the personality factors (i.e. $31 \times 5 \times 3 = 465$ text blocks). Each of these texts emphasizes an aspect of the activity in question that is especially well suited to the corresponding personality trait of the user (see Table 16.9).

Of course, it would be even more accurate if these text blocks would not address whole categories but rather single activities, because in this case they could go into detail about the differences between certain museums or the like, while at the same time the explanations would become more varied and more interesting to read. However, the relatively high number of 200 single activities in the database would require a huge effort in order to create 3000 text blocks that would be required. Nevertheless, the underlying principle could be transferred to this scenario without any change.

When the right text for the current customer has been selected based on his or her factor interval classification, TourBO fits them together in the sequence extraversion, openness and neuroticism before attaching them to the direct explanations (see above). A user with very low values in extraversion and neuroticism but a high openness, to whom the system recommended the visit at the zoo because of the collaborative search, could get an explanation looking like the following:

Table 16.9. Exemplary text blocks for the category 'Zoos'.

	Rating	
Factor	Very low	Very high
Neuroticism	And is not it really thrilling to watch the cats of prey and other wild beasts just across a trench?	And, finally, is there anything more tranquilizing than to sit and watch the dolphins play in their basin?
Extraversion	*There is always a secluded corner in the zoo where one can take a walk in peace.*	*In the zoo, there are youth groups, families and tourist parties around at all times, so it rarely gets boring.*
Openness	Furthermore, a visit to the zoo has always been one of the favourite leisure activites of children and adults alike.	Furthermore, you may always learn something new about the animals at the zoo.

Although your profile shows only *average* interest in visits to the *zoo*, the other 12 users with a taste similar to yours have given the *Nuremberg zoo* an average rating of 8 out of ten points. *There is always a secluded corner in the zoo where one can take a walk in peace.* Furthermore, you may always learn something new about the animals at the zoo. And, isn't it really thrilling to watch the cats of prey and other wild beasts just across a trench?

6. Outlook

The work described above differs from the mainly empirical focus of Northern American literature in this field. Unlike, for example, Hu and Brent Ritchie (1993) or Madrigal and Kahle (1994), we did not conduct a survey of our own in order to establish connections between a destination's attributes and the traveller's decision to go there or between personal values and leisure preferences, respectively. Rather, we took their work as a basis upon which to build our advising system. The prototype implemented in Nuremberg is to be improved according to the users' feedback. We hope to produce results with a practical use as the system gathers its data in a 'real-time' environment instead of a laboratory. In the future we want to incorporate the presented concepts and prototypical modules into our operative 'Nix-Verpassen' system together with the city of Nuremberg. The first module, which is already completed, mainly addresses inhabitants of Nuremberg, but tourists may profit from its services too. They can subscribe to an individual e-mail newsletter, which regularly informs them about events and other cultural news (push functionality). In a further step, the findings of this regional tourism and spare time portal are to be generalized and transferred to other regions in Bavaria or Germany. A long-term goal will be the integration of these regional platforms in order to provide customers with the same services, wherever they happen to be.

Chapter Summary

This chapter has described TourBO, a prototype tourism advising system that supports the provision of individualized travel information for a tourist region in Germany. The core of the TourBO system is a set of profiling algorithms to categorize tourists into preference groups or roles, such as 'cultural tourists', 'leisure travellers', 'young single travellers', 'adventurers' and 'family tourists'. Fuzzy logic methods are introduced into the stereotyping process in order to make the recommendations more meaningful. These algorithms are further extended to support group profiling. In addition, the system integrates explanation components that tell the user which rules of recommendations lead to the presented result. Finally, directions for future development were discussed.

17 MobyRek: A Conversational Recommender System for On-the-move Travellers

FRANCESCO RICCI AND QUANG NHAT NGUYEN

1. Introduction

Although many e-commerce websites support travel information search and in particular travel planning, most of them simply let users search (e.g. with keywords or with query forms) through their electronic catalogues of products. In fact, e-commerce travel and tourism websites often contain huge quantities of travel items with different characteristics and types. Hence, a user's search request often returns a potentially overwhelming set of options, causing an 'information overload' (Maes, 1994). This problem has three reasons. First, some users may not have enough knowledge to express their needs in accordance with the system language and interface, i.e. to define a query to be processed by the system. Second, the preferences, which are collected at the time of a user's request, are typically a subset of the user's real 'needs and wants', because users (especially mobile users) usually do not like to input data. Third, users often receive poor support in analysing search results, in comparing products and in bundling final choices.

Both leisure and business travellers need system support throughout all travel stages: from pre-travel planning to the on-the-move support during the travel, and even when the travel is finished (Ricci, 2002). We have developed two systems, NutKing and MobyRek, which cooperate to support travellers through their full travel life cycle. NutKing deals with the pre- and post-travel stages. It is a recommender system that combines content-based and collaborative-based filtering methods to support users in building their travel plans (Ricci *et al.*, 2002a, 2003). NutKing helps users in selecting one or more destinations to visit and then adding additional products related to the selected destinations (accommodations, activities, events).

MobyRek, which is described in this chapter, deals with the on-tour stage. On-tour support is needed by travellers when they are on the move to, or during the stay in, their selected destination. In the on-tour stage, travellers typically use mobile devices to search for desired travel products, or to complement their pre-travel plan (which is already built before their leave, using the NutKing system). MobyRek is based on the assumption that the complementary products should conform to what have already been selected in the pre-travel stage. Moreover, we hypothesize that when a traveller is on the move the time span and cognitive effort spent to find his or her desired products should be minimized using appropriate methodologies.

In the MobyRek system the decision support is provided to travellers through personalized recommendations. Given a traveller's request, MobyRek produces those travel product recommendations that are personalized to the traveller in that particular situation. To minimize the user's effort, MobyRek does not require the user to formulate a precise and complete query at the time of the request, but involves the user in a dialogue (i.e. a conversation), which interleaves system's recommendation with user's critique. The ideas of 'recommendation by proposing' and 'similarity-based query revision' have been introduced in previous research (Burke, 2000b; Shimazu, 2001; McGinty and Smyth, 2002). The basic idea is that critique-based elicitation of user preferences (i.e. by interleaving elicitation with recommendation) seems to be more effective in pushing the users to the elicitation of their needs while keeping the interaction alive. Usually, users communicate their needs and preferences when they are convinced that they will benefit from that. Hence, for instance, the request of formulating a precise and complete query right from the beginning of the interaction may not be practical, especially for mobile users.

Our approach in MobyRek is innovative in two aspects: the way the first proposals are computed and the interaction supported. In a recommendation session, the closer the initial proposal is to the user's needs, the higher is the chance that the recommendation is accepted. In user–system interaction, the simpler it is to receive feedback or critiques to the proposal, the more likely the user will interact with the system to improve the recommendation. We propose to exploit different knowledge sources of the user-related data in building the initial representation of the user's preferences. When a user is in a place, which is specified by precise space–time coordinates, MobyRek first selects all the restaurants that are in a given distance range, and then sorts these restaurants according to their similarity to previous restaurant choices of the user (or of similar users). This approach tries to initially offer to the user restaurants similar to those the traveller normally chooses. The system then enables the user to browse the proposals, encouraging him to choose or to criticize each option. A typical critique is, for instance: 'I am interested in this restaurant, but it is a bit too expensive.' Depending on the type of critique (i.e. feedback), the critique is incorporated into the system's representation of the user's preferences as either a must-have requirement or an optional preference. Hence, if the user indicates that a restaurant is too expensive, the system discards those with costs above the criticized restaurant. Whereas, if the user says that he would prefer to pay with credit card, the system uses this preference to order those that accept this payment method first in the recommendation list.

2. Pre-travel Support

The traveller initially defines some trip characteristics and personal interests, such as the travel party, the available budget and means of transportation. NutKing uses these features: (i) to identify similar trips built by other users; and (ii) to set some default constraints in successive query forms. After this initial step, the traveller starts bundling his or her trip by searching for the travel products recommended by the system. The system allows the user to issue a query (with a simple query-by-example form) and retrieves the desired products (see Fig. 17.1). If the query fails because no products satisfy the user's query, the system proposes alternative query relaxations, which, if applied, would retrieve a suitable result set. Conversely, when the query retrieves too many products, NutKing asks the user to provide some additional constraints to narrow the result list. The retrieved products, which satisfy the user's (explicit) constraints, are then sorted and presented to the user, ordering the products most similar to those selected by other users who have expressed similar general travel wishes (see Fig. 17.2).

Although NutKing has been validated successfully in the web context for pre-travel planning (Ricci *et al.*, 2003), it cannot be used, as it is, by on-the-move travellers. Indeed, the mobile context imposes a number of peculiar constraints and requirements (Passani, 2002):

- the limitation of mobile devices (e.g. small screen size, limited computation capability);
- the graphical user interface and interaction supported (e.g. compact layout, limited input modality);
- the behaviour of mobile users (e.g. like to input less, but to receive results quickly); and
- the external environment impacts (e.g. noise, interruptions, light).

A recommender system designed to support on-the-move travellers should take into consideration, among other things, the following characteristics:

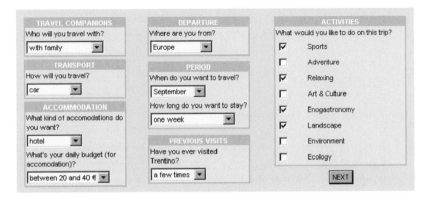

Fig. 17.1. NutKing interface to define the trip characteristics.

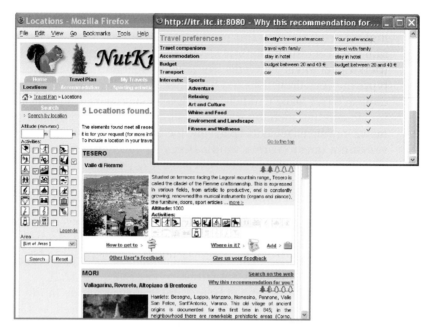

Fig. 17.2.   List of recommended products.

- Mobile users do not like to input lots of data; rather, they prefer answering to Yes/No questions with one click.
- A mobile user's interaction session should be kept (very) short in time.
- Mobile travellers should receive a useful recommendation within about 2–3 recommendation cycles.
- The preferences are only valid for a specific session, and could be rather different in another situation.

For these reasons, we have designed a completely different recommendation methodology. We see that NutKing contributes to this new methodology in the initialization of the on-the-move recommendation process by providing a set of preferences extracted from the product choices made by users in the past. In this respect, NutKing and the proposed mobile recommender system, MobyRek, provide an integrated solution to support travel decision choices.

3. On-tour Support

3.1 User preferences representation

A travel product is represented as a vector of feature values $x = (x_1, ..., x_n)$, where a feature value x_i may be numeric, nominal or symbol-set. Hereafter, we shall illustrate system functionality using a restaurant recommendation as an example. For the sake of simplicity, we represent a restaurant with six features (in reality, MobyRek describes a restaurant with 15 features): Name (nominal), Type (symbol-set), Location (nominal), MaxCost (numeric), OpeningDays (symbol-set) and Characteristics (symbol-set). Hence, the restaurant x = ('Pizzeria Ristorante al Vesuvio', {pizzeria}, 'Trento', 10, {1,2,3,4,6,7}, {parking, animals allowed}) has name x_1 = 'Pizzeria Ristorante al Vesuvio', type x_2 = {pizzeria}, location x_3 = 'Trento', maximum cost x_4 = 10, opening days x_5 = {1,2,3,4,6,7} and characteristics x_6 = {parking, animals allowed}.

To produce recommendations personalized to a particular user, recommender systems need a representation of the user's preferences. Preferences vary from user to user; and even the same user, in different situations (sessions), may have different preferences. A user's preferences are represented as a composite query containing three components: logical query, favourite pattern and feature importance weights vector.

- The logical query (Q_L) models must-have conditions that need to be independently satisfied by any of the products recommended. The logical query is constructed by a conjunction of logical constraints:

$$Q_L = c_1 \cdots c_m$$

where c_j is a constraint on a feature. Each feature type has a corresponding constraint representation. A constraint deals with only one feature, and a feature appears in only one constraint.

- The favourite pattern (p) models wish conditions that are expected to match as many as possible the products recommended. Differently from 'must-have' conditions, wish conditions allow trade-offs to be made. The preferred pattern is represented in the same vector space in which travel products are present:

$$p = (p_1, \ldots, p_n)$$

where p_i is a preference value for the ith feature; and x_i and p_i belong to the same feature type, $\forall_i = 1 \cdots n$. A value p_i may be unknown (denoted as '?') to indicate that the MobyRek system does not know about the user's preference on the ith feature. Such unknown values are, therefore, ignored in the similarity computation.

- The feature importance weights (w) model how much each feature is important with respect to the others:

$$w = (w_1, \ldots, w_n)$$

where w_i ($\in [0,1]$) is the importance weight of the ith feature.

For example, the representation of a user's preferences $<Q_L = (x_3 = \text{'Trento'}) \wedge (x_5 \supseteq \{7,1\})$, $p = (?, \{\text{spaghetteria}\}, ?, ?, ?, ?)$, $w = (0, 0.6, 0, 0.4, 0, 0)>$ indicates that the user is interested in only those restaurants in Trento that are open on Saturday and Sunday, and he or she prefers spaghetti restaurants to the others. The user considers the feature 'Type' as most important, the cost feature as the second most important and the remaining as unimportant.

When a traveller is on the move and starts searching for a desired travel product, MobyRek builds an initial representation of the user's preferences exploiting different knowledge sources of the user's data (i.e. the past on-tour product selections, the pre-travel plan, the spatial–temporal constraints and the initial preferences explicitly specified). The system's initial representation of the user's preferences (i.e. the initial query) is refined as the user proceeds with the dialogue, where MobyRek proposes candidate products and the user criticizes them or accepts one.

3.2 On-tour recommendation process

In our application scenario, on-tour support is offered when a traveller who has possibly built a pre-travel plan before leaving is at the selected destination (or on the move towards it). On-tour support is provided by the MobyRek system in cooperation with the pre-travel planning aid system (NutKing). The cooperation between these two systems allows the pre-travel information (in terms of knowledge of the user's decisions) to be exploited in the process of providing on-tour support.

An on-tour recommendation session starts when an on-the-move traveller requests the MobyRek system to find some desired travel products and ends when the traveller either selects a travel product or gives up the current session with no product selected. The recommendation process evolves in cycles. At each recommendation cycle, the system's representation of the user's preferences is used to produce a set of recommended products that are presented to the user. MobyRek models the on-tour recommendation process as in Fig. 17.3.

A recommendation session is initiated by the traveller's request for a generic product recommendation (e.g. 'I need a restaurant for lunch'). The

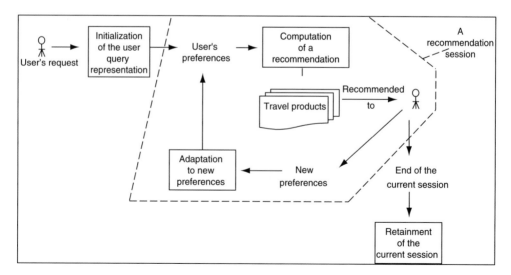

Fig. 17.3.   The on-tour recommendation process.

MobyRek system builds an initial representation of the user's preferences without querying the user and is aimed at minimizing the user input (effort). In MobyRek, the logical query (Q_L) is initialized using the spatial–temporal constraints detected from the traveller's position and current time. The favourite pattern (p) is initialized as a blank pattern (i.e. the preference value for every feature is unknown). The feature importance weights (w) are initialized in such a way that all the features are considered equally important.

The MobyRek system uses the initial representation of the user's preferences to produce the first recommendation set. In the computation of a recommendation, those products not satisfying the logical query (Q_L) are first excluded, and only those Q_L-satisfying products are ranked according to their similarity to the favourite pattern (p) taking into account the feature importance weights (w). Those (Q_L-satisfying) products most similar to (p) appear at the top of the ranked list; in the case where two products score the same, the least expensive product appears first in the ranked list. Only the k best products in the ranked list are shown to the user as recommendation result for the current cycle. The cut-off value (k) is a system parameter which is determined so that the recommendation list fits the screen size of the traveller's mobile device. Hence, the traveller can easily and quickly consider the recommendation list.

With a recommendation list, the user is supposed to browse the details of these products. In response, the user can execute one of the three actions: selection, critique or quit. A *selection* action is done when the user is satisfied with one of the recommended products. This selected product is added to the user's travel notes, and the current session ends successfully. A *critique* action is done when the user is somewhat interested in one of the recommended products, but unsatisfied with one (or more) feature(s) of this product. By criticizing the interested product, the user exposes preference on the unsatisfactory features. The MobyRek system uses such critiques to refine the previous representation of the user's preferences. Based on the refined representation, a new recommendation set that is expected to be closer to the user's real needs is produced. MobyRek's adaptation to a critique depends on the type of that critique and on the type of the feature criticized.

A *quit* action is made when no recommended products satisfy the user and he or she does not want to proceed with the dialogue. The session terminates with a failure. When an on-tour recommendation session finishes, either successfully or with a failure, it is retained as a case for future references. In this way, past recommendation sessions can be exploited by the system in building the initial representation of the user's preferences. We are in the process of addressing this problem (i.e. building the system's initial representation of the user's preferences) by exploiting different available knowledge sources of the user-related data (Nguyen and Ricci, 2004).

When the user criticizes a recommended product, it means that the criticized product interests the user but lacks some features (e.g. parking or live music) or some particular one is unsatisfactory (e.g. the price is too high). In our model, a user critique is supposed to express 'must-have' or 'wish-to-have' conditions, thereby indicating that the feature is either a non-compensatory or a compensatory decision criterion (Edwards and Fasolo, 2001). Non-compensatory criteria are such conditions that should be satisfied completely and independently; whereas compensatory ones are such conditions that would be satisfied to some extent (i.e. not necessarily to be completely satisfied) and one can be traded off against another. Non-compensatory criteria are encoded in MobyRek as logical constraints in Q_L, whereas compensatory ones are encoded in the favourite pattern (p) and the feature importance weights (w).

An important issue that should be considered and verified carefully is the number of critiques per cycle. In our approach, the user can express only one critique per cycle. In other words, after the user has criticized one product, with respect to one feature, the system acquires this input and recomputes the recommendation list. One may argue that the system should allow the user to express all the critiques before revising the user's preferences representation and producing a new recommendation set. Our design choice (i.e. to acquire only one critique per cycle) is motivated by some characteristics of the user behaviour and the mobile context. First, at the time of criticizing, the user usually does not know perfectly the distribution of products available in the catalogue; hence, as new products are recommended to the user, these may change his or her mind and suggest new preferences. In many real recommendation sessions, it is not surprising to observe that a user starting with some preferences ends with (very) different ones. Second, users are usually not good at making multi-objective decisions. In fact, users usually find it very difficult to take decisions that involve more than one feature where they must consider simultaneously both: (i) trade-offs between different values of the features and (ii) the probability that alternative outcomes occur. Third, mobile users typically do not like to have to input a lot before seeing something interesting. In particular, users only make explicit their preferences when they are convinced that they will immediately benefit from that. Hence, a mobile recommender system should play a more active and interactive role in the user–system dialogues, rather than wait (i.e. with no response) until the (mobile) user makes explicit all his   preferences. Because of these characteristics, the user can criticize only one feature of a single product; after that, MobyRek immediately incorporates the critique to produce a new recommendation set. The adaptation method proposed here can be described as the instance-to-instance learning mode in the machine learning domain (as opposed to the batch learning mode).

More formally, the user can express his or her preference regarding a feature of a criticized product using the following critique types:

F1 – Positive critique on a nominal feature. The user states that he or she likes the value l_i of the ith feature of a product $l = (l_1, ..., l_n)$. Then the value l_i is assigned for the ith element in the favourite pattern (p):

$$p_i = l_i$$

F2 – Positive critique on a numeric feature: want less. The user states that over-all he or she likes the product, but wants to see some alternatives having a smaller value for the ith feature. Hence the following constraint is included in the logical query (Q_L):

$$c_i \equiv (x_i \le l_i - \delta)$$

where δ (>0) is an adjustment factor that allows to retrieve other products rather than the current one.

F3 – Positive critique on a symbol-set feature. The user states that he or she likes some values (Values_set$_i$) of the ith symbol-set feature (e.g. the feature 'Char-acteristics'), and wants to see some products having these values for the ith feature. So the following constraint is included in Q_L:

$$c_i \equiv (x_i \supseteq \text{Values\_set}_i).$$

The method of eliciting user preferences through critiques has two advan-tages. First, preferences are explicitly stated by the user and, hence, are much more reliable than those implicitly collected (e.g. by mining the user's navigation or browsing). Second, the user effort required in the user–system interaction is not as high as that required by some other methods of eliciting user preferences such as through interviews or early rating.

4. User Interface

We assume that an on-the-move traveller accesses MobyRek to look for a res-taurant. MobyRek, as described above, exploits the traveller's current time and position (achieved via Global Positioning System (GPS) services) to ini-tialize the representation of the traveller's preferences (i.e. speaking more precisely, to initialize the logical query (Q_L)). The initial representation of the traveller's preferences is used to compute an initial recommendation list (as shown in Fig. 17.4A). Then the traveller can view detailed information about the listed restaurants. Figure 17.4B shows the attributes of the 'Pizzeria Ristorante al Vesuvio' restaurant, and Fig. 17.4C shows the restaurant's brief description and customers' opinions. If the traveller accepts this recommen-dation, he or she can add it to the travel notes (a convenient container of all his or her selections); otherwise, he or she can criticize one recommendation (Fig. 17.4D).

In this example, the traveller criticizes the feature 'Characteristics', by checking the two characteristics 'Parking' and 'Air-conditioned' to indicate that he or she is interested in these characteristics (F3 critique in Section 3). Note that only the first characteristic ('Parking') is available at the viewed restaurant, whereas the second ('Air-conditioned') is missing. The critique is then exploited (i.e. incorporated in the representation of the traveller's

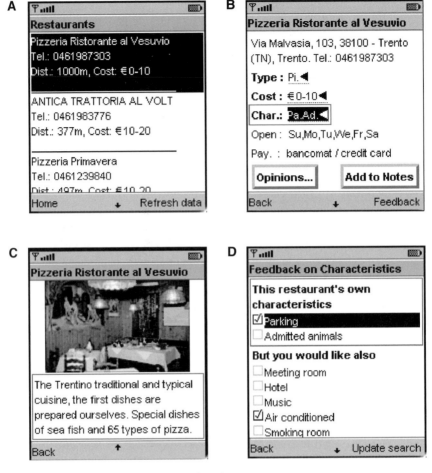

Fig. 17.4. MobyRek's graphical user interface.

preferences) when the traveller clicks on the button 'Update search'. In reply, a new recommendation list with three products is computed where the requested characteristics, if available, are present.

5. Evaluation

The evaluation involved six test users with no experience in applications running on WAP- or Java-enabled mobile phones. The test procedure, which each test user was asked to follow, consists of three phases. In the first phase (i.e. *training*), the test user is introduced to the simulator usage (e.g. the meanings of the buttons, the meaning of the contextual commands and how to execute them). Next, they are introduced to the system functionality and usage through a sample of a recommendation that demonstrates how the prototypical system works. The test users familiarize themselves with the simulator before solving a real task. We note that using the simulator is slightly more difficult than using a real mobile phone. For instance, in the simulator, the navigation buttons (up, down, left and right) and the three command buttons (select, left-ok, right-ok) are mapped to some number keys of the PC keyboard. This causes some difficulties. To test the prototype, test users associate icon buttons on the simulator interface (i.e. on the PC screen) with keys of the PC keyboard; however, on a real mobile phone, the user presses physical buttons on the phone's keypad.

In the second phase (i.e. *testing*), the test users are asked to think about the attributes of the desired restaurant and then to try to use the system to find one as such. If the test users can find the restaurant, they are then asked to add it to their travel notes, and to open these notes to look at that restaurant.

In the third phase (i.e. *evaluating*), the test users are asked to complete a usability survey. The survey form consists of two parts: one for the test users' subjective evaluation of the system's performance; the other for their brief comment on the difficulties they face and on the desirable extensions, and improvements of, the next system version. The test users are asked to state their agreement or disagreement on a 7-point Likert scale regarding the following nine statements:

1. The system was pleasant to use.
2. The organization of information on the system screen was clear.
3. This system has all the functions and capabilities that I expected to have.
4. The information provided by the system was complete.
5. I have found the restaurant that satisfies my needs.
6. I have found the possibility to critique a restaurant and get a new sorting of the offers useful and easy to use.
7. It was simple to use the system.
8. I was able to efficiently complete the tasks and scenarios using this system.
9. If the system were available on my phone, I would use it.

Some of the above statements were extracted directly from the Post-Study System Usability Questionnaire (PSSUQ) following Lewis (1995); the remainder were added to obtain an evaluation on the new functionality specific to the on-tour travel recommendation setting. The results of the experiment are shown in Table 17.1.

All the test users stated that they were able to find such a restaurant that matches their needs (s_5). Moreover, all of them rated the found restaurant at the highest rating score. In addition, all the test users were able to complete the predefined task scenario (s_8). Finally, almost all the test users indicated that they would definitely use the proposed on-tour recommendation service if it is available on their mobile phone (s_9).

On-the-move travellers, who use some kind of mobile devices, need not only to find their desired travel products but also to find them quickly (i.e.

Table 17.1. The experiment results.

| Statement | User | | | | | | Average | Standard deviation |
	u1	u2	u3	u4	u5	u6		
s_1	4	1	1	3	1	3	2.17	1.33
s_2	3	1	3	2	4	3	2.67	1.03
s_3	6	1	1	1	2	3	2.33	1.97
s_4	5	2	1	1	2	4	2.50	1.64
s_5	1	1	1	1	1	1	1.00	0.00
s_6	1	2	7	1	3	1	2.50	2.35
s_7	2	2	3	3	4	2	2.67	0.82
s_8	1	1	1	1	1	1	1.00	0.00
s_9	1	3	1	1	1	1	1.33	0.82
Average	2.67	1.56	2.11	1.56	2.11	2.11	2.02	0.42

after a few recommendation cycles). By mining the log file (which records the test users' recommendation sessions), we saw that all the test users had found their desired restaurant within three recommendation cycles. It should be noted that a critique required only 2–3 button clicks. Therefore, being able to find the desired restaurant within three recommendation cycles (i.e. maximum of three critiques) is a convincing result.

However, the experiment results also show some critical issues that are extracted from their comments. First, some of the test users found it difficult to use the on-screen commands, which are embedded in the screen. In the traditional web interface, users execute a command by first moving their pointing device (e.g. mouse) to that command, and then activating it. As shown in Fig. 17.4B, to execute an on-screen command, users have to navigate through several display objects (using the device's 'go-down' button) and then activate the command (using the device's 'select' button). Second, some of the test users preferred to initialize the search by explicitly specifying some preferences (see Fig. 17.5). In a traditional web interface, users usually state their conditions before the system's retrieval. The first prototype of MobyRek, which was used in the experiment, automatically recommends candidate products (i.e. those cheapest amongst the restaurants close to the users' position). Hence, the first recommendation set is produced without any consultation with the users. This manner of producing the first recommendation set was not liked by some testers who wanted to have more control on the search initialization process.

Some of the test users also preferred a longer (even the full) list of recommended products at each recommendation cycle. This seems to disprove the hypothesis that mobile users prefer to reduce the time and cognitive effort spent to fulfil a task. There could be two explanations for this preference. First, the search's goals and the acceptable trade-offs vary from user to user. Some users simply search for a 'good-enough' item while some others want to find the 'optimal' solution. Small recommendation sets could be acceptable for the

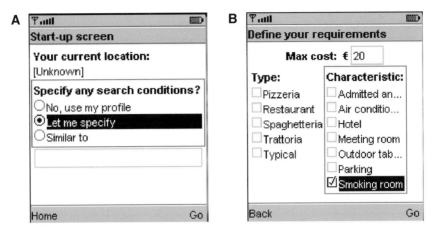

Fig. 17.5. Preferences initialization.

first class of users, but not for the second one. Second, some test users might be too familiar with traditional web interfaces that offer the possibility to browse complete lists of items. Therefore, they were surprised to find such a different interface. Third, all of the test users asked for a map-based navigation support to reach their selected restaurant from their position. This is a missing function in the prototype that should be supported in a next version of the system.

6. Conclusion and Future Work

In this chapter we have shown that MobyRek provides a usable approach to recommend tourism products to travellers when they are on the move to (or in the stay at) the selected destination. However, a number of open issues will need to be tackled in future work. First, we would like to perform a more extensive user evaluation: exploiting a real mobile phone to evaluate the system, and defining an appropriate methodology to assess the accuracy of the system in recommending products. Second, we would like to refine the system's initialization of the user preferences representation. In this initialization step, the system should exploit the knowledge about the user's preferences contained in past recommendation sessions, as well as the user's information and preferences that are specific to the current session and available at the time of the request. Third, we would like to improve the capability of the system to capture the user's preferences. In fact, the user's preferences could change during the interaction session (i.e. from an unclear state to a more refined state) and, therefore, some methods to tackle this 'drift' effect must be put in place (Montaner *et al.*, 2002). A final issue we expect to tackle to improve the quality of the recommendations is an analysis of the relationships among the critiqued items in the same interaction session.

Chapter Summary

Users of travel and tourism websites often experience difficulty in selecting desired travel products. This difficulty is especially true for on-the-move travellers who use some kind of mobile devices to browse travel products information repositories. On the one hand, travellers are overwhelmed by a huge number of options to consider. On the other hand, travellers lack system support in filtering information and comparing among candidate products. Given the inherent limitations of the mobile usage context, mobile travellers need system support in making travel decision choices. In this chapter we present a computational approach for providing personalized travel product recommendations to on-the-move travellers. The system employs a dialogue approach whereby a set of candidate products are proposed and the user is asked to critique the recommended products. A user's critiques elicited through a dialogue are incorporated in the system's representation of the user's preferences so that the system, step by step, better models users' needs. A prototype that implements the proposed approach is presented and the results of its empirical evaluation are discussed.

IV Recommendation Systems and Travel – An Exciting Future

18 Futuring Travel Destination Recommendation Systems

OLIVIERIO STOCK, HANNES WERTHNER AND
MASSIMO ZANCANARO

1. Introduction

The goal of a destination recommendation system (DRS) can be formulated as to guide a tourist or traveller in terms of the destination and other trip-related products. This book provides an overview of the state of the art in this field, looking at both theory and application. The work suggests that there exists already a rich field of research, although the topic itself, being heavily dependent on computer science and information technology, is rather young. This also reflects the high level of interest that is brought forward by both academia and industry.

When looking at the different theories that lay the foundation for this research, the multi- and interdisciplinarity of the work becomes obvious (as in many fields of science where new phenomena are explored or new types of information technology (IT) applications are developed): it ranges from the theory in travel and destination decision-making, customer and/or destination choice models, information search behaviour (especially on the Web), human–computer interaction (HCI), user modelling, collaborative and content-based recommendations to case-based reasoning (CBR), just to name some. The overall goal of such systems is in the context of information search in the case of rather unspecified user needs, where, in addition, user decision-making cannot, explicitly, be based on the rationality axiom. Tourists are not – at least to some extent – rational beings; their decisions are based on emotional – and very often also hidden – criteria. In this context recommendation systems try to address the problem of information overload, and to narrow down the search space, either by restructuring information or by proposing specific steps in the problem-solving process. This becomes rather complicated (maybe also unsolvable) as one has to deal with different types of users (with the described mindsets such as deliberative, implemental, exploratory or hedonic) and also, sometimes – but not always – related search styles (such as holistic or analytical).

Already, this short description uncovers a multidimensional solution space of methodologies and technologies, which points also at future developments. Many challenges remain untackled, are probably not even explored, and most of them need the already interdisciplinary approach, including the problem of system evaluation and user satisfaction rating. In this final chapter, instead of summarizing the content, we try to provide a look into the future – following an IT point of view. This description of a potential future is based on technological forecast and a prototypical application.

We foresee intelligent mobile systems that are embedded, personalized and adaptive, which try to anticipate visitors' needs. We also see our frontiers at the borderline of IT and cognitive science, it includes mobile systems and architectures, user modelling, learning (of user interests), adaptation (to specific user types and search styles), multimodal flexible content presentation, recommendation strategies, communication and persuasion. Although our focus is more in this direction, we do acknowledge the challenges in tourist decision-making or destination modelling. However, our approach is another one, somehow like entering from the backdoor. Thus, we do not follow, for example, the choice model with its seven steps based upon the understanding that there is a choice to be made up to action taking and feedback giving; future mobile systems will rather follow their user in a non-obtrusive way, probably unconscious and invisible to the user. This information will be put into broader context (sitiuational, personal, technical) and used for proposing specific actions, even in the case where the user may not even know that there are alternatives.

Our approach follows from, and is put into the context of, the (European) vision of Ambient Intelligence, which posits that the environment will become intelligent. In technical terms Ambient Intelligence represents the convergence of ubiquitous computing and communication and intelligent user-friendly interfaces. We elaborate on two important topics of intelligent interfaces and recommendation systems: information presentation and persuasive communication. This is followed by the description of an example of what we intend by such potential future systems: a project called PEACH from the context of cultural tourism (employing usage scenarios in order to provide the tourism context). The system, taking as a major source of input the movements of a museum visitor, guides the visitor by means of personalized video sequences. The system learns while observing the user, dynamically adapts the content and interface and provides hints for exhibits to be seen next. Thus, since nearly none or a very limited explicit input is needed, the interaction is somehow 'unconscious' to the user.

2. Technological Progress

IT has changed and penetrated our life, business and society so much that even our visions cannot exist without technology and its applications – and this process is accelerating. The Web and the related e-commerce pheno-mena are just the 'latest' examples of this development. It highlights two phenomena of our time, constituting the context of e-commerce: *accelera-tion* and *complexity* (Werthner and Klein, 1999). We are witnessing rapidly evolving technological progress, steadily shrinking time intervals between the introduction of new inventions and innovative products. Today, more information is written through digital media than the total cumulative and printing during all of the recorded human history (Fayyad, 2001). Accelera-tion is a historic phenomenon: taking the three major technologies of man-kind – hunting, farming and industry – each one has grown 100 times faster than its predecessor (Varian, 2001; based on Hansen, 1998). This is paralleled by the growth of the so-called knowledge-based industries. Knowledge, acquired through investments in research and development (R&D) as well as education, has become a critical factor and source of competition. Indeed, international R&D spending has grown over the last 15 years and R&D-oriented companies have shown a strong performance.

The second phenomenon is *complexity*. When trying to identify a single aspect of our society by using a social, economic, ecological or even cultural point of view, one realizes an ongoing trend towards organization with a simultaneous growth of interdependencies. There exists a relationship between the growth of organizations and complexity. As in the case of the developments in technology and information processing, these are at the same time cause as well as result of industrial changes. Large organizations are also large information-processing systems. The ability to digest informa-tion is one of the preconditions for their functioning. In fact, the work of most of them is predominantly in information processing. The evolution of the Web is a further example of this phenomenon; its development could be described as an ongoing interaction of order and disorder – on different levels:

- Technology with periods of standardization, e.g. the work of W3C or IETF and then (or in parallel) breakthroughs as now with wireless communica-tion and the different proposed communication protocols.
- Services, where, for example, search engines could be identified as tools to create order (at least for the user) and, on the other side, individualized recommendation systems or individual pricing (e.g. Priceline).
- Structure with a tendency to concentration, where *the Winners take it all*, and the simultaneous entering of new players. The crucial issue is that websites are rewarded for rather small differences in their relative per-formances, not on their absolute performance (Acamic and Huberman, 1999). The disordering element, the permanent appearance of new ser-vices, leads to a 'deconstruction' of value chains, where new services tend to become commodities, where with increased quality prices tend to decrease.

Thus, the complexity of today's society is directly correlated with the infor-mation-processing machinery, which, however, produces also an overabun-dance of information. In that sense IT-based information processing increases complexity as well as uncertainty. There is an obvious paradox: on the one hand, IT increases complexity of information; on the other hand, it appears to be the only means to reduce uncertainty, which implies again more IT applications. This is also the case with intelligent interfaces or, specifically, with recommendation systems, which should ease the human–machine interaction and guide users by reducing complexity and uncertainty. In the best case, this should be invisible to the user. Of course, the tourism domain is an excellent example for the trend towards increasingly personalized services. It reflects that users become part of the product creation process, the trend from customer-focused to customer-driven.

3. A Look into the Technological Future – Ambient Intelligence

We have observed the metamorphosis of the computer from a calculator to a media machine. Computers changed from being tools to become communication machines due to transparent technology and access. We have a doubling of computing power every 18 months, of bandwidth every 12 months and of IP addresses every 9 months, and many more chips go to other devices than to simple PCs. The PC will not be the major access device, but rather nearly any human artefact you can imagine, linking users to the Internet. This is exactly the vision of the EU-funded research: Ambient Intelligence, the surrounding becomes the interface:

> We can make huge numbers of inexpensive computing devices which can exchange data very fast; If we could integrate fixed and mobile communication/services in a seamless way; And if we could link these devices to the basis infrastructure and embed them in our surrounding; And if we could incorporate value added services we make the devices to understand the people they serve, we would have an Ambient Intelligence Landscape.[11]

Ambient Intelligence is the convergence of ubiquitous computing, communication and intelligent user interfaces. Whereas today the dominant mode of interaction is lean-forward (i.e. tense, concentrated), it will become laid-back (i.e. relaxed, enjoyable). People should enjoy, and technology should go to the background. At the end: Why should not your washing machine talk to your dirty linen?

Taking this vision, how would the future look? An exercise was conducted on behalf of the Information Society Technology Advisory Group (ISTAG) in order to describe potential future trajectories or scenarios (Ducatel *et al.*, 2001). These scenarios provide insights into the technical, social and political aspects of Ambient Intelligence. A series of necessary characteristics permitting the eventual societal acceptance of such technologies were identified such as the facilitation of human contact, the capability to build knowledge and skills for work, citizenship and consumer choice, the need for trust and confidence as well long-term sustainability (psychological, societal and

---

[11] www.cordis.lu, website of DG INFSOC, European Commission.

environmental). In addition, such a development should be within human control and enjoyable. The social aspects raise major issues that require precautionary research, particularly in the areas of privacy, control and social cohesion. It is not assumed that these scenarios will become reality – at least not entirely. They serve to identify potential elements of the future and their very general (technical) requirements, apart from the necessary social and economic preconditions described.

The main structuring differentials between the scenarios are shown in Fig. 18.1, where these scenarios are not on the same time line (e.g. Carmen seems to be rather near in the future, whereas the others seem to be more distant):

- Economic and personal efficiency vs sociability or humanistic drivers.
- Communal vs individual as the user orientation driver.

1. Maria is a business lady, travelling via airplane to a business meeting. She uses her personal communicator or recommender; her virtual agent has arranged the trip and links permanently to the necessary networks and systems. She can use her fingerprint to unlock and start the rented car; her P-Com shows the way to the hotel, and the respective room, which also opens automatically, and adapts light and temperature to her needs. This scenario is rather incremental and not so distant in time. Crucial issues are privacy, trust and security. Also there has to be an 'off switch'.

2. Dimitrios is an employee taking a coffee break; he has his D-Me (embedded in his cloth) and this learning recommendation device takes phone calls and answers them automatically – giving advice for as long as possible,

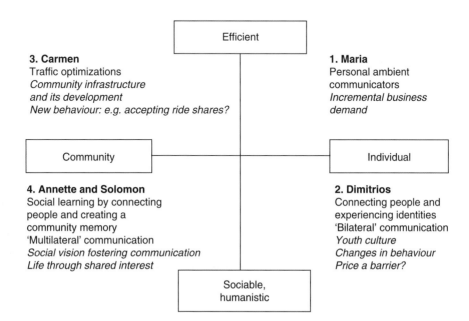

Fig. 18.1. The four Ambient Intelligence scenarios and their focus.

using also Dimitrios' voice. This scenario is on connecting people and experiencing different identities: communication is 'bilateral'. We have network-supported relationships; crucial are access privacy, authenticity and ethics.

3. **Carmen** is a young woman travelling to work, disposed to accept vehicle sharing. Waking up in the morning, her agent connects to the traffic system, which recommends her the next car passing by; she can – based on an in-car sensor checking whether or not the driver is smoking – decide to accept it. The focus is on traffic optimization and multimodal transport. Here we have smart materials and tagging, an advanced traffic infrastructure and urban management services (with all the necessary investments). New behaviour is required as well as – at least to some extent – the acceptance of control by the citizen (e.g. optimized intermodality).

4. **Annette and Solomon** are two persons in this last scenario, which is about social learning by connecting people and creating a community memory. Communication is 'multilateral' based on a vision of life through shared interest. Annette (known to the group) and Solomon (a new member) are automatically introduced to the group; there are automatic negotiations going on. All different means of communication infrastructure and tools are used. It puts emphasis on the social side, and both efficiency and fun are considered. There is also a wide choice as well as personalization of learning approaches.

All these scenarios have in common an underlying seamless mobile or fixed communications infrastructure as well as dynamic and massively distributed device networks. In our context the most important aspects are, however, natural-feeling human interfaces (using voice, gestures, and perhaps smell and eye movements) guiding the user, recommending specific actions, functions and content, without asking for specific user input. People and their movements are sensed, as are anticipated their potential needs and wishes. Recommendations are based on different input devices, sophisticated behaviour analysis, decision styles as well as user models. As such, they are a step forward with respect to today's technologies, where users still have to guide and direct systems.

4. Intelligent Interfaces and Information Presentation

What we want are interfaces that understand us, that are non-intrusive, natural and powerful, that adapt to us, that help us focus our attention and memorize, and that are pleasant and entertaining. Natural language as a means of communication is an obvious aspiration. As such, it has been a focus of research for many years, which generated many ideas and potentiality in the area of interaction, especially with the development of the field of computational dialogue. The last decade has seen a transformation of the field, due to mainly two factors: (i) availability of a large quantity of linguistic data, and dramatic increase of computer power and memory that enables fast processing; and (ii) the introduction of short-term competition in the field, basically imported from the speech research tradition. These factors have been at the centre of a more engineering-oriented development, as opposed to an ambition of understanding cognitive processes, and specifically to the prevailing emphasis on statistical methods rather than knowledge-based methods. Speech technology, a culturally different area, has in the meanwhile produced notable results, and speech recognition can be realistically integrated in many interfaces. Yet we speak of limited dialogue capabilities, currently appropriate only for certain applications. As such, the Natural Language Processing (NLP) community has contributed also to the emergence of intelligent user interfaces.

At the root of the theme of Intelligent Information Presentation (see Stock *et al.*, 2004) we can consider several scientific areas, but at least three are fundamental. Probably the first to be mentioned is Natural Language Generation, the branch of natural language processing that deals with the automatic production of texts. The field normally is described as investigating communicative goals, the dynamic choice of what to say, the planning of the overall rhetorical structure of the text (called sometimes strategic planning), the actual realization of sentences on the basis of grammar and lexicon (sometimes called tactical planning) and so on. With a similar objective but with different means, the field of Adaptive Hypermedia combines hypertext (hypermedia) and user modelling. Adaptive Hypermedia systems build a model of the goals, preferences and knowledge of the individual user and use this throughout the interaction for adaptation of the hypermedia to the needs of the user. By keeping a model of some aspects of the user's characteristics, the system can adapt to, and aid the user in navigating and filtering information that best suits his or her goals. A third important field is Computer Graphics; it has experienced a fundamental passage towards the end of the 1980s, when it was understood that graphics production should start from internal representations and communicative goals in a way similar to language production. This has led to the possibility of developing multimodal systems, which in output would consider the available modalities, possibly the context and the user characteristics, and operate so that the message is allocated and realized in a coordinated way on several media.

Intelligent Interactive Information Presentation has gone further along that line; it relates to the ability of a computer system to automatically produce multimodal information presentations, taking into account the specifics about the user, such as needs, interests and knowledge, and engaging the user in a collaborative interaction that helps the retrieval of relevant information and its understanding on the part of the user. It may include dimensions such as entertainment and education, opening important connections to areas that were not related to the world of HCI, such as broadcasting or cinematography. This vision has led to novel concrete aggregations and is evident in a number of projects where the teams have included very diverse expertise.

5. Automating Persuasive Communication

Future intelligent interfaces will have contextual goals to pursue. They may aim at inducing the user – or in general the audience – to perform some actions in the real world. They will have to take into account the 'social environment', exploit the situational context and value emotional aspects in communication. Some foreseeable scenarios of this kind are dynamic advertisement, preventive medicine and social action. In all these scenarios rational reasoning is not enough for intention adoption; often what really matters is not only the content but also the overall impact of the communication. A similar situation is in an educational context. In a museum, for example, the curator may wish to influence the visitor so that he or she does not miss some masterpiece on special display. Or a system of visual sensors (see also Section 6 about PEACH) may have signalled to the system that a certain room is overcrowded and the system will have to persuade the visitor to go to a different room.

We want to provide the interface with the capability of reasoning on the effectiveness of the message, as well as on the high-level goals and content (Guerini *et al.*, 2003). According to Perelman and Olbrechts-Tyteca (1969), persuasion is a skill that human beings use in order to make their partners perform certain actions or collaborate in various activities. Argumentation has often been considered as addressing similar points. In our view persuasion is a wider concept: argumentation can be regarded as a resource for persuasion, while negotiation puts the accent on interactivity in argumentation. It is a 'superset' of argumentation, while argumentation is concerned with the goal of making the receiver believe that a certain proposition and persuasion is concerned with the goal of making the receiver perform a certain action. The link relies on the fact that, apart from coercion, the only way to make someone do something is to change his or her beliefs.

'It is impossible to directly modify the Goals ... of an Autonomous Cognitive Agent. In order to Influence him (to modify his goals) another Agent is obliged to modify the former's beliefs supporting those Goals' (Castelfranchi, 1996). In this prospect argumentation is a resource for persuasion. The statement that there is more than argumentation in persuasion refers as well to the fact that persuasion is concerned also with irrational elements. Examples are inducing emotions as a factor for obtaining a given result, or the use of specific language for threatening or promising. They all can be regarded as resources for inducing the receiver to act in a desired way.

6. An Example of a Future Recommendation System: The PEACH Project

Personal Experience with Active Cultural Heritage (PEACH) is a project with the objective of studying and experimenting with various advanced technologies that can enhance cultural heritage appreciation.[12] In our view it represents a next step in designing and implementing recommendation systems, using moves and gestures of users as 'implicit' input, guiding the user in a museum visit, and also hinting at specific paintings. As such, it incorporates the previously described techniques of information presentation as well as persuasive communication.

6.1 The context: cultural tourism

Cultural tourism has not changed much for centuries. If one looks back at the reported experiences of 18th-century travellers, or the organization of museums in the 19th century, the real, striking difference is that now the cultural visit experience has become a mass phenomenon. In museums we have seen visitor signs with exhibit illustrations, guidebooks and then the introduction of some technology: audio material through cassettes and discs (the latter having the advantage of being random access devices) and dynamic visual material through various forms of kiosks, screens or presentation rooms.

Modern personal digital assistant (PDA) technology and wireless communication increasingly reduce the gap in computational power between mobile and stationary devices. Sensors can provide fine-grained localization and orientation, and are improving on gaze recognition, as an indicator of the user's focus of attention. Crucially, intelligent systems can be conceived for the individual, building on a wealth of developments in artificial intelligence, HCI and NLP. So the aim is to provide the individual with a companion that is knowledgeable but non-intrusive when monitoring movements, is also sensitive to the interests and the taste of the person by recommending context-specific and interesting information as well as locations, and is capable of communicating flexibly in an attractive and entertaining manner.

6.2 The project

The research activity (Stock *et al.*, 2004) focuses on two technology mainstreams: *natural interactivity* (encompassing NLP, perception, image understanding, intelligent systems, etc.) and *microsensory systems*. These two basic technologies are combined in order to interact (non-obtrusive) and guide the user, and to recommend personalized and anticipative content and tours through the museum. Throughout the project, synergy and integration of different research sectors are emphasized. Two general areas of research are highlighted:

- The study of techniques for individual-oriented information presentation: (i) use of formalisms and technologies derived from the field of natural language generation in order to build contextual presentations; (ii) use of

---

[12] The project is funded by the Autonomous Province of Trento, Italy, and mainly based on IRST research. DFKI, Saarbrücken, Germany, is partner in the project.

speech and gestures as input and audio and animated characters as output; and (iii) use of multi-agent architectures to provide suggestions and propose new topics.

- The study of techniques for multisensorial analysis and modelling of physical spaces; i.e. the use of visual sensors such as video cameras, laser telemetry, infrared sensors and audio sensors such as microphone arrays and ultrasonic signals for monitoring a dynamic environment, and collecting information about objects and about the environment for accurate virtual reconstruction.

This project is based on a rather long history of research and development of intelligent interfaces in the context of cultural heritage (Stock, 2001) such as techniques for producing a coherent language-based information presentation that would take into substantial consideration what the user had seen in the visit and his or her actual position and attitude (Not *et al.*, 2000). These techniques are further developed and enhanced by dynamic multimodal mobile presentations. The overall aim of the project is to significantly increase the quality of cultural heritage appreciation in such a way as to transform passive objects into active ones that can be manipulated by the observer.

The traditional modes of cultural heritage appreciation impose numerous limitations that are not always obvious. For instance, in observing a large statue, notwithstanding physical proximity, the observer most likely will be unable to capture details from every angle, as these may be too far from his or her viewpoint. In these cases, direct observation creates limitations that can be overcome with augmented reality, such as by using a palm computer to observe the details of the statue, taken from cameras or reconstructed in a virtual environment. Moreover, access to some objects can be difficult or even impossible for some visitors, such as disabled or elderly people. Creating an accurate virtual representation of the objects would extend fruition of the exhibit to these visitors as well.

In general, remote appreciation opens interesting possibilities for the study of an artefact that due to its fragile nature must be kept under restricted conditions and is thus not accessible to everyone. The possibility of interacting with an accurate virtual representation allows the non-invasive access to a work of art in the manner, time and place most appropriate for the visitor. Objects can be manipulated in an innovative, didactic and fun way such as by modifying a work of art, partially or in its entirety.

It is particularly important for the individual to be able to 'navigate' an independent information course based on individually and dynamically created presentations. One of the scopes of the project is transcending a museum's restrictive environment by transforming a passive object observed by the visitor into an active subject capable of providing new information in a context-sensitive manner, a kind of hyperlink for accessing additional situation-specific information to be presented coherently. Much of the technology for accessing information on the Internet today (e.g. adaptive user profiling, information promotion, database browsing, query by example) has a natural place of application in this environment.

6.3 The mobile guide prototype

We now describe some particular aspects of the project that have been at the core of some recent activity, and have been implemented in a prototype experimented in Torre Aquila in the Buonconsiglio Castle in Trento, Italy. The prototype tackles the issue of the seamless interleaving of interaction with a mobile device and stationary devices (Rocchi *et al.*, 2000).

The following describes a scenario of a prototypical museum visit, highlighting major features of the system:

> Mary, a young tourist visiting Trento decides to visit Torre Aquila. When she first enters the Castle of the Buonconsiglio, she receives a PDA, yet she is not required to read instructions, neither to fill in a questionnaire on her personal interests. Mary just switches on the PDA and walks through the castle to reach Torre Aquila. As soon as she approaches a large computer screen few rooms away from Torre Aquila, something captures her attention. Two cartoon-like characters, one dressed as a medieval lady and one as a painter, are greeting her. Mary decides to stop and listen, and the characters explain what she is going to find in Torre Aquila. Mary already knew that in the tower there is a wall-size fresco depicting scenes of life in the Middle Ages and she now understands that the two characters are two 'experts' respectively in Middle Ages history, the lady, and in painting techniques, the artist. When both the characters offered to accompany Mary, she realizes that she can choose between two rather different ways of visiting the Torre Aquila. She chooses the lady and the artist invites her, with a tone of voice lightly sad, to come back later for his services.
>
> The lady jumps from the computer screen to the PDA with a *Star Trek*-like beaming sound. Mary now enters Torre Aquila, while the lady, from her PDA, starts illustrating the reason why the bishop Giorgio di Lichtenstein commissioned this fresco back in the 15th century. Mary freely moves in the frescoed room and whenever she gets closer to a particular scene, the lady from the PDA tells her amazing stories about life in the Middle Ages. The lady also suggests that Mary look for unexpected connections among the scenes by zooming in details on the PDA display. Sometimes, the lady, instead of talking, offers Mary the possibility of watching a video. Mary soon realizes that the videos take into account what she had previously seen. For example, one video compares the fox hunting scene in the month of January to the falconry she saw a few minutes earlier in the month of July. She never thought how much the hunting techniques change in different seasons! When she decides to leave Torre Aquila, she stops at the large computer screen, the so-called Virtual Window, to bid farewell to the lady. She declines the invitation of the artist and both of them reminded her to collect the written report of her visit: a personal diary of her own visit to Torre Aquila. This report is produced electronically in natural language, integrated with images and suggested links available for successive elaboration. For instance, it will allow her to re-follow on a virtual environment what she has seen and to explore related material at a deeper level, and it will help her to remain in contact with the site.

Although many research projects are exploring the new possibilities offered by PDAs in a museum setting (see, e.g. Cheverst *et al.*, 2000 and Grinter *et al.*, 2002), usually these multimedia guides use static images, while others employ pre-recorded short video clips about museum exhibits. In our approach, we have focused on automatically produced video clips that are played on the small screen of the mobile device and using lifelike characters either as an anchor or a presenter.

Figure 18.2 shows the PEACH architecture that explains this adaptation process. It is designed as a client–server architecture, where all mobile devices and Virtual Windows have to register with a central presentation server. One of its particular features is the ability to generate presentations both for the mobile devices and the Virtual Windows simultaneously.

Given a visitor-specific context, the presentation server first selects the appropriate content and the degree of adaptation that is necessary. For this purpose, we make use of different strategies that adapt the presentation not only to the location and the interest of the visitor but also to the available modalities. The strategies also take into account technical resources of the output media, i.e. the screen resolution and display size.

The content for presentations at the Virtual Window is selected according to the visitor's interests during the visit. Instead of providing only additional material according to the stereotype (e.g. general vs artistic view), the system provides further detailed information on the exhibits that were of specific interest to the visitor (according to the *visiting history*). Meta-strategies allow providing the visitors with information that helps to change their situative context if necessary. The system could, for example, advise the visitors to look at an image that is displayed on the mobile device. One specific strategy

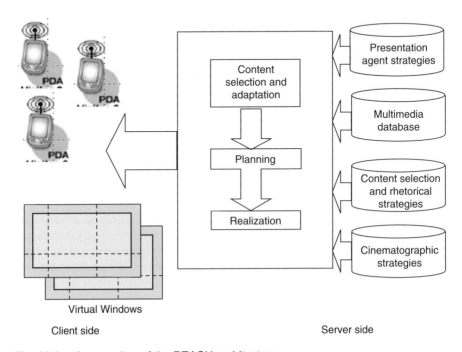

Fig. 18.2. An overview of the PEACH architecture.

even allows the system to guide the visitors to the next Virtual Window, where the content may be presented more appropriately. After having determined the content and structure of the presentation, the server starts to plan the behaviour and role of the lifelike character and where appropriate also plans the structure of a video clip.

For this purpose, the server relies on the cinematographic strategies described above. The behaviour of the lifelike character is captured in its own set of strategies, helping the system to decide, for example, which of the two roles (presentation agent or anchorman, see Section 6.5) the character should play during a piece of presentation. Finally, the server renders the overall presentation with material retrieved from a multimedia database that contains graphics and text. At this point the video clips are generated from static graphics and the text for the character is transformed into spoken language using a speech synthesizer. The final presentations are then delivered either to the mobile devices (via wireless network) or to the Virtual Windows. The lifelike-character engine is implemented in Macromedia Flash MX. The transition of the character from the mobile device to the Virtual Window (also realized in Flash MX) is also fully implemented. Two characters, representing different stereotypes in our scenario, namely an artist and an aristocrat woman, were developed and integrated into our prototype. The video clip generation is implemented with Flash under PocketPC.

6.4 Personalized video clips

Information about the discourse structure of the dynamically produced text is exploited for automatically producing video clips (Zancanaro *et al.*, 2003). At presentation time, a sequence of pictures is synchronized with the audio commentary and the transitions among them are planned according to cinematic techniques. The language of cinematography (Metz, 1974), including shot segmentation, camera movements and transition effects, is employed in order to plan the animation and to synchronize the visual and the verbal parts of the presentation. In building the animations, a set of strategies similar to those used in documentaries were thus employed. Two broad classes of strategies have been identified: the first encompasses constraints, imposed by the grammar of cinematography, while the second deals with conventions normally used in guiding camera movements in the production of documentaries.

The input for the video clips planner is a text annotated at discourse level, made of non-overlapping spans (*segments*), where each segment has a *topic* (the entity the text is about) and the *rhetorical relation* that links it to the previous text span. Besides the annotated text, the planner takes into input a repository of images. The annotation schema provides general features of each image (height, width and source file) as well as information about details, relevant portions of an image illustrating one or more topics.

Video clips (see Fig. 18.3) are built by first searching for the sequence of details mentioned in the audio commentary, deciding the segmentation in

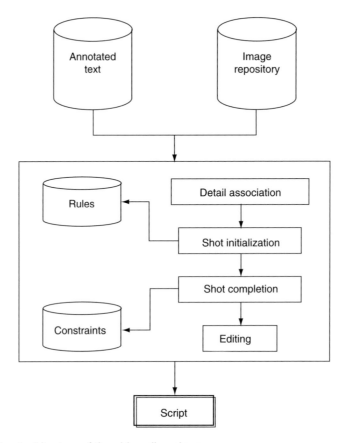

Fig. 18.3. Architecture of the video clips planner.

shots, and then planning the camera movements (employing a rule-based system) in order to smoothly focus on each detail in synchrony with the verbal part. The planning process is divided into four phases:

- Detail association. A detail is associated to each segment of text.
- Shot initialization and structure planning. A candidate structure (a sequence of shots) for the final presentation is elaborated according to the rules and the rhetorical structure of the text.
- Shot completion. Camera movements between details in each shot are planned; in this phase the constraints are applied.
- Editing. Transitions among shots are selected according to the rhetorical tree configuration.

While constraints are just forbidden sequences of camera movements, conventions are expressed in terms of the rhetorical structures of the audio commentary. The example in Fig. 18.4 illustrates the strategy based on the background relation that forces segmentation of the two text spans in different shots with a long fade between them. It is worth noting that, in the example in Fig. 18.4, the shot segmentation was not necessary for the

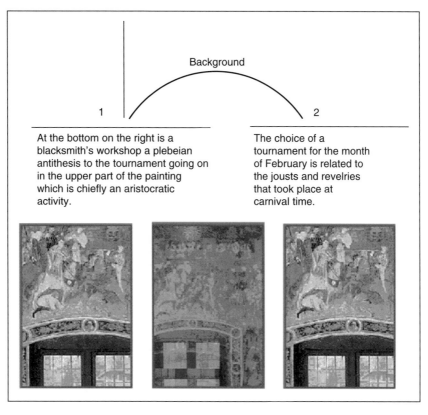

Fig. 18.4. From audio commentary to video clips.

purpose of detail identification (both text spans talk about the tournament); yet the long fade quite effectively remarks the rhetorical difference between the main information provided by the first part and the background information expressed in the second.

For instance, a strategy in the first class would discourage a zoom-in immediately followed by a zoom-out, while a different strategy in the second class would recommend the use of sequential scene cuts, rather than a fade-out effect, to visually enumerate different characters in a scene. In order to formally use discourse structure, we employ the Rhetorical Structure Theory (Mann and Thompson, 1987; for more information, see Rocchi and Zancanaro, 2003).

6.5 The role of lifelike characters during presentations

While the dynamically arranged video clips are a basic element of our dynamic presentation, we have also experimented with a lifelike character that plays the role of an accompanying agent, ready to move on the mobile device or to jump onto the Virtual Window, in order to provide continuous assistance and continuity to the presentation. The character helps in solving problems like how to reach a certain exhibit, and yielding explanations. User evaluations (van Mulken *et al.*, 1998) have shown that the introduction of a life-like character makes presentations more enjoyable and attractive (something that we regard as very important to keep younger visitors also engaged).

The use of lifelike characters on portable devices has to be carefully weighted because of the small dimension of the display. Nevertheless, there are specific roles that a properly designed character can play on a mobile device to improve the level of engagement with the presentation. In particular, following the TV metaphor, two main roles can be recognized: the *presenter* and the *anchorman*. When playing the role of the presenter, the character introduces new media assets and uses pointing gestures. When playing the role of the anchorman, the character just introduces video presentations without interfering with them any further. Although simpler than the role of the presenter, the role of an anchor can help the visitor understand many different presentations, providing a context in which they all make sense. Similar to a TV presenter who walks around the studio to present different content, the character is able to move between the mobile device and the Virtual Window. Besides the specific role that the character may play, it is also a metaphor for the actual interests of the visitor. By providing different characters and giving the visitor the choice among them, the different views on the exhibits are transparently conveyed and selected. For example, in our demo scenario we have an aristocratic woman (see Fig. 18.5) for the generally interested visitor and an artist for visitors who are more interested in explanations on artistic techniques.

6.6 User evaluation

The first phase of a formal evaluation of the cinematic part of the system in Torre Aquila was realized with the main objective of investigating the benefits

Fig. 18.5. Lifelike characters in the Virtual Window (left) and on a PDA (right).

of the use of cinematic techniques in a multimedia presentation. A study was designed to measure the level, if any, of the PDA interference with the visitor's exploration of the fresco. A major concern was to understand whether a cinematic-based presentation differs from a standard multimedia presentation in the capacity to guide the user's attention, as measured by the number and pattern of eye shifts caused by corresponding stimulus situations.

Results confirm the hypothesis that the time spent looking at the device rather than the fresco does not depend on the way the information is presented (i.e. cinematographic or slideshow), while the number of eye shifts is significantly greater in the slideshow version (Alfaro *et al.*, 2004). This effect might be interpreted as a sign that the cinematic presentation induces a more relaxed attentional behaviour, which can be attributed to the expectation created by the camera movements and the transition effects about the moment when a subsequent piece of information will be displayed on the device. The user is less worried about missing important visual information. Even the most naive user is, in fact, familiar with the language of cinematography as it is commonly used in television and movies. For example, a user can guess the communicative goal of a panning movement towards a detail of the fresco by simply watching the initial direction of the movement. It is for this reason that the slideshow presentation demands more eye shifts.

It is worth noting that since in both conditions the time spent looking at the fresco is significantly greater than that spent on the device, it can be suggested that our multimedia guide does not hinder the appreciation of the actual artwork in a museum. Qualitative observations conducted while the visitors interacted with the system revealed some interesting insights related to the design of location-aware mobile guides. All users were able to comfortably interact with the system after only a brief demonstration of usage. This was the case even for people with an extremely low technological background.

7. Conclusions

Tourism has to do with fun, relaxation and enjoyment, being freed from the normal constraints of daily life. The future of technological progress points to environments with electronic artefacts, which may extend and enrich this pleasant experience. The move will be from user-driven systems – where the user has to decide, to be active and aware that the respective system's state is active – to systems that will guide the user and actively propose and prepare actions. Presentations and interaction styles will adapt. This is shown by a concrete prototype that helps users to understand respective sites and enrich this experience. A further dimension not discussed is that most tourist experiences are group experiences. This group dimension needs more attention in terms of how a family (or any other group) can be best exposed in individually different ways to the material in the environment so that they enjoy what they have seen and have a conversation that enriches their individual experience, bringing in new interests and curiosity. There is also the question of the infrastructure, for sharing the experience, knowing where other members of the group are, providing synchronous and asynchronous communication, like virtual 'post-its' to be left at a place for others to hear or see when they get there. There is the issue of presenting material to the individual knowing what the other members of the group have been, or are being, exposed to.

Not only this chapter but the entire book shows that an interdisciplinary approach needs to be followed, as already expressed in the beginning. In addition, experimental (user) studies and simulations are essential, as it is not easy to predict the acceptability of new interfaces and the behaviour of visitors. Entertainment and aesthetics are of importance too. The case presented in this chapter shows that technology not only guides users and recommends specific actions but also helps to improve our appreciation of artefacts and nature in a pleasant and entertaining way and to enrich our experience.

This book is an excellent example of the reciprocal relationship between information technology and tourism: tourism is at the forefront of new technology development and may open a new market perspective. That is, the challenging scenarios developed specifically for tourism may foster novel applications in other markets. On the other side, computer science and information technology offer exciting possibilities for tourism, not only in the field of decision-making and guidance but also in extending and enriching our experiences.

References

Aaker, J. (1997) Dimensions of brand personality. *Journal of Marketing Research* 34, 347–356.

Aamodt, A. and Plaza, E. (1994) Case-based reasoning: foundational issues, methodological variations, and system approaches. *AI Communications* 7(1), 39–59.

Abowd, G. and Beale, R. (1991) Users, systems, and interfaces: a unifying framework for interaction. In: Diaper, D. and Hammond, N. (eds) *HCI'91: People and Computers*, Vol. VI. Cambridge University Press, Cambridge, UK, pp. 73–87.

Acamic, L. and Huberman, B. (1999) The nature of markets in the World Wide Web. Working paper, eCommerce Research Forum. Available at: http://ecommerce.mit.edu/forum/

Achrol, R. and Kotler, Ph. (1999) Marketing in the network economy. *Journal of Marketing* 63(Special Issue), 146–163.

Adaval, R. and Wyer, R.S. Jr (1998) The role of narratives in consumer information processing. *Journal of Consumer Psychology* 7(3), 207–245.

Agarwal, R. and Karahanna, E. (2000) Time flies when you're having fun: cognitive absorption and beliefs about information technology usage. *MIS Quarterly* 24(4), 665–694.

Aha, D.W. (1998) The omnipresence of case-based reasoning in science and application. *Knowledge-Based Systems* 11(5–6), 261–273.

Aha, D.W. and Breslow, L. (1997) Refining conversational case libraries. In: *Case-Based Reasoning Research and Development, Proceedings of the 2nd International Conference on Case-Based Reasoning (ICCBR-97)*. Springer, Berlin, pp. 267–278.

Aha, D.W., Kibler, D. and Albert, M.K. (1991) Instance-based learning algorithms. *Machine Learning* 6, 37–66.

Aimeur, E. and Vézeau, M. (2000) Short-term profiling for a case-based reasoning recommendation system. In: de Mántaras, R.L. and Plaza, E. (eds) *Machine Learning: 2000, 11th European Conference on Machine Learning*. Springer, Berlin, pp. 23–30.

Ainscough, T. and Luckett, M.G. (1996) The Internet for the rest of us: marketing on the World Wide Web. *Journal of Consumer Marketing* 13, 36–47.

Ajzen, I. (1991) The theory of planned behavior. *Organizational Behavior and Human Decision Processes* 50(2), 179–211.

Ajzen, I. and Driver, B.L. (1991) Prediction of leisure participation from behavioral, normative, and control beliefs: an application of the theory of planned behavior. *Leisure Sciences* 13(3), 185–204.

Ajzen, I. and Fishbein, M. (1980) *Understanding Attitudes and Predicting Social Behavior*. Prentice-Hall, Englewood Cliffs, New Jersey.

Alba, J. and Hutchinson, W. (1987) Dimensions of consumer expertise. *Journal of Consumer Research* 13, 411–454.

Alfaro, I., Nardon, M., Pianesi, F., Stock, O. and Zancanaro, M. (2004) Using cinematic techniques on mobile devices for cultural tourism. In: Frew, A.J. (ed.) *Information and Communication Technologies for Tourism*. Springer, Vienna.

Allen, B.L. (1996) From research to design: a user-centered approach. In: Ingwersen, P. and Pors, N.O. (eds) *Colis2: 2nd International Conference on Conceptions of Library and Information Science: Integration in Perspective, 13–16 October, Copenhagen, Denmark*. Royal School of Librarianship, Copenhagen, Denmark, pp. 45–59.

Amelang, M. and Bartussek, D. (2001) *Differentielle Psychologie und Persönlichkeitsforschung*, 5th edn. Stuttgart, Germany.

Anderson, J.R. (2000) *Cognitive Psychology and Its Implications*. Worth Publishers, New York.

Ankomah, P.K., Crompton, J.L. and Baker, D. (1996) Influence of cognitive distance in vacation choice. *Annals of Tourism Research* 23(1), 138–150.

Ansari, A., Essegaier, S. and Kohli, R. (2000) Internet Recommendation Systems. *Journal of Marketing Research* 37 (August), 363–375.

Arslan, B., Mirzadeh, N. and Venturini, A. (2002) CBR component design. Technical Report D4.2, DieToRecs IST-2000–29474.

Assael, H. (1984) *Consumer Behavior and Marketing Action*. Kent, Boston, Massachusetts.

Assael, H. (1998) *Consumer Behavior and Marketing Action*, 6th edn. South-Western College Publishing, Cincinnati, Ohio.

Backhaus, K., Erichson, B., Plinke, W. and Weiber, R. (2000) *Multivariate Analysemethoden – Eine anwendungsorientierte Einführung*, 9th edn. Springer, Berlin.

Bakos, Y. (1997) Reducing buyer search costs: implications for electronic marketplace. *Management Science* 43(12), 1676–1692.

Balabanovic, M. and Shoham, Y. (1997) Fab: content-based, collaborative recommendation. *Communications of the ACM* 40(3), 66–72.

Barnett, L.A. (1991) The playful child: measurement of a disposition to play. *Play and Culture* 4, 51–74.

Bauer, C. and Scharl, A. (2000) Quantitative evaluation of web site content and structure. *Internet Research* 10(1), 31–43.

Bauernfeind, U. (2002) A comparison of quantitative and qualitative methods for the evaluation of tourism web sites. Master thesis at the Institute for Tourism and Leisure Studies, Vienna University of Economics and Business Administration, Vienna, Austria.

Bauernfeind, U., Wöber, K.W., Scharl, A., Bauer, C., Natter, M. and Taudes, A. (2002) The evaluation of European cities' tourism offices' web sites. In: Wöber, K.W., Frew, A.J. and Hitz, M. (eds) *Information and Communications Technologies in Tourism*. Springer, Vienna and New York, pp. 323–334.

Beaulieu, M. (2000) Interaction in information searching and retrieval. *Journal of Documentation* 56(4), 431–439.

Bellman, S., Lohse, G.L. and Johnson, E.J. (1999) Predictors of online buying behavior. *Communications of the ACM* 42(12), 32–38.

Ben-Akiva, M. and Lerman, S.R. (1985) *Discrete Choice Analysis: Theory and Application to Tourism Demand*. MIT Press, Cambridge, Massachusetts.

Benbunan-Fich, R. (2001) Using protocol analysis to evaluate the usability of a commercial web site. *Information and Management* 39(2), 151–163.

Bendixen, M. (1996) A practical guide to the use of correspondence analysing in marketing research. *Marketing Research On-Line* 1, 16–38. Available at: http://www.xlstat.com/corres3.pdf.

Berners-Lee, T., Hendler, J. and Lassila, O. (2001) The semantic Web. *Scientific American* (May), 34–43.

Bettman, J.R. (1979) *An Information Processing Theory of Consumer Choice*. Addison-Wesley, Reading, Massachusetts.

Bettman, J.R., Johnson, E.J. and Payne, J.W. (1991) Consumer decision-making. In: Robertson, T.S. and Kassarjian, H.H. (eds) *Handbook of Consumer Behavior*.

Prentice-Hall, Englewood Cliffs, New Jersey, pp. 50–84.

Bettman, J.R., Luce, M.F. and Payne, J.W. (1998) Constructive consumer choice processes. *Journal of Consumer Research* 25(3), 187–217.

Bieger, T. and Laesser, C. (2004) Information search for travel decisions: toward a source process model. *Journal of Travel Research* 42, 357–371.

Bilal, D. (2000) Children's use of the Yahooligans! Web search engine. I. Cognitive, physical, and affective behaviors on fact-based tasks. *Journal of the American Society for Information Science* 51(7), 646–665.

Bishop, Ch.M. (1995) *Neural Networks for Pattern Recognition*. Clarendon Press, Oxford, UK.

Björk, P. and Guss, Th. (1999) The Internet as a marketspace – the perception of the consumers. In: Buhalis, D. and Schertler, W. (eds) *Information and Communication Technologies in Tourism 1999*. Springer, Vienna, pp. 54–65.

Blackmon, M.H., Polson, P.G., Kitajima, M. and Lewis, C. (2002) Cognitive walkthrough for the Web. In: *Proceedings of the ACM Conference on Human Factors in Computing Systems (CHI 2002)*, pp. 463–470.

Bloch, P.H., Sherrell, D.L. and Ridgway, N.M. (1986) Consumer search: an extended framework. *Journal of Consumer Research* 13(1), 119–126.

Blythe, M.A., Overbeeke, K., Monk, A.F. and Wright, P.C. (2003) Funology – from usability to enjoyment. In: Blythe, M.A., Overbeeke, K., Monk, A.F. and Wright, P.C. (eds) *Human–Computer Interaction Series, 3*. Kluwer Academic Publishers, Dordrecht, The Netherlands.

Bockenholt, U. and Hynan, L.S. (1994) Similarities and differences between SI and SM: a reply to Payne and Bettman. *Journal of Behavioral Decision Making* 7, 123–127.

Boechler, P.M. (2001) How spatial is hyperspace? Interacting with hypertext documents: cognitive processes and concepts. *Cyberpsychology & Behavior* 4, 23–46.

Bollen, J. (2001) A cognitive model of adaptive Web design and navigation: a shared knowledge perspective. Doctoral dissertation, Free University of Brussels, Brussels.

Börcsök, J. (2000) *Fuzzy-Control – Theorie und Industrieeinsatz*. Springer, Berlin.

Borgman, C.L. (1986) The user's mental model of an information retrieval system: an experiment on a prototype online catalog. *International Journal of Man–Machine Studies* 24, 47–64.

Borkenau, P. and Ostendorf, F. (1993) NEO-Fünf-Faktoren-Inventar (NEO-FFI) nach Costa und McCrae – Handanweisung. Göttingen, Hogrefe.

Borkenau, P. and Ostendorf, F. (2001) NEO-FFI – NEO-Fünf-Faktoren-Inventar. Available at: http://www.unifr.ch/ztd/HTS/inftest/catalogs/neo-ffi.1.de.pck/1.pdf

Börner, K., Pippig, E., Tammer, E.-C. and Coulon, K.-H. (1996) Structural similarity and adaptation. In: *European Workshop on CBR*. Lausanne.

Bower, G.H. and Bryant, D.J. (1991) On relating the organizational theory of memory to levels of processing. In: Kessen, W., Ortony, A. and Craik, F. (eds) *Memories, Thoughts, and Emotions: Essays in Honor of George Mandler*. Lawrence Erlbaum Associates, Hillsdale, New Jersey, pp. 149–168.

Bowers, K.S. (1993) Situationism in psychology: an analysis and a critique. *Psychological Review* 80(5), 307–336.

Breese, J., Heckerman, D. and Kadie, C. (1998) Empirical analysis of predictive algorithms for collaborative filtering. In: *Proceedings of the 14th Conference on Uncertainty in Artificial Intelligence*. Morgan Kaufmann Publishers, Madison, Wisconsin.

Brewer, W.F. (1988) Imagery and text genre. *Text* 8, 431–438.

Brewer, W.F. (1995) To assert that essentially all human knowledge and memory is represented in terms of stories is certainly wrong. In: Wyer, R.S. Jr (ed.) *Knowledge and Memory: The Real Story, Advances in Social Cognition*, Vol. VIII. Lawrence Erlbaum Associates, Hillsdale, New Jersey, pp. 109–119.

Brewer, W.F and Lichtenstein, E.H. (1982) Stories are to entertain: a structural-affect theory of stories. *Journal of Pragmatics* 6, 473–486.

Bridge, D. (2001) Product recommendation systems: a new direction. In: *Proceedings of the Workshop Programme at the Fourth International Conference on Case-Based Reasoning*, pp. 79–86.

Bridge, D. and Ferguson, A. (2002) Diverse product recommendations using an expressive language for case retrieval. In: Craw, S. and Preece, A. (eds) *Advances in Case-Based Reasoning, Proceedings of the 6th European Conference on Case Based Reasoning, ECCBR 2002*. Springer, Aberdeen, Scotland, pp. 43–57.

Bristow, R.S., Liever, S.R. and Fesenmaier, D.R. (1995) The compatibility of recreation activities in Illinois. *Geografiska Annaler B* 77(1), 3–15.

Brooke, J. (1986) SUS – a quick and dirty usability scale. Available at: http://www.cee.hw.ac.uk/~ph/sus.html

Brucks, M. (1985) The effects of product class knowledge on information search behavior. *Journal of Consumer Research* 12, 1–16.

Brynjolfsson, E. and Smith, M.D. (2000) Frictionless commerce? A comparison of Internet and conventional retailers. *Management Science* 46(4), 563–585.

Buchta, Ch. and Mazanec, J.A. (2001) SIMSEG/ACM: a simulation environment for artificial consumer markets. Working Paper No. 79, Special Research Programme on Adaptive Systems and Modelling, Vienna University of Economics and Business Administration, March, Australia.

Buhalis, D. (2003) *eTourism: Information Technology for Strategic Tourism Management*. Prentice-Hall, Upper Saddle River, New Jersey.

Buhalis, D. and Spada, A. (2000) Destination management systems: criteria of success – an exploratory research. *Information Technology and Tourism* 3(1), 41–58.

Bunke, H. and Messmer, B. (1994) Similarity measures for structured representations. In: Wess, S., Althoff, K.-D. and Richter, M.M. (eds) *Topics in Case-Based Reasoning*. Springer, Kaiserslautern, Germany.

Burke, R.D. (2000a) A case-based approach to collaborative filtering. In: *Advances in Case-Based Reasoning: Proceedings of the 5th European Workshop, EWCBR-2000, 6–9 September, Trento, Italy*. Springer, Berlin.

Burke, R.D. (2000b) Knowledge-based recommender systems. In: Daily, J.E., Kent, A. and Lancour, H. (eds) *Encyclopedia of Library and Information Science*, Vol. 69. Marcel Dekker, New York, pp. 180–200.

Burke, R.D. (2002) Hybrid recommender systems: survey and experiments. *User Modeling and User-Adapted Interaction* 12, 331–370.

Burke, R.D., Hammond, K.J., Kulyukin, V.A., Lytinen, S.L., Tomuro, N. and Schoenberg, S. (1997) Question answering from frequently asked question files. *AI Magazine* 18(2), 57–66.

Cacioppo, J.T. and Petty, R.E. (1982) The need for cognition. *Journal of Personality and Social Psychology* 42(1), 116–131.

California Tourism (2005) California fun. Available at: http://www.visitcalifornia.com/state/tourism/tour_homepage.jsp

Calishain, T. and Dornfest, R. (2003) *Google Hacks. 100 Industrial-Strength Tips & Tools*. O'Reilly, Sebastopol, California.

Cantor, N. and Mischel, W. (1979) Prototypes in person perception. In: Berkowitz, L. (ed.) *Advances in Experimental Social Psychology*, Vol. 12. Academic Press, New York, pp. 3–52.

Capella, L.M. and Greco, A.J. (1987) Information Sources for elderly vacation decisions. *Annals of Tourism Research* 14, 148–151.

Card, S.K., Moran, T.P. and Newell, A. (1983) *The Psychology of Human–Computer Interaction*. Lawrence Erlbaum Associates, Hillsdale, New Jersey.

Card, S.K., Pirolli, P., Van Der Wege, M., Morrison, J.B., Reeder, R.W., Schraedley, P. and Boshart, J. (2001) Information scent as a driver of web behavior graphs: results of a protocol analysis method for web usability. In: Jacko, J., Sears, A., Beaudouin-Lafon, M. and Jacob, R.J.K. (eds) *Proceedings of the ACM Conference on Human Factors in Computing Systems*. ACM, Seattle, Washington, DC, pp. 498–505.

Carley, K. and Palmquist, M. (1992) Extracting, representing, and analyzing mental models. *Social Forces* 70(3), 601–636.

Carpenter, G.A. and Grossberg, S. (1995) Adaptive resonance theory (ART). In:

Arbib, M.A. (ed.) *The Handbook of Brain Theory and Neural Networks*. MIT Press, Cambridge, Massachusetts, pp. 79–82.

Carroll, J. and Thomas, J. (1982) Metaphors and the cognitive representation of computing systems. *IEEE Transactions on Systems Man and Cybernetics* 12(2), 107–116.

Caspi, A. (1987) Personality in the life course. *Journal of Personality and Social Psychology* 53(6), 1203–1213.

Cassell, J. and Smith, J. (1999) The Victorian laptop: narrative engagement through place and time. In: *Proceedings of the AAAI Fall Symposium 1999 'Narrative Intelligence'*. American Association of Artificial Intelligence, Cape Cod, Massachusetts.

Castelfranchi, C. (1996) Reasons: beliefs structure and goal dynamics. *Mathware & Soft Computing* 3(2), 233–247.

Catarci, T., Costabile, M., Levialdi, S. and Batini, C. (1997) Visual query systems for databases: a survey. *Journal of Visual Languages and Computing* 8(2), 215–260.

Cavnar, W.B. and Trenkle, J.M. (1994) N-Gram-based text categorization. In: *Proceedings of the International Symposium on Document Analysis and Information Retrieval (SDAIR'94)*. Las Vegas, Nevada, pp. 161–175.

Celsi, R. and Olsen, J. (1988) The role of involvement in attention and comprehension processes. *Journal of Consumer Research* 15, 37–47.

Cha, S., McLeary, K.W. and Uysal, M. (1995) Travel motivations of Japanese overseas travelers. *Journal of Travel Research* 34(2), 33–39.

Chakrabarti, S. (2003) *Mining the Web. Discovering Knowledge from Hypertext Data*. Morgan Kaufmann Publishers, Amsterdam.

Chakrabarti, S., van den Berg, M. and Dom, B. (1999) Focused crawling: a new approach to topic-specific web resource discovery. *Computer Networks* 31(11–16), 1623–1640.

Chaturvedi, A., Carroll, J.D., Green, P.E. and Rotondo, J.A. (1997) A feature-based approach to market segmentation via overlapping K-centroids clustering. *Journal of Marketing Research* 34(August), 370–377.

Chau, M. and Chen, H. (2003a) Comparison of three vertical search spiders. *IEEE Computer* 36(5), 56–62.

Chau, M. and Chen, H. (2003b) Personalized and focused web spiders. In: Zhong, N., Liu, J. and Yao, Y. (eds) *Web Intelligence*. Springer, Vienna and New York, pp. 197–217.

Chau, M., Zeng, D., Chen, H., Huang, M. and Hendriawan, D. (2003) Design and evaluation of a multi-agent collaborative web mining system. *Decision Support Systems* 35(1), 167–183.

Chen, H., Houston, A., Sewell, R. and Schatz, B. (1998) Internet browsing and searching: user evaluations of category map and concept space techniques. *Journal of the American Society for Information Science* 49(7), 582–603.

Chen, H., Wigand, R.T. and Nilan, M.S. (1999) Optimal experience of web activities. *Computers in Human Behavior* 15, 585–608.

Chen, H., Fan, H., Chau, M. and Zeng, D. (2001) MetaSpider: meta-searching and categorization on the Web. *Journal of the American Society for Information Science and Technology* 52(13), 1134–1147.

Cheverst, K., Davies, N., Mitchell, K., Friday, A. and Efstratiou, C. (2000) Developing a context-aware electronic tourist guide: some issues and experiences. In: *Proceedings of the CHI 2000*. Amsterdam, pp. 17–24.

Chi, E.H., Pirolli, P., Chen, K. and Pitkow, J. (2001) Using information scent to model user information needs and actions on the Web. In: *Proceedings of the ACM CHI 2001 Conference on Human Factors in Computing Systems*. ACM Press, Seattle, Washington, DC, pp. 490–497.

Chin, J.P., Diehl, V.A. and Norman, K.L. (1988) Development of a tool measuring user satisfaction of the human–computer interface. In: *Proceedings of the ACM SIG-CHI '88 Conference on Human Factors in Computing*, New York.

Cho, Y., Wang, Y. and Fesenmaier, D.R. (2002) Searching for experiences: the web-based virtual tour in tourism marketing. *Journal of Travel and Tourism Marketing* 12(4), 1–18.

Christianini, N. and Shawe-Taylor, J. (2000) *Support Vector Machines and Other Kernel-Based Learning Methods*. Cambridge University Press, Cambridge, Massachusetts.

Clemons, E.K. and Il-Horn, H. (1999) Rosenbluth International: strategic transformation of a successful enterprise. *Journal of Management Information Systems* 16(2), 9–27.

Cohen, E. (1972) Towards a sociology of international tourism. *Social Research* 39, 164–182.

Collins, D. (1995) *Designing Object-Oriented User Interfaces.* Benjamin/Cummings, Redwood City, California.

Collins, A.M. and Quillian, M.R. (1972) Experiments on semantic memory and language comprehension. In: Gregg, L.W. (ed.) *Cognition in Learning and Memory.* Wiley, New York, pp. 117–138.

Conklin, J. (1987) Hypertext: an introduction and survey. *Computer, III Computing Society* 20(9), 17–41.

Cooley, R., Mobasher, B. and Srivastava, J. (1997) Web mining: information and pattern discovery on the World Wide Web. In: *Proceedings of the 9th IEEE International Conference on Tools with Artificial Intelligence (ICTAI'97).* IEEE, Newport Beach, California, pp. 558–567.

Cooper, C.P. (1981) Spatial and temporal patterns of tourist behaviour. *Regional Studies* 15(3), 359–371.

Correia, A. (2002) How do tourists choose? *Tourism* 50(1), 21–29.

Costa, P.T. and McCrae, R.R. (1992) *Revised NEO Personality Inventory (NEO PI-R) and NEO Five Factor Inventory – Professional Manual.* Odessa, Florida.

Cotte, J. and Ratneshwar, S. (2001) Timestyle and leisure decisions. *Journal of Leisure Research* 33(4), 396–409.

Crawford, C. (2003a) *On Game Design.* New Riders, Indianapolis, Indiana.

Crawford, C. (2003b) *The Art of Interactive Design: A Euphonious and Illuminating Guide to Building Successful Software.* No Starch Press, San Francisco, California.

Crompton, J.L. (1979) Motivations for pleasure vacation. *Annals of Tourism Research* 6, 408–422.

Crompton, J.L. (1992) Structure of vacation destination choice sets. *Annals of Tourism Research* 19, 420–434.

Crompton, J.L. and Ankomah, P.K. (1993) Choice set propositions in destination decisions. *Annals of Tourism Research* 20, 461–476.

Crotts, J.C. (1999) Consumer decision-making and prepurchase information search. In: Pizam, A. and Masfeld, Y. (eds) *Consumer Behavior in Travel and Tourism.* The Haworth Hospitality Press, Binghamton, New York, pp. 149–168.

Crouch, G.I. and Louviere, J.J. (2001) A review of choice modelling research in tourism, hospitality and leisure. In: Mazanec, J.A., Crouch, G.I., Ritchie, J.R.B. and Woodside, A.G. (eds) *Consumer Psychology of Tourism, Hospitality and Leisure.* CAB International, Wallingford, UK, pp. 67–86.

Csikszentmihalyi, M. (1975) *Beyond Boredom and Anxiety.* Jossey-Bass, San Francisco, California.

Csikszentmihalyi, M. (1990) *Flow: The Psychology of Optimal Experience.* Harper & Row, New York.

Csikszentmihalyi, M. and Csikszentmihalyi, I.S. (1988) *Optimal Experience: Psychological Studies of Flow in Consciousness.* Cambridge University Press, Cambridge, UK.

Csikszentmihalyi, M. and LeFevre, J. (1989) Optimal experience in work and leisure. *Journal of Personality and Social Psychology* 56(5), 815–822.

Cunningham, P., Bergmann, R., Schmitt, S., Traphöner, R., Breen, S. and Smyth, B. (2001) Websell: intelligent sales assistants for the World Wide Web. In: Weber, R. and Wangenheim, C. (eds) *Proceedings of the Workshop Programme at the Fourth International Conference on Case-Based Reasoning, Vancouver, Canada.*

Dabholkar, P.A. (1994) Incorporating choice into an attitudinal framework: analyzing models of mental comparison processes. *Journal of Consumer Research* 21(June), 100–118.

Dabholkar, P.A. (1996) Consumer evaluations of new technology-based self-service options: an investigation of alternative models of service quality. *International Journal of Research in Marketing* 13, 29–51.

Dalgleish, J. (2000) *Customer-Effective Web Sites.* Prentice-Hall, Upper Saddle River, New Jersey.

Daniels, J.J. and Rissland, E.L. (1997) What you saw is what you want: using cases to seed information retrieval. In: *ICCBR*, pp. 325–336.

Darden, W.R. and Ashton, D. (1974–1975) Psychographic profiles of patronage preference groups. *Journal of Retailing* 50(Winter), 99–112.

Dautenhahn, K. (1999) The Lemur's tale – story-telling in primates and other socially intelligent agents. In: *Proceedings of the AAAI Fall Symposium 1999 Narrative Intelligence*. American Association of Artificial Intelligence, Cape Cod, Massachusetts.

Dautenhahn, K. (2002) The origins of narrative: in search of the transactional format of narratives in humans and other social animals. *International Journal of Cognition and Technology* 1(1), 97–123.

Davies, F., Goode, M., Mazanec, J.A. and Moutinho, L. (1999) LISREL and neural network modelling: two comparison studies. *Journal of Retailing and Consumer Services* 6(Special Issue on Marketing Applications of Neural Networks), 249–261.

Davis, F.D. (1989) Perceived usefulness, perceived ease of use, and user acceptance of information technology. *MIS Quarterly* 13(3), 319–340.

Davis, F.D., Bagozzi, R.P. and Warshaw, P.R. (1989) User acceptance of computer technology: a comparison of two theoretical models. *Management Science* 35(8), 982–1003.

Davulcu, H., Vadrevu, S., Nagarajan, S. and Ramakrishnan, I.V. (2003) OntoMiner: bootstrapping and populating ontologies from domain-specific web sites. *IEEE Intelligent Systems* (September/October), 24–33.

Day, H.I. (1981) Play. In: Day, H.I. (ed.) *Advances in Intrinsic Motivation and Aesthetics*. Plenum Press, New York, pp. 225–250.

Debbage, K. (1991) Spatial behavior in a Bahamian resort. *Annals of Tourism Research* 18, 251–268.

Decrop, A. (1999) Tourists' decision-making and behavior processes. In: Pizam, A. and Mansfeld, Y. (eds) *Consumer Behavior in Travel and Tourism*. The Haworth Hospitality Press, Binghamton, New York, pp. 103–134.

Deighton, J., Romer, D. and McQueen, J. (1989) Using drama to persuade. *Journal of Consumer Research* 16, 335–343.

Delgado, J. and Davidson, R. (2002) Knowledge bases and user profiling in travel and hospitality recommender systems. In: Wöber, K., Frew, A. and Hitz, M. (eds) *Information and Communication Technologies in Tourism*. Springer, Vienna, pp. 1–16.

Dellaert, B.G.C. and Häubl, G. (2004) Consumer product search with personalized recommendations. Working paper, Department of Marketing, University of Alberta, Edmonton, Alberta.

Dellaert, B.G.C. and Wendel, S. (2004) Tourists' hedonic and utilitarian use of the Internet as a travel information channel. In: Mosey, R.N., Joppe, M., Andereck, K.L. and McGehee, N.G. (eds) *Measuring the Tourism Experience: When Experience Rules, What is the Metric of Success? Proceedings of the 35th Annual TTRA Conference*. Travel and Tourism Research Association, Boise, Idaho.

Dellaert, B.G.C., Borgers, A. and Timmermans, H. (1997) Consumer activity pattern choice: development and test of state-dependent conjoint choice experiments. *Journal of Retailing and Consumer Services* 4(1), 25–37.

Dellaert, B.G.C., Ettema, D.F. and Lindh, C. (1998a) Multi-faceted tourist travel decisions: a constraint-based conceptual framework to describe tourists' sequential choices of travel components. *Tourism Management* 19(4), 313–320.

Dellaert, B.G.C., Arentze, T., Bierlaire, M., Borgers, A. and Timmermans, H. (1998b) Investigating consumer's tendency to combine multiple shopping purposes and destinations. *Journal of Marketing Research* 35, 177–188.

De Mey, M. (1977) The cognitive view point: its development and its scope. In: de Mey, M., Pinxten, R., Poriau, M. and Vandamme, F. (eds) *CC77: International Workshop on the Cognitive Viewpoint, 24–26 March, Ghent, Belgium*. University of Ghent, Ghent, Belgium, pp. xvi–xxxi, 7–23.

Depner, U. (2002) Konzeption und prototypische Implementierung eines Moduls zur Zuordnung von Kunden auf Stereotypprofile im Rahmen eines Freizeit- und Tourismusberatungssystems mithilfe der Fuzzy-Technologie. Diploma thesis, Nuremberg.

Dewey, J. (1913) Play. In: Monroe, P. (ed.) *A Cyclopedia of Education*. Macmillan, New York, pp. 725–727.

Dholakia, U. and Bagozzi, R.P. (2001) Consumer behavior in digital environments. In: Wind, J. and Mahajan, V. (eds) *Digital Marketing*. Wiley, New York, pp. 163–200.

Dholakia, R.R., Zhao, M., Dholakia, N. and Fortin, D.R. (2000) Interactivity and revisits to websites: a theoretical framework. RITIM working paper. Available at: http://ritim.cba.uri.edu/wp2001/wpdone3/wpdone3.htm

Diem, G. (1996) Wirtschafts- und Tourismusleitbild Bregenz. Available at: http://www.bbn.at/Wigem/Texte/Konzepte/Leitbild.pdf

Dittenbach, M., Merkl, D. and Berger, H. (2003) A natural language query interface for tourism information. In: Frew, A.J., Hitz, M. and O'Connor, P. (eds) *Proceedings of the 10th International Conference on Information Technologies in Tourism (ENTER'03), 29–31 January, Helsinki, Finland*. Springer, Vienna and New York, pp. 152–162.

Dix, A., Finlay, J., Abowd, G. and Beale, R. (1998) *Human–Computer Interaction*, 2nd edn. Prentice-Hall, Upper Saddle River, New Jersey.

Don, A. (1990) Narrative and the interface. In: Laurel, B. (ed.) *The Art of Human–Computer Interface Design*. Addison-Wesley, Reading, Massachusetts, pp. 383–392.

Doyle, M. and Cunningham, P. (2000) A dynamic approach to reducing dialog in on-line decision guides. In: *Advances in Case-based Reasoning: Proceedings of the 5th European Workshop, EWCBR-2000, 6–9 September, Trento, Italy*. Springer, Berlin.

Dreyer, A. (2000) *Kulturtourismus*, 2nd edn. Munich.

Driver, B.L., Brousseau, K.R. and Hunsaker, P.L. (1990) *The Dynamic Decision-Maker: Five Decision Styles for Executive and Business Success*. Harper & Row, New York.

Ducatel, K., Bogdanowicz, M., Scapolo, F., Leijten, J. and Burgelman, J.-C. (2001) Scenarios for ambient intelligence in 2010. Final Report, Version 2, IPTS-Seville, 2001.

EC (2003) The European e-Business market watch, Newsletter 13 II/July 2003, European Commission. Available at: http://www.ebusiness-watch.org

Edson Escalas, J. (2004a) Imagine yourself in the product: mental simulation, narrative transportation, and persuasion. *Journal of Advertising* 33(2), 37–48.

Edson Escalas, J. (2004b) Narrative processing: building consumer connections to brands. *Journal of Consumer Psychology* 14(1–2), 168–180.

Edwards, W. and Fasolo, B. (2001) Decision technology. *Annual Review of Psychology* 52, 581–606.

Einhorn, H.J. and Hogarth, R.M. (1981) Behavioral decision theory: processes of judgment and choice. *Annual Review of Psychology* 32, 53–88.

Einhorn, H.J., Kleinmuntz, D.N. and Kleinmuntz, B. (1979) Linear regression and process-tracing models of judgment. *Psychological Review* 86, 465–485.

Etzel, M.J. and Wahlers, R.G. (1985) The use of requested promotional material by pleasure travelers. *Journal of Travel Research* 23(Spring), 2–6.

Fahrmeir, L. and Tutz, G. (1997) *Multivariate Statistical Modelling Based on Generalized Linear Models*. Springer, New York.

Fayyad, U. (2001) The digital physics of data mining. *Communications of the ACM* 44(3), 62–65.

Ferrari, J.R. and Dovidio, J.F. (2001) Behavioral information search by indecisives. *Personality and Individual Differences* 30, 1113–1123.

Fesenmaier, D.R. (1990) Theoretical and methodological issues in behavioral modeling: introductory comments. *Leisure Sciences* 12, 1–7.

Fesenmaier, D.R. and Jeng, J. (2000) Assessing structure in the pleasure trip planning process. *Tourism Analysis* 5, 13–17.

Fesenmaier, D.R. and Johnson, B. (1989) Involvement-based segmentation: implications for travel marketing in Texas. *Tourism Management* 10, 293–300.

Fesenmaier, D.R. and Lieber, S.R. (1985) Spatial structure and behavior response in outdoor recreation participation. *Geografiska Annaler B* 67, 131–138.

Fesenmaier, D.R. and Lieber, S.R. (1988) Destination diversification as an indicator of activity compatibility: an exploratory analysis. *Leisure Sciences* 10(3), 167–168.

Fesenmaier, D.R., Grabler, K., Gretzel, U., Hwang, Y., Mazanec, J., Pan, B. and Zins, A. (2002) Tourist decision model. Technical Report D2.2 DieToRecs IST-2000–29474, EU IST project. Available at: http://dietorecs.itc.it/PubDeliverables/D2.2-V1.0.pdf

Fesenmaier, D.R., Ricci, F., Schaumlechner, E., Wöber, K. and Zanella, C. (2003) DIETORECS: travel advisory for multiple decision styles. In: Frew, A.J., Hitz, M. and O'Connor, P. (eds) *Information and Communication Technologies in Tourism*. Springer, Vienna, pp. 232–241.

Finn, D. (1983) Low involvement isn't low involving. In: Bagozzi, R.P. and Tybout, A. (eds) *Advances in Consumer Research*. Association for Consumer Research, Ann Arbor, Michigan, pp. 419–424.

Fishbein, M. and Ajzen, I. (1975) *Belief, Attitude, Intention, and Behavior: An Introduction to Theory and Research*. Addison-Wesley, Reading, Massachusetts.

Flowerday, T. and Schraw, G. (2003) Effect of choice on cognitive and affective engagement. *Journal of Educational Research* 96(4), 207–215.

Fodness, D. and Murray, B. (1997) Tourist information search. *Annals of Tourism Research* 37(2), 108–119.

Fodness, D. and Murray, B. (1998) A typology of tourist information search strategies. *Journal of Travel Research* 37, 108–119.

Fogg, B.J. (2003) *Persuasive Technology*. Morgan Kaufmann Publishers, San Francisco, California.

Fotheringham, A.S. (1985) Spatial competition and agglomeration in urban modeling. *Environmental Planning A* 17, 213–230.

Franke, Th. (2002) Extended personalized services in an online regional tourism consulting system. In: Wöber, K.W., Frew, A.J. and Hitz, M. (eds) *Information and Communication Technologies in Tourism*. Springer, Vienna, pp. 346–355.

Franke, Th. and Mertens, P. (2001) User modelling and personalization – some experiences in German industry and public administration. In: Tseng, M.M. and Piller, F.T. (eds) *Proceedings of the 1st World Congress on Mass Customization and Personalization, Hong Kong*.

Franke, Th. and Mertens, P. (2003) User modelling and personalization – experiences in German industry and public administration. In: Tseng, M.M. and Piller, F.T. (eds) *The Customer Centric Enterprise – Advances in Mass Customization and Personalization*. Springer, Berlin, pp. 85–108.

Frese, M., Albrecht, K., Altmann, A., Lang, L., Papstein, P.V., Peyerl, R., Pruemper, J., Schulte-Goecking, H., Wankmueller, I. and Wendel, R. (1988) The effects of an active development of the mental model in the training process: experimental results in a word processing system. *Behaviour and Information Technology* 7, 295–304.

Gaasterland, T., Godfrey, P. and Minker, J. (1992) An overview of cooperative answering. *Journal of Intelligent Information Systems* 1(2), 123–157.

Gardner, B. and Levy, S.J. (1955) The product and the brand. *Harvard Business Review* 33, 33–39.

Garrett, J.J. (2003) *The Elements of User Experience*. New Riders, Indianapolis, Indiana.

Gebhardt, F., Voß, A., Gräther, W. and Schmidt-Belz, B. (1997) *Reasoning with Complex Cases*. Kluwer Academic Publishers, Amsterdam.

Gershon, N. and Page, W. (2001) What storytelling can do for information visualization. *Communications of the ACM* 44(3), 31–37.

Gibson, H. and Yiannakis, A. (1992) Roles tourists play. *Annals of Tourism Research* 19(2), 287–303.

Gibson, H. and Yiannakis, A. (2002) Tourist roles – needs and the lifecourse. *Annals of Tourism Research* 29(2), 358–383.

Gilbert, A. and Bacheldor, B. (2000) The big squeeze. *InformationWeek* 779, 46–56.

Gitelson, R.J. and Crompton, J.L. (1983) The planning horizons and sources of information used by pleasure vacationers. *Journal of Travel Research* 21(Winter), 2–7.

Gitelson, R. and Kerstetter, D. (1994) The influence of friends and relatives in travel decision-making. *Journal of Travel and Tourism Marketing* 3(3), 59–68.

Glover, E., Lawrence, S., Gordon, M., Birmingham, W. and Giles, C.L. (1999) Recommending web documents based on user preferences. In: *ACM SIGIR 99 Workshop on Recommender Systems, Berkeley, California.* Available at: http://www.csee.umbc.edu/%7Eian/sigir99-rec/

Göker, M.H. and Thomson, C.A. (2000) Personalized conversational case-based recommendation. In: *Advances in Case-Based Reasoning: Proceedings of the 5th European Workshop, EWCBR-2000, 6–9 September, Trento, Italy.* Springer, Berlin, pp. 99–111.

Good, N., Schafer, J.B., Konstan, J., Borchers, A., Sarwar, B. and Herlocker, J. (1999) Combining collaborative filtering with personal agents for better recommendations. In: *Proceedings of the 1999 Conference of the American Association for Artificial Intelligence (AAAI-99)*, pp. 439–446.

Google (2004) Search result for keyword 'travel'. Available at: http://www.google.com

Google (2005) Google maps beta. Available at: http://maps.google.com

Gosling, S.D., Rentfrow, P.J. and Swann, W.B. Jr (2003) A very brief measure of the big-five personality domains. *Journal of Research in Personality* 37, 504–508.

Grabler, K. and Zins, A.H. (2002) Vacation trip decision styles as basis for an automated recommendation system: lessons from observational studies. In: Wöber, K., Frew, A. and Hitz, M. (eds) *Information and Communication Technologies in Tourism.* Springer, Vienna, pp. 458–469.

Graesser, A.C. and Ottati, V. (1995) Why stories? Some evidence, questions and challenges. In: Wyer, R.S. Jr (ed.) *Knowledge and Memory: The Real Story, Advances in Social Cognition*, Vol. VIII. Lawrence Erlbaum Associates, Hillsdale, New Jersey, pp. 121–132.

Green, M.C. and Brock, T.C. (2002) In the mind's eye: transportation-imagery model of narrative persuasion. In: Green, M.C., Strange, J.J. and Brock, T.C. (eds) *Narrative Impact: Social and Cognitive Foundations.* Lawrence Erlbaum Associates, Mahwah, New Jersey, pp. 315–181.

Gretzel, U. and Fesenmaier, D.R. (2002a) Store-telling in destination recommendation systems: concepts and implications of narrative design: user modeling and decision-making in travel and tourism emergent systems. eCTRL Workshop, April, Trento, Italy, pp. 5–7.

Gretzel, U. and Fesenmaier, D.R. (2002b) Building narrative logic into tourism information systems. *IEE Intelligent Systems* 17(6), 59–61.

Gretzel, U. and Fesenmaier, D.R. (2003) Experience-based Internet marketing: an exploratory study of sensory experiences associated with pleasure travel to the Midwest United States. In: Frew, A., Hitz, M. and O'Connor, P. (eds) *Information and Communication Technologies in Tourism 2003.* Springer, Vienna, pp. 49–57.

Gretzel, U. and Wöber, K.W. (2004) Intelligent search support: building search term associations for tourism-specific search engines. In: Frew, A.J. (ed.) *Proceedings of the 11th International Conference for Information and Communication Technologies in Tourism – ENTER 2004.* Springer, Vienna and New York.

Griffith, D.A. and Albanese, P.J. (1996) An examination of plog's psychographic travel model within a student population. *Journal of Travel Research* 34(4), 47–51.

Grinter, R.E., Aoki, P.M., Hurst, A., Szymanski, M.H., Thornton, J.D. and Woodruff, A. (2002) Revisiting the visit: understanding how technology can shape the museum visit. In: *Proceedings of the ACM Conference on Computer Supported Cooperative Work.* New Orleans, Louisiana.

Guerini, M., Stock, O. and Zancanaro, M. (2003) Toward intelligent persuasive interfaces. In: *Proceedings of the IJCAI 2003 Workshop on Natural Argumentation, Acapulco, 2003.*

Gunn, C.A. (1994) *Tourism Planning: Basics, Concepts, Cases*. Taylor & Francis, Washington, DC.

Gursoy, D. and Chen, J. (2000) Competitive analysis of cross cultural information search behavior. *Tourism Management* 21, 583–590.

Gursoy, D. and McCleary, K.W. (2004) An integrative model of tourists' information search behavior. *Annals of Tourism Research* 31(2), 353–373.

Haas, S.W. and Grams, E.S. (2000) Readers, authors, and page structure: a discussion of four questions arising from a content analysis of web pages. *Journal of the American Society for Information Science* 51(2), 181–192.

Haider, W. and Ewing, G.O. (1990) A model of tourist choices of hypothetical Caribbean destinations. *Leisure Sciences* 12, 33–47.

Hansen, R. (1998) *Long-Term Growth as a Sequence of Exponential Modes*. George Mason University, Fairfax, Virginia.

Hartson, H.R., Andre, T.S. and Williges, R.C. (2001) Criteria for evaluating usability evaluation methods. *International Journal of Human–Computer Interaction* 13(4), 373–410.

Häubl, G. and Dellaert, B.G.C. (2004) Electronic recommendation agents and tourist choice. In: Weiermair, K. and Mathies, C. (eds) *The Tourism and Leisure Industry: Shaping the Future*. The Haworth Hospitality Press, Binghamton, New York, pp. 317–324.

Häubl, G. and Murray, K.B. (2003) Preference construction and persistence in digital marketplaces: the role of electronic recommendation agents. *Journal of Consumer Psychology* 13(1), 75–91.

Häubl, G. and Trifts, V. (2000) Consumer decision making in online shopping environments: the effects of interactive decision aids. *Marketing Science* 19(1), 4–21.

Häubl, G., Dellaert, B.G.C., Murray, K.B. and Trifts, V. (2004) Buyer behavior in personalized shopping environments: insights from the Institute for Online Consumer Studies. In: Karat, C.M., Blom, J. and Karat, J. (eds) *Designing Personalized User Experiences in eCommerce*. Kluwer Academic Publishers, Amsterdam, pp. 207–229.

Hauser, J.R. and Wernerfelt, B. (1990) An evaluation cost model of consideration sets. *Journal of Consumer Research* 16(March), 393–408.

Hawaii Visitors and Convention Bureau (2005) Send a message of Aloha. Available at: http://www.gohawaii.com/culture/hula.php

Hawkins, D.I., Best, R.J. and Coney, K.A. (1995) *Consumer Behavior: Implications for Marketing Strategy*. Irwin Publishing, Homewood, Illinois.

Hay, B., Wets, G. and Vanhoof, K. (2003) Segmentation of visiting patterns on websites using a sequence alignment method. *Journal of Retailing and Consumer Services* 10, 145–153.

Hendler, J., Berners-Lee, T. and Miller, E. (2002) Integrating applications on the semantic web. *Journal of the Institute of Electrical Engineers of Japan* 122(10), 676–680.

Herbrich, R., Keilbach, M., Graepel, Th., Bollmann-Sdorra, P. and Obermayer, K. (1999) Neural networks in economics. In: Brenner, Th. (ed.) *Computational Techniques for Modelling Learning in Economics: Advances in Computational Economics*. Kluwer Academic Publishers, Boston/Dordrecht/London, pp. 169–196.

Hibbard, J. (1997) Straight line to relevant data. *InformationWeek* 657, 21–25.

Hilbert, D.M. and Redmiles, D.F. (2000) Extracting usability information from user interface events. *ACM Computing Surveys* 32(4), 384–421.

Hinch, T.D. and Higham, J.E.S. (2001) Sport tourism: a framework for research. *International Journal of Tourism Research* 3(1), 45–58.

Hirschman, E. (1980) Attributes of attributes and layers of meaning. In: Olsen, J.C. (ed.) *Advances in Consumer Research*, Vol. 7. Association for Consumer Research, Ann Arbor, Michigan.

Hoch, S.J. and Deighton, J.A. (1989) Managing what consumers learn from experience. *Journal of Marketing* 53(2), 1–20.

Hoff, G. and Mundhenk, M. (2001) Creating a virtual library with HPSearch and Mops. In: *Proceedings of the 19th Annual International Conference of Computer Documentation,*

Communicating in the New Millennium, Santa Fe, New Mexico, pp. 201–207.

Hoffman, D.L. and Novak, T.P. (1996) Marketing in hypermedia computer-mediated environments: conceptual foundations. *Journal of Marketing* 60(July), 50–68.

Holbrook, M.B. (1980) Some preliminary notes on research in consumer esthetics. In: Olsen, J.C. (ed.) *Advances in Consumer Research*, Vol. 7. Association for Consumer Research, Ann Arbor, Michigan.

Holyoak, K.J. and Thagard, P. (1995) Mental leaps: analogy in creative thought. MIT Press, Cambridge, Massachusetts.

Howard, J.A. and Sheth, J.N. (1969) *The Theory of Buyer Behavior*. Wiley, New York.

Hruschka, H. (1996) *Marketing-Entscheidungen*. Vahlen, Munich.

Hruschka, H. (2001) An Artificial Neural Net Attraction Model (ANNAM) to analyze market share effects of marketing instruments. *Schmalenbach Business Review-ZFBF*, 27–40.

Hruschka, H. and Mazanec, J. (1990) Computer-assisted travel counseling. *Annals of Tourism Research* 17(2), 208–227.

Hruschka, H. and Probst, M. (2001) Interpretation aids for multilayer perceptron neural nets. Regensburger Diskussionsbeiträge zur Wirtschaftswissenschaft, Nr. 364. Universität Regensburg.

Hsieh-Yee, I. (2001) Research on web search behavior. *Library and Information Science Research* 23, 167–185.

Hu, Y. and Brent Ritchie, J.R. (1993) Measuring destination attractiveness: a contextual approach. *Journal of Travel Research* 32(2), 25–34.

Huang, M. (2003) Designing website attributes to induce experiential encounters. *Computers in Human Behavior* 19, 425–442.

Huizinga, J. (1938) *Homo Ludens*. Harper & Row, New York.

Human Factors Research Group (1993/2000) Software Usability Measurement Inventory (SUMI). Available at: http://www.ucc.ie/hfrg/questionnaires/sumi/index.html

Hunt, R.G., Krzystofiak, F.J., Meindl, J.R. and Yousry, A.M. (1989) Cognitive style and decision making. *Organizational Behavior and Human Decision Processes* 44, 436–453.

Hutchins, E. (1989) Metaphors for interface design. In: Taylor, M.M., Neel, F. and Bouwhuis, D.G. (eds) *The Structure of Multimodal Dialogue*. Elsevier Science, Amsterdam, pp. 11–28.

Hwang, Y.H. and Fesenmaier, D.R. (2001) Collaborative filtering: strategies for travel destination bundling. In: Sheldon, P., Woeber, K. and Fesenmaier, D.R. (eds) *Information Technology and Communication Technologies in Tourism 2001*. Springer, Berlin, pp. 167–175.

Hwang, Y.-H., Gretzel, U. and Fesenmaier, D.R. (2002) Behavioural foundations for human-centric travel decision-aid systems. In: Wöber, K.W., Frew, A.J. and Hitz, M. (eds) *Information and Communication Technologies in Tourism*. Springer, Vienna, pp. 356–365.

Hwang, Y.H., Gretzel, U. and Fesenmaier, D.R. (2003) Behavioral foundations for destination recommendation systems. Working paper. National Laboratory for Tourism and eCommerce, Champaign, Illinois.

Ingwersen, P. (1992) *Information Retrieval Interaction*. Taylor Graham, London.

Ivory, M.Y. (2003) *Automated Web Site Evaluation. Researchers' and Practitioners' Perspectives*. Kluwer Academic Publishers, Dordrecht and London.

Ivory, M.Y. and Hearst, M.A. (2001) The state of the art in automating usability evaluation of user interfaces. *ACM Computing Surveys* 33(4), 470–516.

Ivory, M.Y., Sinha, R.R. and Hearst, M.A. (2000) Preliminary findings on quantitative measures for distinguishing highly rated information-centric web pages. In: *Proceedings of the 6th Conference on Human Factors and the Web, Austin, Texas*.

Ivory, M.Y., Sinha, R.R. and Hearst, M.A. (2001) Empirically validated web page design metrics. In: *Proceedings of the ACM SIGCHI, Seattle, Washington, DC*.

Jacob, E.K. and Shaw, D. (1998) Sociocognitive perspectives on representation. *Annual Review of Information Science and Technology* 33, 131–185.

Jacobsen, N.E. and John, B.E. (2000) Two case studies in using cognitive walkthrough for interface evaluation. School of Computer

Science Technical Report CMU-CS-00-132. Carnegie Mellon University, Pittsburgh, Pennsylvania. Available at: http://reports-archive.adm.cs.cmu.edu/anon/2000/CMU-CS-00-132.pdf

Jamrozy, U., Backman, S. and Backman, K. (1996) Involvement and opinion leadership in tourism. *Annals of Tourism Research* 23, 908–924.

Jansen, B.J., Spink, A. and Saracevic, T. (2000) Real life, real user, and real needs: a study and analysis of user queries on the Web. *Information Processing and Management* 36(2), 207–227.

Jeng, J. (1999) Exploring the travel planning hierarchy: an interactive web experiment. Doctoral dissertation, University of Illinois, Urbana, Illinois.

Jeng, J. and Fesenmaier, D.R. (1996) A neural network approach to discrete choice modeling. *Journal of Travel and Tourism Marketing* 15(1/2), 119–144.

Jeng, J. and Fesenmaier, D.R. (1998) Destination compatibility in multidestination pleasure travel. *Tourism Analysis* 3, 77–87.

Jeng, J. and Fesenmaier, D.R. (2002) Conceptualizing the travel decision making hierarchy: a review of recent developments. *Tourism Analysis* 7, 15–32.

Jeong, M. and Lambert, C.U. (2001) Adaptation of an information quality framework to measure customers' behavioral intentions to use lodging web sites. *International Journal of Hospitality Management* 20, 129–146.

Jiang, J., Havitz, M.E. and O'Brien, R.M. (2000) Validating the international tourist role scale. *Annals of Tourism Research* 27(4), 964–981.

Johnson, E.J., Bellman, S. and Lohse, G.L. (2003) Cognitive lock-in and the power law of practice. *Journal of Marketing* 67(April), 62–75.

Johnson, K.L. and Misic, M.M. (1999) Benchmarking: a tool for web site evaluation and improvement. *Internet Research: Electronic Networking Applications and Policy* 9(5), 383–392.

Johnson-Laird, P.N. (1983) *Mental Models: Toward a Cognitive Science of Language, Inference, and Consciousness.* Harvard University Press, Cambridge, Massachusetts.

Jung, T.H., Louvieris, P. and Oppewal, H. (2002) Channel management strategy in the e-commerce environment – a portfolio management approach. In: Wöber, K.W., Frew, A.J. and Hitz, M. (eds) *Proceedings of the 9th International Conference for Information and Communication Technologies in Tourism – ENTER 2002.* Springer, Vienna and New York, pp. 17–26.

Jutla, D., Bodorik, P. and Wang, Y. (1999) Developing Internet e-commerce benchmarks. *Information Systems* 24(6), 475–493.

Kansas Travel and Tourism (2005) Kansas points of interest. Available at: www.travelks.com

Kearsley, G. (2001) Mental models. In: *Encyclopedia of Psychology.* Available at: http://tip.psychology.org/models.html

Keller, P.A. and McGill, A.L. (1994) Differences in the relative influence of product attributes under alternative processing conditions: attribute importance versus ease of imagining. *Journal of Consumer Psychology* 3(1), 29–49.

Kendall, E. and Sproles, G.B. (1986) Learning styles of secondary vocational home economics students: a factor analytic test of experiential learning theory. *The Journal of Vocational Education Research* 11(3), 1–15.

Kendall, E. and Sproles, G.B. (1990) Consumer decision-making styles as a function of individual learning styles. *The Journal of Consumer Affairs* 24(1), 134–147.

Kerstetter, D. and Cho, M.-H. (2004) Prior knowledge, credibility and information search. *Annals of Tourism Research* 31(4), 961–985.

Kiani-Kress, R. (2003) Der neue Libero. *Focus* 10(3), 88.

Kim, H. and Hirtle, S.C. (1995) Spatial metaphors and disorientation in hypertext browsing. *Behaviour and Information Technology* 45(2), 93–102.

Kim, S. and Fesenmaier, D.R. (1990) Evaluating spatial structure effects in recreational travel. *Leisure Sciences* 12, 367–381.

Kim, B.D. and Kim, S.O. (2001) A new recommender system to combine content-based and collaborative filtering systems. *Journal of Database Marketing* 8(3), 244–252.

King, J. (2002) Destination marketing organizations – connecting the experience rather than promoting the place. *Journal of Vacation Marketing* 5(3), 105–108.

Klein, L.R. (1998) Evaluating the potential of interactive media through a new lens: search versus experience goods. *Journal of Business Research* 41(March), 195–203.

Klicek, B. (2001) Tourist's decision-making process assisted by the Web and multimedia intelligent advisory system. In: Sheldon, P., Wöber, K. and Fesenmaier, D.R. (eds) *Proceedings of the ENTER'2001 in Montreal, Canada*. Springer, New York, pp. 358–367.

Kohonen, T. (1982) Self-organized formation of topologically correct feature maps. *Biological Cybernetics* 43, 59–69.

Kolb, D.A. (1984) *Experiential Learning: Experience as the Source of Learning and Development*. Prentice-Hall, Englewood Cliffs, New Jersey.

Kolodner, J. (1993) *Case-Based Reasoning*. Morgan Kaufmann Publishers, San Mateo, California.

Konstan, J.A. and Riedl, J. (1999) Research resources for recommender systems. In: *CHI '99 Workshop Interacting with Recommender Systems, 15–16 May*.

Kosala, R. and Blockeel, H. (2000) Web mining research: a survey. *SIGKDD Explorations* 2(1), 1–15.

Kramer, T. (2003) The effect of preference measurement on preference construction and responses to customized offers. Dissertation, Stanford University, Stanford, California.

Kruger, A., Giles, C.L., Coetzee, F., Glover, E., Flake, G., Lawrence, S. and Omlin, C. (2000) DEADLINER: building a new niche search engine. In: *Proceedings of the Conference on Information and Knowledge Management, Washington, DC*.

Kubey, R. and Csikszentmihalyi, M. (1990) *Television and Quality of Life: How Viewing Shapes Everyday Experience*. Lawrence Erlbaum Associates, Hillsdale, New Jersey.

Kutsch, Th. (2001) Wellness-Forschung – Gesundheit, Freizeit, Wohnen. Available at: http://www.agp.uni-bonn.de/wiso/8967WS20002001Abstracts.pdf

Lake, D. (2001) American go online for travel information. CNN, June 14. Available at: http://www.cnn.com/2001/TECH/internet/06/14/travelers.use.net.idg/index.html

Lakoff, G. and Johnson, M. (1980) *Metaphors We Live By*. University of Chicago Press, Chicago, Illinois.

Lamarque, P. (2004) On not expecting too much from narrative. *Mind & Language* 19(4), 393–408.

Lastovicka, J.L. (1982) On the validation of lifestyle traits: a review and illustration. *Journal of Marketing Research* 19(February), 126–138.

Laurel, B. (1986) Interface as mimesis. In: Norman, D.A. and Draper, S. (eds) *User-Centered System Design: New Perspectives on Human–Computer Interaction*. Lawrence Erlbaum Associates, Hillsdale, New Jersey.

Laurillard, D. (1998) Multimedia and the learner's experience of narrative. *Computers & Education* 31, 229–242.

Lawrence, S. (2000) Context in web search. *IEEE Data Engineering Bulletin* 23(3), 25–32.

Lawrence, S. and Giles, C.L. (1999) Accessibility and distribution of information on the Web. *Nature* 400, 107–109.

Lawrence, S., Giles, C.L. and Bollacker, K. (1999) Digital libraries and autonomous citation indexing. *IEEE Computer* 32(6), 67–71.

Lederer, A.L., Maupin, D.J., Sena, M.P. and Zhuang, Y. (2000) The technology acceptance model and the World Wide Web. *Decision Support Systems* 29(3), 269–282.

Leiper, N. (1990) Tourist attraction systems. *Annals of Tourism Research* 17(3), 367–384.

Lenz, M. (1996) Imtas – intelligent multimedia travel agent system. In: *Information and Communication Technologies in Tourism (Proceedings of the ENTER-96)*. Springer, pp. 11–17.

Lenz, M. (1999) Experiences from deploying CBR applications in electronic commerce. In: *Proceedings of the German Workshop on CBR*, Wurzburg, Germany.

Lenz, M. and Burkhard, H.D. (1997) CBR for document retrieval-the FAllQ project. In: Leake, D.B. and Plaza, E. (eds) *Case-Based Reasoning Research and Development (ICCBR-97), Lecture Notes in Artificial Intelligence No. 1266*. Springer, Berlin, pp. 84–93.

Lepper, M.R., Green, D. and Nisbett, R.E. (1973) Undermining children's intrinsic interest with extrinsic rewards: a test of the over justification hypothesis. *Journal of Personality and Social Psychology* 28, 129–137.

Levitt, T. (1981) Marketing intangible products and product intangibles. *Harvard Business Review* (May–June), 94–102.

Levy, S.J. (1959) Symbols for sale. *Harvard Business Review* 37, 117–119.

Levy, S.J. (1963) Symbolism and life style. In: Greyser, S.A. (ed.) *Toward Scientific Marketing*. American Marketing Association, Chicago, Illinois, pp. 27–28.

Levy, S.J. (1983) *Play Behavior*. Robert E. Krieger, Malabar, Florida.

Lewis, J.R. (1995) IBM computer usability satisfaction questionnaires: psychometric evaluation and instructions for use. *International Journal of Human–Computer Interaction* 7(1), 57–78.

Li, H., Daugherty, T. and Biocca, F. (2001) Characteristics of virtual experience in electronic commerce: a protocol analysis. *Journal of Interactive Marketing* 15(3), 13–30.

Lieberman, J.N. (1977) *Playfulness*. Academic Press, New York.

Lin, C.S., Wu, S. and Tsay, R.J. (2005) Integrating perceived playfulness into expectation-confirmation model for web portal context. *Information and Management* 42(5), 683–693.

Lin, H.X., Choong, Y.-Y. and Salvendy, G. (1997) A proposed index of usability: a method for comparing the relative usability of different software systems. *Behaviour and Information Technology* 16(4/5), 267–278.

Lindgaard, G. (1994) *Usability Testing and System Evaluation. A Guide for Designing Useful Computer Systems*. Chapman & Hall, London, Glasgow.

Lo, L. (1992) Destination interdependence and the competing-destinations model. *Environment and Planning A* 24, 1191–1204.

Loban, S. (1997) A framework for computer-assisted travel counseling. *Annals of Tourism Research* 24(4), 813–831.

Lohmann, M. (1997) Gesundheitsurlaub, Wellness-Urlaub: Marktsituation und Perspektiven. In: Kagelmann, H.-J. (ed.) *Tourismus und Gesundheit*. Gießen, Frankfurt, pp. 22–29.

Louviere, J.J. (1988) *Analyzing Decision Making, Metric Conjoint Analysis, Quantitative Applications in the Social Sciences*. Sage Research Productions, Beverly Hills, Cambridge.

Louviere, J.J. and Hensher, D.A. (1983) Using logistic regressions with experimental design data to forecast consumer demand for a unique cultural event. *Journal of Consumer Research* 10, 350–367.

Lovelock, C.H. and Wright, C. (1999) *Principles of Service, Marketing and Management*. Prentice-Hall, Englewood Cliffs, New Jersey.

Lue, C.C., Crompton, J.L. and Fesenmaier, D.R. (1993) Conceptualization of multi-destination pleasure trip decisions. *Annals of Tourism Research* 20, 289–301.

Lue, C.C., Crompton, J.L. and Stewart, W.P. (1996) Evidence of cumulative attraction in multidestination recreational trip decision. *Journal of Travel Research* 35(1), 41–49.

Macedo, L. and Cardoso, A. (1998) Nested graph-structured representations for cases. In: Smyth, B. and Cunningham, P. (eds) *Advances in Case-Based Reasoning*, Vol. 1488 of *Lecture Notes in Computer Science*. Springer, Berlin, pp. 1–12.

Madrigal, R. (1995) Personal values, traveler personality type, and leisure travel style. *Journal of Leisure Research* 27(2), 125–142.

Madrigal, R. and Kahle, L.R. (1994) Predicting vacation activity preferences on the basis of value-system segmentation. *Journal of Travel Research* 32(3), 22–28.

Maedche, A. and Staab, S. (2002) Applying semantic web technologies for tourism information systems. In: Wöber, K.W., Frew, A.J. and Hitz, M. (eds) *Proceedings of the 9th International Conference for Information and Communication Technologies in Tourism – ENTER 2002*. Springer, Vienna and New York, pp. 311–319.

Maedche, A., Staab, S., Stojanovic, N., Studer, R. and Sure, Y. (2003) SEmantic PortAL – the SEAL approach. In: Fensel, D., Hendler, H. and Wahlster, W. (eds) *Spinning the Semantic Web*. MIT Press, Cambridge, Massachusetts, pp. 317–359.

Maes, P. (1994) Agents that reduce work and information overload. *Communications of the ACM* 37(7), 31–40.

Magnusson, D. (1981) *Toward a Psychology of Situations: An Interactional Perspective*. Lawrence Erlbaum Associates, Hillsdale, New Jersey.

Mahmood, M.A., Burn, J.M., Gemoets, L.A. and Jacqez, C. (2000) Variables affecting information technology end-user satisfaction: a meta-analysis of the empirical literature. *International Journal of Human–Computer Studies* 52, 751–771.

Malhotra, N.K. (1988) Self-concept and product choice: an integrated perspective. *Journal of Economic Psychology* 61, 13–25.

Mandler, G. (1975) *Mind and Emotion*. Wiley, New York.

Manfredo, M.J. (1989) An investigation of the basis for external information search in recreation and tourism. *Leisure Sciences* 11, 29–45.

Mann, W.C. and Thompson, S. (1987) Rhetorical structure theory: a theory of text organization. In: Polanyi, L. (ed.) *The Structure of Discourse*. Ablex Publishing Corporation, Norwood, New Jersey.

Manolescu, I., Florescu, D. and Kossmann, D.K. (2001) Answering XML queries over heterogeneous. In: *2001 International Conference on Very Large Data Bases (VLDB)*, pp. 241–250.

Manovich, L. (2001) *The Language of New Media*. MIT Press, Cambridge, Massachusetts.

Mansfeld, Y. (1992) From motivation to actual travel. *Annals of Tourism Research* 19(3), 399–419.

Marsh, T. and Wright, P. (1999) Co-operative evaluation of a desktop virtual reality system. In: Harrison, M. and Smith, S. (eds) *Workshop on User-Centered Design and Implementation of Virtual Environments*. The University of York, New York, pp. 99–108.

Martinetz, Th. and Schulten, K. (1994) Topology representing networks. *Neural Networks* 7(5), 507–522.

Martinetz, Th., Berkovich, St.G. and Schulten, K. (1993) 'Neural gas' network for vector quantization and its application to time-series prediction. *IEEE Transactions of Neural Networks* 4(4), 558–569.

Masden, K.H. (1994) A guide to metaphorical design. *Communications of the ACM* 37(12), 57–62.

Mateas, M. (2004) A preliminary poetics for interactive drama and games. In: Wardrip-Fruin, N. and Harrigan, P. (eds) *First Person: New Media as Story, Performance, and Game*. MIT Press, Cambridge, Massachusetts, pp. 19–33.

Mateas, M. and Sengers, P. (1999) Narrative intelligence. Report of the AAAI Fall Symposium on Narrative Intelligence, American Association for Artificial Intelligence, 5–7 November, North Falmouth, Massachusetts.

Mathwick, C. and Rigdon, E. (2004) Play, flow, and the online search experience. *Journal of Consumer Research* 31(September), 324–332.

Mattila, A.S. (2000) The role of narratives in the advertising of experiential services. *Journal of Service Research* 3(1), 35–45.

Mayo, E.J. and Jarvis, L.P. (1981) *The Psychology of Leisure Travel*. CBI Publishing, Boston, Massachusetts.

Mazanec, J.A. (1990) An expert system approach to travel counseling. In: Travel & Tourism Research Association (ed.) *The Tourism Connection: Linking Research and Marketing, 21st Annual Conference, Salt Lake City, Utah*, pp. 81–87.

Mazanec, J.A. (1999) TRN32. Available at: http://tourism.wu-wien.ac.at/cgi-bin/ift.pl?charly/http/software/trn32.html

Mazanec, J.A. (2001) Neural market structure analysis: novel topology-sensitive methodology. *European Journal of Marketing* 35(7–8), 894–914.

McCallum, A., Nigam, K., Rennie, J. and Seymore, K. (1999) A machine learning approach to building domain-specific search engines. In: Dean, T. (ed.) *Proceedings of the 16th International Joint Conference on Artificial Intelligence – IJCAI 99, Vol 2*. Morgan Kaufmann Publishers, San Francisco, California, pp. 662–667.

McDonald, M. (1995) *Marketing Plans: How to Prepare Them, How to Use Them*, 3rd edn. Butterworth-Heinemann, Oxford.

McDonald, W.J. (1993) The roles of demographics, purchase histories and shopper decision making styles in predicting consumer catalog loyalty. *Journal of Direct Marketing* 7(3), 55–65.

McFadden, D. (1986) The choice theory approach to market research. *Marketing Science* 5(4), 275–297.

McGinty, L. and Smyth, B. (2002) Deep dialogue vs. casual conversation in recommender systems. In: Ricci, F. and Smyth, B. (eds) *Proceedings of the Workshop on Personalization in e-Commerce, at the 2th International Conference on Adaptive Hypermedia and Web-Based Systems, AH-02*. Universidad de Malaga, Malaga, Spain, pp. 80–89.

McGinty, L. and Smyth, B. (2003) On the role of diversity in conversational recommender systems. In: Aamodt, A., Bridge, D. and Ashley, K. (eds) *ICCBR 2003, the 5th International Conference on Case-Based Reasoning*. Trondheim, Norway, pp. 276–290.

McGrath, J.E. and Kelly, J.R. (1986) *Time and Human Contraction*. The Guilford Press, New York.

McKercher, R. (1998) The effect of market access on destination choice. *Journal of Travel Research* 37, 39–47.

McKercher, B. (2002) Towards a classification of cultural tourists. *International Journal of Tourism Research* 4(1), 29–38.

McSherry, D. (2002) Diversity-conscious retrieval. In: Craw, S. and Preece, A. (eds) *Advances in Case-Based Reasoning, Proceedings of the 6th European Conference on Case Based Reasoning, ECCBR 2002*. Springer, Aberdeen, UK, pp. 219–233.

McSherry, D. (2003) Similarity and compromise. In: Aamodt, A., Bridge, D. and Ashley, K. (eds) *ICCBR 2003, the 5th International Conference on Case-Based Reasoning*. Trondheim, Norway, pp. 291–305.

Meadows, M.S. (2003) *Pause & Effect: The Art of Interactive Narrative*. New Riders, Indianapolis, Indiana.

Mertens, P. and Höhl, M. (1999) Wie lernt der Computer den Menschen kennen? – Bestands-aufnahme und Experimente zur Benutzermodellierung in der Wirtschaftsinformatik. *WIRTSCHAFTSINFORMATIK* 41(3), 201–209.

Metz, C. (1974) *Film Language: A Semiotics of the Cinema*. Oxford University Press, New York.

Mihalich, J.C. (1982) *Sports and Athletics*. Littlefield, Adams & Company, Totowa, New Jersey.

Miller, G.A. (1956) The magical number seven, plus or minus two: some limits on our capacity for processing information. *Psychological Review* 63(2), 81–97.

Minsky, M. (1986) *The Society of Mind*. Simon & Schuster, New York.

Mitsche, N. (2001) Personalized traveling counseling system: providing decision support features for travelers. In: Sheldon, P., Wöber, K. and Fesenmaier, D.R. (eds) *Information and Communication Technologies in Tourism 2001*. Springer, Vienna, pp. 160–166.

Mittal, B. (1988) The role of affective choice mode in the consumer purchase of expressive products. *Journal of Economic Psychology* 9, 499–524.

Mittal, B. (1994) The study of the concept of affective choice mode for consumer decisions. In: Allen, C. and Roedder, J.D. (eds) *Advances in Consumer Research*, Vol. 21. Association for Consumer Research, Provo, Utah.

Mo, C.-M., Havitz, M.E. and Howard, D.R. (1994) Segmenting travel markets with the international tourism role (ITR) scale. *Journal of Travel Research* 33(1), 24–31.

Montaner, M., López, B. and De La Rosa, J.L. (2002) Improving case representation and case base maintenance in recommender systems. In: Craw, S. and Preece, A. (eds) *Proceedings of the 6th European Conference on Case Based Reasoning, ECCBR 2002*. Springer, Aberdeen, UK, pp. 234–248.

Moorthy, S., Ratchford, B. and Talukdar, D. (1997) Consumer information search revisited: theory and empirical analysis. *Journal of Consumer Research* 23, 263–277.

Moschis, G.P. (1976) Shopping orientations and consumer uses of information. *Journal of Retailing* 52(Summer), 61–70.

Moutinho, L. (1987) Consumer behaviour in tourism. *European Journal of Marketing* 21(10), 3–44.

Murray, J.H. (2001) *Hamlet on the Holodeck: The Future of Narrative in Cyberspace*. MIT Press, Cambridge, Massachusetts.

Murray, K.B. (1991) A test of services marketing theory: consumer information acquisition activities. *Journal of Marketing* 55, 10–25.

Murray, K.B. and Häubl, G. (2003) Skill acquisition and interface loyalty: a human capital perspective. *Communications of the ACM* 46(12), 272–278.

Nakayama, T., Kato, H. and Yamane, Y. (2000) Discovering the gap between web site designers' expectations and users' behavior. *Computer Networks* 33, 811–822.

Neale, D.C. and Carroll, J.M. (1997) The role of metaphors in user interface design. In: Helander, M.G., Landauer, T.K. and Prabhu, P. (eds) *Handbook of Human–Computer Interaction*, 2nd edn. Elsevier Science, Amsterdam.

Nestorov, S. and Tsur, S. (1999) Integrating data mining with relational DBMS: a tightly coupled approach. In: Pinter, R.Y. and Tsur, S. (eds) *Proceedings of the 4th Workshop on Next Generation Information Technologies and Systems (NGITS)*. Springer, Berlin, pp. 295–311.

NeuralWare Inc (1993) *NeuralWorks Professional II/Plus*. Technical Publications Group, Pittsburgh, Pennsylvania.

Nguyen, Q.N. and Ricci, F. (2004) User preferences initialization and integration in critique-based mobile recommender systems. In: *Proceedings of the 5th Workshop on Artificial Intelligence in Mobile Systems, AIMS 2004, in conjunction with UbiComp 2004*. Nottingham, UK.

Nickerson, N.P. and Ellis, G.D. (1991) Traveler types and activation theory: a comparison of two models. *Journal of Travel Research* 29(3), 26–31.

Nielsen, J. (1990) The art of navigating through hypertext. *Communications of the ACM* 33(3), 196–310.

Nielsen, J. (1993) *Usability Engineering*. Harcourt Brace & Company, Academic Press, Boston, Massachusetts.

Nielsen, J. (1995) *Multimedia and Hypertext: The Internet and Beyond*. AP Professional, Boston, Massachusetts.

Nielsen, J. (1999) *Designing Web Usability: The Practice of Simplicity*. New Riders, Indianapolis, Indiana.

Norman, D.A. (1988) *The Psychology of Everyday Things*. Basic Books, New York.

Norman, D.A. (1990) *The Design of Everyday Things*. Doubleday Publishing, New York.

Norman, D.A. (2004) *Emotional Design*. Basic Books, New York.

Norman, K.L. and Chin, J.P. (1988) The effect of tree structure on search in a hierarchical menu selection system. *Behaviour and Information Technology* 7, 51–65.

Not, E., Petrelli, D., Stock, O., Strapparava, C. and Zancanaro, M. (2000) The environment as a medium: location-aware generation for cultural visitors. In: *Proceedings of the Workshop on 'Coherence in Generated Multimedia', held in conjunction with INLG '2000*. Mitzpe Ramon, Israel.

Novak, T.P., Hoffman, D.L. and Yung, Y.F. (2000) Measuring the customer experience in online environments: a structural modeling approach. *Marketing Science* 19(1), 22–42.

Novak, T.P., Hoffman, D.L. and Duhachek, A. (2003) The influence of goal-directed and experiential activities on online flow experiences. *Journal of Consumer Psychology* 13(1–2), 3–16.

Olsina, L. (2003) Methods for quality assessment of web sites and applications. Presentation held at the University of Trento, 2 April. Available at: http://www.economia.unitn.it/etourism/eventi/olsina.pdf

Olsina, L. and Rossi, G. (2001) A quantitative method for quality evaluation of web applications. In: *Proceedings of the Argentinean Symposium on Software Engineering (ASSE 2001), Buenos Aires, Argentina*.

Opaschowski, H.-W. (2002) *Tourismus – Eine systematische Einführung, Analysen und Prognosen*, 3rd edn. Leske Verlag, Opladen.

Oppermann, M. (1992) Intranational tourist flows in Malaysia. *Annals of Tourism Research* 19, 482–500.

Oppermann, M. (1995) A model of travel itineraries. *Journal of Travel Research* 33, 57–61.

Oppermann, M. (1998) Travel horizon – a valuable analysis tool? *Tourism Management* 19(4), 321–329.

Oppermann, R. and Reiterer, H. (1997) Software evaluation using the 9241 evaluator. *Behaviour and Information Technology* 16(4/5), 232–245.

Oren, T. (1990) Designing a new medium. In: Laurel, B. (ed.) *The Art of Human–Computer Interface Design*. Addison-Wesley, Reading, Massachusetts, pp. 467–479.

Osborne, H. (1979) Some theories of aesthetic judgment. *Journal of Aesthetics and Art Criticism* 38, 135–144.

Overbeeke, K., Djajadiningrat, T., Hummels, C., Wensveen, S. and Frens, J. (2003) Let's make things engaging. In: Blythe, M.A., Monk, A.F., Overbeeke, K. and Wright, P.C. (eds) *Funology: From Usability to Enjoyment*. Kluwer Academic Publishers, Dordrecht, The Netherlands, pp. 7–17.

Oyama, S., Kokubo, T. and Ishida, T. (2003) Domain-specific web search with keyword spices. *IEEE Transactions on Knowledge and Data Engineering* 16(1), 17–27.

Packer, R. and Jordan, K. (2001) Multimedia: from Wagner to virtual reality. W.W. Norton, New York.

Palkoska, J., Pühretmair, F., Tjoa, A.M., Wagner, R.R. and Wöß, W. (2002) Advanced query mechanisms in tourism information systems. In: Wöber, K., Frew, A.J. and Hitz, M. (eds) *Information and Communication Technologies in Tourism 2002*. Springer, Vienna and New York, pp. 438–447.

Palmer, A. and McCole, P. (2000) The role of electronic commerce in creating virtual tourism destination marketing organizations. *International Journal of Contemporary Hospitality Management* 12(3), 198–204.

Pan, B. (2003) Travel information search on the Internet: an exploratory study. Doctoral dissertation, University of Illinois, Urbana-Champaign, Illinois.

Pan, B. and Fesenmaier, D.R. (2000) A typology of tourism-related web sites: its theoretical background and implications. *Information Technology and Tourism* 3(3/4), 155–176.

Pan, B. and Fesenmaier, D.R. (2002) Semantics of online tourism and travel information search on the Internet: a preliminary study. In: Wöber, K., Frew, A. and Hitz, M. (eds) *Information and Communication Technologies in Tourism 2002*. Springer, Vienna, pp. 320–328.

Park, W.C. and Lessig, V.P. (1981) Familiarity and its impact on consumer decision biased and heuristics. *Journal of Consumer Research* 8, 223–230.

Park, W.C. and Lutz, R.J. (1982) Decision plans and consumer choice dynamic. *Journal of Marketing Research* 16, 108–115.

Park, W.C., Gardner, M.P. and Thukral, V.K. (1988) Self-perceived knowledge: some effects on information processing for a choice task. *American Journal of Psychology* 101, 401–424.

Passani, L. (2002) Building usable wireless applications for mobile phones. In: Paterno, F. (ed.) *Proceedings of the 4th International Symposium on Human–Computer Interaction with Mobile Devices, Mobile HCI*. Springer, Pisa, Italy, pp. 9–20.

Payne, J.W. (1976) Task complexity and contingent processing in decision making: an information search and protocol analysis. *Organizational Behavior and Human Performance* 16, 366–387.

Payne, J.W., Bettman, J.R. and Johnson, E.J. (1988) Adaptive strategy selection in decision making. *Journal of Experimental Psychology: Learning, Memory and Cognition* 14, 534–552.

Pazzani, M.J. (1999) A framework for collaborative, content-based and demographic filtering. *Artificial Intelligence Review* 13, 393–408.

Pearrow, M. (2000) *Web Site Usability Handbook*. Charles River Media, Rockland, Massachusetts.

Pennington-Gray, L. and Vogt, C. (2003) Examining welcome center visitors' travel and information behaviors: does location of centers or residency matter? *Journal of Travel Research* 41(3), 272–280.

Pennock, D.M., Horvitz, E., Lawrence, S. and Giles, C.L. (2000) Collaborative filtering by personality diagnosis: a hybrid memory- and model-based approach. In: *Proceedings of the 16th Conference on Uncertainty in Artificial Intelligence (UAI-2000)*. Morgan Kaufmann Publishers, San Francisco, California, pp. 473–480.

Perdue, R.P. (1993) External information search in marine recreational fishing. *Leisure Sciences* 15, 169–187.

Perelman, C. and Olbrechts-Tyteca, L. (1969) *The New Rhetoric: A Treatise on Argumentation*. University of Notre Dame Press, Notre Dame, Illinois.

Pervin, L.A. (1985) Personality: current controversies, issues, and directions. *Annual Review of Psychology* 36, 83–114.

Pervin, L.A. (2000) *Persönlichkeitstheorien*, 4th edn. Reinhardt, Munich.

Peterson, R.A. and Merino, M.C. (2003) Consumer information search behavior and the Internet. *Psychology & Marketing* 20(2), 99–121.

Philips, D.M., Olson, J.C. and Baumgartner, H. (1995) Consumption visions in consumer decision making. In: Kardes, F. and Sujan, M. (eds) *Advances in Consumer Research*. Association for Consumer Research, Provo, Utah, pp. 280–284.

Picard, R.W. (1997) *Affective Computing*. MIT Press, Cambridge, Massachusetts.

Picard, R.W. (1998) *Affective Computing*, 2nd edn. MIT Press, Cambridge, Massachusetts.

Pine, B.J. and Gilmore, J. (1999) *The Experience Economy*. Harvard Business School Press, Cambridge, Massachusetts.

Pirolli, P. and Card, S.K. (1999) Information foraging. *Psychological Review* 106(4), 643–675.

Plaza, E. (1995) Cases as terms: a feature term approach to the structured representation of cases. In: *International Conference on Case-Based Reasoning (ICCBR-95), 26–29 October*. Springer, Sesimbra, Portugal.

Plog, S.C. (1974) Why destination areas rise and fall in popularity? *The Cornell Hotel and Restaurant Administration Quarterly* 14(4), 55–58.

Plog, S.C. (1994) Developing and using psychographics in tourism research. In: Ritchie, J.R.B. and Goeldner, C.R. (eds) *Travel, Tourism and Hospitality Research: A Handbook for Managers and Researchers*, 2nd edn. Wiley, New York.

Poon, A. (1993) *Tourism, Technology and Competitive Strategies*. CAB International, Wallingford, UK.

Pröll, B. and Retschitzegger, W. (2000) Discovering next generation tourism information systems: a tour on TIScover, *Journal of Travel Research* 39(2), 182–191.

Punj, G. and Staelin, R. (1983) Central and peripheral routes to advertising effectiveness. *Journal of Consumer Research* 9, 366–380.

Radosevich, L. (1997) Fixing web-site usability. *InfoWorld* 19(50), 81–82.

Rangarajan, S.K., Phoha, V.V., Balagani, K.S., Selmic, R.R. and Iyengar, S.S. (2004) Adaptive neural network clustering of web users. *IEEE Computer* 37(4), 34–40.

Ratchford, B.T., Talukdar, D. and Shocker, A. (1996) Goal-derived categories and the antecedents of across-category consideration. *Journal of Consumer Research* 23, 240–250.

Ratchford, B.T., Lee, M.-S. and Talukdar, D. (2003) The impact of the Internet on information search for automobiles. *Journal of Marketing Research* 40(May), 193–209.

Raudys, S. (2000) How good are support vector machines? *Neural Networks* 13, 17–19.

Reid, I.S. and Crompton, J.L. (1993) A taxonomy of leisure purchase decision paradigms based on level of involvement. *Journal of Leisure Research* 25(2), 182–202.

Rennie, J. and McCallum, A. (1999) Using reinforcement learning to spider the web efficiently. In: *Proceedings of the 16th International Conference on Machine Learning*, pp. 335–343.

Ricci, F. (2002) Travel recommender systems. *IEE Intelligent Systems* 17(6), 55–57.

Ricci, F. and Senter, L. (1998) Structured cases, trees and efficient retrieval. In: Smyth, B. and Cunningham, P. (eds) *Advances in Case-Based Reasoning*, Vol. 1488 of *Lecture Notes in Computer Science*. Springer, pp. 88–99.

Ricci, F. and Werthner, H. (2001) Case-based destination recommendations over an XML data repository. In: Sheldon, P., Wöber, K. and Fesenmaier, D.R. (eds) *Proceedings of the ENTER '2001 in Montreal*. Springer, Vienna and New York, pp. 150–159.

Ricci, F. and Werthner, H. (2002) Case base querying for travel planning recommendation. *Information Technology and Tourism* 4, 215–226.

Ricci, F., Arslan, B., Mirzadeh, N. and Venturini, A. (2002a) ITR: a case-based travel advisory system. In: Craw, S. and Preece, A. (eds) *Proceedings of the 6th European Conference on Case-Based Reasoning, ECCBR 2002*. Springer, Berlin, pp. 613–627.

Ricci, F., Blaas, D., Mirzadeh, N., Venturini, A. and Werthner, H. (2002b) Intelligent query management for travel products selection. In: Wöber, K.W., Frew, A.J. and Hitz, M. (eds) *Information and Communication*

Technologies in Tourism. Springer, Vienna, pp. 448–457.

Ricci, F., Mirzadeh, N. and Venturini, A. (2002d) Intelligent query management in a mediator architecture. In: 2002 First International IEEE Symposium 'Intelligent Systems'. Varna, Bulgaria, pp. 221–226.

Ricci, F., Venturini, A., Cavada, D., Mirzadeh, N., Blaas, D. and Nones, M. (2003) Product recommendation with interactive query management and twofold similarity. In: Aamodt, A., Bridge, D. and Ashley, K. (eds) Proceedings of the 5th International Conference on Case-Based Reasoning, ICCBR 2003, Trondheim, Norway, pp. 479–493.

Rieman, J., Franzke, M. and Redmiles, D. (1995) Usability evaluation with the cognitive walkthrough. In: ACM (ed.) CHI 95 Conference Companion 1995 ACM. Denver, Colorado, pp. 387–388.

Ripley, B.D. (1996) Pattern Recognition and Neural Networks. Cambridge University Press, Cambridge, Massachusetts.

Roberts, J.H. and Lilien, G.L. (1993) Explanatory and predictive models of consumer behavior. In: Eliashberg, J. and Lilien, G.L. (eds) Handbooks in Operations Research and Management Science: Marketing, Vol. 5. North-Holland, Amsterdam, pp. 27–82.

Rocchi, C. and Zancanaro, M. (2003) Generation of video documentaries from discourse structures. In: Proceedings of the 9th European Workshop on Natural Language Generation. Budapest.

Rocchi, C., Stock, O., Zancanaro, M., Kruppa, M. and Krüger, A. (2000) The museum visit: generating seamless personalized presentations on multiple devices. In: Proceedings of the Intelligent User Interfaces 2004, 13–16 January. Island of Madeira, Portugal.

Roehl, W.S. and Fesenmaier, D.R. (1992) Risk perception and pleasure travel: an exploratory analysis. Journal of Travel Research 30(4), 17–26.

Ross, G.F. (1994) The Psychology of Tourism. Hospitality Press, Melbourne, Australia.

Rudd, J. and Isensee, S. (1994) Twenty-two tips for a happier, healthier prototype. Journal of Interactions 1(1), 35–40.

Ruefli, T.W., Whinston, A. and Wiggins, R.R. (2001) The digital technological environment. In: Wind, J. and Mahajan, V. (eds) Digital Marketing: Global Strategies from the Worlds' Leading Experts. Wiley, New York, pp. 26–58.

Rumelhart, D.E. (1980) Schemata: the building blocks of cognition. In: Spiro, R.J., Bruce, B.C. and Brewer, W.F. (eds) Theoretical Issues in Reading Comprehension, Vol. 1. Lawrence Erlbaum Associates, Hillsdale, New Jersey.

Rumetshofer, H., Pühretmair, F. and Wöß, W. (2003) Individual information presentation based on cognitive styles for tourism information systems. In: Frew, A.J., Hitz, M. and O'Connor, P. (eds) ENTER 2003, Information and Communication Technologies in Tourism 2003. Springer, Helsinki, Finland, pp. 440–449.

Ryan, M.-L. (2001) Narrative as Virtual Reality. Johns Hopkins University Press, Baltimore, Maryland.

Sandelands, L.E., Ashford, S.J. and Dutton, J.E. (1983) Reconceptualizing the over justification effect: a template-matching approach. Motivation and Emotion 7, 229–255.

Sasse, M.A. (1997) Eliciting and describing users' models of computer systems. Doctoral dissertation, University of Birmingham, Birmingham, UK.

Schafer, J.B., Konstan, J.A. and Riedl, J. (2001) E-commerce recommendation applications. Data Mining and Knowledge Discovery 5(1/2), 115–153.

Schank, R. (1982) Dynamic Memory. Cambridge University Press, Cambridge, Massachusetts.

Schank, R. (1990) Tell Me a Story: A New Look at Real and Artificial Memory. Charles Scribner's Sons, New York.

Schank, R. and Abelson, R.P. (1977) Scripts, Plans, Goals, and Understanding: An Inquiry into Human Knowledge Structures. Lawrence Erlbaum Associates, Hillsdale, New Jersey.

Schank, R. and Abelson, R.P. (1995) Knowledge and memory: the real story. In: Wyer, R.S. (ed.) Advances in Social Cognition, Vol. VIII. Lawrence Erlbaum Associates, Hillsdale, New Jersey, pp. 1–86.

Schank, R. and Berman, T.R. (2002) The pervasive role of stories in knowledge and action. In: Green, M.C., Strange, J.J. and Brock, T.C. (eds) *Narrative Impact: Social and Cognitive Foundations.* Lawrence Erlbaum Associates, Hillsdale, New Jersey, pp. 287–313.

Scharl, A. (2000) *Evolutionary Web Development.* Springer, London.

Schlosser, A.E. (2003) Experiencing products in the virtual world: the role of goal and imagery in influencing attitudes versus purchase intentions. *Journal of Consumer Research* 30(September), 35–42.

Schlosser, A.E. and Shavitt, S. (1999) The effect of interactive advertising on attitude resistance. Presentation given at the NLTeC Workshop on Advertising and Technology in Tourism, Urbana-Champaign, Illinois, November.

Schmidt, J. and Spreng, R. (1996) A proposed model of external consumer information search. *Journal of the Academy of Marketing Science* 24, 246–256.

Schmitt, B. (1999) *Experiential Marketing.* Free Press, New York.

Schmoll, G.A. (1977) *Tourism Promotion.* Tourism International Press, London.

Schuhbauer, H. (1999) Ein WWW-basiertes Stadtinformationssystem zur individuellen Frei-zeitberatung – Grundlagen und Prototyp TourBO. Dissertation, Nürnberg.

Selin, S. and Beason, K. (1990) Interorganizational relations in tourism. *Annals of Tourism Research* 18(4), 639–652.

Sengers, P. (2000) Narrative intelligence. In: Dautenhahn, K. (ed.) *Human Cognition and Social Agent Technology.* John Benjamins, Amsterdam, The Netherlands, pp. 1–26.

Sengers, P. (2003) The engineering of experience. In: Blythe, M.A., Monk, A.F., Overbeeke, K. and Wright, P.C. (eds) *Funology: From Usability to Enjoyment.* Kluwer Academic Publishers, Dordrecht, The Netherlands, pp. 19–29.

Shaw, S.M. and Dawson, D. (2001) Purposive leisure: examining parental discourses on family activities. *Leisure Sciences* 23(4), 217–231.

Shedroff, N. (2001) *Experience Design.* New Riders, Indianapolis, Indiana.

Shera, J.H. (1965) Putting knowledge to work. In: Shera, J.H. (ed.) *Libraries and Organization of Knowledge.* Archon Books, Hamden, Connecticut.

Shimazu, H. (1998) A textual case-based reasoning system using XML on the World Wide Web. In: Smyth, B. and Cunningham, P. (eds) *Advances in Case-Based Reasoning,* Vol. 1488 of *Lecture Notes in Computer Science.* Springer, Vienna, pp. 274–285.

Shimazu, H. (2001) Expertclerk: navigating shoppers buying process with the combination of asking and proposing. In: Nebel, B. (ed.) *Proceedings of the 17th International Joint Conference on Artificial Intelligence, IJCAI 2001.* Morgan Kaufmann Publishers, Seattle, Washington, pp. 1443–1448.

Shneiderman, B. (1992) *Designing the User Interface. Strategies for Effective Human–Computer Interaction,* 2nd edn. Addison-Wesley, Reading, Massachusetts.

Si, J., Lin, S. and Vuong, M.-A. (2000) Dynamic topology representing networks. *Neural Networks* 13, 617–627.

Silverman, B.G., Bachann, M. and Al-Akharas, K. (2001) Implications of buyer decision theory for design of e-commerce websites. *International Journal of Human–Computer Studies* 55(5), 815–844.

Simmons, A. (2001) *The Story Factor.* Perseus Publishing, Cambridge, Massachusetts.

Singh, N. (2004) *Electronic Commerce: Economics and Strategy.* Prentice-Hall, Englewood Cliffs, New Jersey.

Slawinski, N. (2001) 'PowerBuying wird zunehmen' – Neue Handelsformen erobern das Internet. Available at: http://www.symposion.de/ecommerce/roh_18.htm

Smith, P.A. (1996) Towards a practical measure of hypertext usability. *Interacting with Computers* 8(4), 365–381.

Smyth, B. and Cotter, P. (2000) A personalized television listing service. *Communications of the ACM* 43(8).

Smyth, B. and Keane, M.T. (1996) Design à la déjà vu: reducing the adaptation overhead. In: Leake, D. (ed.) *Case-Based Reasoning: Experiences, Lessons, and Future Directions.* AAAI Press/MIT Press, California.

Snepenger, D., Meged, K., Snelling, M. and Worrall, K. (1990) Information search strategies by destination-naive tourists. *Journal of Travel Research* 29(Summer), 13–16.

Sniezek, J.A., Paese, P.W. and Switzer, F.S. III (1990) The effect of choosing on confidence in choice. *Organizational Behavior and Human Decision Processes* 46, 264–282.

Spiekermann, S. and Paraschiv, C. (2002) Motivating human-agent interaction: transferring insights from behavioral marketing to interface design. *Electronic Commerce Research* 2, 255–285.

Spiliopoulou, M. (2000) Web usage mining for web site evaluation. *Communications of the ACM* (Association for Computing Machinery) 43(8), 127–134.

Sproles, G.B. (1985) From perfectionism to fadism: measuring consumer's decision-making styles. In: *Proceedings of the American Council on Consumer Interests*, pp. 79–85.

Sproles, G.B. and Kendall, E.L. (1986) A methodology for profiling consumers' decision-making styles. *The Journal of Consumer Affaires* 20(2), 267–279.

Srinivasan, N. (1990) Pre-purchase external information search for information. In: Zeithaml, V.E. (ed.) *Review of Marketing*. American Marketing Association, Chicago, Illinois.

Srivastava, J., Cooley, R., Deshpande, M. and Tan, P.-N. (2000) Web usage mining: discovery and applications of usage patterns from web data. *SIGKDD Explorations* 1(2), 12–23.

Stahl, A. and Bergman, R. (2000) Applying recursive CBR for the customization of structured products in an electronic shop. In: *Advances in Case-Based Reasoning: Proceedings of the 5th European Workshop, EWCBR-2000, 6–9 September, Trento, Italy*. Springer, Vienna, pp. 297–308.

Star Tribune (1999) Stakes are high for amazon.com CEO. *Star Tribune Newspaper*. Minneapolis, Minnesota, December 20, D8.

Steele, R. (2001) Techniques for specialized search engines. In: *Proceedings of the Internet Computing '01*, pp. 25–28.

Stephenson, G.A. (1988) Knowledge browsing – front ends to statistical databases. In: Rafanelli, M., Klensin, J.C. and Svensson, P. (eds) *Statistical and Scientific Database Management. Proceedings of the 4th*

International Working Conference SSDBM, pp. 327–337.

Stewart, S.I. and Vogt, C.A. (1997) Multi-destination trip patterns. *Annals of Tourism Research* 24(2), 458–461.

Stock, O. (2000) Intelligent interfaces for the tourist. In: Fesenmaier, D.R., Klein, S. and Buhalis, D. (eds) *Information and Communication Technologies in Tourism 2000*. Springer, Vienna, pp. 1–14.

Stock, O. (2001) Language-based interfaces and their application for cultural tourism. *AI Magazine* 22/1, 85–97.

Stock, O., Zancanaro, M. and Not, E. (2004) Intelligent interactive information presentation for cultural tourism. In: Stock, O. and Zancanaro, M. (eds) *Intelligent Multimodal Information Presentation*. Kluwer Academic Publishers, Dordrecht, The Netherlands.

Stoltz, C. (1999) Each year, a bit less. *Washington Post*, 11 November.

Stone, G.P. (1954) City shoppers and urban identification: observations on the social psychology of city life. *American Journal of Sociology* 60, 36–45.

Strasser, H. (2000) Reduction of complexity. In: Mazanec, J.A. and Strasser, H.A. (eds) *Nonparametric Approach to Perceptions-Based Market Segmentation: Foundations*. Springer, Vienna, pp. 99–137.

Tabatabai, D. and Luconi, F. (1998) Expert-novice differences in searching the Web. In: *Proceedings of the Americas Conference on Information Systems, 14–16 August, Baltimore, Maryland*, pp. 390–392.

Taha, I.A. and Ghosh, J. (1999) Symbolic interpretation of artificial neural networks. *IEEE Transactions on Neural Networks* 11(3), 448–463.

Tay, R., McCarthy, P. and Fletcher, J. (1996) A portfolio choice model of the demand for recreational trips. *Transportation Research B* 30(5), 325–337.

Teare, R. (1992) An exploration of the consumer decision process for hospitality services. In: Teare, R., Moutinho, L. and Morgan, N. (eds) *Managing and Marketing Services in the 1990s*. Cassell Educational, London, pp. 233–248.

Tenopir, C. (1985) Full text database retrieval performance. *Online Review* 9(2), 149–164.

Teo, H., Oh, L., Liu, C. and Wei, K. (2003) An empirical study of the effects of interactivity on web user attitude. *International Journal of Human–Computer Studies* 58, 281–305.

Texas Travel (2005) Texas cams. Available at: http://www.traveltex.com/texas_cams.asp?area = Ft.%20Worth

The Walt Disney Company (2005) Disney online. Available at: http://disney.go.com/home/today/index.html

TIA (2002) *Travelers' Use of the Internet*. Telecommunications Industry Association, Washington, DC.

Tideswell, C. and Faulkner, W. (1999) Multidestination travel patterns of international visitors to queensland. *Journal of Travel Research* 37, 364–374.

Tierney, P. (2000) Internet-based evaluation of tourism web site effectiveness: methodological issues and survey results. *Journal of Travel Research* 39, 212–219.

Turley, S.K. (2001) Children and the demand for recreational experiences: the case of zoos. *Leisure Studies* 20(1), 1–18.

Tversky, A. (1969) Intransitivity of preferences. *Psychological Review* 76, 31–48.

Um, S. and Crompton, J.L. (1990) Attitude determinants in tourism destination choice. *Annals of Tourism Research* 17, 432–448.

Um, S. and Crompton, J.L. (1991) Development of pleasure travel attitude dimensions. *Annals of Tourism Research* 18, 374–378.

Um, S. and Crompton, J.L. (1992) The roles of perceived inhibitors and facilitators in pleasure travel destination decisions. *Journal of Travel Research* 30(3), 18–25.

Umaschi, M. and Cassell, J. (1997) Storytelling systems: constructing the innerface of the interface. In: *Proceedings of the Cognitive Technologies '97, IEEE*, pp. 98–108.

Unger, L.S. and Kernan, J.B. (1983) On the meaning of leisure: an investigation of some determinants of the subjective experience. *Journal of Consumer Research* 9, 381–391.

van Middelkoop, M. (2001) *A Decision-Support System for Outdoor Leisure Planning, Development and Test of a Rule-Based Micro-Simulation Model for the Evaluation of Alternative Scenarios and Planning Options*. Eindhoven University Press, Eindhoven.

van Mulken, S., André, E. and Mueller, J. (1998) The persona effect: how substantial is it. In: *Proceedings of the Human–Computer Interaction Conference*. Springer, Vienna, pp. 53–58.

van Raaij, W.F. (1986) Consumer research on tourism: mental and behavioral constructs. *Annals of Tourism Research* 13, 1–9.

van Hof, K. and Molderez, I. (1994) An advice system for travel agents. In: Schertler, W. et al. (eds) *Information and Communication Technologies in Tourism*. Springer, Vienna, pp. 126–132.

Varian, H. (2001) The computer mediated economy. *Communications of the ACM* 44/3, 92–93.

Venkatesh, V. (2000) Determinants of perceived ease of use: integrating control, intrinsic motivation, and emotion into the technology acceptance model. *Information Systems Research* 11(4), 342–365.

Venkatesh, V. and Davis, F.D. (2000) A theoretical extension of the technology acceptance model: four longitudinal field studies. *Management Science* 46(2), 186–204.

Venkatesh, V., Morris, M.G., Davis, G.B. and Davis, F.D. (2003) User acceptance of information technology: toward a unified view. *MIS Quarterly* 27(3), 425–479.

Vester, H.G. (1988) *Zeitalter der Freizeit – Eine soziologische Bestandsaufnahme*. Darmstadt.

Vogt, C.A. and Fesenmaier, D.R. (1998) Expanding the functional information search model. *Annals of Tourism Research* 25(3), 551–578.

Vogt, C.A., Fesenmaier, D.R. and MacKay, K. (1993) Functional and aesthetic information needs underlying the pleasure travel experience. *Journal of Travel and Tourism Marketing* 2(2), 133–146.

Voigt, U. (1997) Alternativtourismus versus Massentourismus. Available at: http://home.snafu.de/uli.voigt/alternativtourismus.htm

Waes, V.L. (2000) Thinking aloud as a method for testing the usability of websites: the influence of task variation on the evaluation of hypertext. *IEEE Transactions on Professional Communication* 43(3), 279–291.

Wahab, S., Crampon, L.J. and Rothfield, L.M. (1976) *Tourism Marketing*. Tourism International Press, London.

Walker, M., Takayama, L. and Landay, J.A. (2002) Low- or high-fidelity, paper or computer? Choosing attributes when testing web prototypes. In: *Proceedings of the Human Factors and Ergonomics Society, 46th Annual Meeting HFES2002*, pp. 661–665.

Walsh, G., Hennig-Thurau, T., Mitchell, V.-W. and Wiedmann, K.-P. (2001) Consumers' decision-making style as a basis for market segmentation. *Journal of Targeting, Measurement and Analysis for Marketing* 10(2), 117–131.

Wang, P. and Pouchard, L. (1997) End-user searching of web resources: problems and implications. In: *Advances in Classification Research: Proceedings of the 8th ASIS SIG/CR Classification Research Workshop, 2 November 1996, Washington, DC*, pp. 73–85.

Wang, Y. and Fesenmaier, D.R. (2003) Assessing motivation of contribution in online communities: an empirical investigation of an online travel community. *Electronic Markets* 13(1), 33–45.

Wang, Y., Yu, Q. and Fesenmaier, D.R. (2002) Defining the virtual tourist community: implications for tourism marketing. *Tourism Management* 23, 407–417.

Weber, K. and Roehl, W.S. (1999) Profiling people searching for and purchasing travel products on the World Wide Web. *Journal of Travel Research* 37(3), 291–298.

Webster, J. and Martocchio, J.J. (1992) Microcomputer playfulness: development of a measurement of a measure with workplace implications. *MIS Quarterly* 16(2), 201–226.

Wedel, M. and Kamakura, W.A. (1998) *Market Segmentation, Conceptual and Methodological Foundations*. Kluwer Academic Publishers, Boston, Massachusetts.

Weitzman, M. (1979) Optimal search for the best alternative. *Econometrica* 47(May), 641–654.

Welles, J.D. and Fuerst, W.L. (2000) Domain-oriented interface metaphors: designing web interfaces for effective customer interaction. In: *Proceeding of the 33rd Hawaii International Conference on System Sciences*. IEEE Computer Society Press, Maui, Hawaii.

Wells, W.D (ed.) (1974) *Life Style and Psychographics*. American Marketing Association, Chicago, Illinois.

Werthner, H. and Klein, S. (1999) *Information Technology and Tourism – A Challenging Relationship*. Springer, Vienna.

West, P.M., Brockett, P.L. and Golden, L.L. (1997) A comparative analysis of neural networks and statistical methods for predicting consumer choice. *Marketing Science* 16(4), 370–391.

Westbrook, R.A. and Black, W.C. (1985) A motivational-based shopper typology. *Journal of Retailing* 61(1), 78–103.

Williams, A.P. and Palmer, A. (1999) Tourism destination brands and electronic commerce: towards synergy? *Journal of Vacation Marketing* 5(3), 263–275.

Witten, I.H. and Frank, E. (2000) *Data Mining*. Morgan Kaufmann Publishers, San Francisco, California.

Wöber, K.W. (2003) Evaluation of DMO web sites through interregional tourism portals: a European cities tourism case example. In: Frew, A.J., Hitz, M. and O'Connor, P. (eds) *Proceedings of the 10th International Conference for Information and Communication Technologies in Tourism – ENTER 2003*. Springer, Vienna and New York, pp. 76–85.

Wöber, K.W., Scharl, A., Natter, M. and Taudes, A. (2002) Success factors of European tourism web sites. In: Wöber, K.W., Frew, A.J. and Hitz, M. (eds) *Proceedings of the 9th International Conference for Information and Communication Technologies in Tourism – ENTER 2002*. Springer, Vienna and New York, pp. 397–406.

Woodside, A.G. and Lysonski, S. (1989) A general model of traveler destination choice. *Journal of Travel Research* 27, 8–14.

Woodside, A.G. and MacDonald, R. (1994) General system framework of customer choice processes of tourism services. In: Gasser, R.V. and Weiermair, K. (eds) *Spoilt for Choice. Decision Making Processes and Preference Change of Tourist: Intertemporal and Intercountry Perspectives*. Kulturverlag, Thaur, Germany, pp. 30–59.

Woodside, A.G. and Ronkainen, I.A. (1980) Vacation planning segments: self-planning vs. users of motor club and travel agents. *Annals of Tourism Research* 7, 385–393.

Woszczynski, A.B., Roth, P.L. and Segars, A.H. (2002) Exploring the theoretical foundations of playfulness in computer interactions. *Computers in Human Behavior* 18(4), 369–388.

WTO (2001) *E-Business for Tourism. Practical Guidelines for Destinations and Businesses.* World Tourism Organization, Madrid.

Wu, Z., Meng, W., Yu, C. and Li, Z. (2001) Towards a highly scalable and effective metasearch engine. In: *Proceedings of the 10th International Web Conference – WWW10, 1–5 May, Hong Kong.*

Wyer, R.S. (1974) *Cognitive Organization and Change: An Information-Processing Approach.* Lawrence Erlbaum Associates, Hillsdale, New Jersey.

Wyer, R.S., Adaval, R. and Colcombe, S.J. (2002) Narrative-based representations of social knowledge: their construction and use in comprehension, memory and judgment. *Advances in Experimental Social Psychology* 34, 131–197.

Xiang, Z. (2003) Assessing interface metaphors for searching the Web: implications for travel related website design. Master's dissertation, University of Illinois, Urbana-Champaign, Illinois.

Yong, L.T. and Kong, T.E. (1999) The study of cooperative evaluation approach on Internet search. In: *Proceedings of the USM Computer Science Student Symposium on Computer Science and IT.* University of Science, Malaysia.

Zancanaro, M., Rocchi, C. and Stock, O. (2003) Automatic video composition. In: *Proceedings of the 3rd International Symposium on SmartGraphics 2003.* Heidelberg, Germany.

Zaiane, O.R. (1998) *From Resource Discovery to Knowledge Discovery on the Internet. Technical Report.* Simon Fraser University, Canada.

Zhang, P. and Von Dran, G.M. (2000) Satisfiers and dissatisfiers: a two-factor model for website design and evaluation. *Journal of the American Society for Information Science and Technology* 51(14), 1253–1268.

Zins, A.H. (1998) Leisure traveler choice models of theme hotels using psychographics. *Journal of Travel Research* 36(4), 3–15.

Zins, A.H. (2001) Two means to the same end: hierarchical value maps in tourism – comparing the association pattern technique with direct importance ratings. In: Mazanec, J.A., Crouch, G.I., Ritchie, J.R.B. and Woodside, A.G. (eds) *Consumer Psychology of Tourism Hospitality and Leisure,* Vol. 2. CAB International, Wallingford, UK, pp. 123–151.

Zins, A.H. (2003) Adapting to cognitive styles to improve the usability of travel recommendation systems. In: Frew, A.J., Hitz, M. and O'Connor, P. (eds) *Information and Communication Technologies in Tourism.* Springer, Vienna, pp. 289–297.

Zins, A.H., Bauernfeind, U., Del Missier, F., Venturini, A. and Rumetshofer, H. (2004a) An experimental usability test for different destination recommender systems. In: Frew, A.J. (ed.) *Information and Communication Technologies in Tourism 2004. Proceedings of the International Conference in Cairo.* Springer, Vienna, pp. 228–238.

Zins, A.H., Bauernfeind, U., Del Missier, F., Mitsche, N., Ricci, F., Rumetshofer, H. and Schaumlechner, E. (2004b) Prototype testing for a destination recommender system: steps, procedures and implications. In: Frew, A. (ed.) *Proceedings of the 11th International Conference on Information and Communication Technologies in Travel & Tourism (ENTER 2004), Illinois.* Springer, Cairo.

Index